Thirty-Third Edition May 2024

The State of Church Giving through 2021

A Comparison of the Growth in Church Contributions with United States Per Capita Income (1988)

Previous Editions in *The State of Church Giving* Series:

The State of Church Giving, through 1989: "Observations and Reflections" (1991)

The State of Church Giving through 1990: "Church Member Giving in Recession Years: 1970, 1974, 1980, 1982 and 1990" (Second Edition, 1992)

The State of Church Giving through 1991: "Denominational Giving Data and Other Sources of Religious Giving Information"; "Church Member Giving Trends Based on 1968–1991 Data" (Third Edition, 1993)

The State of Church Giving through 1992: "Church Giving in Perspective: Can Church Members Afford to Give More?" (Fourth Edition, 1994)

The State of Church Giving through 1993: "Exploration of Roman Catholic Giving Patterns"; "A Unified Theory of Church Giving and Membership" (Fifth Edition, 1995)

The State of Church Giving through 1994: "Retrospective of *The State of Church Giving* Series" (Sixth Edition, 1996)

The State of Church Giving through 1995: "The Theological Implications of Church Member Giving Patterns" (Seventh Edition, 1997)

The State of Church Giving through 1996: "Church Member Giving in Perspective: Can Religion Influence the Middle Class" (Eighth Edition, 1998)

The State of Church Giving through 1997: "Future of Congregational Giving: The Need for Creative Church Policy" (Ninth Edition, 1999)

The State of Church Giving through 1998: "Systems and Subsystems Analysis: A Case Study" (Tenth Edition, 2000)

The State of Church Giving through 1999: "National Church Leaders Response Form" (Eleventh Edition, 2001)

The State of Church Giving through 2000: "Two Solutions for the Vacuum of Leadership in the Church in the U.S." (Twelfth Edition, 2002)

The State of Church Giving through 2001: "Reversing the Decline in Benevolences Giving: A Country-by-Country Needs Analysis"; (Thirteenth Edition, 2003)

The State of Church Giving through 2002: "Helping Church Members to Care Effectively: Yoking Map Twenty-Year Update"; (Fourteenth Edition, 2004)

The State of Church Giving through 2003: "Giving Trends and the Church's Priorities" (Fifteenth Edition, 2005)

The State of Church Giving through 2004: Will We Will? (Sixteenth Edition, 2006)

The State of Church Giving through 2005: Abolition of the Institutional Enslavement of Overseas Missions (Seventeenth Edition, 2007)

The State of Church Giving through 2006: Global Triage, MDG 4, and Unreached People Groups (Eighteenth Edition, 2008)

The State of Church Giving through 2007: What Are Our Christian Billionaires Thinking — Or Are They? (Nineteenth Edition, 2009)

The State of Church Giving through 2008: Kudos to Wycliffe Bible Translators and World Vision for Global At-Scale Goals, But Will Denominations Resist Jesus Christ And Not Spend $1 to $26 Per Member to Reach The Unreached When Jesus Says, "You Feed Them"? (Twentieth Edition, 2010)

The State of Church Giving through 2009: Jesus Christ, the Church in the U.S., & the 16 No-Progress-in-Child Deaths Nations, 10 Being 84% Christian (Twenty-First Edition, 2011)

The State of Church Giving through 2010: Who's in Charge Here? A Case for a Positive Agenda for Affluence (Twenty-Second Edition, 2012)

The State of Church Giving through 2011: The Kingdom of God, Church Leaders & Institutions, Global Triage Needs, and the Promises of Jesus (Twenty-Third Edition, 2013)

The State of Church Giving through 2012: What Are Christian Seminaries and Intellectuals Thinking — Or Are They? (Twenty-Fourth Edition, 2014)

The State of Church Giving through 2013: Crisis or Potential? (Twenty-Fifth Edition, 2015)

The State of Church Giving through 2014: Speaking Truth to Power (Twenty-Sixth Edition, 2016)

The State of Church Giving through 2015: Understanding the Times (Twenty-Seventh Edition, 2017)

The State of Church Giving through 2016: What Do Denominational Leaders Want to Do with $368 Billion More a Year? (Twenty-Eighth Edition, 2018)

The State of Church Giving through 2017: What a Can-Do Attitude in the Church+$16 Billion Can Do in Jesus' Name for the Children Dying in the Promise Gap (Twenty-Ninth Edition, 2019)

The State of Church Giving through 2018: What If Jesus Comes Back in 2025? (Thirtieth Edition, 2020)

The State of Church Giving through 2019: Serve God with Money At-Scale or Serve Money (Thirty-First Edition, 2022)

The State of Church Giving through 2020: A Theology for an Age of Affluence (Thirty-Second Edition, March 2023)

Note: Special focus chapters, indicated by quote marks above, were not listed as subtitles until the sixteenth edition.

Thirty-Third Edition May 2024

The State of Church Giving through 2021

Intentional Miracles

John L. Ronsvalle

Sylvia Ronsvalle

empty tomb,® inc.
Champaign, Illinois

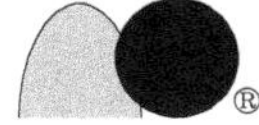

The State of Church Giving through 2021:
Intentional Miracles
by John and Sylvia Ronsvalle
Published by empty tomb, inc.
First printing, May 2024; Second printing, June 2024

empty tomb, inc.
301 N. Fourth Street
P.O. Box 2404
Champaign, IL 61825-2404
Phone: (217) 356-9519
Fax: (217) 356-2344
www.emptytomb.org
See www.emptytomb.org/publications-corrigenda for updates and corrigenda.

ISBN 979-8-3852-2883-6
ISSN 1097-3192

The Library of Congress has catalogued this publication as follows:
The state of church giving through ... — 19uu- Champaign, Ill. : Empty Tomb, Inc.,
v. : ill. ; 28 cm. Annual.
1. Christian giving Periodicals.
2. Christian giving Statistics Periodicals.
3. Church finance—United States Periodicals.
4. Church finance—United States Statistics Periodicals.
BV772 .S32 98-640917

CONTENTS

TABLES, FIGURES AND ABBREVIATIONS

List of Tables

List of Figures:

List of Abbreviations:

BEA ............U.S. Bureau of Economic Analysis
BLS ............U.S. Government Dept. of Labor, Bureau of Labor Statistics
CE ....Consumer Expenditure Survey
CPI ....Consumer Price Index
CU ....Consumer Unit
DPI ....Disposable Personal Income
GDP ....Gross Domestic Product
IGME ....Inter-agency Group for Child Mortality Estimation
MDG ....Millennium Development Goal
NAE ....National Association of Evangelicals
NCC ....National Council of the Churches of Christ in the U.S.A.
NIV ....New International Version of the Holy Bible (1984)
NLT ....New Living Translation
RCMUS........*Religious Congregations & Membership in the United States*
SCG ....*State of Church Giving*
SDG ....Sustainable Development Goal
U5MR ....Under-5 Mortality Rate
UNICEF.......United Nations Children's Fund
YACC ....*Yearbook of American and Canadian Churches*

PREFACE

This series would not be possible without the faithful work of those officials who track the numbers for each of their communions. The series in this edition is able to update data for 11 communions from 1921 through 2021, and for a larger number of communions from 1968 through 2021. This is a remarkable feat, providing valuable information for those concerned with the history, and future, of the church in the U.S. Great credit goes to these individuals who make time in their busy schedules to provide the latest requested data.

Once again, as in so many areas of current life, various issues led to delays in the production and distribution of this thirty-third edition. The goal of Fall 2023 for the present edition was not met. Completed in April 2024, the goal, with unwavering hope, is to return to a Winter schedule for the next edition.

Staff, volunteers, and donors at empty tomb have been supportive in a way that allows this research work to exist side-by-side with the direct efforts to help people in Jesus' name, both locally and internationally, through churches. We thank God for them. Their faithful service continues to provide us with the confidence we have that the church in the U.S. is capable of doing great things in Jesus' name.

Both Becky Ford and Matthew Cosby provided vital assistance with the production of this edition. Their help made it possible to bring this thirty-third edition to completion in April 2024.

Several verses are highlighted in this volume. One is Luke 18:1 that indicates Jesus taught his disciples to pray and never give up. That verse is important on so many levels, from the practical production issues to the hope that the church in the U.S. will mobilize to do intentional miracles at a scale never seen before. These pages once again are offered in the hope of Eph. 3:20-21, that God will do even more than we ask or imagine, and also in light of the direction given in Hebrews 10:24, that the information will stir all of us to even more love for this hurting world, shown in word and deed in Jesus' name. We're looking forward with the hope that it will be so.

John L. Ronsvalle, Ph.D.
Sylvia Ronsvalle

Champaign, Illinois
April 2024

SUMMARY

The State of Church Giving through 2021 is the 33rd edition in an annual series that began with *The State of Church Giving through 1989*. These analyses consider denominational giving data for a set of denominations first analyzed in a study published in 1988. The present report reviews data for a composite set of denominations from 1968 through 2020. As of 2021, this composite group included 23.6 million full or confirmed members across the Protestant theological spectrum. As of the latest year with relevant data available, 2010, these communions included just over 100,000 of the estimated 350,000 religious congregations in the U.S. Analyses in others chapters present additional data that expands the group of communions to include other Protestants and also Catholics. The broadest data set includes membership of 104 million in 2021.

In this edition, the series for population, income, and deflators, and the data series for one large denomination, that were revised for the last edition, are again used. See chapter 1 for details.

- In chapter 1, per member giving for the composite set of denominations was analyzed for 1968 through 2021. The portion of income given in 2021 declined from the 1968 level in the categories of Total Contributions, Congregational Finances, and Benevolences. From 2020 to 2021, per member contributions in current dollars and inflation-adjusted dollars increased to Total Contributions and the two subcategories, while giving as a percent of income decreased to Congregational Finances and increased to Total Contributions and Benevolences.
- In chapter 2, data for an additional 12 denominations was available for 2020-2021. Combining this data with that of 24 composite denominations that provided both 2020 and 2021 information, an analysis was done for an expanded set of 36 Protestant communions, with 30 million members in 2021. The 2020-2021 pattern in both the expanded set and the 24-composite subset was an increase in per member giving in current and inflation-adjusted dollars to Total Contributions and the two subcategories of Congregational Finances and Benevolences. Both the expanded set and the composite set increased from 2020 to 2021 to Total Contributions and Benevolences in giving as a percent of income. In 2021, the composite set decreased 1% from the 2020 base, while the small increase rounded to 0% change for the expanded set, for giving as percent of income to Congregational Finances.
- In chapter 3, an analysis of data for a subset of mainline Protestant denominations and a subset of evangelical Protestant denominations for the data years 1968, 1985, 2002, and 2021 is presented. The analysis found giving higher in the evangelical denominations. However, giving as a portion of income to Total Contributions and Congregational Finances posted a steeper decline among the evangelical denominations from 1968 to 2021. Both the

evangelical and mainline communions posted a similar decline in giving to Benevolences as a portion of income for the 1968 to 2021 period.

- In chapter 4, a review of giving and membership patterns in 11 Protestant denominations from 1921 to 2021 found that giving as a percent of income, and membership as a percent of U.S. population, were lower in 2021 than in both 1921 and 1933, the depth of the Great Depression, for the set of 11 denominations.
- In chapter 5, data was analyzed using both linear and exponential regression. Both giving and membership data were reviewed regarding how past patterns may influence the future for various sets of denominational groups. Expenditures on new religious construction in the U.S. were compared for the period 1964 through 2021.
- In chapter 6, a survey of denominations' overseas missions income in 2003 through 2021 found that, for the group as a whole, denominations' overseas ministries income was again about 2¢ of every dollar donated to congregations in 2021. The cost per church member for addressing global needs, such as world evangelization and helping, in Jesus' name, to close the gap between the reduction goals set and the reported rates of global child deaths, was calculated for church members. If giving increased to 10%, and 6% of that total were directed to mission, $210 billion more would be available to assist both local and global neighbors in need. Using different factors, as discussed later in the chapter, as much as an additional $474 billion could have been available in 2021 for churches' international missions.
- In chapter 7, charitable giving data for the U.S. Bureau of Labor Statistics (BLS) Consumer Expenditure Survey (CE), 2021, was analyzed by age, income level, and region of residence. Americans reported that giving to "church, religious organizations" represented 56% of their contributions in 2021. Three estimates for Total Giving by Living Individuals in 2019, the latest year for which all three sources had available data, were compared: the U.S. BLS CE, the Internal Revenue Service Form 990 series, and the *Giving USA* publication. A review of media coverage of charitable giving found that the media did not present an adequate analysis of available information such that it would provide the public with a useful understanding of charitable giving trends.
- Chapter 8 considers the fact that church members can make this age of affluence an age of intentional miracles. The topics include:
  - What is an intentional miracle?
  - How does pursuing intentional miracles prepare for the future? Various groups are considered: the present-day church; world neighbors; the general good; the youth; each individual church member.
  - What makes this present time so special regarding intentional miracles?
  - What would an intentional miracle look like?
  - Are intentional miracles even possible?

INTRODUCTION

A historical series of financial and membership data in the United States is available through the critically important work of denominational officials. These church statesmen took a broad overview of organized religion as a major social institution. They collected and preserved the data through publications and archives.

Individual congregations initially provide the data to the regional or national denominational office with which the congregation is affiliated. The denominational offices then compile the data. Traditionally, the data was requested, aggregated, and published, in a series that began with the 1916 *Federal Council Year Book*, which reported membership and financial support for foreign missions. In the 1919 *Yearbook of the Churches*, general giving was added to these categories.

This series appeared under a total of five titles until 1973, when the data was published in the *Yearbook of American and Canadian Churches* (*YACC*), of the National Council of the Churches of Christ in the U.S.A.

The analyses in this volume are based on the *YACC* series that continued through the 2012 *YACC* edition, with 2010 data. To supplement that series, data has also been obtained directly from denominational sources (as noted in the tables in Appendix B). The numbers on the following pages represent the actual dollar records included in reports submitted by pastors and lay congregational leaders to their own denominational offices.

By following the same data set of denominations over a period of years, trends can be seen among a broad group of church members. In addition, since the data set includes communions from across the theological spectrum, subsets of denominations within the larger grouping provide a basis for comparing patterns between communions with different perspectives.

In an ongoing fashion, efforts are made to use the latest information available. As a result, *The State of Church Giving through 2021* provides information available to date.

Definition of Terms. The analyses in this report use certain terms that are defined as follows.

Full or Confirmed Members is used in the present analysis because it is a relatively consistent category among the reporting denominations. Certain denominations also report a larger figure for Inclusive Membership, which may include, for example, children who have been baptized but are not yet eligible for confirmation in that denomination. In this report, when the term "per member" is used, it refers to Full or Confirmed Members, unless otherwise noted.

The terms "denomination" and "communion" are used interchangeably. Both refer to a group of church people who share a common identity defined by traditions and stated beliefs.

The phrase "historically Christian church" refers to that combination of believers with a historically acknowledged confession of the faith. The broad spectrum of communions represented in the National Church Leaders Response Form list indicates the breadth of this definition.[1]

Total Contributions Per Member refers to the average contribution donated to the denominations' affiliated congregations by Full or Confirmed Members in a given year.

Total Contributions combines the two subcategories of Congregational Finances and Benevolences. The definitions used in this report for these two subcategories are consistent with the standardized *YACC* data request questionnaire.

The first subcategory of Congregational Finances includes contributions directed to the internal operations of the individual congregation, including such items as the utility bills, salaries and benefits for the pastor and staff, as well as Sunday school materials and capital programs.

The second subcategory is Benevolences. This category includes contributions for the congregation's external expenditures, beyond its own operations, for what might be termed the larger mission of the church. Benevolences includes financial support for international missions as well as national and local charities, through denominational channels as well as programs of nondenominational organizations to which the congregation contributes directly. Benevolences also includes support of denominational administration at all levels, as well as donations to denominational seminaries and schools.

As those familiar with congregational dynamics know, an individual generally donates an amount to the congregation that underwrites both Congregational Finances and Benevolences. During the budget preparation process, congregational leadership considers allocations to these categories. The budget may or may not be reviewed by all the congregation's members, depending on the communion's polity. However, the sum of the congregation's activities serves as a basis for members' decisions about whether to increase or decrease giving from one year to the next. Also, many congregations provide opportunities to designate directly to either Congregational Finances or Benevolences, through fundraising drives, capital campaigns, and special offerings. Therefore, the allocations between Congregational Finances and Benevolences can be seen to fairly represent the priorities of church members.

When the terms "income," "per capita income," and "giving as a percent of income" are used, they refer to the U.S. Per Capita Disposable (after-tax) Personal Income (DPI) series from the U.S. Department of Commerce Bureau of Economic Analysis (BEA), unless otherwise noted.

Analysis Factors. *Chained Dollars.* The analyses in *The State of Church Giving through 2021* are keyed to the U.S. BEA Implicit Price Deflator for Gross National Product series of "chained (2012) dollars" to factor out inflation.

Income Series. The U.S. Department of Commerce BEA published the 15th comprehensive ('benchmark") revision of the national income and product accounts, with the reference year being 2012. The U.S. Per Capita DPI series used in the present *The State of Church Giving through 2021* is drawn from this national accounts data, revising the income series as necessary.

Appendix C includes both U.S. Per Capita DPI figures and the Implicit Price Deflator for Gross National Product figures used in this study.

Rate of Change Calculations, 1985-2021. The following methodology is used to calculate the rate of change between 1985 and the most recent calendar year for which data is available, in the present case, 2021.

The rate of change between 1968 and 1985 was calculated by subtracting the 1968 giving as a percent of income figure from the 1985 figure and then dividing the result by the 1968 figure.

The rate of change between 1985 and 2021 was calculated as follows. The 1968 giving as a percent of income figure was subtracted from the 2021 figure and divided by the 1968 figure, producing a 1968-2021 rate of change. Then, the 1968-1985 rate of change was subtracted from the 1968-2021 figure. The result is the 1985-2021 rate of change, which may then be compared to the 1968-1985 figure.

Rounding Calculations. In most cases, aggregate Total Contributions, Total Congregational Finances, and Total Benevolences for the denominations being considered were divided by Full or Confirmed Membership in order to obtain per capita, or per member, data for that set of denominations. This procedure occasionally led to a small rounding discrepancy in one of the three related figures. That is, by a small margin, rounded per capita Total Contributions did not equal per capita Congregational Finances plus per capita Benevolences. Similarly, rounding data to the nearest dollar for use in tables and graphics led on occasion to a small rounding error in the data presented in tabular or graphic form.

Giving as a Percent of Income. The most useful way to look at church member giving is in terms of giving as a percent of income. Rather than indicating how much money the congregation has to spend, as when one considers dollars donated, giving as a percent of income indicates where the congregation stands in terms of church members' total available incomes. Has the church sustained the same level of support from its members in comparison to previous years, as measured by what portion of income is being donated by members from the changing total resources available to them?

Percent of income is a valuable measure because incomes change. Just as inflation changes the value of the dollar so that $5 in 2021 did not purchase the same amount as $5 in 1968, incomes, influenced by inflation and real growth, also change. For example, per capita DPI in 1968 was $3,208 in current dollars; if a church member gave $321 that year, that member would have been tithing, or giving the standard of ten percent. In contrast, 2021 per capita DPI had increased to $52,857 in current dollars; and if that church member had still given $321, the member would have been giving less than 0.57% of income. The church would have commanded a smaller portion of the member's overall resources.

Thus, while dollars donated provide a limited picture of how much the church has to spend, giving as a percent of income provides both a measure of the church member's level of commitment to the church in comparison to other spending priorities, as well as a measure of whether the church's income is keeping up with inflation and growth in the economy. One might say that giving as a percent of income is an indication of the church's "market share" of church members' lives.

In most cases, to obtain giving as a percent of income, total income for a set of denominations was divided by the number of Full or Confirmed Members in the set. This yielded the per member giving amount in dollars. This per member giving amount was divided by per capita DPI.

Giving in Dollars. Per member giving to churches can be measured in dollars. The dollar measure indicates, among other information, how much money religious institutions have to spend.

Current dollars indicate the value of the dollar in the year it was donated. However, since inflation changes the amount of goods or services that can be purchased with that dollar, data provided in current dollars has limited information value over a time span. If someone donated $5 in 1968 and $5 in 2021, on one level that person is donating the same amount of money. On another level, however, the buying power of that $5 has changed a great deal. Since less can be bought with the $5 donated in 2021 because of inflation in the economy, on a practical level the value of the donation has shrunk.

To account for the changes caused by inflation in the value of the dollar, a deflator can be applied. The result is inflation-adjusted 2012 dollars. Dollars adjusted to their chain-type, annual-weighted measure through the use of a deflator can be compared in terms of real growth over a time span since inflation has been factored out.

The deflator most commonly applied in this analysis designated the base period as 2012, with levels in 2012 set equal to 100. Thus, when adjusted by the deflator, the 1968 gift of $5 was worth $25.53 in inflation-adjusted 2012 dollars, and the 2021 gift of $5 was worth $4.21 in inflation-adjusted 2012 dollars.

Data Appendix and Revisions. Appendix B includes the aggregate denominational data used in the analyses in this study. When available, the data for the denominations included in these analyses appears as it was reported in editions of the *YACC*. Data for one or more years was also obtained directly from the denominational office. In addition, the denominational giving data set has been refined and revised as additional information has become available. Where relevant, this information is noted in the appendix.

Endnote to Introduction

[1] John Ronsvalle and Sylvia Ronsvalle; "National Church Leaders Response Form"; *The State of Church Giving through 1998* (2000 edition); <https://www.emptytomb.org/survey1.html>.

chapter 1

Church Member Giving, 1968–2021

"I tell you the truth, anyone who has faith in me will do what I have been doing. He will do even greater things than these, because I am going to the Father." — Jesus in John 14:12

"However, when the Son of Man comes, will he find faith on the earth?"
— Jesus in Luke 18:8

Introduction

Last year's edition, the 32nd, incorporated revisions to some of the data analyzed in *The State of Church Giving* series.

One factor was a revision of the Implicit Price Deflators for Gross Domestic Product for 1929 through 2020 released by the U.S. Bureau of Economic Analysis (BEA). In addition, the BEA revised the current-dollar U.S. per capita Disposable (after-tax) Personal Income (DPI) series for Data Years 1999 through 2020.

The other change was a revision of the 1999 through 2019 data series for the Southern Baptist Convention, the largest Protestant denomination in the U.S.[1]

This 33rd edition in *The State of Church Giving* series builds on these revisions.

The first three chapters in this 33rd edition consider different aspects of church member giving numbers from 1968 through 2021.

In chapter 4, long-term trends, over a period of 101 years, are observed in both church giving and membership in the U.S. for a data set of 11 denominations.

Chapter 5 considers what the trends in the first four chapters suggest will be patterns in the future. Chapter 6 explores the potential of church members to intentionally change the observed patterns.

Chapter 7 explores philanthropy for the entire population in the U.S. Of note is that the analysis of charitable giving patterns in the U.S. Bureau of Labor Statistics Consumer Expenditure Survey found once again that Americans generally identified giving to "Church, religious organizations" as the single largest recipient category. This finding lends urgency to understanding what church giving patterns mean because of the apparent broader relationship to giving in general.

Chapter 8 explores the idea that church members could choose to turn this age of affluence into the age of intentional miracles.

To begin the discussion, chapter 1 lays a groundwork of giving trends from 1968 through 2021 for a set of composite denominations that have provided data during that period.

Overview of Church Member Giving, 1968 through 2021

Giving Categories. When a dollar is given to the church, it may be categorized by one of two major subcategories, using the long-standing annual reporting form definitions of the *Yearbook of American and Canadian Churches* (YACC) series.

Giving can be considered as a percent of income, which places the amount given in the context of the total income resources available to the donor.

The first subcategory is Congregational Finances. This subcategory refers to those expenditures that support the operations of the local congregation, such as building and utilities, pastor and staff salaries, insurance, music, and Sunday school materials.

The second subcategory is Benevolences, which generally refers to expenditures for what might be termed the broader mission of the church, beyond the local congregation. Benevolences includes everything from support of regional and national denominational offices to the local soup kitchen, from seminaries to international ministries.

Total Contributions is the sum of Congregational Finances and Benevolences.

Giving can be considered as a percent of income, which places the amount given in the context of the total income resources available to the donor. Giving as a percent of income is the preferred category in this volume, although per member giving in both current and inflation-adjusted dollars are also considered. For a discussion about these three approaches to considering giving, see the "Details of Church Member Giving, 1968-2021" section below.

Giving as a Percent of Income, 1968-2021. Figure 1 presents per member giving as a portion of income to churches among the members of the basic set of denominations in this analysis, referred to as the composite set. As can be observed from this chart, between 1968 and 2021, giving as a portion of income declined to Total Contributions, Congregational Finances, and Benevolences. Giving as a percent of income to Congregational Finances was at its lowest point in 2021, with Total Contributions and Benevolences up slightly from their low points in 2020. The overall decline in giving as a portion of income from 1968 to 2021 suggests that the church is commanding less of church members' attention, as evidenced by giving to churches compared to other spending priorities that absorbed an increasing share of their incomes.

Giving in Dollars, 1968 through 2021. Per member giving measured in current dollars (the value the dollar had in the year it was given) increased overall from 1968 through 2021.[2] This increase was evident in giving to Total Contributions, and to the two subcategories of Congregational Finances and Benevolences. Generally, giving in current dollars increased every year to churches, until 2008 when the first decrease occurred in the 1968-2021 period.

Figure 1: Per Member Giving to Total Contributions, Congregational Finances, and Benevolences, Percent of Income, 1968-2021

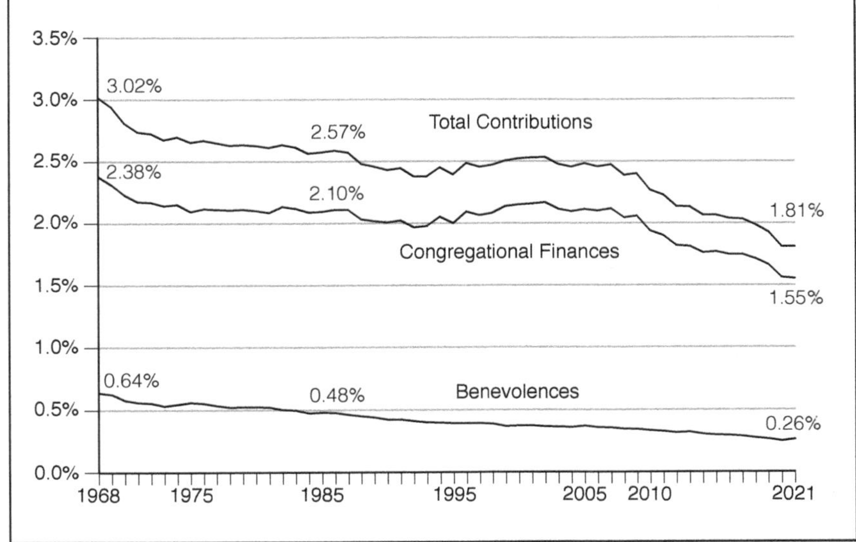

Source: empty tomb analysis; *YACC* adjusted series; U.S. BEA   empty tomb, inc., 2024

By applying a "deflator" to convert each year's current dollars to the value they would have had in a standard year, in the present case the year 2012, the effect of inflation can be factored out of the current dollars. Figure 2 presents the changes in inflation-adjusted dollar contributions to Total Contributions, and the two subcategories of Congregational Finances and Benevolences. As can be observed in Figure 2, giving to each of the categories of Total Contributions, Congregational Finances, and Benevolences declined in some years throughout the 1968-2021 period.

Of the total inflation-adjusted dollar increase between 1968 and 2021, 95% was directed to Congregational Finances. Stated another way, of each additional inflation-adjusted dollar donated in 2021 compared to 1968, 95¢ was directed to Congregational Finances. This emphasis on the internal operations of the congregation helps explain the finding that Benevolences represented 21% of all church activity in 1968, and 14% in 2021.

From 1968 to 2021, per member giving to Total Contributions increased 73% in inflation-adjusted dollars. However, during this same period, U.S. Per Capita Disposable (after-tax) Personal Income

Figure 2: Changes in Per Member Giving in Inflation-Adjusted 2012 Dollars, Total Contributions, Congregational Finances, and Benevolences, 1968-2021

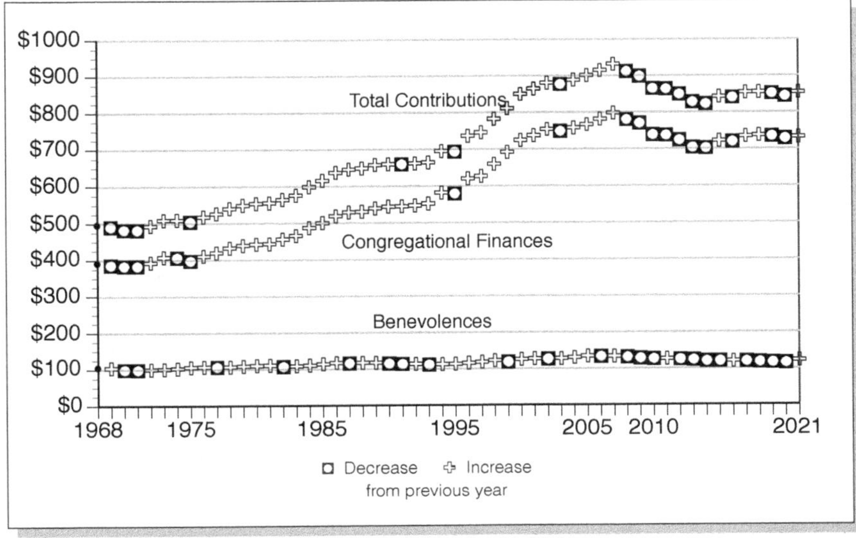

Source: empty tomb analysis; *YACC* adjusted series; U.S. BEA   empty tomb, inc., 2024

Figure 3: Per Member Giving to Congregational Finances, and Benevolences, and U.S. Per Capita Disposable Personal Income, Inflation-Adjusted 2012 Dollars, 1968-2021

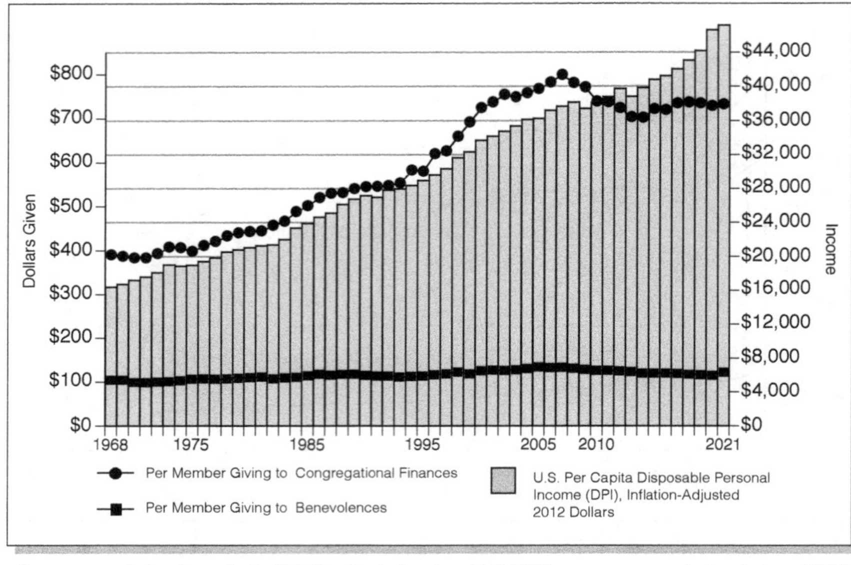

Source: empty tomb analysis; *YACC* adjusted series; U.S. BEA empty tomb, inc., 2024

(DPI) increased 188%, over twice as much as per member giving to churches. The fact that incomes increased faster than giving explains why per member giving increased in dollars overall from 1968 through 2021, but shrank as a portion of income.

Figure 3 provides a comparison of per member giving to the categories of Congregational Finances and Benevolences with changes in U.S. per capita DPI, all in inflation-adjusted 2012 dollars.

Details of Church Member Giving, 1968 through 2021

The Composite Denominations. The first study that provided a basis for the present series was published in 1988. The *YACC* series provides a church member giving data series extending back to 1921. Data for the years 1968 and 1985 could be confirmed for 31 denominations.[3] The data year 1968 was selected because, beginning that year, a consistent distinction was made between Full or Confirmed Membership and Inclusive Membership in the *YACC* series. The denominations that published data for both 1968 and 1985 included 30,226,853 Full or Confirmed Members in 1985. Data for 2010 indicates that the composite denomination set comprised approximately 100,000 of the estimated 350,000 religious congregations in the U.S.

The present church member giving report series extended the analysis for the original set of denominations beyond 1985. The current report analyzes the data set through 2021, the most recent year for which data was available at the time this report was written.[4] Also, data for the intervening years of 1969 through 1984, and 1986 through 2020, was included in the composite set, as available.[5]

Financial Categories. Calculating contributions on a per member basis accounts for any changes in membership which might have taken place during the period under review, either through growth or decline. The dollars given can be considered from two points of view. The *number of dollars given* by members indicates how much money the church has to spend. On the other hand, *giving as a percent of income* places donations in the larger context of the income available to church members, and demonstrates how church giving fared compared to other church member spending priorities.

The key general category is giving as a percent of income. This category considers not only the dollars given, but also what portion those dollars represent of the resources available to the church member who gave them. One might say that considering giving as a percent of income reflects how the donation rated in the donor church member's overall lifestyle choices, a sort of thermometer to gauge the warmth of the member's commitment. Therefore, since the point of interest is in the level of priority members place on their church giving, the more useful category is giving as a percent of income.

Even factoring out inflation, few people had the same amount of income in 2021 as in 1968. This real growth in income is taken into account in giving as a percent of income, since the number of dollars given is placed in the context of the total amount of resources available to the donor. If income goes up faster than the amount of dollars given, in a very real sense giving has decreased in the donor's priorities, because the dollars given represent a smaller portion of the donor's total spending.

If the rate of increase in income slows, and yet church giving remains steady or even increases, then the percent of income given will increase, thus suggesting a sustained level of commitment to the church even in difficult economic times.

Considering giving as a percent of income provides insight not only into the amount given by church members, but also into the priority that the members are placing on those donations, compared to other categories that attract the church members' spending. To understand how much church members have available to address, in Jesus' name, the needs before them, the percent of income given provides a better overview.

> Considering giving as a percent of income provides insight not only into the amount given by church members, but also into the priority that the members are placing on those donations ...

Giving as a percent of income is, of course, based on the dollars given, set in the context of dollars available as income. Within the category of dollars given, there are two approaches: (1) current dollars; and (2) inflation-adjusted dollars.

Current dollars refers to the value that the dollar had in the year it was donated.

The fact that dollars did not have the same purchasing power in both 1968 and 2021 should be considered. To be able to compare dollars across different years, a deflator is used to factor out the effects of inflation. When inflation is factored out, the value that the dollars had in the same year the dollars were given ("current" dollar value) is converted to the value those adjusted dollars would have in a standard year ("inflation-adjusted" dollar value). The U.S. Bureau of Economic Analysis (U.S. BEA) publishes the Implicit Price Deflator for Gross National Product series that is used to factor out inflation in this volume. For example, a current dollar gift of $5.00 in 1968 had the value, or purchasing power, of $25.53 in the year 2012, and a current dollar gift of $5.00 in the year 2021 had the value of $4.21 in the year 2012. By factoring out inflation, the value of gifts in dollars can be compared across years in a more meaningful way.

Giving as a Percent of Income, 1968-2021. The first approach to considering church member giving is giving as a portion of income. Unlike dollars, there is no distinction between current or inflation-adjusted when one is considering

Table 1: Per Member Giving as a Percent of Income,1968-2021

Year	Per Full or Confirmed Member Giving as a Percent of Income					
	Total Contrib.	↑↓	Cong. Finances	↑↓	Benevol.	↑↓
1968	3.02%	—	2.38%	—	0.64%	—
1969	2.94%	↓	2.31%	↓	0.63%	↓
1970	2.81%	↓	2.23%	↓	0.58%	↓
1971	2.74%	↓	2.18%	↓	0.56%	↓
1972	2.73%	↓	2.17%	↓	0.55%	↓
1973	2.68%	↓	2.14%	↓	0.53%	↓
1974	2.70%	↑	2.15%	↑	0.55%	↑
1975	2.65%	↓	2.09%	↓	0.56%	↑
1976	2.67%	↑	2.12%	↑	0.55%	↓
1977	2.65%	↓	2.11%	↓	0.54%	↓
1978	2.63%	↓	2.11%	↓	0.52%	↓
1979	2.64%	↑	2.11%	↑	0.52%	↑
1980	2.63%	↓	2.10%	↓	0.53%	↑
1981	2.61%	↓	2.09%	↓	0.52%	↓
1982	2.64%	↑	2.13%	↑	0.50%	↓
1983	2.62%	↓	2.12%	↓	0.50%	↓
1984	2.56%	↓	2.09%	↓	0.48%	↓
1985	2.57%	↑	2.10%	↑	0.48%	↑
1986	2.59%	↑	2.11%	↑	0.48%	↓
1987	2.57%	↓	2.11%	↑	0.46%	↓
1988	2.48%	↓	2.03%	↓	0.45%	↓
1989	2.46%	↓	2.02%	↓	0.44%	↓
1990	2.43%	↓	2.01%	↓	0.42%	↓
1991	2.44%	↑	2.02%	↑	0.42%	↓
1992	2.38%	↓	1.97%	↓	0.41%	↓
1993	2.38%	↓	1.98%	↑	0.40%	↓
1994	2.45%	↑	2.05%	↑	0.40%	↓
1995	2.39%	↓	2.00%	↓	0.39%	↓
1996	2.49%	↑	2.09%	↑	0.39%	↓
1997	2.46%	↓	2.06%	↓	0.39%	↓
1998	2.47%	↑	2.08%	↑	0.39%	↓
1999	2.51%	↑	2.14%	↑	0.37%	↓
2000	2.52%	↑	2.15%	↑	0.37%	↑
2001	2.53%	↑	2.16%	↑	0.37%	↓
2002	2.53%	↑	2.17%	↑	0.36%	↓
2003	2.48%	↓	2.12%	↓	0.36%	↓
2004	2.46%	↓	2.10%	↓	0.36%	↓
2005	2.48%	↑	2.11%	↑	0.37%	↑
2006	2.46%	↓	2.10%	↓	0.36%	↓
2007	2.47%	↑	2.12%	↑	0.35%	↓
2008	2.39%	↓	2.04%	↓	0.35%	↓
2009	2.40%	↑	2.06%	↑	0.34%	↓
2010	2.27%	↓	1.94%	↓	0.33%	↓
2011	2.23%	↓	1.90%	↓	0.33%	↓
2012	2.14%	↓	1.82%	↓	0.32%	↓
2013	2.13%	↓	1.81%	↓	0.32%	↑
2014	2.06%	↓	1.76%	↓	0.30%	↓
2015	2.07%	↑	1.77%	↑	0.29%	↓
2016	2.04%	↓	1.75%	↓	0.29%	↓
2017	2.03%	↓	1.75%	↑	0.29%	↓
2018	1.98%	↓	1.71%	↓	0.27%	↓
2019	1.93%	↓	1.66%	↓	0.26%	↓
2020	1.81%	↓	1.56%	↓	0.25%	↓
2021	1.81%	↑	1.55%	↓	0.26%	↑

Details in table may not compute to numbers shown due to rounding. empty tomb, inc., 2024
Source: empty tomb analysis; *YACC* adjusted series; U.S. BEA

giving as a percent of income. So long as one compares current dollar giving to current dollar income when calculating the percent of income — or inflation-adjusted giving to inflation-adjusted income — the percent will be the same.

In Table 1, giving as a percent of income is presented for per member Total Contributions, and the two subcategories of Congregational Finances and Benevolences. The arrows indicate whether the percent of income in that category increased or decreased from the previous year. Inasmuch as the percent figures are rounded to the second decimal place, the arrows indicate the direction of a slight increase or decrease, including for those values in which the percent provided appears to be the same numerical figure as the previous year.

A review of Table 1 yields the following information.

Overall, per member giving to Total Contributions as a percent of income decreased from 3.02% in 1968 to 1.81% in 2021, a change of -40% in the portion of income donated to the church compared to the 1968 base. Giving to Total Contributions as a percent of income decreased 34 of a possible 53 times, or 64% of the time, between 1968 and 2021.

Unlike measuring only the dollars given, considering giving as a percent of income takes into account changes in the resources available to the donor as well. U.S. per capita Disposable (after-tax) Personal Income (DPI) serves as an average income figure for the broad spectrum of church members included in the composite denominations data set.

U.S. per capita DPI was $3,208 in current dollars in 1968. When that figure was calculated in inflation-adjusted 2012 dollars, U.S. per capita DPI in 1968 was $16,381.

The current-dollar DPI figure for 2021 was $56,065. When inflation was factored out, 2021 U.S. per capita DPI was $47,165.

After-tax per capita income in inflation-adjusted dollars increased by $30,784, an increase of 188% from 1968 to 2021. During the same period, per member Total Contributions increased 73% in inflation-adjusted dollars. This difference suggests church members applied only a portion of their increased incomes to their church giving, and explains how church member contributions could be increasing in inflation-adjusted dollars in most of the years from 1968 to 2021, and yet be decreasing as a percent of income in most of the years from 1968 to 2021.

As a percent of income, giving to Congregational Finances, the amount spent to maintain the operations of the local congregation, decreased from one year to the next 60% of the time in the 1968-2021 period. Congregational Finances declined from 2.38% in 1968 to 1.55% in 2021, a percent change of -35% from the 1968 base in giving as a percent of income.

This difference suggests church members applied only a portion of their increased incomes to their church giving ...

As a percent of income, giving to Benevolences, church members' investment in the larger mission of the church, declined from 0.64% of income in 1968 to 0.26% in 2021, a change of 59% as a portion of income from the 1968 base. In the 1968-2021 period, the portion of income that went to Benevolences declined 83% of the time, from one year to the next.

In Data Year 2021, giving as a percent of income increased to Total Contributions and Benevolences from 2020. The category of Congregational Finances continued the pattern of decline evident in Data Years 2018 through 2020. In 2021, Congregational Finances was at its lowest point in the 1968-2021 period.

Giving as a percent of Benevolences declined in 2014 through 2020 when it reached the lowest point in the 1968-2021 period. This category increased in 2021. An increase in giving to Benevolences as a percent of income in 2005 is also evident. This increase could have been a function of disaster response opportunities. The year 2005 included the Indian Ocean earthquake and related tsunami that occurred the day after Christmas in 2004, Hurricanes Katrina, Rita and Wilma, and the Pakistani earthquake. These events were presented as opportunities for compassionate response in churches.

Giving in Current Dollars, 1968-2021. Table 2 presents per member contributions in current dollars for the composite denominations data set, that is, in the value the dollars had in the year donated. Per member giving is presented as Total Contributions, and the two subcategories of Congregational Finances and Benevolences. U.S. per capita DPI is also included. The last column includes the Benevolences dollar figures divided by the DPI, yielding Benevolences as a percent of income, which is also presented in Table 1.

Table 2: Per Member Giving to Total Contributions, Congregational Finances, and Benevolences, U.S. Per Capita Disposable Personal Income, Current Dollars, and Per Member Giving to Benevolences as Percent of Income, 1968-2021

Year	Current Dollars				Per Member Giving to Benevolences as % of Income
	Per Full or Confirmed Member Giving			U.S. Per Capita Disposable Personal Income	
	Total Contrib.	Cong. Finances	Benevol.		
1968	$96.79	$76.35	$20.44	$3,208	0.64%
1969	$100.82	$79.34	$21.47	$3,432	0.63%
1970	$104.36	$82.87	$21.49	$3,715	0.58%
1971	$109.55	$87.08	$22.48	$4,002	0.56%
1972	$116.97	$93.16	$23.81	$4,291	0.55%
1973	$127.37	$102.01	$25.36	$4,758	0.53%
1974	$138.87	$110.79	$28.08	$5,146	0.55%
1975	$150.19	$118.45	$31.73	$5,657	0.56%
1976	$162.87	$129.15	$33.72	$6,098	0.55%
1977	$175.82	$140.23	$35.60	$6,634	0.54%
1978	$193.05	$154.74	$38.31	$7,340	0.52%
1979	$212.42	$170.17	$42.25	$8,057	0.52%
1980	$233.57	$186.90	$46.67	$8,888	0.53%
1981	$256.59	$205.15	$51.44	$9,823	0.52%
1982	$276.72	$223.93	$52.79	$10,494	0.50%
1983	$293.52	$237.68	$55.83	$11,216	0.50%
1984	$316.25	$257.63	$58.62	$12,330	0.48%
1985	$335.43	$272.95	$62.48	$13,027	0.48%
1986	$354.20	$288.73	$65.47	$13,691	0.48%
1987	$367.87	$301.73	$66.14	$14,297	0.46%
1988	$382.54	$313.15	$69.40	$15,414	0.45%
1989	$403.23	$331.06	$72.16	$16,403	0.44%
1990	$419.65	$346.48	$73.17	$17,264	0.42%
1991	$433.57	$358.67	$74.90	$17,734	0.42%
1992	$445.00	$368.28	$76.72	$18,714	0.41%
1993	$457.47	$380.54	$76.94	$19,245	0.40%
1994	$488.83	$409.35	$79.48	$19,943	0.40%
1995	$497.71	$416.00	$81.71	$20,792	0.39%
1996	$538.39	$453.34	$85.05	$21,658	0.39%
1997	$554.44	$465.92	$88.52	$22,570	0.39%
1998	$588.10	$495.76	$92.34	$23,806	0.39%
1999	$618.52	$527.77	$90.75	$24,684	0.37%
2000	$663.09	$564.89	$98.19	$26,274	0.37%
2001	$689.47	$587.85	$101.61	$27,255	0.37%
2002	$713.08	$610.54	$102.55	$28,160	0.36%
2003	$724.19	$618.43	$105.76	$29,230	0.36%
2004	$753.56	$642.70	$110.86	$30,674	0.36%
2005	$788.23	$670.56	$117.66	$31,732	0.37%
2006	$824.69	$704.61	$120.09	$33,558	0.36%
2007	$863.06	$739.28	$123.77	$34,899	0.35%
2008	$860.52	$736.21	$124.31	$36,021	0.35%
2009	$853.36	$731.44	$121.93	$35,568	0.34%
2010	$831.30	$709.79	$121.52	$36,654	0.33%
2011	$847.39	$723.21	$124.19	$38,059	0.33%
2012	$848.62	$723.45	$125.17	$39,732	0.32%
2013	$841.56	$715.62	$125.94	$39,474	0.32%
2014	$852.07	$727.47	$124.60	$41,276	0.30%
2015	$881.28	$755.46	$125.82	$42,672	0.29%
2016	$887.67	$760.45	$127.23	$43,556	0.29%
2017	$919.72	$790.74	$128.98	$45,252	0.29%
2018	$942.33	$812.50	$129.83	$47,473	0.27%
2019	$955.46	$824.71	$130.75	$49,585	0.26%
2020	$959.31	$828.32	$130.99	$53,034	0.25%
2021	$1,015.16	$869.91	$145.25	$56,065	0.26%

Details in table may not compute to numbers shown due to rounding. empty tomb, inc., 2024
Source: empty tomb analysis; *YACC* adjusted series; U.S. BEA

As can be seen in Table 2, the per member amount given to Total Contributions, Congregational Finances, and Benevolences increased overall in current dollars between 1968 and 2021.

From 1968 to 2021, Total Contributions to the church in current dollars increased $918.37 on a per member basis. That amounted to an increase of 949% from the 1968 base.

Of this increase, $793.56 was allocated to Congregational Finances, for the benefit of members within the congregation, an increase of 1039% for this category from its 1968 base.

Benevolences, or outreach activities of the congregation, increased by $124.81, an increase of 611% over the 1968 base.

Meanwhile, U.S. per capita DPI increased from $3,208 in 1968, to $56,065 in 2021, an increase of 1648% from the 1968 base.

In 2008, per member giving to Total Contributions decreased in current dollars for the first time in the 1968-2021 period. Declines were also observed in 2009, 2010, and 2013. It may be of interest to note, in light of the COVID pandemic, that per member giving in current dollars increased from 2019 to 2020, the first year of the pandemic.

Per member contributions to Congregational Finances in current dollars increased each year from 1968 through 2007. Declines occurred in each of the years 2008, 2009, 2010, and 2013.

The fairly consistent decline in giving as a percent of income to

Benevolences in the 1968-2021 period might lead to the assumption that current dollar giving also declined. However, in the 2008 through 2021 period, per member giving to Benevolences in current dollars declined only in 2009, 2010, and 2014. During the 1968 through 2021 period, the declines in giving as a percent of income that occurred 83% of the time to this category were apparently due not to declines in per member giving in current dollars to Benevolences, but to a consistent pattern of low levels of increase in giving that did not keep up with expanding incomes.

As noted earlier, considering changes in giving in current dollars provides a limited evaluation tool. For example, while a congregation or denomination might accurately state that members in general gave more current dollars from one year to the next, the reality of inflation's impact should be taken into account, to understand how the buying power of those dollars given might be affected.

Giving in Inflation-Adjusted Dollars, 1968-2021. Table 3 presents the current dollar per member giving converted to inflation-adjusted dollars, as well as U.S. per capita DPI, also in inflation-adjusted dollars. The arrows next to the three inflation-adjusted giving category columns are included to provide a quick reference as to whether giving increased or decreased from one year to the next.

When the effects of inflation were removed, one may note that per member giving decreased in a number of years.

When the effects of inflation were removed, one may note that per member giving decreased in a number of years. Per member giving to Total Contributions did increase overall from 1968 to 2021. However, when inflation was factored out, the percent increase was smaller than in current dollars. Per member giving to Total Contributions in inflation-adjusted dollars increased from $494.23 in 1968 to $854.00 in 2021, an increase of 73% from the 1968 base.

Congregational Finances also increased in inflation-adjusted 2012 dollars from 1968 to 2021. Overall, per member giving to Congregational Finances increased in inflation-adjusted dollars from $389.87 in 1968 to $731.81 in 2021, an increase of $341.94 or 88% from the 1968 base.

Benevolences also increased from 1968 to 2021 when adjusted for inflation, although proportionately less than Congregational Finances. From 1968 to 2021, per member giving to Benevolences in inflation-adjusted dollars increased from $104.35 in 1968 to $122.19 in 2021, an increase of $17.83, that is, 17% from the 1968 base.

U.S. per capita DPI, considered in inflation-adjusted dollars, increased from $16,381 in 1968, to $47,165 in 2021, an increase of 188% from the 1968.

Per member giving to Benevolences as a percent of income is again included in Table 3. The figures for this category are the same in both Tables 2 and 3. Because the same deflator is applied to both the giving dollars and the income dollars, per member giving to Benevolences as a percent of income is proportionally the same, whether the information is considered as current or inflation-adjusted dollars. As long as current dollar giving is compared to current dollar income, or inflation-adjusted giving is compared to inflation-adjusted income, giving as a percent of income will be the same for both series.

Table 3: Per Member Giving to Total Contributions, Congregational Finances, and Benevolences, U.S. Per Capita Disposable Personal Income, Inflation-Adjusted 2012 Dollars, and Per Member Giving to Benevolences as a Percent of Income, 1968-2021

	Inflation-Adjusted 2012 Dollars							Per Member Giving to Benevolences as % of Income
	Per Full or Confirmed Member Giving						U.S. Per Capita Disposable Personal Income	
Year	Total Contrib.	↑↓	Cong. Finances	↑↓	Benevol.	↑↓		
1968	$494.23	—	$389.87	—	$104.35	—	$16,381	0.64%
1969	$490.76	↓	$386.23	↓	$104.53	↑	$16,706	0.63%
1970	$482.54	↓	$383.17	↓	$99.37	↓	$17,177	0.58%
1971	$482.06	↓	$383.15	↓	$98.91	↓	$17,610	0.56%
1972	$493.37	↑	$392.95	↑	$100.42	↑	$18,099	0.55%
1973	$509.24	↑	$407.85	↑	$101.39	↑	$19,024	0.53%
1974	$509.47	↑	$406.46	↓	$103.01	↑	$18,880	0.55%
1975	$504.25	↓	$397.70	↓	$106.55	↑	$18,993	0.56%
1976	$518.22	↑	$410.92	↑	$107.30	↑	$19,402	0.55%
1977	$526.67	↑	$420.04	↑	$106.63	↓	$19,872	0.54%
1978	$540.25	↑	$433.05	↑	$107.20	↑	$20,541	0.52%
1979	$548.89	↑	$439.72	↑	$109.18	↑	$20,820	0.52%
1980	$553.61	↑	$443.00	↑	$110.61	↑	$21,067	0.53%
1981	$555.55	↑	$444.18	↑	$111.37	↑	$21,268	0.52%
1982	$564.28	↑	$456.64	↑	$107.64	↓	$21,399	0.50%
1983	$575.92	↑	$466.37	↑	$109.55	↑	$22,007	0.50%
1984	$598.91	↑	$487.89	↑	$111.02	↑	$23,351	0.48%
1985	$615.76	↑	$501.06	↑	$114.70	↑	$23,914	0.48%
1986	$637.32	↑	$519.53	↑	$117.80	↑	$24,635	0.48%
1987	$645.77	↑	$529.67	↑	$116.10	↓	$25,097	0.46%
1988	$648.62	↑	$530.95	↑	$117.67	↑	$26,135	0.45%
1989	$657.82	↑	$540.10	↑	$117.72	↑	$26,760	0.44%
1990	$659.78	↑	$544.74	↑	$115.04	↓	$27,143	0.42%
1991	$659.26	↓	$545.36	↑	$113.89	↓	$26,965	0.42%
1992	$661.57	↑	$547.51	↑	$114.06	↑	$27,822	0.41%
1993	$664.39	↑	$552.65	↑	$111.73	↓	$27,950	0.40%
1994	$695.11	↑	$582.10	↑	$113.02	↑	$28,359	0.40%
1995	$693.13	↓	$579.34	↓	$113.79	↑	$28,956	0.39%
1996	$736.27	↑	$619.96	↑	$116.31	↑	$29,618	0.39%
1997	$745.37	↑	$626.37	↑	$119.00	↑	$30,343	0.39%
1998	$781.79	↑	$659.04	↑	$122.75	↑	$31,646	0.39%
1999	$810.74	↑	$691.79	↑	$118.95	↓	$32,355	0.37%
2000	$849.89	↑	$724.03	↑	$125.86	↑	$33,676	0.37%
2001	$864.24	↑	$736.87	↑	$127.37	↑	$34,164	0.37%
2002	$880.14	↑	$753.57	↑	$126.57	↓	$34,757	0.36%
2003	$876.54	↓	$748.53	↓	$128.01	↑	$35,379	0.36%
2004	$888.25	↑	$757.58	↑	$130.67	↑	$36,157	0.36%
2005	$900.84	↑	$766.37	↑	$134.47	↑	$36,266	0.37%
2006	$914.30	↑	$781.17	↑	$133.13	↓	$37,204	0.36%
2007	$931.63	↑	$798.02	↑	$133.61	↑	$37,672	0.35%
2008	$911.36	↓	$779.71	↓	$131.66	↓	$38,149	0.35%
2009	$898.11	↓	$769.79	↓	$128.32	↓	$37,433	0.34%
2010	$864.48	↓	$738.12	↓	$126.37	↓	$38,117	0.33%
2011	$863.23	↓	$736.73	↓	$126.51	↑	$38,770	0.33%
2012	$848.62	↓	$723.45	↓	$125.17	↓	$39,732	0.32%
2013	$827.11	↓	$703.33	↓	$123.78	↓	$38,796	0.32%
2014	$822.05	↓	$701.84	↓	$120.21	↓	$39,822	0.30%
2015	$841.87	↑	$721.68	↑	$120.19	↓	$40,764	0.29%
2016	$839.59	↓	$719.25	↓	$120.34	↑	$41,197	0.29%
2017	$853.68	↑	$733.96	↑	$119.72	↓	$42,003	0.29%
2018	$854.15	↑	$736.47	↑	$117.68	↓	$43,031	0.27%
2019	$850.81	↓	$734.38	↓	$116.43	↓	$44,154	0.26%
2020	$843.24	↓	$728.10	↓	$115.15	↓	$46,617	0.25%
2021	$854.00	↑	$731.81	↑	$122.19	↑	$47,165	0.26%

Details in table may not compute to numbers shown due to rounding.
Source: empty tomb analysis; *YACC* adjusted series; U.S. BEA

empty tomb, inc., 2024

Implications of Giving in 2020 Compared to 2021. In light of the COVID pandemic that began in 2020, it is of interest to note that per member giving in current dollars increased to Total Contributions and to the two subcategories of Congregational Finances and Benevolences in 2020, and again in 2021.

When inflation was factored out, per member giving in inflation-adjusted dollars decreased from 2019 to 2020 to each of the three categories. One may observe In Table 3 that giving in inflation-adjusted dollars decreased from 2018 to 2019 as well. However, from 2020 to 2021, per member giving in inflation-adjusted dollars increased to all three categories.

Giving as a portion of income to Congregational Finances decreased from 2020 to 2021. However, giving as a portion of income increased to Total Contributions and Benevolences in 2021 compared to 2020.

Sometimes the change in the portion of income given can be very small from one year to the next. Yet, because there are so many members donating, even small changes are magnified. To explore the implications of these changes, consider the impact of the difference in the portion of income given to Benevolences between 2020 and 2021. For this analysis, information for the 24 denominations that reported data for both 2020 and 2021 is compared.

In 2020, per member giving to Benevolences as a portion of income measured 0.25%. In 2021, the amount measured 0.26%.

The implications of this change can be understood when translated to dollars. The unrounded difference between 2020 and 2021 Benevolences as a portion of income was an increase of 0.012067% of per capita income. When multiplied by the 2021 current dollar U.S. per capita income figure of $56,065, that change translated into an increase of about $6.77 more given in 2021 by each of the 22,228,332 members in these denominations. The combination of these average individual donations meant that the composite communions had $150.4 million more to spend in 2021 on the larger mission of the church, because of the increase in percent given.

Potential Giving at 1968 Levels. Another approach is to consider what would have been the situation in 2021 if giving had at least maintained the 1968 percentages of income donated.

The implications of the difference become clearer when aggregate totals are calculated. The 2021 current dollar DPI was multiplied by each giving category's 1968 percent of income. Each of the three resulting per member giving dollar figures was then multiplied by the number of members reported by these denominations in 2021. The result was a theoretical 2021 aggregate giving level based on the 1968 level of giving as a percent of income.

Sometimes the change in the portion of income given can be very small from one year to the next. Yet, because there are so many members donating, even small changes are magnified.

If the same portion of income had been donated in 2021, as was donated in 1968, aggregate Total Contributions would have been $37.1 billion for these denominations, rather than the actual amount given of $22.6 billion, a difference of $14.6 billion, or an increase of 65%.

Aggregate Congregational Finances would have been $29.3 billion rather than $19.3 billion, a difference of $10 billion, or an increase of 52%.

There would have been a 142% increase in the total amount received for Benevolences. Instead of receiving $3.2 billion in 2021, the amount would have been $7.8 billion available for the larger mission of the church. The additional $4.6 billion for Benevolences would have resulted, not from an increase in the portion of income given, but if giving as a percent of income had not eroded between 1968 and 2021. The additional $4.6 billion could have provided the millions of dollars that some denominations lament are not available for global evangelization. The balance could have had a significant impact on reducing the number of under-age five child deaths around the globe.

It may be tempting for denominational officials to reflect on how the additional $4.6 billion in Benevolences giving could have benefited their organizational structures, as many denominations cut back on operations during this period. However, a word of caution may be in order on that point. Church members were offered the opportunity to maintain those structures at the same level, by donating the same percent of income in 2021 as they did in 1968. They chose not to do so, as evidenced by the actual giving patterns. Whatever denominations were offering, it did not encourage church members in 2021 to maintain the level of income donated to their churches in 1968.

The answer to a follow-up question could impact how denominations relate to congregations from this point forward. That is, would church members have maintained the 1968 level of giving as a portion of income if they had the option, through the denominations, to apply the entire amount of those additional funds to the global triage tasks of expanding global evangelization and/or the prevention of child deaths from treatable causes, working through denominational structures?

The difference between the 1968 and 2021 portions of income given impacts the ministry of the church today in very real ways.

Chapters 6 and 8 of this volume consider some of the implications and consequences of the difference between actual and potential giving levels among church members.

Giving in Inflation-Adjusted Dollars, 1968 and 2021. The first report, which served as the basis for the present series on church member giving, considered data for the denominations in the composite data set for the years 1968 and 1985. With data now available through 2021, a broader trend can be reviewed for the period under discussion, the 54-year range of 1968 through 2021.

The per member amount donated to Total Contributions in inflation-adjusted 2012 dollars was $359.77 greater in 2021 than it was in 1968 for the denominations in the composite data set. This amount represented an average increase of $6.79 a year in per member contributions over this 53-year interval.

Gifts to Congregational Finances also increased between 1968 and 2021. Per member contributions to Congregational Finances increased $341.94, with an average annual rate of change of $6.45.

In inflation-adjusted 2012 dollars, gifts to Benevolences increased $17.83, with an annual average rate of change of $0.34.

Table 4 presents per member gifts to Total Contributions, Congregational Finances, and Benevolences in inflation-adjusted 2012 dollars for the years 1968 and 2021.

Table 4: Total Contributions, Congregational Finances, and Benevolences, Per Member Giving in Inflation-Adjusted 2012 Dollars, 1968 and 2021

	Per Member Giving in Inflation-Adjusted 2012 Dollars								
	Total Contributions			Congregational Finances			Benevolences		
Year	Per Member Giving	Difference from 1968 Base	Average Annual Diff. in $ Given	Per Member Giving	Difference from 1968 Base	Average Annual Diff. in $ Given	Per Member Giving	Difference from 1968 Base	Average Annual Diff. in $ Given
1968	$494.23			$389.87			$104.35		
2021	$854.00	$359.77	$6.79	$731.81	$341.94	$6.45	$122.19	$17.83	$0.34

Details in table may not compute to numbers shown due to rounding.
Source: empty tomb analysis; *YACC* adjusted series; U.S. BEA

empty tomb, inc., 2024

Giving as a Percent of Income, 1968 and 2021. Between 1968 and 2021, Total Contributions declined from 3.02% to 1.81% as a portion of income, an absolute change of 1.21%, a decrease of one percent of income donated to the church. The percent decline in the portion of income donated to the church in the 53-year interval was 40%.

Per member gifts to Congregational Finances measured 2.38% of income in 1968, and 1.55% in 2021. The absolute change in giving as a percent of income was -0.83%. The percent change in the portion of income to Congregational Finances, from the 1968 base, was -35%.

Table 5: Per Member Giving to Total Contributions, Congregational Finances, and Benevolences, Percent of Income, 1968 and 2021

Year	Per Member Giving as a Percent of Income		
	Total Contributions	Congregational Finances	Benevolences
1968	3.02%	2.38%	0.64%
2021	1.81%	1.55%	0.26%
Absolute Difference in Per Member Giving as a Percent of Income from 1968 Base	-1.21%	-0.83%	-0.38%
Percent Change in Giving as a Percent of Income, Calculated from 1968 Base	-40%	-35%	-59%

Details in table may not compute to numbers shown due to rounding. empty tomb, inc., 2024
Source: empty tomb analysis; *YACC* adjusted series; U.S. BEA

From 1968 to 2021, the portion of member income directed to Benevolences decreased from 0.64% to 0.26%, an absolute difference of -0.38%. The decline in the portion of income given to Benevolences translated to a percent change in giving as a percent of income of -59% from the 1968 base.

Table 5 presents per member giving to Total Contributions, Congregational Finances, and Benevolences as a percent of income in 1968 and 2021.

Endnotes for Chapter 1

[1] *The State of Church Giving through 2020: A Theology for an Age of Affluence* (Champaign, IL: empty tomb, inc., March 2023), pp. 7-8 presents more detail about both the BEA and Southern Baptist Convention data revisions.

[2] No adjustment was made in the composite data for missing denominational data in the 1968-2021 analysis. The 2021 composite data set membership represented 98.49% of the benchmark 1985 membership of the composite data set.

[3] John Ronsvalle and Sylvia Ronsvalle, *A Comparison of the Growth in Church Contributions with United States Per Capita Income* (Champaign, IL: empty tomb, inc., 1988).

[4] Two of the original 31 denominations merged in 1987, bringing the total number of denominations in the original data set to 30. As of 1991, one denomination reported that it no longer had the staff to collect national financial data, resulting in a maximum of 29 denominations from the original set, which could provide data for 1991 through 2020. Of these 29 denominations, one reported data for 1968 through 1997, but did not have financial data for 1998 through 2020. A second denomination merged with another communion not included in the original composite set but has since been added; having merged, this new denomination has not collected financial data for 2001-2020 from its congregations, although it did do a survey of congregations for one year. A third denomination indicated that the national office would no longer provide data after 2006 in order to focus on other priorities. Another denomination did not provide financial data for 2008 through 2021, although did provide membership data for 2017 through 2021. One additional denomination did not provide data after 2013. One denomination that did not report data for 2014 was able to report again starting in 2015. One denomination indicated that 2016 data was not available, but was again able to report starting with 2017 data. Therefore, the composite data for 2021 includes financial information from 24 communions in the data set. Throughout this report, what was an original set of 31 denominations in 1985 will be referred to as the composite denominations. Data for up to 31 denominations will be included for 1968 and 1985, as well as for intervening years, as available.

[5] For 1986 through 2021, annual denominational data has been obtained which represented for any given year at least 97.9% (the 2014 percent) of the 1985 Full or Confirmed Membership of the denominations included in the 1968-1985 study. The 2021 percent was 98.49%. For 1986 through 2021, the number of denominations for which data was available varied from a low of 23 denominations of a possible 30 in 2014 to a high of 29 in 1987 through 1997. For the years 1969 through 1984, the number of denominations varied from a low of 28 denominations of a possible 31 in 1971-1972 and 1974-1975 to 31 in 1983, representing at least 99.59% of the membership in the data set. No computation was made to adjust the series for missing data in this chapter. The denominational giving data considered in this analysis was obtained either from the *Yearbook of American and Canadian Churches* series, or directly in correspondence with a denominational office. For a full listing of the data used in this analysis, including the sources, see Appendix B-1.

chapter 2

Church Member Giving, for 36 Denominations 2020 to 2021

Overview of Giving for 36 Denominations, 2020-2021

The composite set of denominations considered in chapter 1 provides a longer-term view of giving patterns by church members. Having data for 1968 through 2021 allows a multi-decade review that can help inform church leaders and those concerned with levels of giving whether trends and patterns are temporary in nature, or are of longer duration, perhaps reflecting deeper changes in the giving habits of church members.

Expanding the composite set to include additional denominations with 2020 and 2021 data can provide a basis to evaluate if the 1968-2021 trends in the composite set are likely also evident in a broader sector of the church as well.

In the composite set considered in chapter 1 reported, 24 denominations reported data for both 2020 and 2021. An additional 12 denominations also provided 2020 and 2021 data.

The comparison of the composite set and the expanded set of 36 denominations is as follows.

Details of Giving for 36 Denominations, 2020-2021

The 1968-2021 analysis in chapter 1 considers data for a group of denominations that published their membership and financial information for 1968 and 1985 in the *Yearbook of American and Canadian Churches* (YACC) series. That initial set of communions, considered in the first report on which the present series of church giving is based, has served as a denominational composite set analyzed for subsequent data years.

Table 6: Per Member Giving in 36 Denominations, in Current, Inflation-Adjusted 2012 Dollars, and as a Percent of Income, 2020 and 2021

	Total Contributions			Congregational Finances			Benevolences		
Year	$ Given in Current $	$ Given in Inflation-Adj. '12 $	Giving as % of Income	$ Given in Current $	$ Given in Inflation-Adj. '12 $	Giving as % of Income	$ Given in Current $	$ Given in Inflation-Adj. '12 $	Giving as % of Income
2020	$1,023.48	$899.65	1.93%	$883.88	$776.94	1.67%	$139.60	$122.71	0.26%
2021	$1,089.71	$916.71	1.94%	$935.88	$787.31	1.67%	$153.82	$129.40	0.27%
Difference from the 2020 Base	$66.22	$17.07	0.01%	$52.00	$10.37	0.00%	$14.22	$6.70	0.011%
% Change in Giving from the 2020 Base	6.47%	1.90%	0.71%	5.88%	1.34%	0.16%	10.19%	5.46%	4.23%

Details in table may not compute to numbers shown due to rounding. empty tomb, inc., 2024
Source: empty tomb analysis; *YACC* adjusted series; U.S. BEA

For the two most recent years, 24 denominations in the composite set reported data for both 2020 and 2021.

Data for both 2020 and 2021 for an additional 12 denominations was obtained directly from denominational offices, in the absence of a YACC edition. By adding the data for these 12 denominations to that of the composite subset for these two years, giving patterns in an expanded set of 36 communions can be considered.

In this enlarged comparison, the number of 2021 Full or Confirmed Members increased from 22.2 million in the composite set to 30.0 million in the expanded set, a 35% increase in the number of members considered. The larger group of denominations included both The United Methodist Church and The Episcopal Church, which were not included in the original 1968-1985 composite set because of the unavailability of confirmed 1968 data at the time of the initial study. A list of the denominations included in the present analysis is contained in Appendix A.

Table 6 presents the data for the 36 denominations in tabular form, including per member giving in current and inflation-adjusted 2012 dollars, and giving as a percent of income.

Per Member Giving as a Percent of Income. For the 24 denominations in the composite set that provided data for both 2020 and 2021, giving as a percent of income changed from the 2020 base as follows.

- Total Contributions: 1.81% in 2020 to 1.81% in 2021, representing a slight increase of 0.1% from the 2020 base.
- Congregational Finances: 1.56% in 2020 to 1.55% in 2021, a percent change from the 2020 base of -0.7%.
- Benevolences: 0.25% in 2020 to 0.26% in 2021, a percent change of 5%.

As can be seen in the Table, in the expanded set of 36 denominations, giving as a percent followed a similar pattern to that of the composite set.

In the expanded set, the percent of income given on a per member basis to Total Contributions measured 1.93% in 2020 and 1.94% in 2021. The increase registered as a percent change of 0.7% in giving as a percent of income from the 2020 base, compared to the composite set percent change of 0.1% from the 2020 base.

Congregational Finances for the expanded set was 1.67% in 2020 and 1.67% in 2021. The percent change from the 2020 base measured 0.2%, compared to -0.7% in the composite set. Although the expanded set posted a positive increase in contrast to the composite set, the variation between the two groups was less than 1%.

Benevolences measured 0.26% in 2020 and 0.27% in 2021, a percent change from the 2020 base of 4.2%, compared to the composite set change of 4.9% from the 2020 base. Of the three giving categories, both the expanded set and the composite set posted the largest increase in per member giving as a percent of income to Benevolences.

Giving in Dollars. Per member giving in current dollars for the 24 denominations in the composite set changed from the 2020 base as follows:

- Total Contributions: from $959.31 in 2020 to $1,015.16 in 2021, an increase of $55.84, or a percent change of 6% from the 2020 base.
- Congregational Finances: from $828.32 in 2020 to $869.91 in 2021, an increase of $41.59, or a percent change of 5% from the 2020 base.
- Benevolences: from $130.99 in 2020 to $145.25 in 2021, an increase of $14.25, or a percent change of 11% from the 2020 base.

Of the three giving categories, both the expanded set and the composite set posted the largest increase in per member giving as a percent of income to Benevolences.

When the 2020 and 2021 data was adjusted to 2012 dollars to account for inflation, per member giving in the composite set changed from the 2020 base as follows.

- Total Contributions: from $843.24 in 2020 to $854.00 in 2021, an increase of $10.76, or a percent change of 1% from the 2020 base.
- Congregational Finances: from $728.10 in 2020 to $731.81 in 2021, an increase of $3.71, or a percent change of 0.5% from the 2020 base.
- Benevolences: from $115.15 in 2020 to $122.19 in 2021, an increase of $7.04, a percent change of 6% from the 2020 base.

As can be seen in Table 6, in the expanded set, per member giving in current dollars demonstrated a similar pattern when compared to that of the composite group, of increase to Total Contributions and the two subcategories of Congregational Finances and Benevolences. Overall, the expanded set posted a higher number of per member current dollars given, compared to the composite set.

In inflation-adjusted 2012 dollars, the expanded set posted increases to Total Contributions, Congregational Finances, and Benevolences, as did the composite set.

Summary. From 2020 to 2021, the composite set posted an increase in current dollar per member contributions to Total Contributions, Congregational Finances, and Benevolences. When the group was expanded to 36 denominations from the composite set of 24, with a 35% increase in membership, the expanded group also posted increases to the three giving categories in current dollars.

When the per member current dollar giving figures were adjusted to 2012 dollars to account for inflation, both the composite set and the expanded set posted increases in per member giving in inflation-adjusted dollars to Total Contributions, Congregational Finances, and Benevolences from the 2020 base. The expanded set's per member giving contribution to Congregational Finances was higher than that of the composite set. Meanwhile per member giving to Benevolences was similar in both the composite set and the expanded sets.

When considered as a percent of income, the percent change in giving as a percent of income showed only a small change to Total Contributions and Congregational Finances in both the composite set and the expanded set from 2020 to 2021. Both the composite set and the expanded set posted increases in the percent change in per member giving as a percent of income to Benevolences from 2020 to 2021: 5% in the composite set; 4% in the expanded set.

chapter 3

Church Member Giving in Denominations Defined by Organizational Affiliation, 1968, 1985, 2002, and 2021

Overview of Giving by Organizational Affiliation, 1968, 1985, 2002, and 2021

Recently, a great deal of attention has been paid to the divisions in U.S. society. People disagree on a large number of topics. Some of these divisions are also visible in the church in the U.S.

There is, however, one area on which church members across the theological spectrum appear to evidence similar attitudes. This area is money. The attitude is apparent in church member giving behavior. Over the past five decades, giving as a percent of income to churches has been declining regardless of theological perspective.

The communions included in the composite denominations data set considered in chapter 1 of this volume span the theological spectrum. Reviewing data for defined subsets within the composite group allows for additional analysis.

For example, the theory that evangelical Protestants donate more money to their churches than do members of mainline Protestant denominations can be tested by comparing giving patterns in two subgroups of communions within the composite denominations data set.

Of course, there is diversity of opinion within any denomination, as well as in multi-communion groupings. For purposes of the present analysis, however, two groups may serve as general standards for comparison, since they have been characterized as representing certain types of denominations. Specifically, the National Association of Evangelicals (NAE) has, by choice of its title, defined its denominational constituency. And traditionally, the National Council of the Churches of Christ in the U.S.A. (NCC) has counted mainline denominations among its members.

Recognizing that there are limitations in defining a denomination's theological perspectives merely by membership in one of these two organizations, a review of giving patterns of the two subsets of denominations may nevertheless provide some insight into how widely spread current giving patterns may be. Therefore, an analysis of 1968, 1985, 2002, and 2021 giving patterns was completed for two subsets of the composite denominations that were affiliated with one of these two interdenominational organizations.[1]

During the 1968-2021 period, members of evangelical Protestant denominations gave larger portions of income to their churches than did members of mainline Protestant denominations.

Also of note, the 1968-2021 decline in giving as a portion of income to Total Contributions was greater among the members of the evangelical denominations than it was among the members of the mainline denominations.

Giving as a portion of income to Congregational Finances declined among the NAE-affiliated denominations from 1968 to 1985, from 1985 to 2002, and from 2002 to 2021.

The level of giving to Congregational Finances in the NCC-affiliated denominations declined from 1968 to 1985, increased from 1985 to 2002, and then declined from 2002 to 2021.

Per member giving as a portion of income to Benevolences declined in both the evangelical and the mainline communions from 1968 to 1985, from 1985 to 2002, and again from 2002 to 2021.

Figure 4: Per Member Giving as a Percent of Income to Total Contributions, Congregational Finances, and Benevolences, Seven NAE and Eight NCC Denominations, 1968, 1985, 2002, 2021

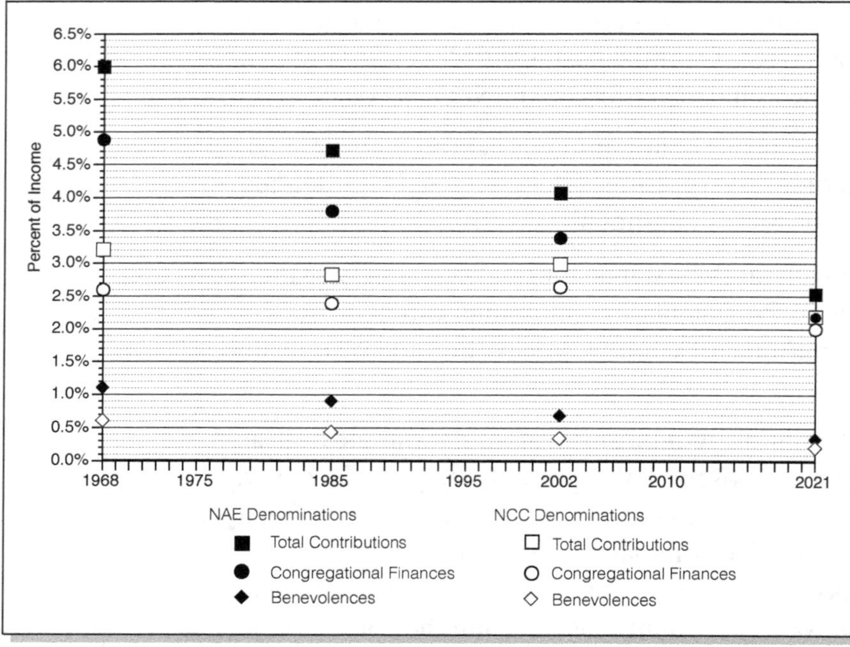

Source: empty tomb analysis; *YACC* adjusted series; U.S. BEA

empty tomb, inc., 2024

Figure 4 presents data for giving as a percent of income to Total Contributions, Congregational Finances and Benevolences for both the NAE- and NCC-affiliated denominations in graphic form for the years 1968, 1985, 2002, and 2021.

In the NAE-affiliated denominations, per member giving in inflation-adjusted dollars increased to all three categories in 1985, and again in 2002. In 2021, per member giving in these communions decreased to Total Contributions and the two subcategories of Congregational Finances and Benevolences.

In the NCC-affiliated denominations, per member giving in inflation-adjusted dollars increased to all three categories in 1985 and in 2002. From 2002 to 2021, the NCC denominations posted an increase to Congregational Finances, and a decrease to Total Contributions and Benevolences. Figure 5 presents the data for per member contributions in inflation-adjusted 2012 dollars in graphic form for the years 1968, 1985, 2002, and 2021 for both the NAE-affiliated and NCC-affiliated denominations.

By using the category of "per member," changes in membership were considered in combination with the giving patterns.

Figure 5: Per Member Giving to Total Contributions, Congregational Finances, and Benevolences, Seven NAE and Eight NCC Member Denominations, Inflation-Adjusted 2012 Dollars, 1968, 1985, 2002, and 2021

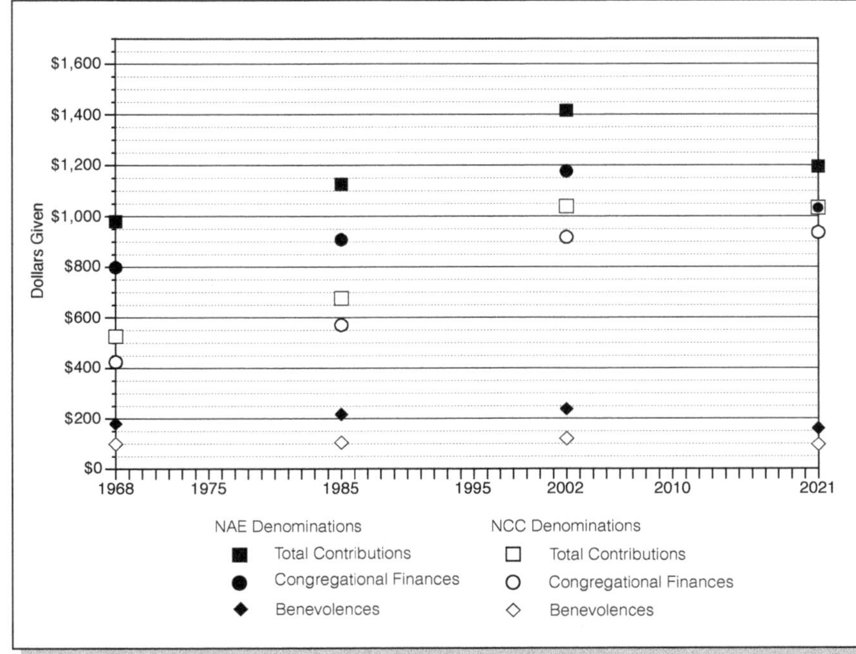

Source: empty tomb analysis; *YACC* adjusted series; U.S. BEA — empty tomb, inc., 2024

Membership in the evangelical denominations grew between 1968 and 2021. Therefore, although evangelicals were receiving a smaller portion of income per member in 2021 than was donated in 1968, aggregate donations in inflation-adjusted dollars were higher in 2021 than in 1968 for this group.

Among the mainline denominations, membership decreased from 1968 to 2021. This fact, in combination with the increase in inflation-adjusted dollars being directed to Congregational Finances, may account in part for the finding that aggregate Benevolences donations in inflation-adjusted dollars were 64 percent smaller in 2021 than in 1968 for these communions. Aggregate dollars to Total Contributions and Congregational Finances also declined, although to a lesser extent.

Details of Giving by Organizational Affiliation, 1968-2021

In the composite group, membership and financial data was available for 1968, 1985, 2002, and 2021 for seven communions affiliated with the National Association of Evangelicals (NAE).

Eight communions affiliated with the National Council of the Churches of Christ in the U.S.A. (NCC) in the composite set had membership and financial data available for 1968, 1985, 2002, and 2021.

Using 1985 data as the reference point, the seven denominations affiliated with the NAE in the present analysis represented 16% of the total number of NAE constituent bodies listed in the *Yearbook of American and Canadian Churches* (YACC) series. These seven denominations represented 18% of the NAE constituent bodies with membership data listed in the YACC, and approximately 21% of the combined membership of those NAE constituent bodies.[2]

Data for these four years was also available for eight NCC-member denominations. In 1985, these eight denominations represented 24% of the total number of NCC constituent bodies listed in the YACC; 27% of the NCC constituent bodies with membership data listed in the YACC; and approximately 29% of the combined membership of those NCC constituent bodies.[3]

Per Member Giving to Total Contributions, 1968, 1985, 2002, and 2021. As noted in Table 7, per member giving as a percent of income to Total Contributions for the seven NAE-member denominations averaged 5.99% in 1968. That year, per member giving as a percent of income to Total Contributions averaged 3.21% for the eight NCC-member denominations.

In 1985, the NAE denominations' per member giving as a percent of income level was 4.71% while the NCC level was 2.83%.

The data shows the NAE-member denominations received a larger portion of their members' incomes than did NCC-affiliated denominations in both 1968 and 1985. This information supports the assumption that denominations identifying with an evangelical perspective received a higher level of support than denominations that may be termed mainline.

The analysis also indicates that the decline in levels of giving observed in the total composite denominations set was evident among both the NAE-member

Table 7: Per Member Giving as a Percent of Income to Total Contributions, Seven NAE and Eight NCC Denominations, 1968, 1985, 2002, and 2021

	Total Contributions									
	NAE Denominations					NCC Denominations				
Year	Number of Denom. Analyzed	Total Contrib. Per Member as % of Income	Diff. in Total Contrib. as % of Income from Previous Base	Percent Change in Total Contrib. as % of Income, 1968-2021, Rate during Years from Previous Base	Avg. Annual Percent Change in Total Contrib. as % of Income from Previous Base	Number of Denom. Analyzed	Total Contrib. Per Member as % of Income	Diff. in Total Contrib. as % of Income from Previous Base	Percent Change in Total Contrib. as % of Income, 1968-2021 Rate during Years from Previous Base	Avg. Annual Percent Change in Total Contrib. as % of Income from Previous Base
1968	7	5.99%				8	3.21%			
1985	7	4.71%	-1.28%	-21.32% from '68	-1.25%	8	2.83%	-0.38%	-11.86% from '68	-0.70%
2002	7	4.07%	-0.64%	-10.64% from '85	-0.63%	8	2.99%	0.16%	4.96% from '85	0.29%
2021	7	2.53%	-1.54%	-25.70% from '02	-1.35%	8	2.19%	-0.80%	-24.84% from '02	-1.31%

Details in table may not compute to numbers shown due to rounding. empty tomb, inc., 2024
Source: empty tomb analysis; *YACC* adjusted series; U. S. BEA

denominations and the NCC-member denominations. While giving as a percent of income decreased for both sets of denominations between 1968 and 1985, the decrease in per member giving to Total Contributions as a percent of income was more pronounced in the NAE-affiliated communions. The percent change in the percent of income donated in the NAE-member denominations, in comparison to the 1968 base, was -21% between 1968 and 1985, while the percent change in percent of income given to the NCC-member denominations was -12%.

The NAE-member and NCC-member denominations posted different trends from 1985 to 2002. In the NAE-member communions, giving as a percent of income decreased to Total Contributions. In the NCC-member denominations, giving as a percent of income increased to Total Contributions.

In the NAE-affiliated communions, Total Contributions decreased from 4.71% in giving as a percent of income in 1985 to 4.07% in 2002, a decrease of 11% in the portion of income given.

In the NCC-affiliated communions, Total Contributions increased from 2.83% in giving as a percent of income in 1985 to 2.99% in 2002, an increase of 5% in the portion of income given.

The annual rate of increase in the NCC-affiliated denominations to Total Contributions from 1985 to 2002 was 0.29% while the annual rate of decrease in the NAE-affiliated denominations was -0.63%.

A decline in giving as a percent of income occurred among the seven NAE-member denominations during the 2002-2021 period. By 2021, per member giving as a percent of income to Total Contributions had declined from the 2002 level of 4.07% to 2.53% a percent decrease of -26% in the portion of members' incomes donated over that 19-year interval.

In 2021 the difference in per member giving as a percent of income between the NAE-affiliated denominations and the NCC-affiliated denominations was not as large as it had been in 1968.

The eight NCC-affiliated denominations also declined in giving as a percent of income to Total Contributions during 2002-2021, from the 2002 level of 2.99% to 2.19% in 2021. The percent decrease from the 2002 base was -25%.

In 2021 the difference in per member giving as a percent of income between the NAE-affiliated denominations and the NCC-affiliated denominations was not as large as it had been in 1968. Comparing the two rates in giving as a percent of income to Total Contributions between the NAE-member denominations and the NCC-member denominations in this analysis, the NCC-affiliated denominations received 54% as much of per capita income as the NAE-member denominations did in 1968, 60% as much in 1985, 73% as much in 2002, and 86% in 2021.

For the NAE-affiliated denominations, during the 2002 to 2021 period, the rate of decrease in the average annual percent change in per member giving as a percent of income to Total Contributions was larger in comparison to the 1968-1985 annual percent change from the 1968 base. The 1968-1985 average annual percent change was -1.25%. The annual rate of change for 2002-2021 was -1.35%.

In the NCC-member denominations, during the 1968-1985 period, the average annual percent change from the 1968 base in giving as a percent of income to Total

Contributions was -0.70%. Between 2002 and 2021, the average annual change from the 2002 base was -1.31%.

Per Member Giving to Congregational Finances and Benevolences, 1968, 1985, 2002, and 2021. Were there any markedly different patterns between the two subsets of denominations defined by affiliation with the NAE and the NCC in regard to the distribution of Total Contributions between the subcategories of Congregational Finances and Benevolences?

In 1968, the NAE-affiliated members were giving 5.99% of per capita income to their churches. Of that, 4.88% went to Congregational Finances, while 1.11% went to Benevolences. In 1985, of the 4.71% of income donated to Total Contributions, 3.80% was directed to Congregational Finances. This represented a percent change in the portion of income going to Congregational Finances of -22% from the 1968 base. Per member contributions to Benevolences among these NAE-member denominations declined from 1.11% in 1968 to 0.91% in 1985, representing a percent change of -18% from the 1968 base in the portion of income donated to Benevolences.

In the subcategory of Benevolences, both groups posted declines in the portion of income directed to that category between 1968 and 2021.

In 2002, the 4.07% of income donated to Total Contributions in the NAE-affiliated denominations was divided as 3.39% to Congregational Finances, a decrease of 8% from the 1985 base, and 0.69% to Benevolences, a decrease of 20%.

In 2021, the 2.53% of income donated in the NAE-affiliated denominations was divided between Congregational Finances and Benevolences at the 2.19% and 0.34% levels, respectively. The percent change between 2002 and 2021 in contributions to Congregational Finances as a percent of income was a change of -24%. That compares to the percent change in contributions to Benevolences as a percent of income of -31% over the same 19-year interval. The annual rate in the percent change in giving as a percent of income to Benevolences changed from -1.04% from 1968 to 1985, to -1.20% from 1985 to 2002, and to -1.63% from 2002 to 2021.

In 1968, the NCC-member denominations were giving 3.21% of per capita incomes to their churches. Of that, 2.60% went to Congregational Finances. In 1985, of the 2.83% of income donated to these communions, 2.39% went to Congregational Finances. This represented a percent change from the 1968 base in the portion of income going to Congregational Finances of -8%. In contrast, per member contributions as a percent of income to Benevolences among these same NCC-affiliated denominations had declined from 0.61% in 1968 to 0.44% in 1985, representing a percent change of -28% from the 1968 base in the portion of income donated to Benevolences.

In 2002, giving as a percent of income to Total Contributions in the NCC-affiliated denominations increased to 2.99%, and was divided as 2.64% to Congregational Finances, an increase of 10% from the 1985 base, and 0.35% to Benevolences, a decrease of 15%.

In 2021, the 2.19% of income donated by the NCC-affiliated members to their churches was divided between Congregational Finances and Benevolences at the

1.99% and 0.21% levels, respectively. The 2021 percent change in contributions to Congregational Finances as a percent of income from 2002 was a decrease of -25%.

The portion of income directed to Benevolences by these NCC-member denominations continued to decline in 2021, although at a slower rate than the 1968-1985 rate. The contributions to Benevolences as a percent of income declined from 0.35% in 2002 to the 2021 level of 0.21%, a decline of 23% over this 19-year period. The annual percent change from the 2002 base in giving as a percent of income to Benevolences was -1.22% between 2002 and 2021, compared to the 1968-1985 annual rate of -1.64%, and the 1985 to 2002 rate of -0.90%.

In the subcategory of Congregational Finances, both the NAE-affiliated and the NCC-affiliated denominations declined in giving as a portion of income between 1968 and 2021. The NAE-affiliated denominations started from a higher percent, and posted a steeper decline than the NCC-affiliated denominations. Therefore, the percent of per capita income for Congregational Finances that the NCC-affiliated denominations received in 1968 was 53% of the percent received by the NAE-affiliated denominations, 63% in 1985, 78% in 2002, and 91% in 2021. Table 8 presents the Congregational Finances giving data for the NAE and NCC denominations in 1968, 1985, 2002, and 2021.

In the subcategory of Benevolences, both groups posted declines in the portion of income directed to that category between 1968 and 2021. The NCC-affiliated denominations' portion of per capita income donated to Benevolences was 55% of the level of per capita income for Benevolences received by the NAE-affiliated denominations in 1968. Because the annual rate of decrease was faster from 1968-1985 in the NCC denominations, in 1985 those denominations received a portion of income to Benevolences that measured 48% of the portion received by the NAE-

Table 8: Per Member Giving as a Percent of Income to Congregational Finances, Seven NAE and Eight NCC Denominations, 1968, 1985, 2002, and 2021

	Congregational Finances									
	NAE Denominations					NCC Denominations				
Year	Number of Denom. Analyzed	Cong. Finances Per Member as % of Income	Diff. in Cong. Finances as % of Income from Previous Base	Percent Change in Cong. Finances as % of Income Figured for Period Noted	Avg. Annual Percent Change in Cong. Finances as % of Income	Number of Denom. Analyzed	Cong. Finances Per Member as % of Income	Diff. in Cong. Finances as % of Income from Previous Base	Percent Change in Cong. Finances as % of Income Figured for Period Noted	Avg. Annual Percent Change in Cong. Finances as % of Income
1968	7	4.88%				8	2.60%			
1985	7	3.80%	-1.08%	-22.16% from '68	-1.30%	8	2.39%	-0.21%	-8.11% from '68	-0.48%
2002	7	3.39%	-0.41%	-8.41% from '85	-0.49%	8	2.64%	0.25%	9.71% from '85	0.57%
2021	7	2.19%	-1.20%	-24.49% from '02	-1.29%	8	1.99%	-0.65%	-25.22% from '02	-1.33%

Details in table may not compute to numbers shown due to rounding.
Source: empty tomb analysis; *YACC* adjusted series; U. S. BEA

empty tomb, inc., 2024

affiliated denominations. In 2002, the annual rate of decline in giving as a percent of income to Benevolences declined in the NCC-affiliated denominations, and increased in NAE-affiliated denominations. Therefore, the NCC-affiliated denominations received a portion of income that was 51% of the portion of income received by the NAE-denominations. From 2002 to 2021, the NAE-affiliated denominations continued a faster annual rate of decline in giving as a portion of income to Benevolences than did the NCC-affiliated denominations. As a result, the NCC denominations received a portion of income that was 60% of the portion of income to Benevolences received by the NAE-affiliated denominations. Table 9 presents the Benevolences giving data for the NAE and NCC denominations in 1968, 1985, 2002, and 2021.

Table 9: Per Member Giving as a Percent of Income to Benevolences, Seven NAE and Eight NCC Denominations, 1968, 1985, 2002, and 2021

	Benevolences									
	NAE Denominations					NCC Denominations				
Year	Number of Denom. Analyzed	Benevol. Per Member as % of Income	Diff. in Benevol. as % of Income from Previous Base	Percent Change in Benevol. as % of Income Figured for Period Noted	Avg. Annual Percent Change in Benevol. as % of Income	Number of Denom. Analyzed	Benevol. Per Member as % of Income	Diff. in Benevol. as % of Income from Previous Base	Percent Change in Benevol. as % of Income Figured for Period Noted	Avg. Annual Percent Change in Benevol. as % of Income
1968	7	1.11%				8	0.61%			
1985	7	0.91%	-0.20%	-17.61% from '68	-1.04%	8	0.44%	-0.17%	-27.83% from '68	-1.64%
2002	7	0.69%	-0.22%	-20.44% from '85	-1.20%	8	0.35%	-0.09%	-15.25% from '85	-0.90%
2021	7	0.34%	-0.35%	-31.03% from '02	-1.63%	8	0.21%	-0.14%	-23.25% from '02	-1.22%

Details in table may not compute to numbers shown due to rounding.
Source: empty tomb analysis; *YACC* adjusted series; U. S. BEA

empty tomb, inc., 2024

Changes in Per Member Giving as a Percent of Income, 1968 to 2021. For the NAE-affiliated denominations, per member giving as a percent of income to Total Contributions declined from 5.99% in 1968 to 2.53% in 2021, a percent change in the portion of income given of -58% from 1968 to 2021. For these communions, Congregational Finances declined from 4.88% in 1968 to 2.19% in 2021, a change of 55% from the 1968 base. In Benevolences, the -69% change reflected a decline in the portion of income given to this category from 1.11% in 1968 to 0.34% in 2021.

For the NCC-affiliated denominations, per member giving as a percent of income to Total Contributions declined from 3.21% in 1968 to 2.19% in 2021, a percent change in the portion of income given of -32% from 1968 to 2021. In the subcategory of Congregational Finances, per member giving as a percent of income was 2.60% in 1968, and 1.99% in 2021, a change of -24%. In the subcategory of Benevolences, the level of giving decreased from 0.61% in 1968 to 0.21% in 2021, which produced a slightly smaller decline compared to that of the NAE-affiliated denominations, that is, a -66%

change in the portion of income donated to this subcategory in 2021 compared to 1968.

Table 10 presents the 1968-2021 percent change in per member giving as a percent of income to Total Contributions, Congregational Finances and Benevolences in both the NAE- and NCC-affiliated communions.

Table 10: Percent Change in Per Member Giving as a Percent of Income, Seven NAE and Eight NCC Denominations, 1968 to 2021

	NAE Denominations				NCC Denominations			
Year	Number of Denom. Analyzed	Total Contrib.	Cong. Finances	Benevol.	Number of Denom. Analyzed	Total Contrib.	Cong. Finances	Benevol.
1968	7	5.99%	4.88%	1.11%	8	3.21%	2.60%	0.61%
2021	7	2.53%	2.19%	0.34%	8	2.19%	1.99%	0.21%
% Chg. 1968-'21	7	-58%	-55%	-69%	8	-32%	-24%	-66%

Details in table may not compute to numbers shown due to rounding. empty tomb, inc., 2024
Source: empty tomb analysis; *YACC* adjusted series; U. S. BEA

Per Member Giving in Inflation-Adjusted 2012 Dollars. The NAE-affiliated group's level of per member support to Total Contributions in inflation-adjusted 2012 dollars was $980.41 in 1968. This increased to $1,126.10 in 1985 to $1,415.43 in 2002, and decreased to $1,195.27 in 2021.

For the NAE-affiliated denominations, per member contributions in inflation-adjusted 2012 dollars to the subcategory of Congregational Finances increased from 1968 to 1985, and from 1985 to 2002, and then decreased from 2002 to 2021. Per member contributions in inflation-adjusted 2012 dollars to Benevolences increased between 1968 and 1985, and from 1985 to 2002, and then decreased between 2002 and 2021. Of the increased per member giving in inflation-adjusted dollars between 1968 and 2021, 109% went to Congregational Finances.

The NCC-affiliated group also experienced an increase in inflation-adjusted per member Total Contributions between 1968 and 2021. The 1968 NCC level of per member support in inflation-adjusted 2012 dollars was $525.83. In 1985, this had increased to $676.64, in 2002 increased to $1,038.84, but decreased in 2021 to $1,033.53.

The NCC-member denominations experienced an increase in inflation-adjusted per member donations to Congregational Finances from 1968 to 1985, from 1985 to 2002, and from 2002 to 2021 as well. Of the increase between 1968 and 2021 to Total Contributions, 101% was directed to Congregational Finances. Gifts to Benevolences increased in inflation-adjusted 2012 dollars between 1968 and 1985, and increased between 1985 and 2002, but decreased from 2002 to 2021.

As a portion of Total Contributions, the NAE-member denominations directed 18% of their per member gifts to Benevolences in 1968, 19% in 1985, 17% in 2002, and 13% in 2021.

The NCC-member denominations directed 19% of their per member gifts to Benevolences in 1968, 16% in 1985, 12% in 2002, and 9% in 2021.

Table 11: Per Member Giving in Seven NAE and Eight NCC Denominations, Inflation-Adjusted 2012 Dollars, 1968, 1985, 2002, and 2021

	NAE Denominations					NCC Denominations				
Year	Number of Denom. Analyzed	Total Contrib.	Cong. Finances	Benevol.	Benevol. as % of Total Contrib.	Number of Denom. Analyzed	Total Contrib.	Cong. Finances	Benevol.	Benevol. as % of Total Contrib.
1968	7	$980.41	$799.26	$181.15	18%	8	$525.83	$425.81	$100.03	19%
1985	7	$1,126.10	$908.20	$217.89	19%	8	$676.64	$571.25	$105.39	16%
2002	7	$1,415.43	$1,177.30	$238.13	17%	8	$1,038.84	$918.01	$120.82	12%
2021	7	$1,195.27	$1,033.99	$161.28	13%	8	$1,033.53	$936.53	$97.00	9%
$ Diff. '68-'21		$214.86	$234.74	-$19.87			$507.69	$510.72	-$3.03	
% Chg. '68-'21		22%	29%	-11%			97%	120%	-3%	

Details in table may not compute to numbers shown due to rounding. empty tomb, inc., 2024
Source: empty tomb analysis; *YACC* adjusted series; U. S. BEA

Table 11 above presents the levels of per member giving to Total Contributions, Congregational Finances and Benevolences, in inflation-adjusted 2012 dollars, and the percent of Total Contributions that went to Benevolences in 1968, 1985, 2002, and 2021, for both sets of denominations. In addition, the percent change from 1968 to 2021, from the 1968 base, in per member inflation-adjusted 2012-dollar contributions is noted.

Aggregate Dollar Donations, 1968 and 2021. The NCC-member denominations and the NAE-member denominations differed in terms of changes in membership. The impact of this difference was evident at the aggregate dollar level.

Table 12 considers aggregate giving data for the seven NAE-member denominations included in this analysis. Membership in these seven NAE-member denominations increased 46% from 1968 to 2021.

As measured in current aggregate dollars, giving in each of the three categories of Total Contributions, Congregational Finances and Benevolences was greater in 2021 than in 1968 for the NAE-member denominations. This was true even though per member giving as a portion of income declined to all three categories during this period.

Table 12: Aggregate Giving, Seven NAE Denominations, Current and Inflation-Adjusted 2012 Dollars, 1968 and 2021

			Current Dollars			Inflation-Adjusted 2012 Dollars		
Year	Number of Denom. Analyzed	Membership	Total Contributions	Congregational Finances	Benevolences	Total Contributions	Congregational Finances	Benevolences
1968	7	534,153	$102,559,195	$83,608,888	$18,950,307	$523,688,700	$426,924,469	$96,764,231
2021	7	777,280	$1,104,383,970	$955,366,217	$149,017,753	$929,060,890	$803,699,992	$125,360,898
% Chg.		46%	977%	1043%	686%	77%	88%	30%

Details in table may not compute to numbers shown due to rounding. empty tomb, inc., 2024
Source: empty tomb analysis; *YACC* adjusted series; U. S. BEA

The same can be said for the three aggregate categories when inflation was factored out by converting the current dollars to inflation-adjusted 2012 dollars. These denominations have been compensated for a decline in giving as a percent of income to all three categories by the increase in total membership. As long as these denominations continue to grow in membership, their national and regional programs may not be affected in the immediate future by the decline in the portion of income donated.

Table 13 below considers aggregate data for the eight NCC-member denominations. The NCC-related denominations experienced a membership change of -63% between 1968 and 2021. The increase in current dollar donations was sufficient to result in an increase in aggregate current dollars in each of the three categories of Total Contributions, Congregational Finances and Benevolences.

However, the inflation-adjusted 2012-dollar figures account for any acknowledged financial organizational difficulties in many of these communions, particularly in the category of Benevolences. The impact of the decline in membership was evident at the aggregate dollar level. Between 1968 and 2021, while the NCC-related communions experienced an increase of 97% in per member giving to Total Contributions in inflation-adjusted 2012 dollars — from $525.83 in 1968 to $1,033.53 in 2021 — aggregate Total Contributions in 2021 to these eight denominations changed by -27% in inflation-adjusted 2012 dollars in 2021 compared to 1968.

Further, Congregational Finances absorbed almost all of the increased giving at the aggregate level. Even so, aggregate inflation-adjusted dollars to Congregational Finances posted a -18% change from 1968 to 2021. A change of -64% in aggregate inflation-adjusted dollars to Benevolences between 1968 and 2021 impacted activities at the denominational level.

Table 13: Aggregate Giving, Eight NCC Denominations, Current and Inflation-Adjusted 2012 Dollars, 1968 and 2021

Year	Number of Denom. Analyzed	Membership	Current Dollars			Inflation-Adjusted 2012 Dollars		
			Total Contributions	Congregational Finances	Benevolences	Total Contributions	Congregational Finances	Benevolences
1968	8	12,876,821	$1,326,045,714	$1,073,798,710	$252,247,004	$6,771,066,759	$5,483,040,799	$1,288,025,960
2021	8	4,798,178	$5,894,863,874	$5,341,635,862	$553,228,012	$4,959,042,890	$4,493,640,890	$465,402,000
% Chg.		-63%	345%	397%	119%	-27%	-18%	-64%

Details in table may not compute to numbers shown due to rounding.
Source: empty tomb analysis; *YACC* adjusted series; U. S. BEA

empty tomb, inc., 2024

Endnotes for Chapter 3

[1] The denominations considered in this chapter are listed in Appendix A.

[2] The 1985 total church membership estimate of 3,388,414 represented by NAE denominations includes YACC 1985 membership data for each denomination where available or, if 1985 membership data was not available, membership data for the most recent year prior to 1985. Full or Confirmed membership data was used except in those instances where this figure was not available, in which case Inclusive Membership was used.

[3] The 1985 total church membership estimate of 39,621,950 represented by NCC denominations includes *YACC* 1985 membership data for each denomination where available or, if 1985 membership data was not available, membership data for the most recent year prior to 1985. Full or Confirmed membership data was used except in those instances where this figure was not available, in which case Inclusive Membership was used.

chapter 4

Church Member Giving and Membership in 11 Denominations, 1921–2021

Overview of Giving and Membership, 1921-2021

A continuing feature in this ongoing series on church member giving is an analysis of available giving data for the 101 years since 1921. Because of the fixed nature of the data source, the overall analysis remains fairly static. However, the data can now be updated to include information through 2021. Further, repeated reviews of the data may suggest additional perspectives.

For the period 1921 through 2021, the preferable approach would be to analyze the entire composite denominations data set considered in chapter 1 of this volume. Unfortunately, comparable data since 1921 is not readily available for all of these communions. However, data over an extended period of time is available in the *Yearbook of American and Canadian Churches (YACC)* series for a group of 11 Protestant communions or their historical antecedents. This set includes ten mainline Protestant communions and the Southern Baptist Convention.

The available data has been reported fairly consistently over the time span of 1921 to 2021.[1] The most recent years were obtained directly from the denominations in order to extend the series through 2021. The value of the multiyear comparison is that it provides a historical time line over which to observe giving patterns.

A review of per member giving as a portion of income during the 1921 through 2021 period found that the portion of income given was above three percent during two multiyear periods. From 1922 through 1933 and then again from 1959 through 1961, per member giving as a percent of income was at or above 3%. This relatively high level of giving is particularly interesting because per capita Disposable (after-tax) Personal Income (DPI) was also increasing from 1922-1927 (with the exception of

Figure 6: Per Member Giving as a Percent of Income in 11 Denominations, and U.S. Per Capita Disposable Personal Income in Inflation-Adjusted 2012 Dollars, 1921-2021

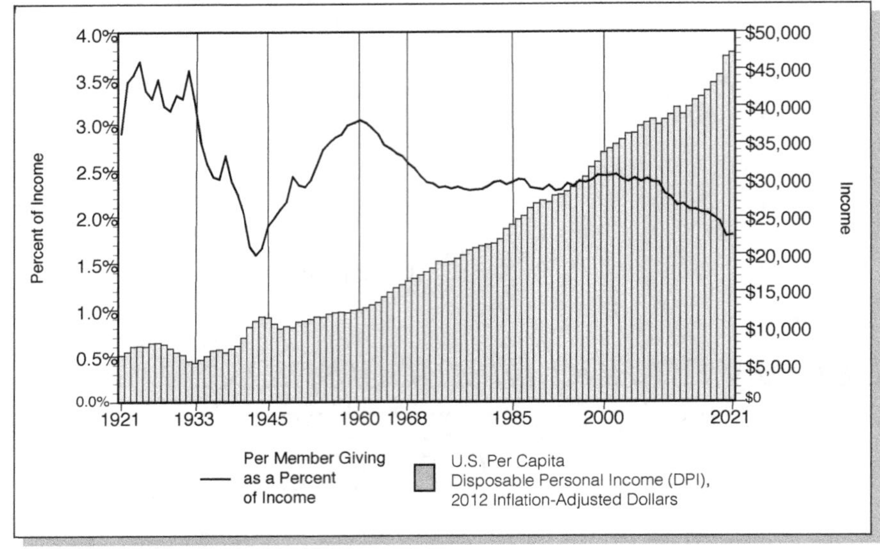

Source: empty tomb analysis; *YACC* adjusted series; U.S. BEA empty tomb, inc., 2024

1925), and from 1950 through 1961, with the exception of 1954 and 1958. However, unlike after 1933, when the country was experiencing the Great Depression followed by World War II, no major national catastrophes explain the drop below 3% after 1961.

Per member giving as a percent of income was at a low point during World War II, recovered during the 1950s, and then declined fairly steadily during the 1960s. The decline in giving as a percent of income that began after the peak in 1960 continued with occasional interruption until 1979. After a period of annual increase from 1980 through 1983, giving began to alternate increases with decreases, and by 1992 was at 2.28%. Giving as a percent of income then increased in more years than it declined from 1993 through 2002. From 2003 through 2021, there were more declines than increases. By 2021, the level of giving as a percent of income was at 1.80%. The years 2020, when giving was 1.79%, and 2021 posted the lowest levels of giving as a percent of income in the 1921-2021 period with the exception of the World War II years of 1942-1944. Giving as a percent of income in 2011 through 2021 measured lower than the 2010 low point of 2.25% in the 1968 through 2010 period.

Figure 6 contrasts per member giving as a percent of income for a group of eleven Protestant denominations, with U.S. per capita DPI in inflation-adjusted 2012 dollars, for the period 1921 through 2021.

By 2021, U.S. per capita DPI had increased 648% since 1921 in inflation-adjusted 2012 dollars, and 792% since 1933 — the depth of the Great Depression.

Meanwhile, by 2021, per member giving in inflation-adjusted 2012 dollars had increased 365% since 1921, and 396% since the depth of the Great Depression.

Consequently, per member giving as a percent of income was lower in 2021 than in either 1921 or 1933. In 1921, per member giving as a percent of income was 2.9%. In 1933, it was 3.2%. In 2021, per member giving as a percent of income was 1.8% for the group of the eleven denominations considered in this chapter. By 2021, the per member portion of income donated to the church had declined by 38% from the 1921 base, and by 44% from the 1933 base.

Membership in absolute numbers increased for the group of 11 denominations on a fairly regular basis from 1921 until 1968, when it peaked at 37.8 million members.

However, as a portion of U.S. population, the group's peak was earlier, in 1961, when the 36.7 million members in the 11 denominations represented 20% of the U.S. population. The decline in membership as a percent of U.S. population that began in 1962 continued through 2021.

Figure 7: Per Member Giving as a Percent of Income and Membership as a Percent of U.S. Population, 11 Denominations, 1921-2021

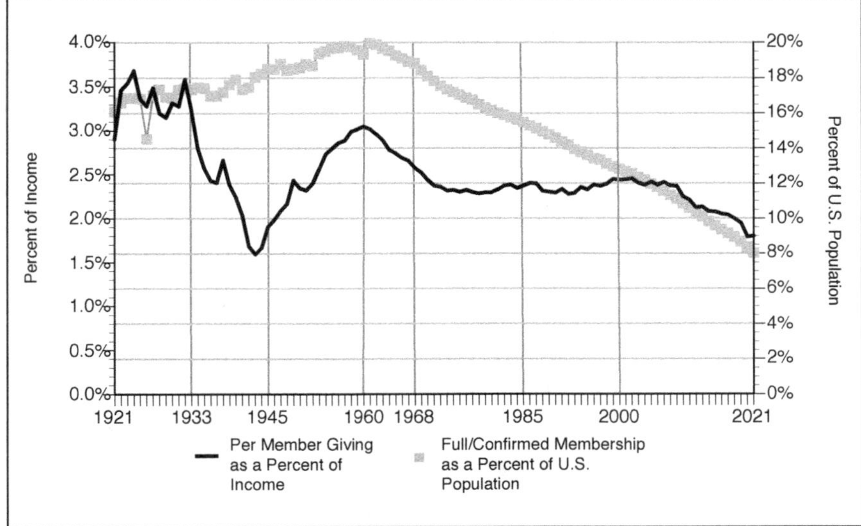

Source: empty tomb analysis; *YACC* adjusted series; U.S. BEA

empty tomb, inc., 2024

It is of some interest to note that the ongoing decline in membership as a percent of U.S. population in the set of 11 denominations began in 1962, one year after the decline in giving as a percent of income that occurred in 1961, the first such decline since 1951. Giving as a portion of income declined 40 of 61 times from 1961 through 2021, increasing 21 times. However, the decline in membership as a percent of U.S. population that began in 1962 continued uninterrupted through the year 2021.

Figure 7 presents both per member giving as a percent of income and membership as a percent of U.S. population for the group of eleven Protestant denominations from 1921 through 2021.

Details of Giving and Membership, 1921-2021

Giving as a Percent of Income. The period under consideration in this section of the report began in 1921. At that point, per member giving as a percent of income was 2.9%. In current dollars, U.S. per capita DPI was $555 and per member giving was $16.10. When inflation was factored out by converting both income and giving to 2012 dollars, per capita income in 1921 measured $6,302 and per member giving was $182.94.

From 1922 through 1933, giving as a percent of income stayed above the 3% level. The high was 3.7% in 1924, followed closely by the amount in 1932, when per member giving measured 3.6% of per capita income. This trend is of particular interest inasmuch as per capita income was generally increasing in inflation-adjusted dollars between 1921 and 1927, with the exception of 1925. Even as people were increasing in personal affluence, they also continued to maintain a giving level of more than 3% to their churches. After income began to decline during the economic reverses in the early years of the Great Depression, giving continued to measure above 3% from 1928 through 1933.

The year 1933 was the depth of the Great Depression. Per capita income was at the lowest point it would reach between 1921 and 2021, whether measured in current or inflation-adjusted dollars. Yet per member giving as a percent of income was 3.2%. Income had decreased by 16% between 1921 and 1933 in inflation-adjusted 2012 dollars, from $6,302 to $5,290. Meanwhile, per member giving decreased 6%, from $182.94 in 1921 to $171.30 in 1933, in inflation-adjusted dollars. Therefore, giving as a percent of income actually increased from 2.9% in 1921 to 3.2% in 1933, an increase of 12% in the portion of income contributed to the church.

Giving in inflation-adjusted 2012 dollars declined from 1933 to 1934, although income began to recover in 1934. Giving then began to increase again in 1935. In inflation-adjusted dollars, giving did not surpass the 1927 level of $280.78 until 1953, when giving grew from $269.12 in 1952 to $296.25 in 1953.

During World War II, incomes improved rapidly. Meanwhile, church member giving increased only modestly in current dollars in the early years of the war, perhaps affected by the war effort. When inflation was factored out, per member giving was $176.85 in 1941, the year the United States entered the war. It declined to $171.26 in 1942, increased in 1943 to $174.77, and then to $192.39 in 1944. During this time, income in inflation-adjusted dollars grew from $8,697 in 1941 to $10,161 in 1942, $10,977 in 1943, and reached a high for this period of $11,554 in 1944, an income level that would not be surpassed again until 1953. Thus, giving as a percent of income reached a low point during the three full calendar years of formal U.S. involvement in World War II, at levels of 1.69% in 1942, 1.59% in 1943, and 1.67% in 1944.

During World War II, incomes improved rapidly. Meanwhile, church member giving increased only modestly in current dollars in the early years of the war, perhaps affected by the war effort.

In 1945, the last year of the war, U.S. per capita income was $11,445 in inflation-adjusted dollars. Giving in inflation-adjusted dollars increased from $192.39 in 1944, to $218.14 in 1945, the highest inflation-adjusted dollar amount it had been since 1930. Although per member giving increased 27% between 1933 and 1945, per capita income increased 116%. Giving as a percent of income therefore declined from the 3.2% level in 1933 to 1.9% in 1945.

The unusually high level of per capita income slumped after the war but had recovered to war levels by the early 1950s. By 1960, U.S. per capita income was 10% higher in inflation-adjusted 2012 dollars than it had been in 1945, increasing from $11,445 in 1945 to $12,534 in 1960. Meanwhile, per member giving in inflation-adjusted dollars increased 75% from $218.14 in 1945 to $381.77 in 1960. Giving as a portion of income recovered to the pattern of 1922 through 1933, that is, above 3%, and stayed above 3% from 1959 through 1961. Giving as a percent of income reached a postwar high of 3.05% in 1960, and then began to decline in 1961, although that year still posted an average of 3.01% of DPI given to the church.

For the second time in the century, giving levels were growing to, or maintaining a level above, three percent of income even while incomes were also expanding. From 1921-1927, incomes expanded 28%. During this time giving grew to above 3% and stayed there. From 1950-1961, incomes grew 18%. Again, giving grew to above 3% in 1959 and stayed there through 1961. In both cases, church members increased or maintained their giving levels even as their incomes increased.

In the 1920s, the economic expansion was interrupted by the Great Depression, followed by World War II.

In contrast to the economic upheaval earlier in the century, however, the economy continued to expand through the 1960s. Yet the portion of income given was not sustained above 3%. By 1968, giving as a percent of income declined to 2.6% for this group of 11 communions. U.S. per capita income increased 31% in inflation-adjusted 2012 dollars between 1960 and 1968, from $12,534 in 1960 to $16,381 in 1968. In comparison, per member giving increased 10% in inflation-adjusted dollars, from the 1960 level of $381.77 to the 1968 level of $421.63.

By 1985, per member giving had increased 35% in inflation-adjusted 2012 dollars, from $421.63 in 1968 to $567.28 in 1985. U.S. per capita income measured $23,914 in 1985, an increase of 46% over the 1968 level of $16,381. Giving as a percent of income, therefore, measured 2.4% in 1985, representing an 8% decline from the 1968 level of 2.6%.

In the 17-year period, 1985-2002, there was a reversal in the pattern of decline. Income increased 45%, from $23,914 in 1985 to $34,757 in 2002. Meanwhile, per member giving in inflation-adjusted dollars increased 50%, from $567.28 in 1985 to $852.25 in 2002. As a result, giving as a percent of income increased 3% during this period, from 2.37% in 1985 to 2.45% in 2002.

The year 2021, nineteen years after 2002, was the latest year for which data was available for the eleven denominations considered in this section. In that year, per member giving as a percent of income was 1.80%, a 27% decrease from the 2002 level. Per member giving declined slightly in inflation-adjusted 2012 dollars, from $852.25 in 2002 to $849.83 in 2021. Meanwhile, U.S. per capita income increased 36% during this period, from the 2002 level of $34,757 to the 2021 level of $47,165.

Between 1921 and 1961, the portion of U.S. population that this group of 11 denominations represented grew from 16.1% of the U.S. population to 20%, or one-fifth of the United States.

Membership and Giving, 1921-2021. Membership was changing for this group of 11 denominations during the 1921-2021 period as well.

Between 1921 and 1961, the portion of U.S. population that this group of 11 denominations represented grew from 16.1% of the U.S. population to 20%, or one-fifth of the United States. Although the set of 11 denominations added members every year from 1949 through 1960, membership as a percent of population decreased in 1952, and then three years in a row, in 1958, 1959, and 1960, from 19.8% to 19.3%. Previously, the longest decline had been two years in a row. Then, the group of 11 denominations added 1.7 million members in 1961, and peaked at 20% of U.S. population.

In that same year of 1961, the first decline in giving as a percent of income occurred since 1951.

The 11 denominations continued to add members during 1962 through 1964, although at a slower pace. Then, from 1969 through 1973, the set of 11 denominations posted a five-year decline in the total number of members. From 1921 through 1968, there had been only six one-year declines in that 48-year period: 1926; 1929; 1936;

1941; 1948; and 1965. During 1974 through 2021, the number of members, from one year to the next, increased 10 times, and decreased 38 times, including every year from 2001 through 2021. Meanwhile, U.S. population continued to expand. Therefore, while this group represented 20% of U.S. population in 1961, by the year 2021, this group represented 8% of U.S. population.

During the 1961-2021 period, the Southern Baptist Convention grew from 9,978,139 to 13,680,493. Meanwhile, the other ten denominations, all of which might be termed mainline Protestant, declined in membership as a group, from 26,683,648[2] in 1961 to 12,997,247 in 2021.

The growth in the number of members in the Southern Baptist Convention offset the mainline Protestant membership loss to some degree, although the SBC also reported membership declines in the most recent years in the period under discussion. For the combined group of 11 denominations, membership declined from 36,661,788 in 1961 to 26,677,740 in 2021. U.S. population increased from 183,742,000 in 1961, when the group of 11 denominations represented 20% of the U.S. population, to 332,351,000 in 2021, when the 11 denominations represented 8% of the U.S. population.

In contrast, membership as a percent of population for the 11 denominations as a group began a decline in 1962 that continued uninterrupted through the year 2021.

Although the decrease in giving as a percent of income that began in 1961 resulted in giving levels varying between 2.28% and 2.30% during 1977 through 1980, the level of giving as a portion of income recovered to 2.38% by 1983 and was at 2.40% in 1986 and 1987. The level of giving as a percent of income decreased to 2.28% by 1992. The percent given measured 2.45% in 2002. From 2002 through 2021, giving as a percent of income decreased 15 out of a possible 19 times. Giving as a percent of income was 1.80% in 2021.

In contrast, membership as a percent of population for the 11 denominations as a group began a decline in 1962 that continued uninterrupted through the year 2021.

Change in Per Member Giving as a Percent of Income and Total Membership as a Percent of U.S. Population. In Table 14, giving as a percent of U.S. per capita DPI is presented for the first and last year in the period noted. The difference between giving in these two years was calculated and then divided by the number of annual intervals in the period to produce the Average Annual Change.

When considered as a portion of income in Table 14, the period of 1950-1955 posted the highest Average Annual Change in giving as a percent of income, followed by the 1955-1960 period. Giving grew to 3.0% in 1959, and a level above 3% was maintained through 1961. However, the 1960-1964 period[3] also was the period within which giving as a portion of income began to decline. It is clear from the Average Annual Change column that giving as a portion of income began a downward trend in the 1960-1964 period that continued through the 1970-1975 period. Posting an increase in the 1980-1985 period, the average annual change was again negative in the 1985-1990 period. During the 1990-1995 and 1995-2000 periods, positive change was measured, but the increases did not recover to the 1950-1960 Average Annual Change levels. The Average Annual Change for the 2005-2010, the 2010-2015, and the 2015-2021 periods were negative.

Meanwhile, during the 1950-2021 period, the group of eleven denominations shrank as a portion of U.S. population. The 1950-1955 period posted an average annual increase of 0.21% in the portion of U.S. population that these denominations represented. The 1955-1960 period posted a decline. The group of 11 denominations peaked in 1961 as a percent of U.S. population. In 1964-1970, a period of decline began that continued through 2021, with the largest annual rate of decline posted in the 2010-2015 and 2015-2021 periods.

Table 14: Average Annual Change in Per Member Giving as a Portion of U.S. Disposable Personal Income and in Membership as a Percent of U.S. Population, 11 Denominations, 1950-2021

	Per Member Giving as % of Income			Membership as % of U.S. Population		
Time Period	First Year in Period	Last Year in Period	Average Annual Change	First Year in Period	Last Year in Period	Average Annual Change
1950-1955	2.34%	2.80%	0.09%	18.58%	19.64%	0.21%
1955-1960	2.80%	3.05%	0.05%	19.64%	19.34%	-0.06%
1960-1964 [3]	3.05%	2.78%	-0.07%	19.34%	19.53%	0.05%
1964-1970 [3]	2.78%	2.44%	-0.06%	19.53%	18.10%	-0.24%
1970-1975	2.44%	2.30%	-0.03%	18.10%	17.05%	-0.21%
1975-1980	2.30%	2.30%	0.00%	17.05%	16.16%	-0.18%
1980-1985	2.30%	2.37%	0.02%	16.16%	15.48%	-0.14%
1985-1990	2.37%	2.29%	-0.02%	15.48%	14.59%	-0.18%
1990-1995	2.29%	2.33%	0.01%	14.59%	13.59%	-0.20%
1995-2000	2.33%	2.44%	0.02%	13.59%	12.82%	-0.16%
2000-2005	2.44%	2.41%	0.00%	12.82%	11.97%	-0.14%
2005-2010	2.41%	2.25%	-0.03%	11.97%	10.87%	-0.22%
2010-2015	2.25%	2.08%	-0.03%	10.87%	9.58%	-0.26%
2015-2021	2.08%	1.80%	-0.05%	9.58%	8.03%	-0.26%

Details in table may not compute to numbers shown due to rounding. empty tomb, inc., 2024
Source: empty tomb analysis; *YACC* adjusted series; U.S. BEA

Change in Per Member Giving and U.S. Per Capita Disposable Personal Income, in Inflation-adjusted 2012 Dollars. For this group of 11 communions, per member giving in inflation-adjusted 2012 dollars increased half the time during the 1921-1947 period. Per member giving in inflation-adjusted dollars decreased from 1924 to 1925. While it increased from 1925 to 1926 and again in 1927, giving began a seven-year decline in 1928. This seven-year period, from 1928 through 1934, included some of the worst years of the Great Depression. Giving increased again in 1935. Declines in 1939, 1940, 1942, 1946, and 1947 alternated with increases in the other years.

Then, in 1948 continuing through 1968,[4] the members in these 11 communions increased per member giving in inflation-adjusted 2012 dollars each year. From 1948 to 1960, per member giving averaged an increase of $13.32 a year. Although giving continued to increase through 1968, it was at the slower rate of $4.98 per year. Overall, in inflation-adjusted 2012 dollars, income grew 60% from 1948 to 1968, while per member giving increased 90%. As a result, giving as a percent of income was 2.16% in 1948 and 2.57% in 1968.

Per member giving in inflation-adjusted dollars declined in 1969, 1970 and 1971, followed by two years of increase and two of decline.

The longest sustained period of average annual increases in per member giving in inflation-adjusted dollars during the 100-year period occurred during the 27 years that include 1976 through 2002. During this time, income increased an average of $590.57 annually in inflation-adjusted 2012 dollars. Meanwhile, per member giving increased $15.44 on average each year, a higher overall rate than from 1948 to 1968, when the annual increase was $9.98. Even so, the 1976-2002 period saw an 89% increase in per member giving in inflation-adjusted dollars from the 1976 base, and the 1948-1968 period saw a 90% increase from the 1948 base. U.S. per capita income increased 79% from 1976 to 2002. Because giving increased at a faster rate than income during the 1976 to 2002 period, giving as a percent of income was 2.32% in 1976 and 2.45% in 2002.

By reviewing this data in smaller increments of the years from 1950 to 2021, the time period in which giving began to decline markedly can be identified. In Table 15, data for the first and last year in each period is presented. The difference between these two years was calculated and then divided by the number of annual intervals in the period. The Average Annual Change in Giving as a Percent of the Average Annual Change in Income column presents the Per Member Giving Average Annual Change divided by the U.S. Per Capita Income Average Annual Change.

As indicated in Table 15, during the 1950 to 2021 period, the highest increase in the average annual change in per member giving measured in inflation-adjusted 2012 dollars occurred from 1995-2000. However, when the average annual change in per member giving was considered as a portion of the average annual change in per capita income, the largest increase occurred in the 1955-1960 period, followed by the 1950-1955 period. In 1995-2000, the annual dollar increase in giving of $29.60 represented 3.1% of the average annual increase in U.S. per capita income, compared to 7.3% during the 1950-1955 period, and 8% during the 1955-1960 period.

Table 15: Average Annual Change in U.S. Per Capita Disposable Personal Income and Per Member Giving, 11 Denominations, Inflation-Adjusted 2012 Dollars, 1950-2021

	U.S. Per Capita Income			Per Member Giving			
Time Period	First Year in Period	Last Year in Period	Average Annual Change	First Year in Period	Last Year in Period	Average Annual Change	Avg. Ann. Chg. Giv. as % Avg. Annual Chg. in Income
1950-1955	$10,843	$11,930	$217.36	$254.00	$333.64	$15.93	7.33%
1955-1960	$11,930	$12,534	$120.80	$333.64	$381.77	$9.63	7.97%
1960-1964 [3]	$12,534	$14,230	$424.03	$381.77	$395.12	$3.34	0.79%
1964-1970 [3]	$14,230	$17,177	$491.14	$395.12	$418.28	$3.86	0.79%
1970-1975	$17,177	$18,993	$363.32	$418.28	$437.34	$3.81	1.05%
1975-1980	$18,993	$21,067	$414.64	$437.34	$483.52	$9.24	2.23%
1980-1985	$21,067	$23,914	$569.51	$483.52	$567.28	$16.75	2.94%
1985-1990	$23,914	$27,143	$645.76	$567.28	$621.41	$10.83	1.68%
1990-1995	$27,143	$28,956	$362.57	$621.41	$673.51	$10.42	2.87%
1995-2000	$28,956	$33,676	$944.04	$673.51	$821.51	$29.60	3.14%
2000-2005	$33,676	$36,266	$517.92	$821.51	$875.68	$10.83	2.09%
2005-2010	$36,266	$38,117	$370.27	$875.68	$857.67	($3.60)	-0.97%
2010-2015	$38,117	$40,764	$529.38	$857.67	$846.20	($2.29)	-0.43%
2015-2021	$40,764	$47,165	$1,066.79	$846.20	$849.83	$0.61	0.06%

Details in table may not compute to numbers shown due to rounding.
Source: empty tomb analysis; *YACC* adjusted series; U.S. BEA

empty tomb, inc., 2024

Between 1960 and 1964 in these communions, the average annual change in per member giving declined markedly from the previous five years. While income was increasing at an annual rate of $424.03 in this four-year period, the average annual increase in per member contributions in inflation-adjusted 2012 dollars was $3.34 in 1960-1964, only about a third of the $9.63 annual rate of increase in the 1955-1960 period.

The 1960-1964 period predates many of the controversial issues often cited as reasons for declining giving as a percent of income. Also, it was in the 1960-1964 period when membership as a percent of population began to decrease in mainline denominations, ten of which are included in this group. Therefore, additional exploration of that period of time might be merited.

Increases in per member giving were consistently low from 1960-1975, compared to the 1950-1960 and 1975-2005 segments. The annual rates of increase of $3.34 per year from 1960 to 1964, $3.86 from 1964 to 1970, and $3.81 from 1970 to 1975, were the lowest in the 1950-1955 through 2000-2005 segments. From 1960 to 1975, the increase in dollars given represented one percent or less of the average annual increase in per capita income.

In the 1975-1980 period, the average annual increase in giving grew to $9.24, representing 2.2% of the average annual increase in per capita income.

From 1980 to 1985, the average annual increase in giving of $16.75 represented 2.9% of the average annual increase in income during this period.

The annual average change in giving as a percent of the average annual income increase during 1985 to 1990 fell from the 1980-1985 figure, while the 1990-1995 level recovered to 2.87%. Although the Average Annual Change in Per Member Giving was comparable in the latter two periods, the slower growth in income during the 1990-1995 period resulted in the increase in dollars given representing a larger portion of the increase in income than during 1985-1990.

The 2015-2021 period posted the highest average annual increase in DPI in the 1950-2021 period. Meanwhile, the average annual change in per member giving of $0.61, while positive, was the lowest average annual increase in the 1950-2021 period.

In the 1995-2000 segment, the average annual change in giving as a percent of the average annual change in income increased from the 1990-1995 period. The average annual change in the number of dollars given on a per member basis was more than double that of the previous period. However, during the 1995-2000 segment, income was increasing at the second highest rate in the 1950-2021 period, in terms of per capita inflation-adjusted dollars. Thus the rate of growth in giving was less than half the rate during the 1950-1960 period, when considered as a portion of the income increases.

For the period 2000-2005, the average annual change in dollars given as a percent of the annual change in income was an increase of 2%.

The 2005-2010 period posted the first annual decrease in per member giving in the 1950-2021 period, with an annual level of decline of -$3.60.

This period included the "Great Recession" years of 2008 and 2009. However, even as per capita income recovered, per member giving continued an average of annual declines in the 2010-2015 period, when the average annual change in per member giving was -$2.29.

The 2015-2021 period posted the highest average annual increase in DPI in the 1950-2021 period. Meanwhile, the average annual change in per member giving of $0.61, while positive, was the lowest average annual increase in the 1950-2021 period.

It may be noted that the years 2008 through 2013 posted six years in a row of decline in per member giving in inflation-adjusted dollars: starting from the 2007 level of $908.03, the highest per member giving level in the 1921-2021 period, declining to $827.63 in 2013. This six-year period was the longest series of annual decline in per member giving since the seven years from 1928 through 1934, which included six years of the Great Depression.

The numbers posted from 2005 through 2021 may suggest a longer term trend has developed among the members of these 11 denominations, although the 2015-2021 numbers suggest that these patterns may be open to change.

Appendix A contains a listing of the denominations contained in the 1921-2021 analysis in this chapter.

Endnotes for Chapter 4

1 Data for the period 1965-1967 was not available in a form that could be readily analyzed for the present purposes, and therefore data for these three years was estimated by dividing the change in per member current dollar contributions from 1964 to 1968 by four, the number of years in this interval, and cumulatively adding the result to the base year of 1964 data and subsequently to the calculated data for the succeeding years of 1965 and 1966 in order to obtain estimates for the years 1965-1967.

2 The difference is due to rounding in the calculated membership. See Appendix B Series introduction, Appendix B-3 for a discussion of the calculation of membership for 1953 through 1964.

3 Use of the intervals 1960-1964 and 1964-1970 allows for the use of years for which there is known data, avoiding the use of the 1965 through 1967 years for which estimated data is used in this chapter.

4 For the years 1965 through 1967, estimated data is used. See Note 1 above.

chapter 5

Church Member Giving and Membership Trends Based on 1968–2021 Data

Overview of Church Member Giving and Membership Trends, 1968-2021

Information as a Tool. The rich historical data series in the *Yearbook of American and Canadian Churches* has, in this volume, been supplemented with and revised by additional denominational data for the 1968-2021 period.

Analysis of this data has been presented in the *State of Church Giving* series since the early 1990s. When first published, the finding that giving as a portion of income was shrinking was received with some surprise and intense interest in many quarters.

Now the series has continued for over a quarter of a century. The trends identified in earlier analyses impact current activities. Various denominations continue to face decisions about staff cuts and, in some cases, whether to decrease missionary forces. The emphasis on local internal operations indicated by the trend in giving to Congregational Finances has, in fact, resulted in changed dynamics between local congregations and national church offices. The numbers did not cause such changes to occur. The numbers only described symptoms of priorities. These priorities produced behaviors resulting in the changed relationships.

It is generally acknowledged that most individuals do not decide how much to give based on academic information such as that contained in these analyses. However, it is possible for institutional leaders at all levels of the church — local, regional, and national — to make use of trend information to formulate strategies in response to the findings. For example, in the composite set of denominations, the data indicated that giving as a percent of U.S. Disposable (after-tax) Personal Income (DPI) to Congregational Finances began to increase as a portion of income in 1993, and continued a general trend in an upward direction through 2002. It is possible that local church leadership had recognized a negative general trend and took steps to address it. The fact that the upturn in giving that began in 1993 essentially benefited local expenses, with only a slowing of the decline to Benevolences, indicates that church leadership may yet be operating with a limited vision of whole-life stewardship. In 2003 through 2021, giving as a percent of income to Congregational Finances declined more frequently from one year to the next than it increased. The more frequent declines in donations for Congregational Finances that began to reoccur in 2003 may suggest support for the internal operations of the congregation will not remain robust over time if not accompanied by a broader vision reflected in support for Benevolences. In either case, the uptick from 1993 through 2002 also indicates that the direction of trends can change.

Facts and figures may be useful to those responsible for promoting the health of the church. The analyses in this chapter are presented in an effort to expand the available information base.

Church leaders and members can then help decide, through action or inaction, what the future will look like.

The Meaning of Trends. Projections produced by statistical regression models are a tool to help leaders plan in response to reported data. Experts evaluate trends in weather to plan strategies that will safeguard agriculture, and people in the path of storms. Demographers map out population change trends to help government at local, national, and international levels plan for needs in education, aging, and trade.

Statistical techniques can also be used to suggest both consequences and possibilities regarding church giving and membership patterns. Of course, trend data only indicates future directions. Data does not dictate what will happen. Available information, including trend analysis, can help formulate intelligent responses to identified factors. Church leaders and members can then help decide, through action or inaction, what the future will look like.

Trend analysis was first included in this series partly in response to developments in national church offices. After talking with a number of denominational officials who were making painful decisions about which programs to cut, in light of decreased Benevolences dollars being received, it seemed useful to see where the present patterns of giving might lead if effective means were not found to alter present behavior. Were current patterns likely to prove a temporary setback, or did the data suggest longer-term implications?

The data for both Benevolences and Congregational Finances can be projected using linear and exponential regression analysis. Linear regression is sometimes called a "straight-line" projection. An exponential regression is also labeled a "decay" model. To determine which type of analysis more accurately describes the data in a category's giving pattern, the data for 1968-1985 was projected using both techniques. Then, the actual data for 1986 through 2021 was plotted. The more accurate projection was judged to be the procedure that produced the trend line most closely resembling the actual 1986-2021 data.

General Trends in Church Member Giving. As noted in chapter 1, the category of Total Contributions from church members is divided into the two general categories of Congregational Finances and Benevolences. In the category of Congregational Finances, giving as a portion of income declined overall between 1968 and 2021 for the composite denominations. More frequent increases in the actual level of giving to this category were observed beginning in 1993. These intermittent increases from one year to the next were in contrast to the decline indicated by an exponential projection through 2021, based on 1968-1985 giving data. However, in 2008, a decline began that brought the numbers closer to the exponential trend. By 2021, the actual data was below both the exponential and linear trends.

In the composite denominations, for the 1986-2021 period, the pattern of decline in actual data for giving to Benevolences as a portion of income initially followed the linear trend based on the 1968-1985 data. In 1993, the rate of decline began to slow, although the reported level of giving as a percent of income remained below the linear trend until 1997. The actual data remained below the exponential trend, despite an uptick in 2005, the year of several natural disasters.

General Trends in Church Membership. Membership trends across the theological spectrum point to a decline when membership was considered as a percent of U.S. population.

Membership trends across the theological spectrum point to a decline when membership was considered as a percent of U.S. population.

Ten mainline Protestant denominations represented 13.2% of the population in 1968, and 3.9% in 2021, a decline of 70% from the 1968 base.

The composite data set communions analyzed in earlier chapters of this volume measured 14.0% of U.S. population in 1968 and 7.1% in 2021, down 49% as a portion of U.S. population from the 1968 base.

A set of fourteen evangelical denominations grew 30% in the number of members between 1968 and 2021, but posted a 22% decline as a portion of U.S. population, since U.S. population expanded at a faster rate. The growth as a percent of population for this group peaked in the mid-1980s, and then began a slow decline, reaching its lowest point of the period in 2021.

Membership in a set of 34 Protestant denominations, including some of the fastest growing denominations in the U.S., and the Roman Catholic Church represented 45% of U.S. population in 1968, and 31% in 2021, a decline of 31% from the 1968 base. An exponential trend line for this set of denominations, based on 1968-2021 data, suggests that the group will represent less than one-quarter of the U.S. population by 2100, and 12% in 2200, if current patterns continue.

New Religious Construction. When considered as a portion of income, spending on new construction of religious buildings was higher in 1965 than in 2021. Per capita spending on new religious construction in 1965 was also higher than in 2021, when considered in inflation-adjusted dollars. Again in inflation-adjusted dollars, the aggregate billions spent in 2001 were the highest annual amount spent in the 1964-2021 period.

Details of Church Giving and Membership Trends, 1968-2021

The Current Trends in Church Giving. The first chapter in this report indicates that per member giving as a percent of income decreased between 1968 and 2021. Further, contributions to the category of Benevolences were declining proportionately faster than those to Congregational Finances between 1968 and 2021.

The data for the composite denominations analyzed for 1968 through 2021 has been projected in *The State of Church Giving* series, beginning with the edition that included 1991 data.[1] The most recent projection is based on data from 1968 through 2021.

The Trend in Congregational Finances. The 1968-2021 church giving data contained in this report indicates that giving for Congregational Finances as a percent of income declined from 2.38% in 1968, to 1.55% in 2021, a decline of 35%.

Both linear and exponential regression were used to analyze the data for giving to Congregational Finances as a percent of income for the 17-year interval of 1968 through 1985. Then the actual data for 1986 through 2021 was plotted. The actual data for 1986-1992 declined more often than it increased but still exceeded the exponential curve, with the exception of 1992. In 1993, giving to Congregational Finances as a percent of income began to increase in some years, unlike either projection.

As discussed in the analysis of new religious construction at the end of this chapter, in 2001 there was a peak in aggregate inflation-adjusted dollars spending on new religious construction, which then began to decline. This religious construction data might help explain an increase in giving to Congregational Finances reported data for that period.

Figure 8: Projected Trends for Composite Denominations, Giving to Congregational Finances as a Percent of U.S. Disposable Personal Income, Using Linear and Exponential Regression Based on Data for 1968-1985, with Actual Data for 1986-2021

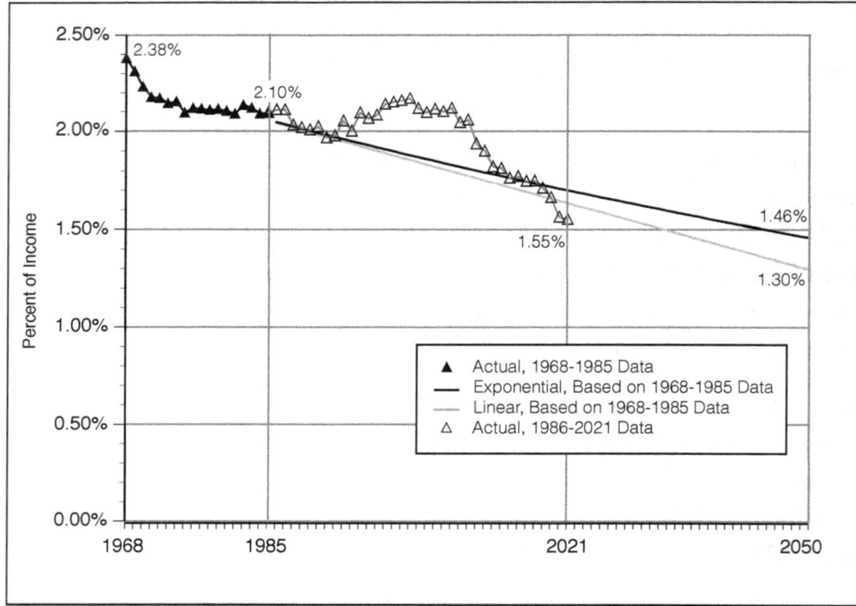

Source: empty tomb analysis; *YACC* adjusted series; U.S. BEA — empty tomb, inc., 2024

Starting in 2003, annual declines in the level of per member giving as a percent of income to Congregational Finances appeared more frequently than increases. The actual data grew closer to the exponential curve, and in 2020 and 2021 was below both the exponential and linear curves. The results are shown in Figure 8.

There may be an interaction between giving and membership that affects the amount of giving to the category of Congregational Finances. The trends in membership are considered below. In cases where membership is declining, levels of giving to Congregational Finances may initially be maintained or even increased on a per member basis, in an effort to keep basic operations at current levels even with fewer members. In these instances, Benevolences may be seen as an optional expenditure and decreased as a cost-cutting strategy. However, over time, Congregational Finances may also decline, since maintenance of congregational operations may not be perceived as a strong enough reason alone to continue giving to the church at the same level, in light of other lifestyle expenditure choices.

This hypothesis suggests that an increase in per member giving to the internal operations of the church, which may initially accompany a decline in membership, will not be maintained over time if there is not also a broader vision attracting church member support for the category of Benevolences as well.

The Trend in Benevolences. Per member contributions to Benevolences as a percent of U.S. DPI decreased from 0.64% in 1968 to 0.26% in 2021. This category reached its lowest point in the 1968-2021 period in 2020. The 2021 level of giving as a percent of income represented a decline of 59% from the 1968 base.

The data for giving to Benevolences as a percent of income for the 17-year interval of 1968 through 1985 was also projected using both linear and exponential regression. The actual data for 1986 through 2021 was then plotted. The results are shown in Figure 9.

Reported per member giving to Benevolences as a percent of income was near or below the projected value of the linear regression for 1987 through 1996. In 1997, the rate of decline slowed to the point that the actual data was above, but still closer to, the linear trend line. From 2000 through 2004, giving to Benevolences as a percent of income was above the linear projection but below the exponential line. Benevolences was above the exponential line in 2005. As discussed in chapter 1, the external factors of tsunami and hurricane relief efforts in 2005 may have put extra focus that year on the types of activities funded through Benevolences. Benevolences was again below the exponential line from 2006 through 2021.

In summary, although giving to Benevolences as a portion of income between 1968 and 2021 exhibited a pattern of decline throughout, the rate slowed in the late 1990s, to be above the linear trend but generally below the exponential trend.

Figure 9: Projected Trends for Composite Denominations, Giving to Benevolences as a Percent of U.S. Disposable Personal Income, Using Linear and Exponential Regression Based on Data for 1968-1985, with Actual Data for 1986-2021

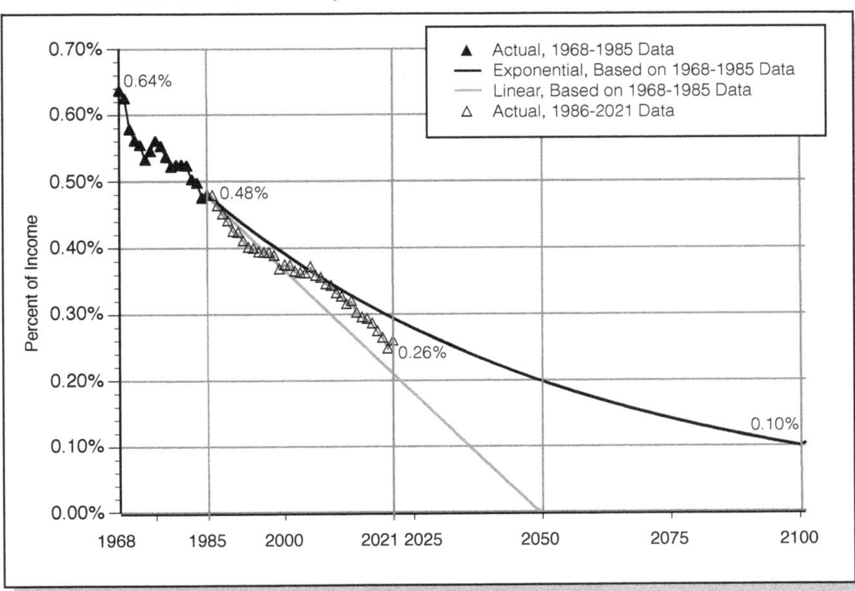

Source: empty tomb analysis; *YACC* adjusted series; U.S. BEA — empty tomb, inc., 2024

In addition to the 1968-1985 projection, shown in Figure 9, a second analysis was done on the entire period from 1968-2021. A linear trend based on the entire period of 1968-2021 data indicated that per member giving as a portion of income to the category of Benevolences would reach 0.07% of income in the year A.D. 2050, based on the 1968-2021 numbers. The exponential curve based on 1968-2021 data indicated that giving in 2050 would be 0.17%, down from the 0.26% level in 2021.[2] Extending the exponential trend to 2100, Benevolences would represent 0.08% of income in that year.

These trend lines may be more useful to predict the general level of giving, rather than precise numbers. However, the overall direction suggests that by 2050 the amount of income going to support Benevolences, including denominational structures, would be severely reduced, if the overall pattern of the last 54 years continues.

Trends in Church Membership as a Percent of U.S. Population, 1968-2021.[3] Membership data for various church groupings is available for review for the years 1968 through 2021. When the reported data is considered as a percent of U.S. population, the membership data is placed in the larger context of the changing environment in which the church exists. This measurement is similar to giving as a percent of U.S. Disposable Personal Income (DPI), which reflects how much a financial donation represents of the resources available to the donor. In a similar way, measuring membership as a percent of U.S. population takes into account the fact that the potential population for church membership also changed as a result of growth in the number of people in the U.S.

However, the overall direction suggests that by 2050 the amount of income going to support Benevolences, including denominational structures, would be severely reduced, if the overall pattern of the last 54 years continues.

The *State of Church Giving through 1993* included a chapter entitled, "A Unified Theory of Giving and Membership."[4] The hypothesis explored in that discussion was that there is a relationship between a decline in church member giving and membership patterns. One proposal considered in that chapter was that a denomination that is able to involve its members in a larger vision, such as mission outreach, as evidenced in levels of giving to support that idea, will also be attracting additional members.

In the present chapter, discussion will focus on patterns and trends in membership as a percent of U.S. population.

Membership in the Composite Denominations, 1968-2021. The composite denominations, which span the theological spectrum, included 28,156,408 Full or Confirmed Members in 1968. By 2021, these communions included 23,585,412 members, representing a decline of 16%.[5] During the same 53-year interval, U.S. population increased from 200,745,000 to 332,351,000, an increase of 66%. As a result, while this church member grouping represented 14% of the U.S. population in 1968, it included 7.1% in 2021, a decline of 49% from the 1968 base. Figure 10 presents membership as a percent of U.S. population, and giving as a percent of U.S. DPI, for the composite denominations, 1968-2021.

Membership Trends in Three Church Groups. Membership data for three subgroups within the historically Christian church in the U.S. is available. Data was analyzed for ten Protestant mainline denominations, fourteen Protestant evangelical denominations, and the Roman Catholic Church. Figure 11 presents the data.

Figure 10: Membership as a Percent of U.S. Population and Giving as a Percent of U.S. Per Capita Disposable Personal Income, Composite Denominations, 1968-2021

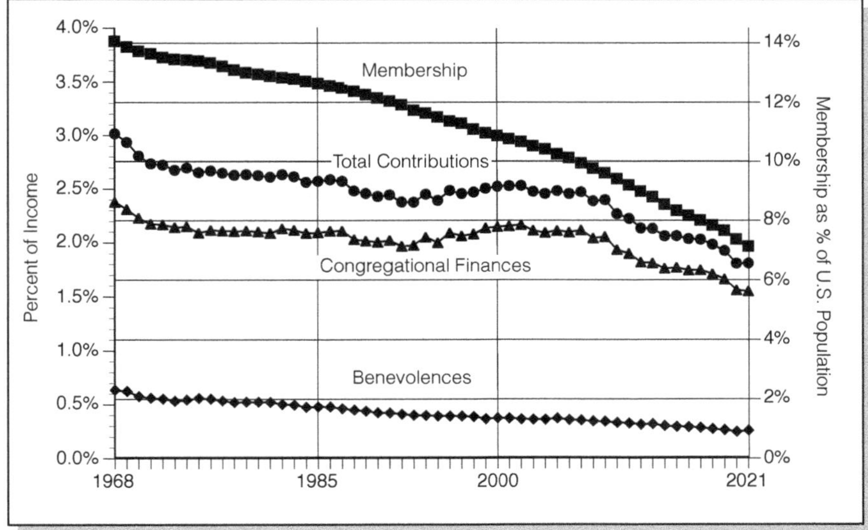

Source: empty tomb analysis; *YACC* adjusted series; U.S. BEA   empty tomb, inc., 2024

The declining membership trends have been noticed most markedly in the mainline Protestant communions. Full or Confirmed Membership in ten mainline Protestant denominations affiliated with the National Council of the Churches of Christ in the U.S.A.[6] decreased as a percent of U.S. population between 1968 and 2021. In 1968, this group included 26,452,819 or 13.2% of U. S. population. In 2021, the 10 denominations included 12,997,247, or 3.9% of U.S. population, a decline of 70% from the 1968 base, as a portion of U.S. population.

Data is also available for a group of fourteen denominations that might be classified on the evangelical end of the theological spectrum.[7] Although one or more of the communions in this grouping might prefer the term "conservative" to "evangelical" as a description, the latter term in its current sociological usage may be useful. These communions included some of the fastest growing denominations in the United States. This group grew 30% in membership, from 15,099,830 in 1968 to 19,602,957 in 2021, while U.S. population grew 66%. As a result, this group measured 7.5% of U.S. population in 1968, and 5.9% in 2021, a decline of 22% in the portion of the U.S. represented by these communions. In the mid-1980s, the group peaked at 8.2% as a portion of U.S. population peaked, and then declined to 5.9% by 2021, a decline of 28% as a portion of U.S. population

Figure 11: Membership as a Percent of U.S. Population, 14 Evangelical Denominations, 10 Mainline Denominations, and the Roman Catholic Church, 1968-2021

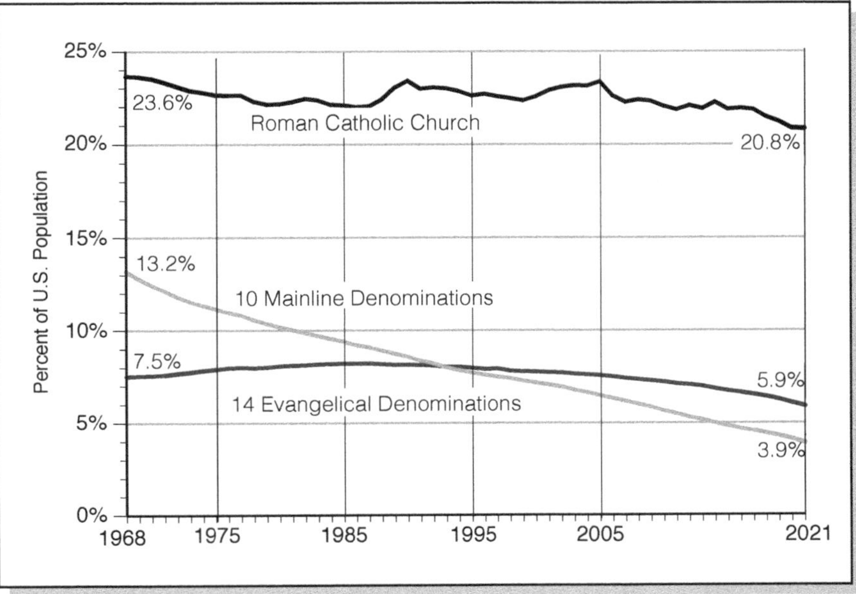

Source: empty tomb analysis; *YACC* adjusted series; U.S. BEA   empty tomb, inc., 2024

from the 1986 peak. In 1993, these 14 evangelical communions surpassed the 10 mainline communions in the portion of U.S. population that they represented.

The Roman Catholic Church counted 47,468,333 members in 1968, or 24% of U.S. population. Although the church's membership grew 46%, to 69,214,513 in 2021, it decreased to 21% as a portion of the faster-growing U.S. population, a decline of 12%.

Projected Membership Trends in Ten Mainline Denominations. As with giving to Congregational Finances and Benevolences as a percent of income, trend lines using both linear and exponential regression were developed for the ten mainline Protestant communions discussed above, using their 1968-1985 membership data. The actual 1986 through 2021 data was also plotted. As shown in Figure 12, the actual 1986-2021 data exceeded the exponential curve for these denominations through 2008. In 2009-2021, the actual membership as a percent of U.S. population was below the exponential trend line.

An exponential curve based on the entire 1968-2021 reported data series suggested that these denominations would represent 2.4% of the U.S. population in 2050, if the present rate of decline continues.

Projected Membership Trends in the Composite Denominations. Eight of the 10 mainline Protestant denominations, as well as nine of the 14 evangelical denominations, discussed above are also included in the composite set of denominations that have been considered in earlier chapters of this report. Regression analysis was carried out on the 1968-1985 membership data for the composite denominations to determine if the trends in the larger grouping differed from the mainline denomination subset. The results were then compared to the actual 1986 through 2021 membership data for the composite data set.

Figure 12: Trend in Membership as a Percent of U.S. Population, 10 Mainline Protestant Denominations, Linear and Exponential Regression Based on Data for 1968-1985, with Actual Data 1986-2021

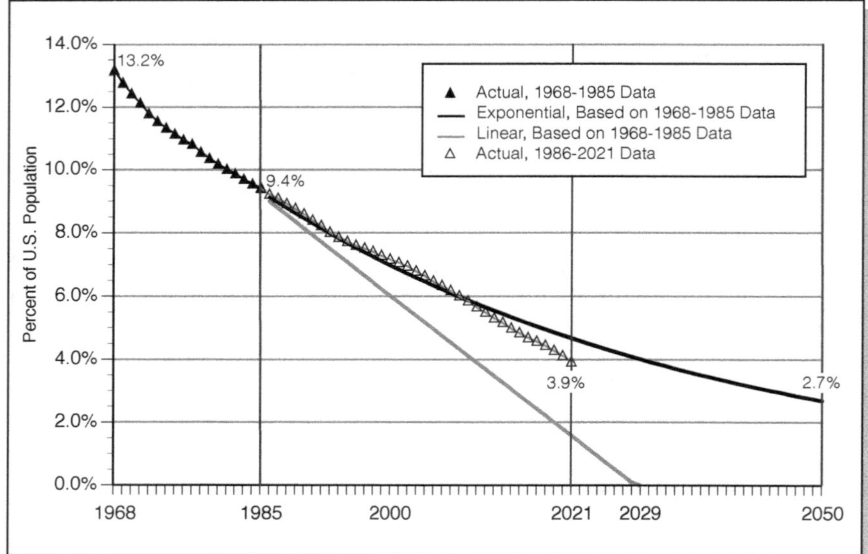

Source: empty tomb analysis; *YACC* adjusted series; U.S. BEA   empty tomb, inc., 2024

The composite denominations represented 14% of the U.S. population in 1968, and 12.6% in 1985. Linear trend analysis of the 1968-1985 data suggested that this grouping would have represented 9.8% of U.S. population in 2021, while exponential regression suggested it would have included 10.2%. In fact, this composite grouping of communions represented 7.1% of the U.S. population in 2021, a smaller figure than that indicated by linear regression, suggesting the trend is closer to that predicted by linear regression than the exponential curve. By 2050, these composite denominations would represent 7.5% of the U.S. population if a linear trend based on the 1968-1985 data remains the more accurate analysis. Figure 13 presents this information in graphic form. However, a linear trend analysis based on the 1968-2021 data suggests the group will represent 4.4% of the population in 2050, if the present trend continues.

Figure 13: Trend in Membership as a Percent of U.S. Population, Composite Denominations, Linear and Exponential Regression Based on Data for 1968-1985, with Actual Data 1986-2021

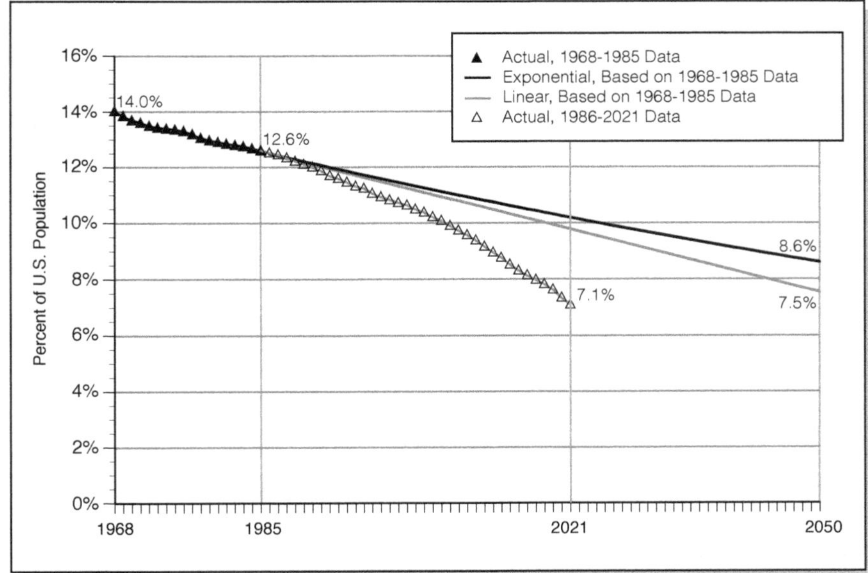

Source: empty tomb analysis; *YACC* adjusted series; U.S. BEA — empty tomb, inc., 2024

Membership and Projected Membership Trends in 35 Communions. Figure 14 presents the following analysis in graphic form.

In 1968, a set of 34 Protestant denominations and the Roman Catholic Church included a total of 90,152,676 members. The Protestant churches in the data set included a broad representation of the theological spectrum, and also included some of the fastest growing denominations in the U.S. With the U.S. population at 200,745,000, these Christians constituted 45% of the 1968 U.S. population. By 2021, the group had grown to 103,713,305 members. However, with U.S. population having grown to 332,351,000 in 2021, these Christians comprised 31% of the American population, a decline of 31% from the 1968 base.

Because of the broad nature of the sampling of these historically Christian communions, a projection was extended to 2200, based on membership data for the entire period of 1968 through 2021. The purpose was

Figure 14: Trend in Membership as a Percent of U.S. Population, 35 Denominations, Linear and Exponential Regression Based on Data for 1968-2021

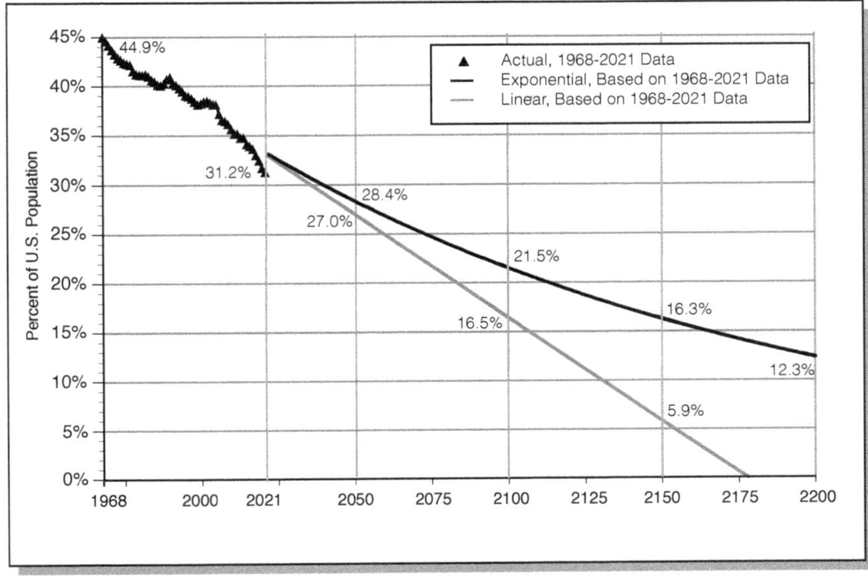

Source: empty tomb analysis; *YACC* adjusted series; U.S. BEA — empty tomb, inc., 2024

to forecast, based on past patterns, the role this group of denominations would play at the end of the next century. By 2050, the linear projection suggested the group will have declined from representing 31% of the U.S. population in 2021 to include 27%. The exponential projection forecasted 28% in 2050. By the year 2100, the linear trend projected 16% while the exponential trend projected 22% of the U.S. population will be affiliated with these 35 communions. In 2150, the figures would be 6% (linear) or 16% (exponential). If the trends continue long term, in 2200 this group of communions will represent 12% of U.S. population, according to the exponential curve, or if the linear trend proves more accurate, a negligible percent. Figure 14 presents these findings in graphic form.

Trends in One Denomination. The quality of trend data will be affected by the measurements taken. An example from one denomination may illustrate the point.

The United Methodist Church resulted from the merger of The Methodist Church and the Evangelical United Brethren in 1968. While The Methodist Church reported data for 1968 in the 1970 *YACC* edition, the Evangelical United Brethren did not. Therefore, data for The United Methodist Church, including both The Methodist Church and the Evangelical United Brethren, was not available in 1968, and as a result this communion was not included in the composite denominations in this volume.[8]

The two different patterns in UMC Benevolences illustrate the point that definitions of the categories being measured are important.

For data year 1971, The United Methodist Church (UMC) changed its reporting methodology for its information published in the *YACC* series. Specifically, the category of Connectional Clergy Support was switched from Congregational Finances to Benevolences. UMC Connectional Clergy Support included district superintendents and episcopal salaries, which would standardly be included in Benevolences for other communions. However, UMC Connectional Clergy Support also included pastor pension and benefits, including health insurance, large categories that would be included in Congregational Finances in most denominations.

In 2008, the last year with data available for the category of "Connectional Clergy Support" in the following analysis,[9] The United Methodist Church was the second largest Protestant denomination, and third largest communion overall in the U.S.

When, as of 1971, UMC Connectional Clergy Support was included in per member giving to the UMC Benevolences series as a percent of income, Benevolences increased from 0.38% in 1969 to 0.43% in 2008, a 13% increase from the 1969 base.

When UMC Benevolences for 1971 to 2008 was adjusted to remove UMC Connectional Clergy Support, giving to UMC Benevolences as a portion of income declined from 0.38% in 1969 to 0.26% in 2008, a decrease of 31%.

This adjustment is only illustrative, since, when UMC Connectional Clergy Support was removed from the Benevolences series, expenses that would traditionally be included in Benevolences were removed as well as those that would more generally be attributed to Congregational Finances. The change in the adjusted data is noticeable because the single category of UMC Connectional Clergy Support increased 40% from 1969 to 2008 when measured as per member giving as a percent of income.

As of 2009, the category of Connectional Clergy Support was no longer used.

In 2017, the UMC General Council on Finance and Administrative (GCFA) office provided a giving data series for 2009 through 2013 that included revised categories,[10] to which data for 2014 through 2021 has now been added. Specifically, the UMC GCFA included "direct-billed clergy non-health benefits" and "direct-billed clergy health benefits" in the category of Congregational Finances rather than Benevolences. These two categories represented two of the largest expenditures that had previously been reported in Connectional Clergy Support.

Figure 15: The United Methodist Church, Per Member Giving to Congregational Finances and Benevolences as a Percent of Income, 1969-2018, Adjusted for Connectional Clergy Support 1971-2008, and Direct-Billed Pastor Benefits in Congregational Finances, 2009-2021

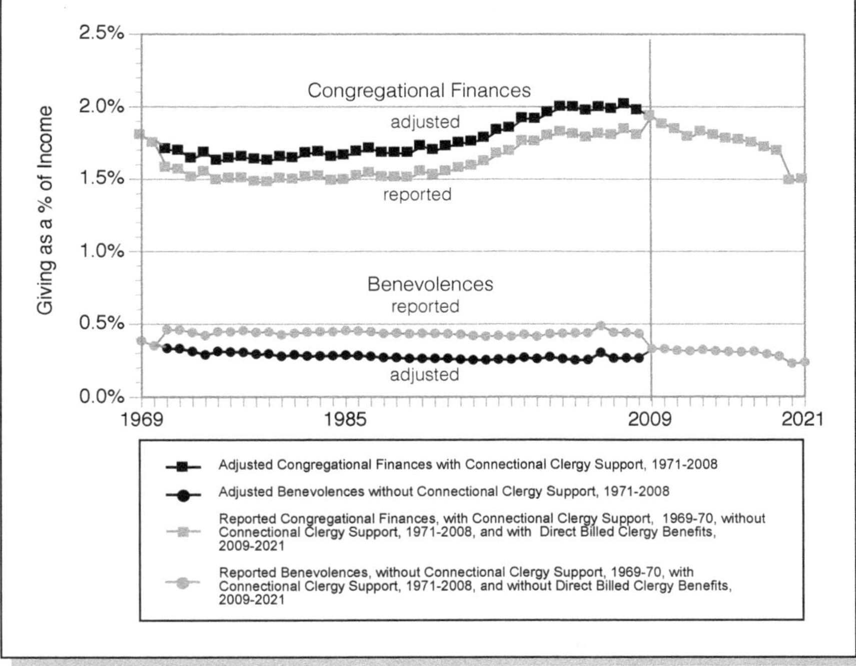

Source: empty tomb analysis; *YACC* adjusted series; U.S. BEA — empty tomb, inc., 2024

Figure 15 illustrates how the trends in Benevolences giving appear, based on which category included Connectional Clergy Support during 1971-2008, and with direct-billed pastor benefit expenses included in Congregational Finances for 2009-2021.

The two different patterns in UMC Benevolences illustrate the point that definitions of the categories being measured are important.

If the generally used definition of Benevolences is used, which would place pastor health insurance and other benefits in Congregational Finances, then giving to Benevolences in The United Methodist Church declined as a portion of income rather than increased between 1969 and 2008 compared to when those expenses were reported in Benevolences.

The definition of Benevolences that excludes those congregationally-based expenses provides a more specific measurement of member support for the larger mission of the church. The latter definition, which combined pastor health insurance and other benefits with more traditional church activities beyond the congregation, indicated a greater level of support for Benevolences than was actually present from 1971-2008.

Therefore the decision by The United Methodist Church to include direct-billed pastor health and non-health benefits in Congregational Finances as of 2009 produced a series that provides data on giving patterns by United Methodists that can be more accurately compared to other communions, resulting in a more precise basis for evaluating giving patterns, and their implications, in the church in the U.S.

New Religious Construction. How does 2021 construction activity among churches in the U.S. compare to other years?

Census Bureau data provides information on the new construction of religious buildings.[11] According to the data, current dollar aggregate construction of religious buildings was $1.135 billion dollars in 1968, the first year in the church member giving and membership analyses series earlier in this chapter, compared to $3.090 billion in 2021. On a current-dollar aggregate level, more building was going on in 2021 than in 1968.

However, as has been emphasized throughout this volume, the context in which data is viewed will influence how meaningful are the conclusions drawn. For example, in the present discussion, one may ask what part of total new construction, and of private construction, did new religious construction represent in 1968 and 2021?

To obtain the most realistic picture about building patterns, changes in population and income also need to be factored into the evaluation.

The aggregate current dollar values of new religious construction put in place, when considered in the context of total and private construction, show that religious construction activity in 2021 represented a smaller portion of total construction than in 1968. In 1968, the $1.135 billion in new religious construction represented 1.2% of the $96.824 billion in total new construction, and 1.6% of the $69.386 billion in new private construction. In 2021, the $3.090 billion in new religious construction represented 0.19% of the $1,653.4 billion in total new construction, and 0.24% of the $1,295.7 billion in new private construction.

Aggregate numbers considered apart from inflation, or that do not take into account changes in population and income, ignore important variables that are needed to obtain the most accurate understanding possible.

Data is available to extend the new religious construction analysis series back to 1964. When inflation was factored out, the data indicated that the aggregate sum of new religious building construction for the most recent five-year period of 2017-2021 was $15.470 billion in inflation-adjusted 2012 dollars, compared to the initial five years in the period under review, 1964-1968, when spending as $31.450 billion. The highest single year inflation-adjusted amount in the 1964-2021 period was the 2001 level of $10.521 billion. The 1965 level of $7.113 billion had been the highest amount of aggregate, inflation-adjusted dollars spent on the construction of new religious buildings from 1964 through 1996. In 1997, aggregate inflation-adjusted spending passed the 1965 level, and religious building expenditures continued to increase through 2001. Expenditures were at or above $9 billion a year in inflation-adjusted 2012 dollars from 1999 through 2004, and decreased to $2.599 billion by 2021.

To obtain the most realistic picture about building patterns, changes in population and income also need to be factored into the evaluation. For example, taking population changes into account, in 1965 the per capita expenditure in the U.S. on religious buildings was $37 dollars per person in inflation-adjusted 2012 dollars. In 2021, it was $8 dollars.

The period 1964 through 1968 posted an average per capita expenditure on new religious buildings of $32 in inflation-adjusted dollars. The period 2017-2021 was $9, suggesting that construction of new religious buildings was higher in the earlier period, when changes in population were taken into account.

Of course, a smaller portion of the entire U.S. population may have been investing in religious buildings in the late 1990s through 2021 than in the mid-1960s. To have the most meaningful comparison, changes in membership as a portion of population would have to be taken into account. Data considered above suggests that membership in historically Christian churches declined as a portion of the U.S. population between 1964 and 2021. However, other religions were added to the religious milieu of the United States during this period. The Census data includes all religious construction, not just Christian churches. So the rough estimate may be fairly useful as a first approximation.

Even comparing per capita inflation-adjusted dollars spent is of limited use because it does not account for the difference in incomes in the two periods. To review, the $37 per capita spent on religious buildings in 1965 represented a different portion of income than the $10 spent in 2021. In fact, as a portion of DPI, Americans spent 0.25% on the construction of new religious buildings in 1965, compared to 0.02% in 2021.

One must conclude, therefore, that the population was investing a higher portion of available resources in religious buildings in the mid-1960s than in the most recent decade. The building activity occurring in the late 1990s through 2021 has to be evaluated in the context of the general affluence produced by decades of economic expansion in the U.S., in order to make an intelligent evaluation of whether religious construction has in fact increased over the mid-1960s level. This fact is clear from the three charts in Figure 16. These charts contrast: (1) the annual aggregate current dollar value of new religious building construction with, (2) the annual aggregate inflation-adjusted 2012 dollar value of new religious building construction, and (3) the per capita expenditure as a portion of U.S. DPI, for the 1964-2021 period. One can observe that the picture is very different when the per person cost of new religious construction is set in the context of the income available to the people paying for the buildings.

Figure 16: Construction of Religious Buildings in the U.S., 1964-2021, Aggregate Current Dollars, Aggregate Inflation-Adjusted 2012 Dollars, and Percent of U.S. Per Capita Disposable Personal Income

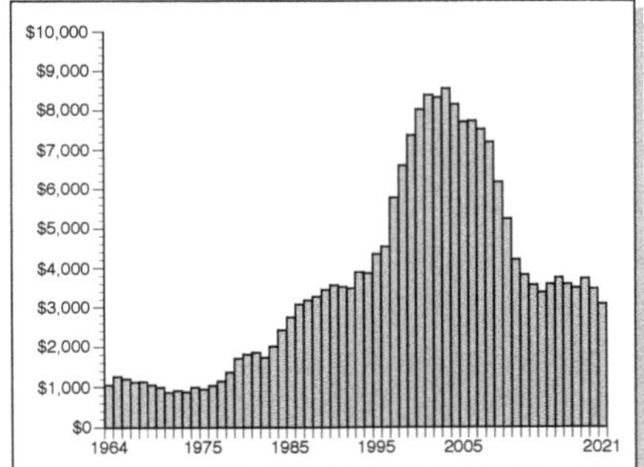

Aggregate Millions of Current Dollars

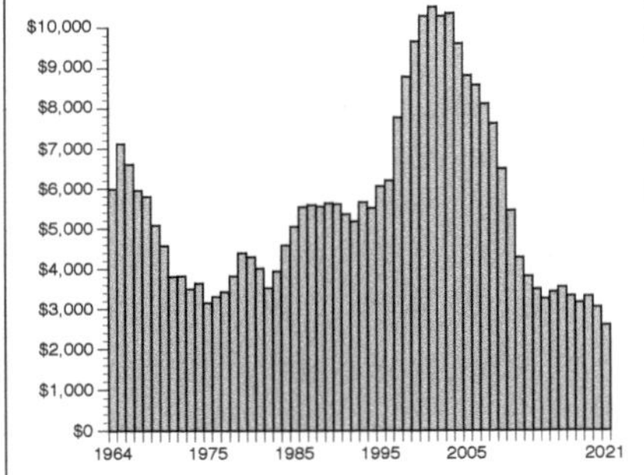

Aggregate Millions of Inflation-Adjusted 2012 Dollars

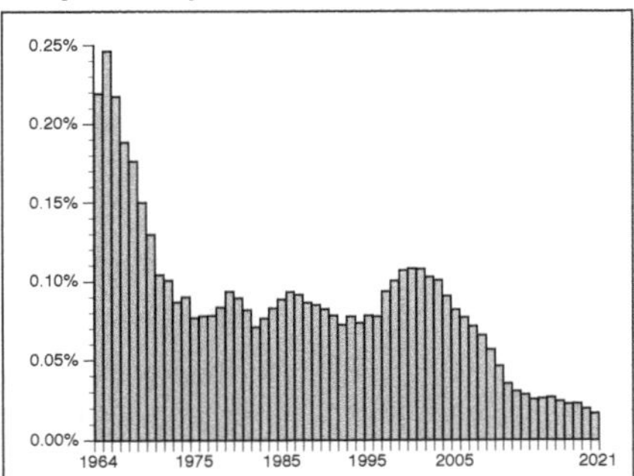

Per Capita as a Percent of DPI

Source: empty tomb analysis; *YACC* adjusted series; U.S. BEA

empty tomb, inc., 2024

The Response to the Trends. As in other sectors, trend lines in church giving and membership are designed to provide an additional source of information. Planning, evaluation and creative thinking are some of the types of constructive responses that can be made in light of projections. The information on church member giving and membership trends is offered as a possible planning tool.[12] The trend lines are not considered to be dictating what must happen, but rather are seen as providing important indicators of what might happen if present conditions continue in an uninterrupted fashion. Trends in church giving and membership, if used wisely, may be of assistance in addressing conditions present in the body of Christ in the United States, and helping to define alternative future possibilities, if deemed advisable.

Endnotes for Chapter 5

[1] John Ronsvalle and Sylvia Ronsvalle, The State of Church Giving through 1991 (Champaign, IL: empty tomb, inc., 1993), and subsequent editions in the series. The edition with data through 1991 provides a discussion of the choice to use giving as a percent of income as a basis for considering future giving patterns.

[2] In the linear regression for the 1968-2021 data, the value for the correlation coefficient, or r_{XY}, for the Benevolences data is -.99. The strength of the linear relationship in the present set of 1968-2021 data, that is, the proportion of variance accounted for by linear regression, is represented by the coefficient of determination, or $r2_{XY}$, of .98 for Benevolences. In the exponential regression, the value for r_{XY}, for the Benevolences data is -.99, while the strength of the exponential relationship is .98. The Benevolences *F*-observed values of 2,044.11 for the linear, and 2,667.65 for the curvilinear, regression are substantially greater than the *F*-critical value of 7.15 for 1 and 52 degrees of freedom for a single-tailed test with an Alpha value of 0.01. Therefore, the regression equation is useful at the level suggested by the $r2_{XY}$ figure in predicting giving as a percent of income.

[3] The denominations analyzed in this section include the composite data set whose financial patterns were analyzed in earlier chapters. The data for the composite communions is supplemented by the data of eight denominations included in an analysis of church membership and U.S. population by Roozen and Hadaway in David A. Roozen and Kirk C. Hadaway, eds., *Church and Denominational Growth* (Nashville: Abingdon Press, 1993), 393-395.

[4] This article is available on the Internet at: <http://www.emptytomb.org/UnifiedTheory.pdf>.

[5] See Appendix B-1 for details of the composite denomination data included in these analyses. Consult Appendix B-4 for the total Full or Confirmed Membership numbers used for the American Baptist Churches in the U.S.A. The year-specific data for the composite denominations are included in the giving as a percent of income analyses. However, some composite denominations were not included in the membership as a percent of population analyses, as indicated in Appendix A. Missing membership data may be calculated for denominations that did not provide complete data sets for the entire period. See Appendix B-3.3 and Appendix B-4 for the membership data of the other denominations included in subsequent analyses in this chapter that are not one of the composite denominations, and that may not have provided giving as well as membership data.

[6] These ten denominations include eight of the communions in the composite set of denominations as well as The Episcopal Church and The United Methodist Church. A list is presented in Appendix A.

[7] A list of the communions in this set is presented in Appendix A.

[8] In correspondence with The United Methodist Church General Council of Administration and Finance (GCFA) in preparation for the original analysis in this series, John Schreiber, Assistant General Secretary, Section on Records and Statistics, GCFA, wrote regarding 1968 data: "Unavailable - - The United Methodist Church was created in mid-year 1968 by the merger of The Evangelical United Brethren Church and The Methodist Church. Reporting categories for the two merging denominations were not compatible in some ways. Therefore, the first full year for which data were gathered on a denomination-wide basis was 1969." John Ronsvalle and Sylvia Ronsvalle, *A Comparison of the Growth in Church Contributions with United States Per Capita Income* (Champaign, IL: empty tomb, inc., 1988), p. 121.

[9] In correspondence dated March 14, 2011, a denominational representative indicated that data for the category of United Methodist Church Connectional Clergy Support was no longer collected as of 2009.

[10] Lauren S. Arieux, Statistician and Research Fellow, Data Services, General Council on Finance and Administration, The United Methodist Church, 3/31/2015 email to empty tomb, inc.

[11] For a series beginning in 1964 titled "Annual Value of Construction Put in Place," the Census Bureau defined its Religious category as follows: "*Religious* includes houses of worship and other religious buildings. Certain buildings, although owned by religious organizations, are not included in this category. These include education or charitable institutions, hospitals, and publishing houses." (U.S. Census Bureau, Current Construction Reports, C30/01-5, *Value of Construction Put in Place*: May 2001, U.S. Government Printing Office, Washington, DC 20402, Appendix A, "Definitions," p. A-2). A 2003 revision of this series presented the definitions as follows: "Religious: Certain buildings, although owned by religious organizations, are not included in this category. These include educational or charitable institutions, hospitals, and publishing houses. House of worship: Includes churches, chapels, mosques, synagogues, tabernacles, and temples. Other religious: In addition to the types of facilities listed below, it also includes sanctuaries, abbeys, convents, novitiates, rectories, monasteries, missions, seminaries, and parish houses. Auxiliary building—includes fellowship halls, life centers, camps and retreats, and Sunday schools." (U.S. Census Bureau; "Definitions of Construction"; July 30, 2003; <http://www.census.gov/const/C30/definitions.pdf>; 8/17/2003 PM printout.) Although documentation for the revised series stated that the 1993 through 2001 data was not comparable to the earlier 1964-2000 data, a comparison of the two series found that there was an average of 0.1% difference between the estimated millions of dollars spent on construction of religious buildings from 1993-2000. For the purposes of the present discussion, the difference in the two series was not deemed sufficient to impact the multi-decade review to the degree that discussion would not be useful. The aggregate current dollar data is as follows:

Table 16: New Religious Construction, Aggregate Millions Current Dollars, 1964-2021

Year	Millions of Current $	Year	Millions of Current $	Year	Millions of Current $	Year	Millions of Current $
1964	$1,044	1979	$1,701	1994	$3,871	2009	$6,177
1965	$1,263	1980	$1,811	1995	$4,348	2010	$5,237
1966	$1,205	1981	$1,853	1996	$4,537	2011	$4,205
1967	$1,118	1982	$1,730	1997	$5,782	2012	$3,819
1968	$1,135	1983	$2,009	1998	$6,604	2013	$3,565
1969	$1,044	1984	$2,418	1999	$7,371	2014	$3,380
1970	$988	1985	$2,751	2000	$8,030	2015	$3,589
1971	$867	1986	$3,076	2001	$8,393	2016	$3,752
1972	$907	1987	$3,178	2002	$8,335	2017	$3,586
1973	$877	1988	$3,271	2003	$8,559	2018	$3,499
1974	$993	1989	$3,449	2004	$8,153	2019	$3,730
1975	$941	1990	$3,566	2005	$7,715	2020	*$3,469*
1976	$1,040	1991	$3,521	2006	$7,740	2021	$3,090
1977	$1,144	1992	$3,485	2007	$7,522		
1978	$1,367	1993	$3,894	2008	$7,197		

The source for the religious construction data is:

- U.S. Census Bureau; Table 1: Annual Value of Construction Put in Place in the U.S.: [Year-Year], p. 1: Current $s & Constant (1996) $s; last revised July 1, 2002;

  1964: 1964-1968; <http://www.census.gov/pub/const/C30/tab168.txt>

  1965-1969: 1965-1969; <http://www.census.gov/pub/const/C30/tab169.txt>

  1970-1974: 1970-1974; <http://www.census.gov/pub/const/C30/tab174.txt>

1975-1979: 1975-1979; <http://www.census.gov/pub/const/C30/tab179.txt>

1980-1984: 1980-1984; <http://www.census.gov/pub/const/C30/tab184.txt>

1985-1989: 1985-1989; <http://www.census.gov/pub/const/C30/tab189.txt>

1990: 1990; <http://www.census.gov/pub/const/C30/tab190.txt>

1991-1992: 1991-1995; <http://www.census.gov/pub/const/C30/tab195.txt>

- 1993-2001: U.S. Census Bureau; Annual Value of Construction Put in Place in the U.S.: 1993-2002, p. 1: Current $s; July 29, 2003; <http://www.census.gov/const/C30/Private.pdf>
- 2002-2010: U.S. Census Bureau; Annual: Annual Value of Construction Put in Place in the U.S.: 2002-2012, p. 1: Current $s; Document Date: 02/01/2013 10:00 AM; <http://www.census.gov/construction/c30/pdf/total.pdf> [URL may vary by year]
- 2011-2020: U.S. Census Bureau; Annual: Annual Value of Construction Put in Place in the U.S.: 2009-2020, p. 1: Current $s; Document Date: 07/01/21 10:00 AM EDT; <https://www.census.gov/construction/c30/xls/total.xls> [URL may vary by year]
- 2021: U.S. Census Bureau; Annual: Annual Value of Construction Put in Place in the U.S.: 2012-2022, p. 1: Current $s; Document Date: 07/03/23 10:00 AM EDT; <https://www.census.gov/construction/c30/xlsx/total.xlsx> [URL may vary by year]

[12] For additional discussion of the implications of the trends, see Ronsvalle and Ronsvalle, *The State of Church Giving through 1991*, pp. 61-67.

chapter 6

The Potential of the Church

This chapter discusses the potential that exists in the church in the U.S. to do intentional miracles.

The declines in church participation have recently received attention in national media. The analyses in the first five chapters of this volume provide an overview of church member giving through the year 2021. The declines in the previous chapters have received attention from church leaders and members alike.

What are less discussed in church circles are the possibilities available to the church in the U.S. in the present age of affluence. Chapter 8 explores this topic. This chapter lays out the numerical support for that discussion.

While the previous chapters have generally reflected on what has happened in church giving in the past, the current chapter considers what potential resources the church has in light of those church member giving numbers. As considered in chapter 8, if church leaders recognized the existence of this potential, they could choose whether or not to mobilize it in Jesus' name, on behalf of God's agenda in this hurting world.

Overview of the Potential of the Church

The analyses in this chapter compare present levels of church member giving with a few standards of potential giving.

One standard of increased giving, by which giving can be evaluated, is the classic tithe, or giving ten percent of income.[1] Calculating that difference between current giving levels and a congregation-wide average of 10%, one analysis suggests that there would have been a low estimate of an additional $210 billion available for the work of the church in 2021, if self-identified Christians had given 10% of income, instead of the 1.81% that was donated by church members. If church members had chosen to allocate 60% of this additional giving to global word and deed need, there would have been an additional $126 billion available for those causes, an amount substantially greater than estimates of the most urgent global word and deed need costs. If 20% had been directed to domestic need in the U.S., an additional $42 billion would have been available to address domestic needs including poverty, with an equal amount available for costs related to the increased international and domestic activity.

In chapter one of this volume, a brief discussion was presented of one standard of potential giving—the resources that would have been available if church members in 2021 gave the same portion of income as church members gave in 1968. If church members had indeed given the same portion of income in 2021 as was given in 1968, an additional $4.6 billion would have been available for the church to spend on the larger mission of the church through Benevolences. In this case, the level of potential giving would have required church members not to increase their giving, but rather, not to let giving decline in relationship to other spending priorities.

In this case, the level of potential giving would have required church members not to increase their giving, but rather, not to let giving decline in relationship to other spending priorities.

These resources presumably provide the opportunity to further kingdom of God priorities. As revealed through Jesus Christ, God's priorities might be summarized in the Great Commission and the Great Commandment. In the Great Commission, Jesus told his followers to go into all the world, baptizing and teaching new converts to obey the tenets of the faith (see Matthew 28:18-20 and Acts 1:8). This assignment sits in the context of the Great Commandment—to love God and therefore love the neighbor (see Mark 12:28-31). Reaching out to others, often summarized by the phrase "the church's mission," and involving both word and deed tasks, seems to be a core responsibility that Jesus passed on to those who would serve God.

One measure of the church's commitment to mission is the level of spending on international missions. In response to a survey sent out by empty tomb, inc., a set of denominations, for which 2003 through 2021 Total Contributions data was available, also provided Overseas Missions Income data for the years 2003 through 2021. The weighted average in 2021 for the group was 2% of Total Contributions being directed to denominational overseas ministries. Stated another way, of every dollar donated to a congregation, about two cents was spent on denominational overseas missions. In 2021, one communion within the group of 28 gave more than 10¢ of each dollar to overseas missions, while eight denominations each gave about 1¢ or less.

In general, the level of support for denominational overseas missions was lower in 2021 than in the 1920s.

One estimate is that an additional $1 billion a year could have a significant impact on the goal of meeting global evangelism needs. The cost would be only cents per day for church members.

If the goal were expanded to include not only evangelization, but also the cost of helping to reduce, in Jesus' name, the number of global child deaths, providing primary education for all children around the world, and providing additional funds for addressing poverty in the U.S., then the bottom line would increase and yet still only require about 49¢ per day per every church member in the U.S. If wealthy church members donated half the costs, then the daily cost would decrease for the other church members.

A potential giving number was calculated for ten Roman Catholic archdioceses in the U.S. led by cardinals as of *The Official Catholic Directory 2005*, or subsequently. The calculation indicated an increased level of giving among Catholics in these ten archdioceses would have resulted in a combined total of $123 billion additional dollars that could be applied to international needs, as well as domestically, for example, to inner-city Catholic schools.

Although there continues to be discussion of "the tithe" in many religious circles, there does not seem to be practical planning for what that money could accomplish if it were given. In 2021, for example, church members gave, on average, less than 2% of income. The tithe would involve church members giving 8% more of income. Suppose that 8% were divided between 2% more for domestic poverty needs and 6% for international needs. Have church leaders given any serious consideration how best to apply, or developed specific plans for, the resulting $474 billion more per year that would be available for critical international needs?

Although there continues to be discussion of "the tithe" in many religious circles, there does not seem to be practical planning for what that money could accomplish if it were given.

Details of the Potential of the Church

Potential Giving at 10% of Income in 2021. Following is one approach to considering potential giving levels among self-identified Christians. At the end of this chapter is another. If members of historically Christian churches had chosen to give 10% to their congregations in 2021, rather than the 1.81% given that year, there would have been a low estimate of an additional $210 billion available for work through the church.[2]

Further, if those members had specified that 60% of their increased giving were to be given to international missions, there would have been an additional $126 billion available for the international work of the church. That would have left an additional $42 billion for domestic missions, including poverty conditions in the U.S., and an equal amount for costs related to the increased missions activity.

It may be noted that the total estimate of $210 billion additional giving at 10% is a conservative estimate. Depending on the definition of religious affiliation used, the estimate might increase, from $773 billion a year using one definition to $1.2 trillion using another.[3]

This level of giving could have made a major impact on global need. Estimates vary on the cost to eliminate extreme poverty, from $70 to $80 billion a year up to $195 billion annually.[4] Basic primary education for all children around the globe could be impacted by an additional $7 billion a year.[5] Of the estimated 5.0 million children under five dying around the globe each year,[6] about two-thirds are dying from causes that could be addressed through low-cost solutions, according to one international study done in 2003. The report stated: "Our findings show that about

Figure 17: Potential Additional Church Giving at a 2021 Average of 10%, and Illustrations of Global Need That Could Be Addressed

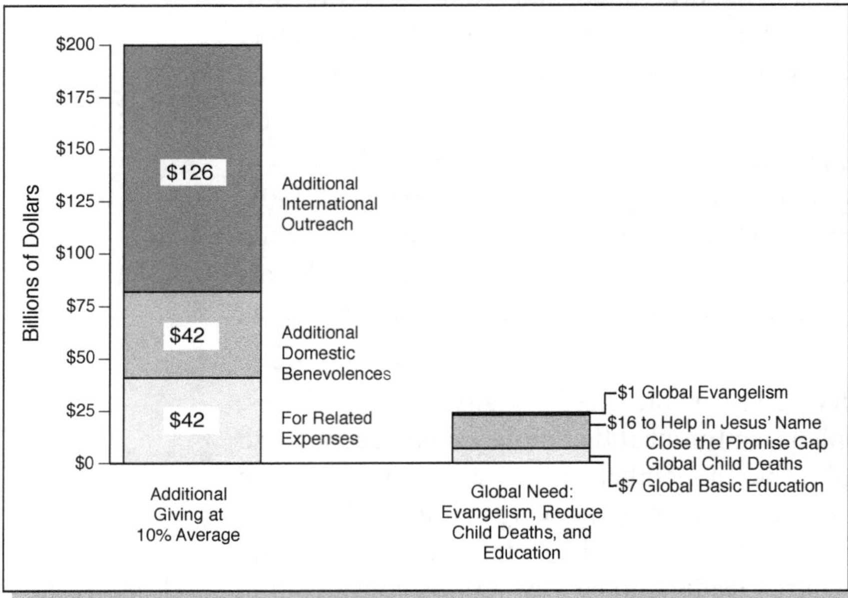

Source: empty tomb analysis; *YACC* adjusted series; U.S. BEA empty tomb, inc., 2024

two-thirds of child deaths could be prevented by interventions that are available today and are feasible for implementation in low-income countries at high levels of population coverage."[7] The cost for these interventions were estimated in 2003 to be about $5 billion a year.[8]

In a paper prepared by the Ad Hoc Study Group for Child Health Cost Validation and published in the World Health Organization *Bulletin* in February 2011, the $5 billion a year estimate made in the year 2003 was updated, "reaching US $14 billion by 2015" (in 2005 dollars[9]; $16 billion in 2011 dollars, the year of publication). Looking ahead to the Millennium Development Goal (MDG) end-year of 2015, the group concluded that efforts would need to accelerate to meet the goals set for 2015. The increase was needed, in part, because "countries with weak health systems need to make the greatest investment; in such countries, the additional resources needed per capita are two to three times greater than countries" with more developed systems.[10]

The 2015 MDGs were not met for reducing the global Under-5 Mortality Rate (U5MR) to target rates. As discussed in chapter 8, the difference between the MDG 2015 level and the actual 2015 U5MR is termed the "Promise Gap," this difference resulting in an estimated 1.5 million child deaths in 2021 that would not have occurred had the MDG been met. Given that acceleration of efforts continues to be needed in order to meet target rates, an estimate of $16 billion annual additional dollars was used for the present model.[11]

In addition to addressing the under-age-5 mortality rate, an annual estimate of $1 billion to cover the costs of global evangelization is discussed below.

Figure 17 displays the potential giving levels, and issues of global need that could be addressed by the increased giving.

Potential Giving Based on Previous Levels. A comparison in chapter 1 considered what would have happened if per member giving as a portion of income in 2021 had been the same as in 1968. That comparison found that Benevolences would have received an additional $4.6 billion in 2021, if church members still gave at the 1968 level of 0.63% of DPI to Benevolences,[12] instead of the actual 2021 level of 0.26%. This additional giving would have resulted not from an increase in the portion of income given, but rather had there not been a decline in the portion of income given between 1968 and 2021.

Another calculation suggests that giving to Benevolences could have been much larger if an earlier trend had continued. Giving as a portion of income was increasing between 1946 and 1960 in the 11-denomination data set analyzed in chapter 4, and then began an overall decline in 1961. If the 1946-1960 rate of increase had been maintained beyond 1960, total giving as a portion of income in 2021 would have been 7.9% instead of 1.81%. If 60% of the resulting additional $75 billion that would have been given in 2021 had been directed to international missions, that allocation would have amounted to $45 billion, with another $15 billion available for domestic outreach.

As noted in the discussion in chapter 1, although it may be tempting to envision how this money not given could have impacted denominational structures, it should be remembered that church members were offered the opportunity to fund those present structures at an increased level, and chose not to do so. It cannot be known if church members would have extended the trend to increase the portion of income given if denominations had offered a challenge to engage global needs, such as evangelization or reducing child mortality, at a scale that might have solved, rather than coped with, the needs.

... Benevolences would have received an additional $4.6 billion in 2021, if church members still gave at the 1968 level of 0.63% of DPI to Benevolences, instead of the actual 2021 level of 0.26%

Per Capita Giving to International Missions. Tables 17-26 provide the data on which the following discussion is based.

A survey of a group of Protestant denominations found that, on average, about two cents of each dollar donated to their affiliated congregations in 2021 funded international missions through the denominations.

The goal of the empty tomb, inc. research survey form was to discern how much of Overseas Missions Income came from living member giving. "Overseas Missions Income" was used in the title of the survey form, and "overseas ministries income" was used in the text of the questions on the survey form. In this volume, the two terms, "overseas missions" and "overseas ministry," are used interchangeably. The following questions were also asked on the denominational Overseas Missions Income survey form for those denominations that had reported 2003 through 2020 data in previous years.

1. What was the amount of income raised in the U.S. during the calendar or fiscal year 2021 for overseas ministries?
2. How many dollars of the total amount on Line 1. came from endowment, foundation, and other investment income?
3. Of the total amount on Line 1., what is the dollar value of government grants, either in dollars or in-kind goods for distribution?
4. Balance of overseas ministries income: Line 1. minus Lines 2. and 3.

The form sent to denominations provided data reported in previous years, in 18 columns labeled "Reported 2003" through "Reported 2020." These columns presented on each line the data previously reported by that denomination. A column to the right of these 18 columns was labeled "Newly Requested 2021" and included blank cells for each of the four lines.

Table 17: Overseas Missions Income, Excluding Any Investment or Government Income, as a Percent of Total Contributions to Congregations, 34 Denominations, 2003 and 2004

	2003				2004			
Denomination	Overseas Missions Income (Line 4)	Total Contributions	Overseas Missions Income as % of Total Contribs.	Cents of Each Dollar for Overseas Ministries	Overseas Missions Income (Line 4)	Total Contributions	Overseas Missions Income as % of Total Contribs.	Cents of Each Dollar for Overseas Ministries
Allegheny Wesleyan Methodist Connection	$262,260	$5,216,941	5.0%	5¢	$266,299	$5,638,852	4.7%	5¢
American Baptist Churches in the U.S.A. [14]	$8,513,838	$452,422,019	1.9%	2¢	$9,491,848	$432,734,941	2.2%	2¢
Associate Reformed Presbyterian Church (General Synod)	$3,332,992	$44,279,992	7.5%	8¢	$3,954,575	$49,290,082	8.0%	8¢
Brethren in Christ Church	$1,606,911	$36,309,353	4.4%	4¢	$1,800,963	$32,235,440	5.6%	6¢
Christian Church (Disciples of Christ)	$4,079,019	$501,756,492	0.8%	1¢	$3,832,092	$493,377,355	0.8%	1¢
Christian and Missionary Alliance [15]	$43,160,960	$381,439,326	11.3%	11¢	$43,534,066	$401,702,995	10.8%	11¢
Church of the Brethren [16]	$1,563,623	$93,876,819	1.7%	2¢	$1,558,320	$90,440,250	1.7%	2¢
Church of God General Conference (Oregon, Ill., and Morrow, Ga.)	$67,193	$4,297,394	1.6%	2¢	$113,497	$4,445,000	2.6%	3¢
Church of the Lutheran Confession	$155,156	$5,855,961	2.6%	3¢	$206,896	$6,187,297	3.3%	3¢
Church of the Nazarene	$45,640,480	$728,931,987	6.3%	6¢	$48,173,085	$743,526,726	6.5%	6¢
Churches of God General Conference [17]	$899,679	$27,444,027	3.3%	3¢	$1,047,148	$28,360,228	3.7%	4¢
Conservative Congregational Christian Conference [18]	$147,805	$52,572,753	See Note 18	See Note 18	$149,299	$59,795,058	See Note 18	See Note 18
Cumberland Presbyterian Church	$290,764	$49,168,885	0.6%	1¢	$323,340	$49,800,171	0.6%	1¢
The Episcopal Church [19]	$13,193,855	$2,133,772,253	0.6%	1¢	$14,781,000	$2,132,774,534	0.7%	1¢
Evangelical Congregational Church	$1,045,237	$19,628,647	5.3%	5¢	$941,409	$22,831,988	4.1%	4¢
Evangelical Covenant Church	$7,913,682	$247,440,270	3.2%	3¢	$8,591,574	$267,267,027	3.2%	3¢
Evangelical Lutheran Church in America [20]	$19,637,381	$2,517,027,671	0.8%	1¢	$23,431,081	$2,568,013,806	0.9%	1¢
Evangelical Lutheran Synod	$246,587	$13,013,890	1.9%	2¢	$266,241	$12,926,484	2.1%	2¢
Fellowship of Evangelical Churches	$912,689	$14,138,539	6.5%	6¢	$847,526	$16,525,789	5.1%	5¢
Free Methodist Church of North America	$9,121,599	$122,723,869	7.4%	7¢	$10,186,619	$131,576,527	7.7%	8¢
General Association of General Baptists	$1,858,866	$35,428,127	5.2%	5¢	$1,768,537	$33,771,637	5.2%	5¢
Lutheran Church-Missouri Synod [21]	$13,079,041	$1,256,382,217	1.0%	1¢	$13,177,379	$1,307,764,010	1.0%	1¢
Moravian Church in America, Northern Province [22]	$467,570	$17,864,570	2.6%	3¢	$528,733	$18,514,925	2.9%	3¢
The Orthodox Presbyterian Church [23]	$1,214,449	$36,644,100	3.3%	3¢	$1,374,254	$38,660,300	3.6%	4¢
Presbyterian Church in America	$24,070,885	$529,220,570	4.5%	5¢	$24,319,185	$544,857,944	4.5%	4¢
Presbyterian Church (U.S.A.) [24]	$23,255,000	$2,743,637,755	0.8%	1¢	$24,588,000	$2,774,907,848	0.9%	1¢
Primitive Methodist Church in the U.S.A. [25]	$536,903	$4,771,104	11.3%	11¢	$526,640	$5,565,638	9.5%	9¢
Reformed Church in America	$7,852,464	$275,354,238	2.9%	3¢	$7,284,560	$296,856,834	2.5%	2¢
Seventh-day Adventists, North Am. Div. [26]	$48,225,234	$1,088,682,947	4.4%	4¢	$46,752,585	$1,121,549,712	4.2%	4¢
Southern Baptist Convention [27]	$239,663,000	$9,648,530,640	2.5%	2¢	$242,140,000	$10,171,197,048	2.4%	2¢
United Church of Christ	$8,373,084	$878,974,911	1.0%	1¢	$7,935,678	$895,654,110	0.9%	1¢
The United Methodist Church [28]	$82,000,000	$5,376,057,236	1.5%	2¢	$91,200,000	$5,541,540,536	1.6%	2¢
The Wesleyan Church	$8,507,914	$260,315,979	3.3%	3¢	$8,881,386	$259,011,346	3.4%	3¢
Wisconsin Evangelical Lutheran Synod	$10,779,163.63	$278,209,035	3.9%	4¢	$10,304,863	$296,791,013	3.5%	3¢
Total/Average for 34 Denominations	$631,675,283	$29,881,390,517	2.1%	2¢	$654,278,678	$30,856,093,451	2.1%	2¢

Source: empty tomb analysis. See endnotes at the end of the chapter. See Appendix B-5 for detail.

empty tomb, inc., 2024

Table 18: Overseas Missions Income, Excluding Any Investment or Government Income, as a Percent of Total Contributions to Congregations, 34 Denominations, 2005 and 2006

	2005				2006			
Denomination	Overseas Missions Income (Line 4)	Total Contributions	Overseas Missions Income as % of Total Contribs.	Cents of Each Dollar for Overseas Ministries	Overseas Missions Income (Line 4)	Total Contributions	Overseas Missions Income as % of Total Contribs.	Cents of Each Dollar for Overseas Ministries
Allegheny Wesleyan Methodist Connection	$399,514	$5,383,333	7.4%	7¢	$286,781	$4,891,827	5.9%	6¢
American Baptist Churches in the U.S.A. [14]	$11,096,481	$336,894,843	3.3%	3¢	$8,779,170	$312,485,013	2.8%	3¢
Associate Reformed Presbyterian Church (General Synod)	$4,516,302	$50,921,233	8.9%	9¢	$3,821,297	$48,592,174	7.9%	8¢
Brethren in Christ Church	$1,920,000	$39,800,056	4.8%	5¢	$2,117,594	$42,357,718	5.0%	5¢
Christian Church (Disciples of Christ)	$4,222,777	$503,045,398	0.8%	1¢	$4,421,669	$539,112,457	0.8%	1¢
Christian and Missionary Alliance [15]	$54,267,422	$442,917,566	12.3%	12¢	$52,505,044	$458,063,183	11.5%	11¢
Church of the Brethren [16]	$2,270,134	$97,940,974	2.3%	2¢	$1,887,202	$92,834,308	2.0%	2¢
Church of God General Conference (Oregon, Ill., and Morrow, Ga.)	$80,000	$4,496,822	1.8%	2¢	$63,355	$4,421,793	1.4%	1¢
Church of the Lutheran Confession	$309,823	$6,551,799	4.7%	5¢	$188,817	$6,965,144	2.7%	3¢
Church of the Nazarene	$52,753,682	$765,434,742	6.9%	7¢	$50,969,965	$792,831,191	6.4%	6¢
Churches of God General Conference [17]	$1,130,100	$32,249,551	3.5%	4¢	$1,233,843	$33,061,351	3.7%	4¢
Conservative Congregational Christian Conference [18]	$166,875	$59,346,227	See Note 18	See Note 18	$123,509	$65,417,224	See Note 18	See Note 18
Cumberland Presbyterian Church	$293,346	$54,148,837	0.5%	1¢	$290,307	$54,727,911	0.5%	1¢
The Episcopal Church [19]	$15,371,967	$2,180,974,503	0.7%	1¢	$14,806,793	$2,187,308,798	0.7%	1¢
Evangelical Congregational Church	$725,089	$21,408,687	3.4%	3¢	$1,326,393	$22,174,004	6.0%	6¢
Evangelical Covenant Church	$9,008,719	$291,847,011	3.1%	3¢	$8,530,245	$313,771,228	2.7%	3¢
Evangelical Lutheran Church in America [20]	$26,084,001	$2,604,798,005	1.0%	1¢	$21,541,809	$2,664,147,210	0.8%	1¢
Evangelical Lutheran Synod	$222,204	$13,831,771	1.6%	2¢	$330,651	$16,412,280	2.0%	2¢
Fellowship of Evangelical Churches	$785,676	$18,426,832	4.3%	4¢	$700,159	$19,031,219	3.7%	4¢
Free Methodist Church of North America	$10,720,240	$138,619,962	7.7%	8¢	$11,878,875	$142,797,105	8.3%	8¢
General Association of General Baptists	$1,924,508	$40,146,583	4.8%	5¢	$2,048,570	$35,905,960	5.7%	6¢
Lutheran Church-Missouri Synod [21]	$17,175,578	$1,296,818,738	1.3%	1¢	$13,432,946	$1,355,458,558	1.0%	1¢
Moravian Church in America, Northern Province [22]	$482,157	$17,835,255	2.7%	3¢	$512,828	$17,780,604	2.9%	3¢
The Orthodox Presbyterian Church [23]	$1,856,529	$40,736,400	4.6%	5¢	$1,706,292	$45,883,300	3.7%	4¢
Presbyterian Church in America	$25,890,591	$586,824,356	4.4%	4¢	$27,627,770	$650,091,428	4.2%	4¢
Presbyterian Church (U.S.A.) [24]	$31,618,000	$2,814,271,023	1.1%	1¢	$20,964,000	$2,854,719,850	0.7%	1¢
Primitive Methodist Church in the U.S.A. [25]	$497,845	$5,541,336	9.0%	9¢	$566,116	$5,080,485	11.1%	11¢
Reformed Church in America	$10,727,347	$310,909,691	3.5%	3¢	$7,486,527	$328,793,517	2.3%	2¢
Seventh-day Adventists, North Am. Div. [26]	$52,130,967	$1,273,399,341	4.1%	4¢	$48,905,616	$1,290,321,473	3.8%	4¢
Southern Baptist Convention [27]	$259,394,000	$10,721,544,568	2.4%	2¢	$275,747,000	$11,372,608,393	2.4%	2¢
United Church of Christ	$7,652,371	$908,726,794	0.8%	1¢	$7,539,124	$920,094,107	0.8%	1¢
The United Methodist Church [28]	$127,600,000	$5,861,722,397	2.2%	2¢	$83,100,000	$6,012,378,898	1.4%	1¢
The Wesleyan Church	$9,769,938	$280,214,570	3.5%	3¢	$13,105,882	$292,826,250	4.5%	4¢
Wisconsin Evangelical Lutheran Synod	$8,794,293	$299,324,485	2.9%	3¢	$10,468,560	$314,016,686	3.3%	3¢
Total/Average for 34 Denominations	$751,858,476	$32,127,053,689	2.3%	2¢	$699,014,709	$33,317,362,647	2.1%	2¢

Source: empty tomb analysis. See endnotes at the end of the chapter. See Appendix B-5 for detail.

empty tomb, inc., 2024

Table 19: Overseas Missions Income, Excluding Any Investment or Government Income, as a Percent of Total Contributions to Congregations, 34 Denominations, 2007, and 33 Denominations, 2008

Denomination	2007				2008			
	Overseas Missions Income (Line 4)	Total Contributions	Overseas Missions Income as % of Total Contribs.	Cents of Each Dollar for Overseas Ministries	Overseas Missions Income (Line 4)	Total Contributions	Overseas Missions Income as % of Total Contribs.	Cents of Each Dollar for Overseas Ministries
Allegheny Wesleyan Methodist Connection	$332,511	$4,973,589	6.7%	7¢	$306,946	$4,756,409	6.5%	6¢
American Baptist Churches in the U.S.A. [14]	$9,866,010	$325,941,205	3.0%	3¢	$9,846,000	$317,338,230	3.1%	3¢
Associate Reformed Presbyterian Church (General Synod)	$4,819,622	$49,424,200	9.8%	10¢	$5,838,994	$46,948,089	12.4%	12¢
Brethren in Christ Church	$2,171,822	$43,936,567	4.9%	5¢	$2,452,498	$44,671,975	5.5%	5¢
Christian Church (Disciples of Christ)	$4,774,004	$519,082,964	0.9%	1¢	$4,527,471	$524,213,682	0.9%	1¢
Christian and Missionary Alliance [15]	$55,964,407	$467,812,148	12.0%	12¢	$52,012,830	$466,388,400	11.2%	11¢
Church of the Brethren [16]	$1,736,654	$88,668,503	2.0%	2¢	$1,748,520	$87,494,968	2.0%	2¢
Church of God General Conference (Oregon, Ill., and Morrow, Ga.)	$103,495	$4,378,745	2.4%	2¢	$101,028	$4,056,759	2.5%	2¢
Church of the Lutheran Confession	$277,600	$7,207,712	3.9%	4¢	$360,323	$7,073,530	5.1%	5¢
Church of the Nazarene	$50,591,155	$817,722,230	6.2%	6¢	$53,761,093	$829,801,861	6.5%	6¢
Churches of God General Conference [17]	$1,118,921	$35,106,856	3.2%	3¢	$1,187,253	$33,239,825	3.6%	4¢
Conservative Congregational Christian Conference [18]	$169,508	$74,467,155	See Note 18	See Note 18	$84,460	$72,677,645	See Note 18	See Note 18
Cumberland Presbyterian Church	$352,644	$57,766,770	0.6%	1¢	$301,245	$57,646,214	0.5%	1¢
The Episcopal Church [19]	$15,028,559	$2,221,167,438	0.7%	1¢	$14,599,354	$2,294,941,221	0.6%	1¢
Evangelical Congregational Church	$1,464,523	$17,180,755	8.5%	9¢	$1,583,478	$18,736,646	8.5%	8¢
Evangelical Covenant Church	$7,954,834	$323,916,976	2.5%	2¢	NA	NA	NA	NA
Evangelical Lutheran Church in America [20]	$21,747,378	$2,725,349,028	0.8%	1¢	$24,160,174	$2,764,009,721	0.9%	1¢
Evangelical Lutheran Synod	$504,018	$16,104,636	3.1%	3¢	$619,754	$15,635,281	4.0%	4¢
Fellowship of Evangelical Churches	$700,590	$19,031,219	3.7%	4¢	$724,626	$24,446,883	3.0%	3¢
Free Methodist Church of North America	$12,478,468	$144,657,810	8.6%	9¢	$13,244,864	$142,838,830	9.3%	9¢
General Association of General Baptists	$2,179,048	$31,385,133	6.9%	7¢	$2,105,841	$33,520,716	6.3%	6¢
Lutheran Church-Missouri Synod [21]	$13,186,920	$1,399,774,702	0.9%	1¢	$14,505,811	$1,343,086,275	1.1%	1¢
Moravian Church in America, Northern Province [22]	$524,149	$19,021,572	2.8%	3¢	$473,520	$18,268,105	2.6%	3¢
The Orthodox Presbyterian Church [23]	$1,824,389	$45,730,400	4.0%	4¢	$1,800,305	$46,035,988	3.9%	4¢
Presbyterian Church in America	$28,456,453	$686,331,677	4.1%	4¢	$29,173,722	$714,356,133	4.1%	4¢
Presbyterian Church (U.S.A.) [24]	$40,366,000	$2,916,788,414	1.4%	1¢	$19,919,000	$2,921,571,493	0.7%	1¢
Primitive Methodist Church in the U.S.A. [25]	$566,810	$4,632,031	12.2%	12¢	$542,438	$4,827,828	11.2%	11¢
Reformed Church in America	$7,611,613	$338,446,877	2.2%	2¢	$7,642,569	$329,904,049	2.3%	2¢
Seventh-day Adventists, North Am. Div. [26]	$52,038,112	$1,259,280,736	4.1%	4¢	$51,501,480	$1,195,419,795	4.3%	4¢
Southern Baptist Convention [27]	$278,313,000	$12,107,096,858	2.3%	2¢	$254,860,000	$12,121,220,925	2.1%	2¢
United Church of Christ	$7,307,090	$936,862,062	0.8%	1¢	$7,244,977	$941,553,540	0.8%	1¢
The United Methodist Church [28]	$79,500,000	$6,295,942,455	1.3%	1¢	$114,500,000	$6,300,722,381	1.8%	2¢
The Wesleyan Church	$13,554,996	$321,461,982	4.2%	4¢	$13,669,461	$333,767,545	4.1%	4¢
Wisconsin Evangelical Lutheran Synod	$10,672,195	$323,082,651	3.3%	3¢	$11,635,379	$319,988,294	3.6%	4¢
Total/Average for 34/33 Denominations	$728,257,498	$34,649,734,056	2.1%	2¢	$717,035,415	$34,381,159,236	2.1%	2¢

Source: empty tomb analysis. See endnotes at the end of the chapter. See Appendix B-5 for detail. empty tomb, inc., 2024

Table 20: Overseas Missions Income, Excluding Any Investment or Government Income, as a Percent of Total Contributions to Congregations, 33 Denominations, 2009 and 2010

	2009				2010			
Denomination	Overseas Missions Income (Line 4)	Total Contributions	Overseas Missions Income as % of Total Contribs.	Cents of Each Dollar for Overseas Ministries	Overseas Missions Income (Line 4)	Total Contributions	Overseas Missions Income as % of Total Contribs.	Cents of Each Dollar for Overseas Ministries
Allegheny Wesleyan Methodist Connection	$275,139	$5,053,282	5.4%	5¢	$313,920	$5,072,039	6.2%	6¢
American Baptist Churches in the U.S.A. [14]	$9,585,000	$288,839,340	3.3%	3¢	$12,121,000	$289,345,336	4.2%	4¢
Associate Reformed Presbyterian Church (General Synod)	$4,234,871	$54,800,721	7.7%	8¢	$4,245,630	$54,229,638	7.8%	8¢
Brethren in Christ Church	$2,473,594	$40,370,797	6.1%	6¢	$2,507,447	$39,432,268	6.4%	6¢
Christian Church (Disciples of Christ)	$3,978,592	$495,988,245	0.8%	1¢	$4,295,675	$489,365,802	0.9%	1¢
Christian and Missionary Alliance [15]	$52,888,984	$464,694,407	11.4%	11¢	$53,693,745	$469,726,502	11.4%	11¢
Church of the Brethren [16]	$1,904,137	$89,631,907	2.1%	2¢	$2,021,630	$92,270,210	2.2%	2¢
Church of God General Conference (Oregon, Ill., and Morrow, Ga.)	$166,433	$4,013,750	4.1%	4¢	$106,015	$4,158,243	2.5%	3¢
Church of the Lutheran Confession	$402,162	$6,974,801	5.8%	6¢	$405,811	$7,082,478	5.7%	6¢
Church of the Nazarene	$43,370,879	$823,915,528	5.3%	5¢	$47,268,270	$774,827,069	6.1%	6¢
Churches of God General Conference [17]	$1,335,598	$35,331,543	3.8%	4¢	$1,697,288	$36,429,878	4.7%	5¢
Conservative Congregational Christian Conference [18]	$18,397	$70,496,255	See Note 18	See Note 18	$10,124	$48,072,539	See Note 18	See Note 18
Cumberland Presbyterian Church	$277,412	$56,383,201	0.5%	0.05¢	$309,000	$52,531,185	0.6%	1¢
The Episcopal Church [19]	$15,611,043	$2,182,330,459	0.7%	1¢	$20,051,263	$2,088,449,676	1.0%	1¢
Evangelical Congregational Church	$1,462,048	$19,594,243	7.5%	7¢	$1,416,294	$20,221,005	7.0%	7¢
Evangelical Covenant Church	NA	NA	NA	NA	NA	NA	NA	NA
Evangelical Lutheran Church in America [20]	$24,665,494	$2,716,085,854	0.9%	1¢	$22,908,625	$2,226,412,989	1.0%	1¢
Evangelical Lutheran Synod	$1,144,111	$15,919,860	7.2%	7¢	$652,338	$14,960,758	4.4%	4¢
Fellowship of Evangelical Churches	$804,057	$24,323,500	3.3%	3¢	$839,881	$24,607,538	3.4%	3¢
Free Methodist Church of North America	$11,720,519	$146,403,342	8.0%	8¢	$12,226,510	$146,613,392	8.3%	8¢
General Association of General Baptists	$1,946,149	$38,261,252	5.1%	5¢	$1,697,759	$35,457,524	4.8%	5¢
Lutheran Church-Missouri Synod [21]	$15,491,786	$1,361,537,807	1.1%	1¢	$16,007,836	$1,375,784,215	1.2%	1¢
Moravian Church in America, Northern Province [22]	$503,817	$18,241,950	2.8%	3¢	$493,168	$18,220,682	2.7%	3¢
The Orthodox Presbyterian Church [23]	$1,979,044	$46,575,856	4.2%	4¢	$1,805,968	$48,356,529	3.7%	4¢
Presbyterian Church in America	$27,219,278	$696,680,887	3.9%	4¢	$25,327,324	$701,995,791	3.6%	4¢
Presbyterian Church (U.S.A.) [24]	$21,986,831	$2,773,343,691	0.8%	1¢	$31,462,380	$2,614,472,933	1.2%	1¢
Primitive Methodist Church in the U.S.A. [25]	$429,530	$4,664,330	9.2%	9¢	$404,770	$5,006,926	8.1%	8¢
Reformed Church in America	$8,187,860	$301,838,760	2.7%	3¢	$8,870,635	$302,162,041	2.9%	3¢
Seventh-day Adventists, North Am. Div. [26]	$49,538,644	$1,275,496,054	3.9%	4¢	$50,392,451	$1,268,582,205	4.0%	4¢
Southern Baptist Convention [27]	$255,427,000	$11,912,179,313	2.1%	2¢	$264,924,000	$11,720,820,320	2.3%	2¢
United Church of Christ	$6,213,752	$928,638,925	0.7%	1¢	$5,812,528	$938,000,522	0.6%	1¢
The United Methodist Church [28]	$96,920,000	$6,218,009,630	1.6%	2¢	$135,240,000	$6,158,084,527	2.2%	2¢
The Wesleyan Church	$14,139,092	$323,061,444	4.4%	4¢	$14,780,950	$316,205,810	4.7%	5¢
Wisconsin Evangelical Lutheran Synod	$11,030,819	$314,982,519	3.5%	4¢	$9,267,581	$314,966,370	2.9%	3¢
Total/Average for 33 Denominations	$687,332,072	$33,754,663,453	2.0%	2¢	$753,577,816	$32,701,924,940	2.3%	2¢

Source: empty tomb analysis. See endnotes at the end of the chapter. See Appendix B-5 for detail.

empty tomb, inc., 2024

Table 21: Overseas Missions Income, Excluding Any Investment or Government Income, as a Percent of Total Contributions to Congregations, 33 Denominations, 2011, and 32 Denominations, 2012

	2011				2012			
Denomination	Overseas Missions Income (Line 4)	Total Contributions	Overseas Missions Income as % of Total Contribs.	Cents of Each Dollar for Overseas Ministries	Overseas Missions Income (Line 4)	Total Contributions	Overseas Missions Income as % of Total Contribs.	Cents of Each Dollar for Overseas Ministries
Allegheny Wesleyan Methodist Connection	$244,376	$4,945,044	4.9%	5¢	$284,379	$5,476,662	5.2%	5¢
American Baptist Churches in the U.S.A. [14]	$10,003,000	$309,967,121	3.2%	3¢	$10,492,000	$322,531,644	3.3%	3¢
Associate Reformed Presbyterian Church (General Synod)	$4,121,650	$66,774,089	6.2%	6¢	$4,133,887	$63,853,050	6.5%	6¢
Brethren in Christ Church	$2,357,759	$45,259,861	5.2%	5¢	$2,475,120	$39,826,190	6.2%	6¢
Christian Church (Disciples of Christ)	$3,022,583	$483,723,029	0.6%	1¢	$2,746,379	$496,930,768	0.6%	1¢
Christian and Missionary Alliance [15]	$51,740,315	$482,474,036	10.7%	11¢	$48,974,794	$432,212,876	11.3%	11¢
Church of the Brethren [16]	$1,813,039	$86,361,373	2.1%	2¢	NA	NA	NA	NA
Church of God General Conference (McDonough, Ga.)	$81,281	$4,102,502	2.0%	2¢	$77,168	$3,995,565	1.9%	2¢
Church of the Lutheran Confession	$389,457	$6,866,506	5.7%	6¢	$176,342	$7,137,149	2.5%	2¢
Church of the Nazarene	$44,769,213	$747,925,798	6.0%	6¢	$42,965,412	$726,061,123	5.9%	6¢
Churches of God General Conference [17]	$1,329,931	$36,994,255	3.6%	4¢	$1,482,648	$37,975,453	3.9%	4¢
Conservative Congregational Christian Conference [18]	$21,855	$51,478,729	See Note 18	See Note 18	$1,750	$55,237,612	See Note 18	See Note 18
Cumberland Presbyterian Church	$429,388	$49,236,085	0.9%	1¢	$1,394,260	$46,827,267	3.0%	3¢
The Episcopal Church [19]	$19,369,172	$2,080,612,044	0.9%	1¢	$15,362,699	$2,084,487,182	0.7%	1¢
Evangelical Congregational Church	$1,502,493	$18,062,552	8.3%	8¢	$1,236,345	$16,591,741	7.5%	7¢
Evangelical Covenant Church	NA	NA	NA	NA	NA	NA	NA	NA
Evangelical Lutheran Church in America [20]	$24,387,446	$2,167,770,306	1.1%	1¢	$23,877,033	$2,148,615,030	1.1%	1¢
Evangelical Lutheran Synod	$254,289	$15,399,301	1.7%	2¢	$264,911	$14,837,123	1.8%	2¢
Fellowship of Evangelical Churches	$719,573	$23,895,325	3.0%	3¢	$602,397	$23,257,146	2.6%	3¢
Free Methodist Church-USA	$13,633,423	$146,081,401	9.3%	9¢	$13,021,413	$150,762,157	8.6%	9¢
General Association of General Baptists	$1,670,928	$44,318,518	3.8%	4¢	$2,151,235	$45,152,556	4.8%	5¢
Lutheran Church-Missouri Synod [21]	$18,663,337	$1,376,155,314	1.4%	1¢	$20,215,817	$1,423,342,829	1.4%	1¢
Moravian Church in America, Northern Province [22]	$491,164	$15,754,854	3.1%	3¢	$439,988	$16,421,999	2.7%	3¢
The Orthodox Presbyterian Church [23]	$1,841,490	$49,363,564	3.7%	4¢	$1,798,267	$50,991,053	3.5%	4¢
Presbyterian Church in America	$24,971,256	$704,611,711	3.5%	4¢	$24,436,050	$710,318,507	3.4%	3¢
Presbyterian Church (U.S.A.) [24]	$22,952,028	$2,620,938,061	0.9%	1¢	$23,014,394	$2,488,199,398	0.9%	1¢
Primitive Methodist Church in the U.S.A. [25]	$340,467	$5,244,894	6.5%	6¢	$418,811	$5,317,027	7.9%	8¢
Reformed Church in America	$6,627,390	$310,520,618	2.1%	2¢	$7,000,872	$336,907,538	2.1%	2¢
Seventh-day Adventists, North Am. Div. [26]	$55,292,154	$1,297,070,070	4.3%	4¢	$50,645,845	$1,323,435,651	3.8%	4¢
Southern Baptist Convention [27]	$256,882,000	$11,805,027,705	2.2%	2¢	$262,104,000	$11,521,418,784	2.3%	2¢
United Church of Christ	$5,678,910	$934,824,110	0.6%	1¢	$5,243,249	$912,804,952	0.6%	1¢
The United Methodist Church [28]	$102,600,000	$6,189,661,943	1.7%	2¢	$81,350,000	$6,216,393,709	1.3%	1¢
The Wesleyan Church	$14,788,726	$329,711,022	4.5%	4¢	$16,556,897	$344,980,569	4.8%	5¢
Wisconsin Evangelical Lutheran Synod	$9,487,614	$311,013,326	3.1%	3¢	$8,633,528	$326,234,605	2.6%	3¢
Total/Average for 33/32 Denominations	$702,477,707	$32,822,145,067	2.1%	2¢	$673,577,890	$32,398,534,915	2.1%	2¢

Source: empty tomb analysis. See endnotes at the end of the chapter. See Appendix B-5 for detail.

empty tomb, inc., 2024

Table 22: Overseas Missions Income, Excluding Any Investment or Government Income, as a Percent of Total Contributions to Congregations, 32 Denominations, 2013 and 2014

	2013				2014			
Denomination	Overseas Missions Income (Line 4)	Total Contributions	Overseas Missions Income as % of Total Contribs.	Cents of Each Dollar for Overseas Ministries	Overseas Missions Income (Line 4)	Total Contributions	Overseas Missions Income as % of Total Contribs.	Cents of Each Dollar for Overseas Ministries
Allegheny Wesleyan Methodist Connection	$266,255	$5,315,850	5.0%	5¢	$270,953	$4,755,035	5.7%	6¢
American Baptist Churches in the U.S.A. [14]	$9,982,000	$291,159,795	3.4%	3¢	$12,977,000	$253,017,729	5.1%	5¢
Associate Reformed Presbyterian Church (General Synod)	$4,390,526	$57,367,421	7.7%	8¢	$4,226,533	$56,829,070	7.4%	7¢
Brethren in Christ Church	$2,656,017	$42,283,647	6.3%	6¢	$3,300,879	$49,324,560	6.7%	7¢
Christian Church (Disciples of Christ)	$2,725,220	$412,720,319	0.7%	1¢	$2,584,483	$401,995,898	0.6%	1¢
Christian and Missionary Alliance [15]	$50,426,684	$427,914,414	11.8%	12¢	$54,324,052	$442,822,428	12.3%	12¢
Church of the Brethren [16]	NA	—	NA	NA	NA	NA	NA	NA
Church of God General Conference (McDonough, Ga.)	$102,207	$3,787,618	2.7%	3¢	$86,086	$3,676,921	2.3%	2¢
Church of the Lutheran Confession	$208,419	$7,388,914	2.8%	3¢	$204,023	$7,321,690	2.8%	3¢
Church of the Nazarene	$41,802,551	$758,116,761	5.5%	6¢	$42,879,133	$750,333,567	5.7%	6¢
Churches of God General Conference [17]	$1,466,619	$38,771,569	3.8%	4¢	$1,432,956	$40,704,505	3.5%	4¢
Conservative Congregational Christian Conference [18]	$2,996	$56,189,324	See Note 18	See Note 18	$9,600	$57,100,123	See Note 18	See Note 18
Cumberland Presbyterian Church	$350,647	$50,439,707	0.7%	1¢	$768,083	$47,940,850	1.6%	2¢
The Episcopal Church [19]	$19,095,769	$2,136,588,352	0.9%	1¢	$20,482,672	$2,154,850,845	1.0%	1¢
Evangelical Congregational Church	$1,188,936	$15,691,414	7.6%	8¢	$1,271,216	$16,509,840	7.7%	8¢
Evangelical Covenant Church	NA	NA	NA	NA	NA	NA	NA	NA
Evangelical Lutheran Church in America [20]	$25,366,486	$2,161,627,227	1.2%	1¢	$26,319,551	$2,176,359,817	1.2%	1¢
Evangelical Lutheran Synod	$246,703	$15,144,771	1.6%	2¢	$265,445	$15,685,299	1.7%	2¢
Fellowship of Evangelical Churches	$465,828	$20,676,498	2.3%	2¢	$257,376	$23,096,122	1.1%	1¢
Free Methodist Church-USA	$12,207,952	$148,799,924	8.2%	8¢	$13,063,585	$149,318,108	8.7%	9¢
General Association of General Baptists	$2,117,145	$40,189,006	5.3%	5¢	$1,012,743	$43,457,886	2.3%	2¢
Lutheran Church-Missouri Synod [21]	$21,272,417	$1,419,687,164	1.5%	1¢	$23,281,641	$1,347,451,761	1.7%	2¢
Moravian Church in America, Northern Province [22]	$447,826	$16,015,888	2.8%	3¢	$478,650	$14,960,386	3.2%	3¢
The Orthodox Presbyterian Church [23]	NA	—	NA	NA	2,111,178$	$54,188,600	3.9%	4¢
Presbyterian Church in America	$25,049,022	$746,446,983	3.4%	3¢	$25,131,181	$747,973,604	3.4%	3¢
Presbyterian Church (U.S.A.) [24]	$20,318,751	$2,356,784,110	0.9%	1¢	$17,888,917	$2,237,307,876	0.8%	1¢
Primitive Methodist Church in the U.S.A. [25]	$440,766	$5,149,726	8.6%	9¢	$339,794	$4,573,688	7.4%	7¢
Reformed Church in America	$7,816,368	$322,697,028	2.4%	2¢	$6,844,816	$332,269,584	2.1%	2¢
Seventh-day Adventists, North Am. Div. [26]	$53,194,898	$1,323,245,575	4.0%	4¢	$48,021,911	$1,355,393,460	3.5%	4¢
Southern Baptist Convention [27]	$265,429,000	$11,209,655,950	2.4%	2¢	$265,633,000	$11,154,665,938	2.4%	2¢
United Church of Christ	$4,763,870	$923,757,089	0.5%	1¢	$4,239,765	$950,538,969	0.4%	0¢
The United Methodist Church [28]	$86,700,000	$6,231,445,829	1.4%	1¢	$76,400,000	$6,315,279,161	1.2%	1¢
The Wesleyan Church	$16,309,860	$347,501,093	4.7%	5¢	$16,186,471	$356,328,403	4.5%	5¢
Wisconsin Evangelical Lutheran Synod	$7,401,896	$330,405,104	2.2%	2¢	$8,151,698	$336,838,227	2.4%	2¢
Total/Average for 32 Denominations	$686,319,473	$31,977,032,072	2.1%	2¢	$680,445,391	$31,902,869,950	2.1%	2¢

Source: empty tomb analysis. See endnotes at the end of the chapter. See Appendix B-5 for detail. empty tomb, inc., 2024

Table 23: Overseas Missions Income, Excluding Any Investment or Government Income, as a Percent of Total Contributions to Congregations, 31 Denominations, 2015, and 30 Denominations, 2016

	2015				2016			
Denomination	Overseas Missions Income (Line 4)	Total Contributions	Overseas Missions Income as % of Total Contribs.	Cents of Each Dollar for Overseas Ministries	Overseas Missions Income (Line 4)	Total Contributions	Overseas Missions Income as % of Total Contribs.	Cents of Each Dollar for Overseas Ministries
Allegheny Wesleyan Methodist Connection	$279,143	$4,500,624	6.2%	6¢	$266,163	$4,657,086	5.7%	6¢
American Baptist Churches in the U.S.A. [14]	$12,405,655	$265,146,678	4.7%	5¢	$12,457,761	$274,875,981	4.5%	5¢
Associate Reformed Presbyterian Church (General Synod)	$4,494,243	$64,763,053	6.9%	7¢	$4,585,724	$60,058,683	7.6%	8¢
Brethren in Christ Church	$1,997,474	$42,913,023	4.7%	5¢	$2,278,831	$35,699,190$	6.4%	6¢
Christian Church (Disciples of Christ)	$2,644,349	$386,639,687	0.7%	1¢	$2,505,260	$381,528,212	0.7%	1¢
Christian and Missionary Alliance [15]	$56,270,007	$456,344,850	12.3%	12¢	$57,675,292	$472,717,978	12.2%	12¢
Church of the Brethren [16]	NA	—	NA	NA	NA	—	NA	NA
Church of God General Conference (McDonough, Ga.)	$218,361	$4,031,562	5.4%	5¢	NA	NA	NA	NA
Church of the Lutheran Confession	$164,708	$7,567,193	2.2%	2¢	$176,019	$7,371,707	2.4%	2¢
Church of the Nazarene	$43,774,637	$733,633,353	6.0%	6¢	$42,108,996	$749,360,820	5.6%	6¢
Churches of God General Conference [17]	$1,332,768	$39,110,943	3.4%	3¢	$1,415,443	$40,778,140	3.5%	3¢
Conservative Congregational Christian Conference [18]	$7,700	$57,315,623	See Note 18	See Note 18	$3,396	$57,439,420	See Note 18	See Note 18
Cumberland Presbyterian Church	$407,780	$47,940,850	0.9%	1¢	$538,979	$54,806,092	1.0%	1¢
The Episcopal Church [19]	$16,469,652	$2,218,134,990	0.7%	1¢	$16,180,397	$2,196,475,669	0.7%	1¢
Evangelical Congregational Church	$1,294,221	$18,404,791	7.0%	7¢	$1,255,320	$16,024,954	7.8%	8¢
Evangelical Covenant Church	NA	NA	NA	NA	NA	NA	NA	NA
Evangelical Lutheran Church in America [20]	$24,517,106	$2,215,993,893	1.1%	1¢	$25,558,226	$2,195,300,461	1.2%	1¢
Evangelical Lutheran Synod	$345,589	$15,850,434	2.2%	2¢	$611,250	$15,043,765	4.1%	4¢
Fellowship of Evangelical Churches	$371,631	*$25,826,489*	*1.4%*	1¢	$631,525	*$29,061,001*	*2.2%*	*2¢*
Free Methodist Church-USA	$13,492,945	$152,314,491	8.9%	9¢	$13,649,495	$156,619,587	8.7%	9¢
General Association of General Baptists	$1,799,695	$46,267,327	3.9%	4¢	$1,641,764	$48,969,862	3.4%	3¢
Lutheran Church-Missouri Synod [21]	$24,194,550	$1,413,399,155	1.7%	2¢	$27,176,684	$1,427,941,128	1.9%	2¢
Moravian Church in America, Northern Province [22]	563,042	$15,057,148	3.7%	4¢	$570,771	$15,619,113$	3.7%	4¢
The Orthodox Presbyterian Church [23]	$2,330,695	$56,853,900	4.1%	4¢	$2,241,587	$57,611,500	3.9%	4¢
Presbyterian Church in America	$25,870,900	$790,629,741	3.3%	3¢	$25,838,573	$819,712,768	3.2%	3¢
Presbyterian Church (U.S.A.) [24]	$20,858,960	$2,109,453,373	1.0%	1¢	$19,239,349	$2,082,391,055	0.9%	1¢
Primitive Methodist Church in the U.S.A. [25]	NA	NA	NA	NA	NA	NA	NA	NA
Reformed Church in America	$7,177,165	$340,325,152	2.1%	2¢	$7,010,249	$332,652,263	2.1%	2¢
Seventh-day Adventists, North Am. Div. [26]	$42,553,150	$1,382,207,609	3.1%	3¢	$42,419,508	$1,394,535,710	3.0%	3¢
Southern Baptist Convention [27]	$285,896,000	$11,545,861,631	2.5%	2¢	$272,292,000	$11,461,572,538	2.4%	2¢
United Church of Christ	$4,408,836	$928,668,423	0.5%	0.5¢	$4,794,472	$920,012,927	0.5%	1¢
The United Methodist Church [28]	$69,993,535	$6,338,036,534	1.1%	1¢	$76,066,535	$6,332,354,673	1.2%	1¢
The Wesleyan Church	$16,269,347	$361,977,836	4.5%	4¢	$16,240,598	$392,625,403	4.1%	4¢
Wisconsin Evangelical Lutheran Synod	$8,382,088	$344,373,376	2.4%	2¢	$7,919,008	$341,735,386	2.3%	2¢
Total/Average for 31/30 Denominations	$690,785,932	*$32,429,543,732*	2.1%	2¢	$685,349,175	*$32,375,553,072*	2.1%	2¢

Source: empty tomb analysis. See endnotes at the end of the chapter. See Appendix B-5 for detail.

empty tomb, inc., 2024

Table 24: Overseas Missions Income, Excluding Any Investment or Government Income, as a Percent of Total Contributions to Congregations, 29 Denominations, 2017 and 2018

	2017				2018			
Denomination	Overseas Missions Income (Line 4)	Total Contributions	Overseas Missions Income as % of Total Contribs.	Cents of Each Dollar for Overseas Ministries	Overseas Missions Income (Line 4)	Total Contributions	Overseas Missions Income as % of Total Contribs.	Cents of Each Dollar for Overseas Ministries
Allegheny Wesleyan Methodist Connection	$280,063	$4,716,051	5.9%	6¢	$218,722	$4,277,567	5.1%	5¢
American Baptist Churches in the U.S.A. [14]	$12,282,858	$271,978,159	4.5%	5¢	$13,342,838	$221,635,829	6.0%	6¢
Associate Reformed Presbyterian Church (General Synod)	$4,441,382	$63,826,184	7.0%	7¢	$4,831,064	$64,894,267	7.4%	7¢
Brethren in Christ Church	$3,673,302	$42,794,063	8.6%	9¢	$1,950,969	$49,091,141	4.0%	4¢
Christian Church (Disciples of Christ)	$2,389,863	$389,248,857	0.6%	1¢	$2,094,583	$277,099,656	0.8%	1¢
Christian and Missionary Alliance [15]	$54,784,666	$484,043,140	11.3%	11¢	$53,675,476	$491,195,600	10.9%	11¢
Church of the Brethren [16]	NA	—	NA	NA	NA	—	NA	NA
Church of God General Conference (McDonough, Ga.)	$131,539	$3,972,103	3.3%	3¢	$187,649	$4,094,781	4.6%	5¢
Church of the Lutheran Confession	$272,236	$7,384,414	3.7%	4¢	$281,732	$7,169,578	3.9%	4¢
Church of the Nazarene	$45,974,585	$751,735,813	6.1%	6¢	NA	—	NA	NA
Churches of God General Conference [17]	$1,547,474	$39,031,837	4.0%	4¢	$1,460,975	$38,931,214	3.8%	4¢
Conservative Congregational Christian Conference [18]	$4,887	$58,574,325	See Note 18	See Note 18	$4,613	$59,836,795	See Note 18	See Note 18
Cumberland Presbyterian Church	$615,472	$46,989,950	1.3%	1¢	$524,663	$50,121,614	1.0%	1¢
The Episcopal Church [19]	$12,973,262	$2,226,690,846	0.6%	1¢	$12,952,606	$2,267,187,403	0.6%	1¢
Evangelical Congregational Church	$1,228,990	$17,563,206	7.0%	7¢	$1,148,753	$18,394,582	6.2%	6¢
Evangelical Covenant Church	NA	NA	NA	NA	NA	NA	NA	NA
Evangelical Lutheran Church in America [20]	$29,642,633	$2,217,104,805	1.3%	1¢	$30,477,408	$2,267,999,764	1.3%	1¢
Evangelical Lutheran Synod	$732,000	$15,016,835	4.9%	5¢	$695,254	$15,818,518	4.4%	4¢
Fellowship of Evangelical Churches	$497,396	$29,011,333	1.7%	2¢	$881,367	$31,174,086	2.8%	3¢
Free Methodist Church-USA	$13,068,299	$159,113,074	8.2%	8¢	$13,217,314	$161,660,039	8.2%	8¢
General Association of General Baptists	$2,046,100	$37,315,539	5.5%	5¢	$1,618,076	$40,651,493	4.0%	4¢
Lutheran Church-Missouri Synod [21]	$25,978,564	$1,461,524,060	1.8%	2¢	$25,314,579	$1,407,068,087	1.8%	2¢
Moravian Church in America, Northern Province [22]	$568,775	$16,205,271	3.5%	4¢	$582,047	$17,102,552	3.4%	3¢
The Orthodox Presbyterian Church [23]	$2,177,855	$60,825,500	3.6%	4¢	$2,544,041	$63,502,600	4.0%	4¢
Presbyterian Church in America	$25,152,705	$833,533,110	3.0%	3¢	$24,703,928	$867,211,101	2.8%	3¢
Presbyterian Church (U.S.A.) [24]	$20,396,077	$2,035,124,371	1.0%	1¢	$17,527,295	$2,189,700,617	0.8%	1¢
Primitive Methodist Church in the U.S.A. [25]	NA	NA	NA	NA	NA	NA	NA	NA
Reformed Church in America	$7,759,403	$361,020,725	2.1%	2¢	$4,323,771	$327,659,475	1.3%	1¢
Seventh-day Adventists, North Am. Div. [26]	NA	NA	NA	NA	NA	—	NA	NA
Southern Baptist Convention [27]	$274,512,000	$11,728,420,088	2.3%	2¢	$279,410,000	$11,811,093,609	2.4%	2¢
United Church of Christ	$4,415,463	$963,940,389	0.5%	1¢	$3,892,889	$967,554,113	0.4%	1¢
The United Methodist Church [28]	$61,433,170	$6,392,738,477	1.0%	1¢	$67,791,284	$6,409,819,537	1.1%	1¢
The Wesleyan Church	$15,129,898	$361,435,481	4.2%	4¢	$16,170,162	$370,675,864	4.4%	4¢
Wisconsin Evangelical Lutheran Synod	$7,560,125	$354,115,699	2.1%	2¢	$9,823,076	$357,245,893	2.7%	3¢
Total/Average for 29 Denominations	$ 631,669,530	$31,434,993,705	2.0%	2¢	$591,647,133	$30,859,867,375	1.9%	2¢

Source: empty tomb analysis. See endnotes at the end of the chapter. See Appendix B-5 for detail.

empty tomb, inc., 2024

Table 25: Overseas Missions Income, Excluding Any Investment or Government Income, as a Percent of Total Contributions to Congregations, 29 Denominations, 2019 and 2020

	2019				2020			
Denomination	Overseas Missions Income (Line 4)	Total Contributions	Overseas Missions Income as % of Total Contribs.	Cents of Each Dollar for Overseas Ministries	Overseas Missions Income (Line 4)	Total Contributions	Overseas Missions Income as % of Total Contribs.	Cents of Each Dollar for Overseas Ministries
Allegheny Wesleyan Methodist Connection	$197,899	$4,565,226	4.3%	4¢	$176,878	$4,532,248	3.9%	4¢
(abc) International Ministries - American Baptist Foreign Mission Society [14]	$13,667,311	$157,178,335	8.7%	9¢	$13,036,110	$174,029,319	7.5%	7¢
Associate Reformed Presbyterian Church (General Synod)	$4,944,343	$66,866,262	7.4%	7¢	$4,809,297	$65,068,384	7.4%	7¢
Brethren in Christ Church	$2,871,335	$50,277,342	5.7%	6¢	$2,756,842	$52,986,802	5.2%	5¢
Christian Church (Disciples of Christ)	$2,172,246	$277,741,541	0.8%	1¢	$2,043,414	$278,122,816	0.7%	1¢
Christian and Missionary Alliance [15]	$58,801,870	$506,468,034	11.6%	12¢	$54,542,430	$498,386,355	10.9%	11¢
Church of the Brethren [16]	NA	—	NA	NA	NA	—	NA	NA
Church of God General Conference (McDonough, Ga.)	$137,881	$4,129,842	3.3%	3¢	$186,137	$4,140,360	4.5%	4¢
Church of the Lutheran Confession	$257,230	$7,859,698	3.3%	3¢	$282,667	$8,305,196	3.4%	3¢
Church of the Nazarene	NA	—	NA	NA	NA	—	NA	NA
Churches of God General Conference [17]	$1,191,554	$39,263,165	3.0%	3¢	$1,224,646	$39,851,574	3.1%	3¢
Conservative Congregational Christian Conference [18]	$4,088	$59,952,863	See Note 18	See Note 18	$14,540	$59,477,316	See Note 18	See Note 18
Cumberland Presbyterian Church	$706,423	$48,467,745	1.5%	1¢	$719,868	$45,898,899	1.6%	2¢
The Episcopal Church [19]	$13,709,163	$2,291,275,165	0.6%	1¢	$16,675,546	$2,139,068,516	0.8%	1¢
Evangelical Congregational Church	$1,100,402	$19,057,044	5.8%	6¢	$1,143,819	$21,365,723	5.4%	5¢
Evangelical Covenant Church	NA	NA	NA	NA	NA	NA	NA	NA
Evangelical Lutheran Church in America [20]	$25,351,981	$2,260,739,392	1.1%	1¢	$25,812,249	$2,127,183,779	1.2%	1¢
Evangelical Lutheran Synod	$399,227	$16,419,011	2.4%	2¢	$384,045	$16,008,080	2.4%	2¢
Fellowship of Evangelical Churches	$590,548	$34,290,648	1.7%	2¢	$583,473	$34,982,033	1.7%	2¢
Free Methodist Church-USA	$12,907,222	$166,486,526	7.8%	8¢	$11,983,519	$167,724,522	7.1%	7¢
General Association of General Baptists	$1,631,662	$51,197,085	3.2%	3¢	$1,859,285	$54,195,382	3.4%	3¢
Lutheran Church-Missouri Synod [21]	$20,781,762	$1,378,737,750	1.5%	2¢	$20,824,675	$1,348,993,840	1.5%	2¢
Moravian Church in America, Northern Province [22]	$579,913	$11,122,574	5.2%	5¢	$529,354	$10,777,147	4.9%	5¢
The Orthodox Presbyterian Church [23]	$2,833,781	$65,431,100	4.3%	4¢	$2,571,817	$67,595,200	3.8%	4¢
Presbyterian Church in America	$26,549,871	$934,034,155	2.8%	3¢	$25,248,587	$931,198,420	2.7%	3¢
Presbyterian Church (U.S.A.) [24]	$16,545,681	$2,188,911,223	0.8%	1¢	$13,142,052	$1,994,454,504	0.7%	1¢
Primitive Methodist Church in the U.S.A. [25]	NA	NA	NA	NA	NA	NA	NA	NA
Reformed Church in America	$6,631,501	$405,032,533	1.6%	2¢	$5,887,946	$384,215,957	1.5%	2¢
Seventh-day Adventists, North Am. Div. [26]	NA	—	NA	NA	NA	—	NA	NA
Southern Baptist Convention [27]	$277,463,000	$11,640,670,559	2.4%	2¢	$284,550,000	$11,526,598,340	2.5%	2¢
United Church of Christ	$3,957,355	$966,999,191	0.4%	Less than 1¢	$3,488,144	$883,577,459	0.4%	Less than 1¢
The United Methodist Church [28]	$54,548,181	$6,378,669,727	0.9%	1¢	$59,953,314	$5,751,405,501	1.0%	1¢
The Wesleyan Church	$15,860,834	$376,374,471	4.2%	4¢	$16,268,002	$384,268,935	4.2%	4¢
Wisconsin Evangelical Lutheran Synod	$10,790,449	$369,952,645	2.9%	3¢	$11,166,031	$375,880,965	3.0%	3¢
Total/Average for 29 Denominations	$577,184,713	$30,778,170,852	1.9%	2¢	$581,864,687	$29,450,293,572	2.0%	2¢

Source: empty tomb analysis. See endnotes at the end of the chapter. See Appendix B-5 for detail.

empty tomb, inc., 2024

Table 26: Overseas Missions Income, Excluding Any Investment or Government Income, as a Percent of Total Contributions to Congregations, 28 Denominations, 2021

		2021			
Denomination		Overseas Missions Income (Line 4)	Total Contributions	Overseas Missions Income as % of Total Contribs.	Cents of Each Dollar for Overseas Ministries
Allegheny Wesleyan Methodist Connection		$220,202	$4,474,114	4.9%	5¢
(abc) International Ministries - American Baptist Foreign Mission Society	14	NA	—	NA	NA
Associate Reformed Presbyterian Church (General Synod)		$5,159,175	$65,484,765	7.9%	8¢
Brethren in Christ Church		$3,482,817	$43,444,240	8.0%	8¢
Christian Church (Disciples of Christ)		$2,230,856	$294,544,397	0.8%	1¢
Christian and Missionary Alliance	15	$55,293,355	$513,462,020	10.8%	11¢
Church of the Brethren	16	NA	—	NA	NA
Church of God General Conference (McDonough, Ga.)		$198,964	$4,723,174	4.2%	4¢
Church of the Lutheran Confession		$225,968	$9,119,470	2.5%	3¢
Church of the Nazarene		NA	—	NA	NA
Churches of God General Conference	17	$1,097,200	$47,031,006	2.3%	2¢
Conservative Congregational Christian Conference	18	$9,600	$59,128,878	See Note 18	See Note 18
Cumberland Presbyterian Church		$733,647	$40,178,068	1.8%	2¢
The Episcopal Church	19	$17,491,209	$2,262,371,419	0.8%	1¢
Evangelical Congregational Church		$1,193,416	$19,377,459	6.2%	6¢
Evangelical Covenant Church		NA	NA	NA	NA
Evangelical Lutheran Church in America	20	$23,880,951	$2,125,660,867	1.1%	1¢
Evangelical Lutheran Synod		$720,060	$13,440,690	5.4%	5¢
Fellowship of Evangelical Churches		$507,130	$35,510,378	1.4%	1¢
Free Methodist Church-USA		$13,731,585	$182,076,964	7.5%	8¢
General Association of General Baptists		$1,675,527	$51,899,730	3.2%	3¢
Lutheran Church-Missouri Synod	21	$19,296,739	$1,473,996,286	1.3%	1¢
Moravian Church in America, Northern Province	22	$535,455	$10,689,601	5.0%	5¢
The Orthodox Presbyterian Church	23	$3,040,180	$75,143,900	4.0%	4¢
Presbyterian Church in America		$25,367,761	$956,168,584	2.7%	3¢
Presbyterian Church (U.S.A.)	24	$11,772,919	$2,038,054,374	0.6%	1¢
Primitive Methodist Church in the U.S.A.	25	NA	NA	NA	NA
Reformed Church in America		$7,182,710	$312,542,470	2.3%	2¢
Seventh-day Adventists, North Am. Div.	26	NA	—	NA	NA
Southern Baptist Convention	27	$283,094,000	$11,830,303,965	2.4%	2¢
United Church of Christ		$3,701,940	$880,489,422	0.4%	Less than 1¢
The United Methodist Church	28	$53,119,404	$5,916,675,766	0.9%	1¢
The Wesleyan Church		$11,833,336	$348,590,727	3.4%	3¢
Wisconsin Evangelical Lutheran Synod		$11,845,184	$410,164,510	2.9%	3¢
Total/Average for 28 Denominations		$558,641,290	$30,024,747,244	1.9%	2¢

Source: empty tomb analysis. See endnotes at the end of the chapter. See Appendix B-5 for detail.

empty tomb, inc., 2024

A total of 28 denominations had complete data available for 2021.[13] The 28 denominations included a combined total of 28 million Full or Confirmed members in 2021.

Data for 34 denominations, including Overseas Missions Income and Total Contributions, is presented in Tables 17 through 26, for the years 2003, 2004, 2005, 2006, and 2007, respectively, for 33 denominations in 2008 through 2011, 32 denominations for 2012, 2013, and 2014, 31 for 2015 and 2016, and 29 for 2017, 2018, 2019, and 2020, and 28 denominations for 2021.

The following observations can be drawn from Tables 17-26 data.

The overall weighted average of Overseas Missions Income as a percent of Total Contributions to the denominations in 2021 was 2.0%. That is, for each dollar of Total Contributions donated to a congregation, about 2¢ was spent on denominational overseas missions.

Table 27: Overseas Missions Income, Excluding Any Investment or Government Income, as a Percent of Total Contributions to Congregations, 28 Denominations, Ranked by Cents per Dollar, 2021

Rank	Denomination		Cents of Each Dollar for Overseas Ministries	Number of Full/Cnfrm Members
1	Christian and Missionary Alliance	29	11¢	194,050
2	Brethren in Christ Church		8¢	15,021
3	Associate Reformed Presbyterian Church (Gen. Synod)		8¢	26,252
4	Free Methodist Church—USA		8¢	64,863
5	Evangelical Congregational Church		6¢	11,162
6	Evangelical Lutheran Synod		5¢	12,748
7	Moravian Church in America, Northern Province	29	5¢	14,530
8	Allegheny Wesleyan Methodist Connection		5¢	973
9	Church of God General Conference (McDonough, Ga.)		4¢	2,672
10	The Orthodox Presbyterian Church	29	4¢	23,664
11	The Wesleyan Church		3¢	109,169
12	General Association of General Baptists		3¢	56,737
13	Wisconsin Evangelical Lutheran Synod		3¢	270,529
14	Presbyterian Church in America		3¢	295,953
15	Church of the Lutheran Confession		2¢	5,367
16	Southern Baptist Convention		2¢	13,680,493
17	Churches of God General Conference	29	2¢	24,091
18	Reformed Church in America		2¢	92,828
19	Cumberland Presbyterian Church		2¢	53,056
20	Fellowship of Evangelical Churches		1¢	7,823
21	Lutheran Church-Missouri Synod	29	1¢	1,395,639
22	Evangelical Lutheran Church in America	29	1¢	2,377,298
23	The United Methodist Church	29	1¢	6,080,352
24	The Episcopal Church	29	1¢	1,083,483
25	Christian Church (Disciples of Christ)		1¢	214,863
26	Presbyterian Church (U.S.A.)	29	1¢	1,193,770
27	United Church of Christ		Less than 1¢	745,230
28	Conservative Congregational Christian Conference	29	See endnote	45,785

Source: empty tomb analysis
See Appendix B-5 for detail.

empty tomb, inc., 2024

Information in the endnotes to Tables 17 through 26 indicates that several of the denominations noted in survey correspondence that the dollar figure for international mission activity provided was only for activities funded through the national denominational office, and did not include overseas missions funded directly by the congregations. That is, some of the national denominational offices were of the opinion that congregations may be doing international mission activity in addition to any contributions sent to their offices.

In at least two instances, past dialogue with the denominational offices resulted in the finding that the national office sends a congregation statistics report form to affiliated congregations, and that this report form does not ask the congregation to distinguish that portion of Benevolences that was spent for international mission activity other than through the national denominational office. One denomination indicated that the national office obtains information from the congregations about missions done both directly by the congregation, and also through the denomination.

Congregational forms, sent by denominations to their congregations to obtain annual reports, could routinely, but apparently do not always, include details of congregational global missions expenditures that are not conducted through the denomination. The denominational structures presumably monitor other congregational expenditures, such as staff compensation and payments for pastor health insurance and pension benefits, as well as the general unified budget assessments requested from the congregations. Therefore, tracking of congregation-direct international mission activity might also be reasonable as well.

Table 27 lists the 28 denominations with complete 2021 data in order of the level of unrounded cents per dollar donated to the congregation that was directed to denominational overseas missions. The membership for each denomination is also listed.

Figure 18 presents, in graphic form, the 2021 cents per dollar donated to the congregation that were directed to denominational overseas missions in 28

Figure 18: Cents Directed to Denominational Overseas Missions, Per Dollar Donated to the Congregation, 28 Denominations in the U.S., 2021, 1 Denomination, 2007, 1 Denomination, 2011, 1 Denomination, 2014, 1 Denomination, 2016, 1 Denomination, 2017, and 1 Denomination, 2020

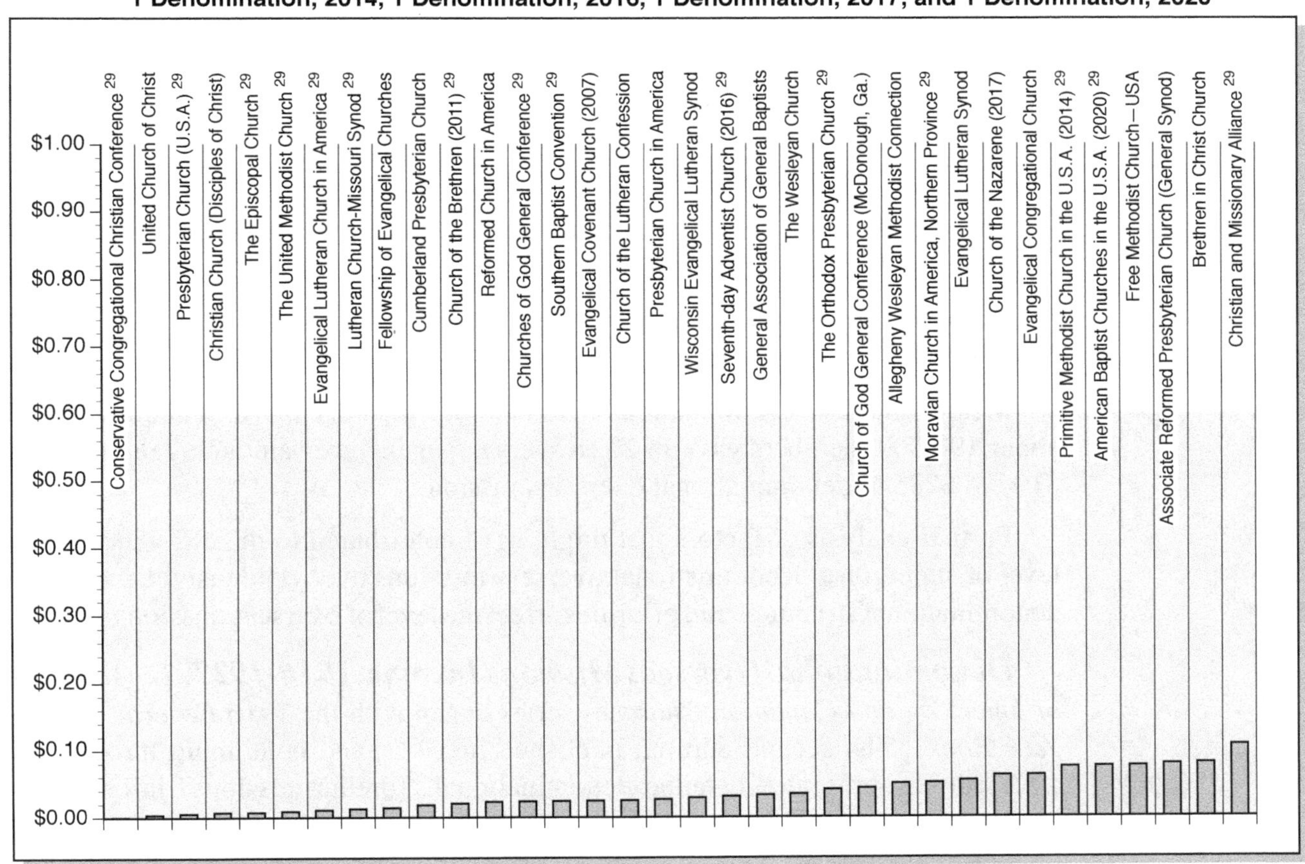

Source: empty tomb analysis; *YACC* adjusted series; U.S. BEA

empty tomb, inc., 2024

denominations in the U.S., reporting data for 2021. One additional denomination that reported data through 2007, one reporting data through 2011, one reporting data through 2014, one reporting through 2016, one reporting through 2017, and one reporting through 2020 are also included in the figure. The gray shading marks a potential standard of giving for overseas missions at 60¢ per dollar. As noted earlier in this chapter, this goal could be achieved if church members increased giving to a congregation-wide average of ten percent and earmarked the major portion of the increase to international missions.

Appendix B-5 lists the four lines of data for the denominations for data years 2003 through 2021.

A Comparison of Per Member Giving to Overseas Missions in Seven Denominations. In the discussion immediately above, aggregate overseas missions income is set in the context of Total Contributions for each denomination.

One can also consider contributions to overseas missions income on a per member basis. A review of the two largest Protestant denominations in the U.S. provided the following results.

The data indicates that denominational overseas missions support was not as high a priority in 2021 as it was in the 1920s ...

The Southern Baptist Convention, with 13,680,493 Full or Confirmed Members in 2021, was the largest Protestant denomination in the U.S. The United Methodist Church, with 6,080,352 Full or Confirmed Members in 2021, was the second largest denomination.

Dividing the amount of overseas missions income by the number of reported members resulted in a per member dollar giving level for each denomination. Since the data is for the year 2021 for both denominations, current dollars can be effectively used in the comparison.

The per member giving dollar figure to denominational overseas missions for the Southern Baptist Convention was $21 in 2021.

The per member giving dollar figure to denominational overseas missions for The United Methodist Church was $9 in 2021.

Meanwhile, five denominations with membership varying from about 1,000 to about 190,000 members gave in 2021 average per member amounts ranging from $197 to $285 to denominational overseas missions.

Further analysis of factors that might have contributed to the difference in the level of support for denominational overseas missions may yield insight about how denominational structures and priorities affect the level of overseas missions support.

Denominational Overseas Missions Income, 1916-1927. The *Yearbook of American and Canadian Churches* series began with the 1916 *Federal Council Year Book*. The second edition, published in 1917, and continuing through the 1927 edition, presented detailed denominational "foreign missions" information. Income as well as geographical placement and type of missionaries were presented on multi-page tables.

Changes in the amount of mission support led a group of denominations to commission a report, published in 1929, about levels of missions giving. As found in Table 28, the 1929 study provided per capita giving to Foreign Missions, Benevolences, and Total Contributions for 11 denominations.[30] With this information, it was possible to calculate per capita Foreign Missions as a percent of per capita Benevolences, and per capita Foreign Missions as a percent of per capita Total Contributions for this group.

Table 28: Foreign Missions, Benevolences, and Total Contributions, 11 Denominations, 1916-1927, Current Dollars

Year	Per Capita Foreign Missions Income from Living Donors	Per Capita Benevolences	Per Capita Foreign Missions as a Percent of Per Capita Benevolences (Calculated)	Per Capita Total Contributions	Per Capita Foreign Missions as a Percent of Per Capita Total Contributions (Calculated)
1916	$0.73	$2.24	32.59%	$10.11	7.22%
1917	$0.74	$2.52	29.37%	$10.75	6.88%
1918	$0.86	$2.89	29.76%	$11.44	7.52%
1919	$1.18	$3.89	30.33%	$12.90	9.15%
1920	$1.66	$5.75	28.87%	$16.45	10.09%
1921	$1.70	$5.51	30.85%	$17.20	9.88%
1922	$1.46	$5.18	28.19%	$17.19	8.49%
1923	$1.44	$5.12	28.13%	$17.69	8.14%
1924	$1.32	$4.97	26.56%	$18.44	7.16%
1925	$1.27	$4.59	27.67%	$18.74	6.78%
1926	$1.32	$4.49	29.40%	$18.94	6.97%
1927	$1.24	$4.17	29.74%	$18.95	6.54%

Source: empty tomb analysis; Charles H. Fahs, *Trends in Protestant Giving* (1929), Tables XVIII and XXIX

empty tomb, inc., 2024

During the 1916-1927 period, for the group of 11 denominations, Foreign Missions Income represented an average of about 29% of all Benevolences. The 1929 study was commissioned in response to the concern of members of the Foreign Missions Conference of North America that giving to foreign missions was declining. As seen in Table 28 per capita Foreign Missions Income had decreased to 6.54% of per capita Total Contributions in 1927.

By 2021, nine decades later, per capita Foreign Missions Income had decreased further, to 2.0% of Total Contributions for a set of 28 Protestant denominations.

The overall average of per capita Foreign Missions Income as a percent of Total Contributions for 11 denominations for the 1916 through 1927 period was 7.9%, compared to 2.0% for the 28 denominations in 2021. The average U.S. per capita Disposable Personal Income (DPI) during the 1916-1927 period was $7,114, in inflation-adjusted 2012 dollars, compared to $47,165 in 2021. Since per capita income was more than six times the average in the 1916-1927 period, Americans had 563% more after-tax income in 2021 than in the earlier period, in inflation-adjusted dollars. The data indicates that denominational overseas missions support was not as high a priority in 2021 as it was in the 1920s, in spite of improved communication about global needs and a higher level of member income in 2021 compared to the 1916-1927 period.

Calculating the Cost of Missions. One area that is exclusively within the realm of the church is the cost of global evangelization. Interestingly, there have been few if any firm cost estimates for insuring that people around the globe have the opportunity to make an informed choice about responding to the Christian message. This has been true even though the accessibility to information about Christianity can be regarded as a justice issue. As a report from the World Council of Churches Commission on World Mission and Evangelism observed:

> There is also a tragic coincidence that most of the world's poor have not heard the Good News of the Gospel of Jesus Christ; or they could not receive it, because it was not recognized as Good News in the way in which it was brought. This is a double injustice: they are victims of oppression of an unjust economic order or an unjust political distribution of power, and at the same time they are deprived of the knowledge of God's special care for them. To announce the Good News to the poor is to begin to render the justice due to them.[31]

One term that is often used to describe the population most excluded from accessibility to the Christian message is "unreached people group" although the term "least-reached" may also be used. The Joshua Project offered a definition that reads:

> An unreached or least-reached people is a people group among which there is no indigenous community of believing Christians with adequate numbers and resources to evangelize this people group without outside assistance.[32]

The Joshua Project Web site also provided a definition for an unreached people group that is also "unengaged":

> An unengaged unreached people group (UUPG) has no known active church planting underway.[33]

If the total cost of evangelization were to be estimated, including not only expanded but also ongoing work, an estimate of $1 billion for the increased total needed might not be unreasonable.

It is difficult to determine the number of unengaged, unreached people groups, as different organizations use a variety of definitions and provide varying numbers.

One denomination that is on record as having a particular concern about unreached people groups is the Southern Baptist Convention (SBC). The SBC is the second largest communion, and the largest Protestant denomination, in the United States. As noted on the Web site of then SBC Executive Committee Director, Dr. Morris Chapman, "In 1845, a network of churches was organized into the Southern Baptist Convention for the purpose of evangelizing the world...."[34] The SBC International Mission Board (IMB) is the group within the Convention that is currently charged with supervising the continuing task of global evangelization.

In 2010, the Executive Committee of the SBC asked its international mission arm, the IMB, about additional needed resources to "reach all of the unreached people groups." The IMB replied that $200 million a year would field the needed additional 3,000 missionaries.[35] The figure of $200 million a year, therefore, may serve as one estimate of the additional word evangelism resources that are needed.

Other communions and para-denominational groups in the U.S. are also focused on the goal of engaging the unreached as well.

If the total cost of evangelization were to be estimated, including not only expanded but also ongoing work, an estimate of $1 billion for the increased total needed might not be unreasonable.[36]

Table 29 illustrates the daily and annual costs based on the population of several groups, for global evangelization as well as three other categories.[37]

Table 29: Great Commandment and Great Commission Outreach Estimated Costs, Calculated Per Member for Selected Church Populations, 2021, and Estimated Christian Household Populations with Selected Levels of Net Worth, Apart from Primary Residence, 2021

Love Expressed in Great Commission Outreach	A. Global Evangelization	B. Helping Close, in Jesus' Name, Promise Gap Global Child Deaths	A. + B. + Global Elementary Education + Domestic Poverty
Global Evangelization	$1,000,000,000		$1,000,000,000
Helping Close, in Jesus' Name, Promise Gap Global Child Deaths		$16,000,000,000	$16,000,000,000
Global Elementary Education			$7,000,000,000
Domestic U.S. Poverty Need: Literacy, Other			$2,000,000,000
Total Per Year			$26,000,000,000
Historically Christian Church Members (44% US Pop. = 146,212,000			
Annual Amount per Historically Christian Church Member	$7	$109	$178
Daily Amount per Historically Christian Church Member	$0.02	$0.30	$0.49
If Wealthy Christian Households provide half:			
Annual Amount per Historically Christian Church Member	$3	$55	$89
Daily Amount per Historically Christian Church Member	$0.01	$0.15	$0.24
Historically Christian Households =>$5 Million (= 902,000)			
Annual Amount	$1,109	$17.738	$28,825
Daily Amount	$3	$49	$79
If Christian Households with =>$5 million provide half:			
Annual Amount	$554	$8,869	$14,412
Daily Amount	$1.52	$24.30	$39.49
Historically Christian Households =>$1 Million (= 6,424,000)			
Annual Amount	$156	$2,491	$4,047
Daily Amount	$0.43	$6.82	$11.09
If Christian Households with =>$1 million provide half:			
Annual Amount	$78	$1,245	$2,204
Daily Amount	$0.21	$3.41	$5.54
Historically Christian Households =>$500,000 (= 9,486,400)			
Annual Amount	$105	$1,687	$2,741
Daily Amount	$0.29	$4.62	$7.51
If Christian Households with =>$500,000 provide half:			
Annual Amount	$53	$843	$1,370
Daily Amount	$0.14	$2.31	$3.75
Three Largest Communions: Roman Catholic, Southern Baptist, and United Methodist (Members = 88,975,358)			
Annual Amount per Member of Three Largest Communions	$11	$180	$292
Daily Amount per Member of Three Largest Communions	$0.03	$0.49	$0.80
If wealthy Christian Households provide half:			
Annual Amount per Member of Three Largest Communions	$6	$90	$146
Daily Amount per Member of Three Largest Communions	$0.02	$0.25	$0.40

Source: empty tomb, inc. analysis — empty tomb inc., 2024

A set of the three largest communions in the U.S. that could accept leadership for the challenge of funding the cost of these needs is also presented.

If creative church leadership were displayed, wealthy Christians might be found who would provide matching funds for donations from the general church population for these needs. In that case, the annual and daily costs would be divided by two, also shown in Table 29.

Of course, the Great Commission, in the context of the Great Commandment, would present the good news of Jesus Christ in both word and deed. Christians generally agree about God's concern for the children of the world. In 2021, about 13,790 children under the age of five died each day around the globe.[38] As discussed earlier in this chapter, the Promise Gap could be closed, at an estimated cost of an additional $16 billion a year, preventing the deaths of 1.5 million children a year. Table 29 also suggests the annual and daily costs for the two groups should they choose to prevent more of these deaths among children under five around the globe, and the option of wealthy paying half.

However, the choice need not be between global evangelization *or* helping to close, in Jesus' name, the Promise Gap that results in global child deaths, *or* primary education, *or* addressing poverty within the United States. When Jesus Christ came in a physical body to announce God's love for the world, Jesus combined the power of the spoken word with healing, feeding, clothing, and freeing those he encountered. Given the resources and the broad base of the church in the U.S., the current body of Jesus Christ, Christians in the 21st century, have the power to choose to follow Jesus' example of loving the whole person in need in a functional equivalent of Jesus' miracles, in what might be termed intentional miracles. The higher cost for combining evangelization, closing the Promise Gap, increasing the number of the world's children receiving primary education, and having $2 billion a year additional to address domestic poverty needs within the U.S. in Jesus' name was estimated at $26 billion a year. Table 29 also displays a model for calculating the annual and daily costs for a set of the three largest communions in the U.S. to step out in leadership to engage all of these needs simultaneously.

... the Promise Gap could be closed, at an estimated cost of an additional $16 billion a year, preventing the deaths of 1.5 million children a year.

In this table, the size of the population with varying degrees of wealth was calculated from available data. Annual and daily costs to meet the outlined needs are presented for households with $5 million net worth, $1 million net worth, and $500,000 net worth, apart from primary residence.[39] As noted, if the general church population were to provide half the funds needed to address these needs, the cost to households with higher levels of wealth would be divided by two.

Potential Roman Catholic Giving. The Roman Catholic Church is the largest single religious body in the United States. Unfortunately, that communion has opted not to publish financial giving data on a regular basis. Therefore, any estimates of giving among this major part of the body of Christ must be only approximations. Given the size of the Catholic Church, however, such an approximation is worth exploring.

At one point, there was some discussion in Catholic circles about the practice of the tithe.[40] To explore that idea further, a review of potential giving levels at an average of 10% per member was conducted for ten archdioceses that were led by a cardinal as of the *Official Catholic Directory 2005*, or subsequently. Each archdiocese comprises certain U.S. counties. As a result, the total population[41] and the U.S. per capita DPI could be obtained for each archdiocese.[42] A general estimate of 1.2% of income was used as the current level of Catholic giving, cited as recently as the 2017 book, *Catholic Parishes in the 21st Century*.[43]

Two observations may be made in regard to the estimate of 1.2% of per capita DPI. First, although the estimate is lower than estimates of Protestant giving, there are certain efficiencies in the way that Catholic parishes are organized, as a previous analysis in *The State of Church Giving* series demonstrated. These efficiencies allow Catholics to maintain basic operations on a par with Protestants, with a smaller per member contribution.[44]

Second, preliminary calculations based on a 2010 Center for Applied Research in the Apostolate survey of Catholic parishes suggest that the per member contribution for "average weekly offering in U.S. parishes" was about 0.3% of income.[45] A 1.2% estimate, for per Catholic giving as a percent of income, therefore, takes into account the possibility of additional charitable contributions, up to three times the amount of weekly offerings, for example, including second collections.

The ten archdioceses combined had an estimated giving level of $16.8 billion in 2021. If Catholics in these archdioceses increased from the current 1.2% of income given to 10% of income, the additional total would have been $123.4 billion in 2021. The additional amounts varied from $3.1 billion in the Archdiocese of Baltimore, to $25.7 billion in the Archdiocese of Los Angeles and $24.4 billion in the Archdiocese of New York.

The results of the calculations are shown in Table 30.

The application of this potential giving could make an impact on international need, as discussed in the description of Table 29, and also in chapter 8.

Table 30: Potential Additional Giving at 10% of Income, Ten Roman Catholic Archdioceses in the U.S., 2021

Area Name	Total U.S. BEA Personal Income for Counties in Archdioceses ($)	% Catholic of Total Population in Area	Calculated U.S. BEA Personal Income Available to Catholics ($)	Estimated Current Catholic Giving at 1.2% of Income ($)	Estimated Potential Additional Catholic Giving at 10% of Income ($)
Archdiocese of Baltimore	$228,372,464,000	15.4%	$35,237,109,193	$422,845,310	$3,100,865,609
Archdiocese of Boston	412,866,814,739	45.0%	185,790,108,658	2,229,481,304	16,349,529,562
Archdiocese of Chicago	443,839,714,000	36.0%	159,782,297,040	1,917,387,564	14,060,842,140
Archdiocese of Detroit	261,584,510,000	26.4%	69,161,083,383	829,933,001	6,086,175,338
Archdiocese of Galveston-Houston	465,292,403,000	23.2%	107,994,884,642	1,295,938,616	9,503,549,848
Archdiocese of Los Angeles	823,429,082,000	35.5%	292,507,970,427	3,510,095,645	25,740,701,398
Archdiocese of New York	617,026,586,000	45.0%	277,661,919,192	3,331,943,030	24,434,248,889
Archdiocese of Newark	251,043,058,000	41.1%	103,113,771,762	1,237,365,261	9,074,011,915
Archdiocese of Philadelphia	321,607,306,000	36.8%	118,292,154,894	1,419,505,859	10,409,709,631
Archdiocese of Washington	239,884,686,000	22.0%	52,774,593,680	633,295,124	4,644,164,244
Total: 10 Archdioceses with Cardinals	$4,064,946,623,739		$1,402,315,892,872	$16,827,790,714	$123,403,798,573

Source: empty tomb analysis

empty tomb, inc., 2024

This additional giving could address domestic needs as well. Consider what additional funds could do to assist Catholic schools in America's inner cities. A news item that cited the views of one expert, Loyola University Associate Professor Carol Ann MacGregor, who has "studied Catholic school enrollment and closures," summarized the problem: "While there's no one single cause of the fall [in Catholic school enrollment], MacGregor said the increased cost of tuition, especially in lower grades, has played a major role." In the past, nuns provided teaching services at low pay, which meant that "increased tuition to pay the salary of lay teachers who were hired" became necessary in the absence of sufficient nuns to fill the teaching roles.[46] Catholic school closings continued to be reported through 2021.[47]

In a 2014 review of *Lost Classroom, Lost Community: Catholic Schools' Importance in Urban America*, Nathan Glazer, professor emeritus of education and sociology at Harvard University, commented on the authors' view that the closing of Catholic schools decreases the "social capital" in the neighborhoods in which they are located. In his careful comments about the book's conclusions, Glazer highlighted the statistical analysis offered by the authors for Chicago and replicated in Philadelphia about Catholic school closing and "the state of order or disorder on the block — and on crime data, at the police-beat level."[48]

"... creating the context with an over arching parish mission and vision can inspire people to work toward something greater" to counter "a lack of spiritual engagement with money."
— Notre Dame Catholic Social and Pastoral Research Initiative report

However, it is not only low-income neighborhoods that are impacted by Catholic school closings. A Catholic girls school in the Los Angeles area, La Reina, was to be closed in June 2024, over the protests of "students, parents and alumnae." With a tuition level of $20,000 a year, the school boasted "a 100% graduation rate into four-year colleges," and had been "named the Ventura County Star's Best Private School in Ventura County for three years in a row." One parent whose daughters graduated from the school was quoted as saying, "The reality is if you take La Reina out of here, you have closed so much Catholic education in the Canejo Valley."[49]

In *Catholic Parishes of the 21st Century*, the authors note that many of the parishes built in the Northeast and Midwest were built by immigrant communities that have "assimilated and moved on." In the South and West, the new churches being built are on a larger scale. Overall, more than half the Catholic parishes in the U.S., according to the authors, have 1,500 registered parishioners or more, with multiple masses each weekend.[50] The larger size, the authors note, addresses the declining number of clergy available: "Bishops have to balance the need for parishes and schools to serve their Catholic population with the reality of limited financial resources and a diminished supply of clergy."[51]

The authors also note that those in smaller parishes, under 300 households, gave a larger weekly donation than those in larger parishes, especially those over 1,500 households.[52]

A 2015 overview of Catholic giving cited a Notre Dame Catholic Social and Pastoral Research Initiative report that suggested, "creating the context with an over arching parish mission and vision can inspire people to work toward something greater" to counter "a lack of spiritual engagement with money."[53]

Aspects of this need for vision, and how it applies to all Christians across the various church traditions, are discussed in chapter 8. Here, it may be noted that the focus on church giving patterns throughout all Christian traditions is generally on coping with the effects of decreased funding. Church leaders have not convinced their members about the power for good that they possess to impact need through increased giving. The analyses in this chapter demonstrate that increased giving at the ten percent level could be allocated so that 60 percent is directed to international ministries and 20 percent to domestic needs. That distribution could direct billions of additional dollars to inner-city Catholic schools, even while providing critical resources for missions that address international need.

Still, the greatest need remains overseas. As shown earlier in Table 29, Catholics, as well as all other Christians, could make a dramatic impact on global word and deed need for much less than the cost of increasing giving to the classic tithe.

Putting Potential into Perspective. Even as this chapter focuses on the potential of church members to give additional money to their churches, an underlying question might be considered. Specifically, how realistic is it to think that church members in the U.S. could actually increase their giving, especially for international missions?

... children dying from treatable causes is a valid place to initiate a movement to tap the additional giving potential among church members on behalf of global neighbors in need.

As described in chapter 4, twice in the twentieth century, per member giving as a percent of income was at or above 3% over a period of years, compared to 1.8% in 2021. Income was increasing during 1922-1927 (with the exception of 1925), when giving as a percent of income was 3% or more, continuing that level of giving through 1933. From 1950 through 1961, with the exception of 1954 and 1958, income was again growing, and giving as a percent of income grew to 3% or more from 1959 through 1961. Increased giving in times of disaster also demonstrates the potential to increase donations, such as in 2005. The current question is whether sustained rather than sporadic increases in giving are possible.

The issue of the number of children under the age of five dying from treatable causes has been highlighted in the foregoing discussion of encouraging church members in the U.S. to act on more of their potential for increased giving. The number of dying children, of course, is not the only crisis facing global neighbors. Yet, this issue may be particularly significant, as noted by James Grant, former Executive Director of UNICEF. He stated: "In practice, it could be argued that the U5MR [Under-5 Mortality Rate] is the best available *single indicator* of social development overall, as most of the factors which it distils are as indicative of the meeting of the essential needs of all human beings as they are of the particular well-being of children" (emphasis in original).[54]

That assessment suggests that children dying from treatable causes is a valid place to initiate a movement to tap the additional giving potential among church members on behalf of global neighbors in need. As discussed in chapter 8, once begun, the growing financial response from Christians can then embrace additional critical needs.

World leaders began to look at the issue of reducing the Under-5 Mortality Rate in 1990. These efforts began with the initial 1990 World Summit for Children that set the goal — termed a "promise" to the world's children — of reducing the Under-5 Mortality Rate (U5MR) by one-third as of the year 2000. Organized by James Grant, the summit was the largest gathering of world leaders and representatives to that time.[55]

That goal was not met. World leaders then convened again in 2000 and established the Millennium Development Goals (MDGs), a broader set of targets which included eight goals, the reduction in the U5MR among them.[56]

Beginning in 2015, the Sustainable Development Goals (SDGs) succeeded the MDGs as targets that world leaders agreed on regarding global needs:

> The SDGs replace the Millennium Development Goals (MDGs), which started a global effort in 2000 to tackle the indignity of poverty. The MDGs established measurable, universally-agreed objectives for tackling extreme poverty and hunger, preventing deadly diseases, and expanding primary education to all children, among other development priorities …
>
> The SDGs are a bold commitment to finish what we started, and tackle some of the pressing challenges facing the world today. All 17 Goals interconnect, meaning success in one affects success for the others.[57]

The 17 SDGs encompass basic needs such as reducing the U5MR to target levels, extending primary education to all children, ending hunger, and providing clean water and sanitation, among others.

The present discussion has considered the issue of reducing the U5MR by 2035 to goal levels, at a cost of $16 billion a year. As shown above in Table 29, a total of $26 billion was estimated as needed to address this need, provide $1 billion for global evangelism efforts, begin to provide primary education for more of the world's children, and to address domestic needs such as basic literacy.

Is that goal of $26 billion realistic? In fact, were church members effectively challenged to promote, in Jesus' name, the good of their neighbors, they are capable of doing a great deal more.

For example, the SDGs set the ambitious goal of universal primary education with an estimated price tag of $26 billion.[58] In light of the fact that $7 billion is already built into the base goal of $26 billion, this more ambitious universal primary education goal would add $19 billion to the total.

Also, ending hunger is another SDG target. One estimate is that it would cost an additional $11.8 billion a year to achieve this goal.[59]

Another goal targets drinking water, sanitation and hygiene. A report on the costs of this goal indicates that estimates for this issue are difficult

Table 31: Estimates for Annual Additional Costs of Addressing, in Jesus' Name, Five Global Needs

Global Needs	Additional Annual Needed, Billions $
Closing the Promise Gap: Reduction of Under-5 Child Deaths to Target Goal Level by 2025	$16.0
Primary Education Availability Total	$26.0
Hunger, Food Security, Nutrition, and Sustainable Agriculture	$11.8
Water, Sanitation, Hygiene, Basic Service, Universal Access, Baseline Estimate	$28.4
Bible Translation and Workers for Unengaged, Unreached People Groups	$1.0
Total:	$83.2

Source: empty tomb analysis empty tomb, inc., 2024

because of varying conditions affecting availability of data within some countries. Therefore, the report offers a range for calculated costs. Further, basic services could be improved by also developing what are termed safely managed services to sustain the improvements. The cost for providing basic services range from a lower estimate of $13.8 billion to a higher estimate of $46.7 billion, with a baseline estimate of $28.4 billion more a year needed to provide adequate water, sanitation, and hygiene universal access in 140 countries. The baseline estimate for safely managed universal access was estimated at $86.9 billion more a year needed, with another calculation in the report suggesting $114 billion (with a range of $74 to $166 billion) a year could be needed for "the total capitalization cost" of meeting SDG water, sanitation, and hygiene targets.[60] For purposes of the present discussion, the $28.4 billion basic service baseline estimate might be used as an immediate starting goal for the church.

The cost of including universal primary education, addressing hunger, and providing adequate water, sanitation, and hygiene in 140 countries totals $59.2 billion. When added to the Table 29 global need figure of $24 billion, the expanded global total would be $83.2 billion as shown in Table 31. Adding the $2 billion domestic figure in Table 29 would bring the overall total estimated need to $85.2 billion.

How realistic is the potential of church members to address these issues at a significant level?

Considering the concept of the tithe, or giving 10% of disposable (after-tax) per capita income as a practical, rather than theoretical, construct can offer an approach to explore that question.

Throughout this chapter, the estimate used has been that 44% of the U.S. population still identifies with historically Christian churches in the U.S. That was 146,212,000 people in 2021.

The church in the U.S. not only has a moral mandate from its Leader to address needs of their global neighbors, but also has been entrusted with great potential resources for impacting global need that rivals any other entity.

An estimate of $18,184,869,381 in religious giving from the U.S. to overseas needs in 2021[61] can be attributed to those approximately 146 million individuals.

U.S. DPI in 2021 was $56,065 in current dollars. Applying 6% of the tithe's 10% to international needs, where the dire circumstances are the most demanding, would result in a gift of $3,363.90 per church member.

The additional 6% of the tithe for the 146 million church members would total $491,918,032,716. Less the estimated $18 billion already given to overseas needs, an additional $473.7 billion was potentially available to increase, in Jesus' name, outreach for global neighbors' needs in 2021, compared to the estimate of $83.2 billion of what a large segment of those global basic needs are.

The church in the U.S. not only has a moral mandate from its Leader to address needs of their global neighbors, but also has been entrusted with great potential resources for impacting global need that rivals any other entity. Looking forward, church leaders effectively challenging their constituents to increase giving to love their neighbors at their points of need could result in an additional $2.4 trillion over the next five years, and $4.7 trillion over ten years.

In light of these numbers, the only resource lacking in church people impacting, in Jesus' name, their neighbors' needs is not the funds but the visionary hope to step out in faith to do it.

Further discussion of the implications of these numbers is presented in chapter 8.

Potential and Reality. The numbers in this chapter document the potential for church members in the U.S. to increase giving, and outline some of the possible impact on global word and deed need, as well as domestic need, that could be made as a result.

Various comparisons in this chapter demonstrate that the issue of meeting global and domestic needs is not one of resources, but of priorities and intentions. Recognizing this potential is a critical first step toward church officials leading church members to consider priorities more in line with their professions of the faith.

Church members need to be informed that they have the potential to make this an age of intentional miracles.

Endnotes for Chapter 6

[1] See Jesus' statement in Matthew 23:23. For a discussion of various views of the tithe, see John and Sylvia Ronsvalle, *Behind the Stained Glass Windows: Money Dynamics in the Church* (Grand Rapids, MI: Baker Book House, 1996), pp. 187-193.

[2] The basis for the calculations of potential giving by self-identified Christians in the U.S. in 2021 is as follows. In chapter seven of this volume titled "Why and How Much Do Americans Give?" a 2021 figure of total giving to religion was presented in the "Denomination-Based series Keyed to 1974 Filer Estimate." That figure was $69.2 billion. A figure of 67% was multiplied by the 2021 figure for giving to religion of $69.2 billion to determine what amount was given by those who identify with the historically Christian church. The result was $46.4 billion. In 2021, if giving had increased to an average of 10% from the actual level of 1.81% given, instead of $46.4 billion, an amount of $256 billion would have been donated to historically Christian churches in the U.S. The difference between the $46.4 billion given and the potential of $256 billion was $210 billion, the additional money that would have been available at an average of 10% giving. The above figure of 67% was an empty tomb calculation based on data in: Gallup World Headquarters; "Religion"; Washington, DC; n.d.; <https://news.gallup.com/poll/1690/religion.aspx>; pp. 1, 6 of 9/25/2022 2:57 PM printout.

[3] It may be noted that the estimate of an additional $210 billion that would be available if average giving were at 10% is at the lower end. Rather than using the calculation detailed in the previous endnote, two other estimates of $773 billion and $1.2 trillion for 2021 were obtained based on alternate assumptions.

An alternative estimate of $773 billion was derived based on the assumption that: (1) 44% of Americans are members of historically Christian churches (empty tomb estimate based on Gallup, 9/25/2022 printout, pp. 1, 6), with aggregate after-tax income of $8.2 trillion; (2) religious giving was $69.2 billion in 2021; and (3) 67% of religious giving was from self-identifying Christians (estimate based on Gallup, 9/25/2022 printout, p. 1), thus attributing the maximum amount of religious giving to church members. The results indicated that the giving level was 0.57% of historically Christian church member after-tax income in 2021, rather than the 1.81% noted in the previous endnote. In that case, the difference between 2021 giving at 0.57% and 10% would have resulting in an additional $773 billion.

Alternatively, one could base the potential giving level calculation on the assumptions that: (1) 67% of Americans identify with the historically Christian church, whether or not they are members (estimate based on Gallup, 9/25/2022 printout, p. 1); (2) this portion of Americans had an aggregate after-tax income of $12.5 trillion; and (3) the calculation considered contributions as possibly available from this 67% of U.S. population. Giving levels would then have been at the 0.37% of income level. In that case, the difference between self-identified Christian giving in 2021 at the 0.37% level and a potential 10% level would have yielded an additional $1.2 trillion in 2021. The 2021 aggregate Disposable Personal Income figure of $18.6 trillion that was multiplied by the church member population figures in the two alternative calculations contained in this endnote above was obtained from U.S. Bureau of Economic Analysis; "Table 2.1. Personal Income and Its Disposition"; Line 27: "Disposable personal income"; National Income and Product Accounts Tables; <https://apps.bea.gov/national/Release/XLS/Survey/Section2All_xls.xlsx>; data published on 4/27/2023.

[4] $70-$80 billion a year: Carol Bellamy, *The State of the World's Children 2000* (New York: UNICEF, 2000), p. 37. $195 billion a year: In *The End of Poverty* (2005), Jeffrey D. Sachs estimated that $135 to $195 billion a year could eliminate the worst of global poverty, according to: Daniel W. Drezner; " 'The End of Poverty': Brother, Can You Spare $195 Billion?"; The New York Times; 4/24/2005; <https://www.nytimes.com/2005/04/24/books/review/the-end-of-poverty-brother-can-you-spare-195-billion.html>; p. 1 of 8/18/2019 3:41 PM printout.

[5] Carol Bellamy, *The State of the World's Children 1999* (New York: UNICEF, 1999), p. 85. Updating the figure for primary education proves to be complicated by definitions, and a tendency to combine primary and secondary education costs. An analysis of one estimate from Julia Gillard, chairwoman of the Global Partnership for Education (see: Joshua Keating; "What Will It Take to Educate Every Kid in the World?"; Slate.com; 10/12/2015; <https://slate.com/news-and-politics/2015/10/Julia-gillard-on-what-it-will-take-to-educate-every-kid-in-the-world.html>; p. 2 of 10/3/2020 11:24 AM printout) suggested that 88% of the costs are being covered by developing countries. That figure would mean an additional $4.7 billion in direct aid is needed for both primary and secondary education. However, Fahad Al-Sulaiti of the Education Above All Foundation suggested that $26 billion in direct aid is needed for primary education only (see: Fahad Al-Sulaiti; "Counting the Cost of Universal Primary Education"; The Guardian; 11/28/2013; <https://www.theguardian.com/global-development-professionals-network/2013/nov/28/universal-primary-education-cost-fund>; p. 2 of 8/18/2019 10:22 AM printout. Based on these numbers, an additional $7 billion could provide the additional funding needed for all children to have a primary education, or provide 27% of the cost for primary education for the 57 million children not now receiving a primary education.

[6] United Nations Inter-agency Group for Child Mortality Estimation (UN IGME); *Levels & Trends in Child Mortality Report 2022*; UNICEF (New York: UNICEF, 2023); <https://childmortality.org/wp-content/uploads/2023/01/UN-IGME-Child-Mortality-Report-2022.pdf>; pp. 6, 13 of 8/27/2023 printout.

[7] Gareth Jones, et al.; "How Many Child Deaths Can We Prevent This Year?"; *The Lancet*, vol. 362; 7/5/2003; <http://www.thelancet.com/journal/vol1362/iss9377/full/llan.362.9377.child_survival.26292.1>; p. 6 of 7/7/03 2:06 PM printout.

[8] James Grant, *The State of the World's Children 1990* (New York: Oxford University Press, 1990), p. 16, estimated that $2.5 billion a year would be needed by the late 1990s to stop preventable child deaths. An updated figure of $5.1 billion was cited in Jennifer Bryce, et al.; "Can the World Afford to Save the Lives of 6 Million Children Each Year?"; *The Lancet*, vol. 365; 6/25/2005; p. 2193; <http://www.thelancet.com/journals/lancet/article/PIIS014065667773/fulltext>; p. 1 of 1/11/2006 printout. Updated estimates for the cost to reduce under-age-five child deaths are not easily available, as discussion of the Sustainable Development Goals, successor to the Millennial Development Goals, combine the goal to reduce child deaths with total health systems. See: Karin Stenberg, et al.; "Financing Transformative Health Systems Towards Achievement of the Health Sustainable Development Goals: A Model for Projected Resource Needs in 67 Low-Income and Middle-Income Countries"; World Health Organization; The Lancet; September 2017; <https://www.thelancet.com/action/showPdf?pii=S2214-109X%2930263-2>; 8/18/2019 download. The cost estimates in the article are not for direct interventions: "About three-quarters of additional investments need to go towards health-systems strengthening" (p. e883). One source for direct intervention costs was a paper that reviewed an initiative in Uganda to reduce child deaths. See: Martina Björkman Nyqvist, et al.; "Reducing Child Mortality in the Last Mile: A Randomized Social Entrepreneurship Intervention in Uganda"; April 2017; <https://yanagizawadrott.com/wp-content/uploads/2017/08/livinggoods_april2017.pdf>; 8/18/2019 download. The study found that the "cost per averted death under-five was $4,237" (p. 24). Using that cost estimate, $5 billion a year in direct interventions could prevent the deaths of 1.18 million children under the age of five years, approximately the number of children in the "Promise Gap."

[9] Liselore van Ekdom, et al., on behalf of the ad hoc Study group for Child Health Cost Validation; "Global Cost of Child Survival; Estimates from Country-Level Validation"; World Health Organization Bulletin; 2/11/2011; <https://www.who.int/bulletin/volumes/89/4/10-081059.pdf>; p. 273 of 8/23/2019 printout.; <https://www.who.int/bulletin/volumes/89/4/10-081059/en/>; p. 9 of 3/31/2019 6:44 PM printout.

[10] Liselore van Ekdom, et al.; "Global Cost of Child Survival"; p. 10.

[11] The "Global Cost of Child Survival" figure of $14 billion was presented in 2005 dollars. The article was published in 2011. For purposes of the present discussion, the $14 billion figure in 2005 dollars was adjusted to 2011 dollars, the year of the article's publication. The resulting figure of $16 billion will be used in chapter 6 discussion.

[12] As explained in chapter 1, for the comparison of 1968 and 2021 giving levels, 24 of the denominations in the composite set provided data for both 1968 and 2021. The difference in denominations resulted in the 1968 figure of 0.63% of DPI to Benevolences used in the giving at previous levels analysis, instead of the complete composite set 1968 figure of 0.64% DPI.

[13] The Friends United Meeting provided Overseas Missions Income through 2012, but not Total Contributions. It should be noted that in 2004, Friends United Meeting changed fiscal years to end June 30, 2004, and so only six months of data was available for 2004. The Mennonite Church-USA provided Overseas Missions Income data for 2003 through 2020. The Evangelical Covenant Church provided Overseas Missions Income, but not Total Contributions, for 2012 through 2021. Data for Tables #6B-#6J, and the three denominations with Overseas Mission Income only, is presented in Appendix B-5.

[14] American Baptist Churches in the U.S.A.: An October 21, 2016, review of Overseas Missions Income data for the American Baptist Churches in the U.S.A. (ABCUSA) resulted in the following note. The Overseas Missions Income tables compare Overseas Missions Income as a percent of Total Contributions. As noted in the Introduction to Appendix B, for the ABCUSA, the membership data used in the calculation for giving as a percent of income was the number of members in congregations reporting Congregational Finances financial data. This partial Congregational Finances figure was added to Total Benevolences to produce a working Total Contributions figure for the communion. This working Total Contributions figure was divided by the number of members in reporting congregations, resulting in the per member giving figure for the ABCUSA. However, this working Total Contributions figure did not reflect the income of non-reporting congregations. As a result, the percent of Overseas Missions Income, the total the national office received from all congregations and individuals, as a percent of Total Contributions presented in the tables was likely higher than it would have been if a Total Contributions figure had included the income of non-reporting churches as well. For example, in 2014, the members in congregations reporting Congregational Finances numbered 166,551, or 13.92%, of the Total Membership figure of 1,196,828. Assuming non-reporting congregations received a similar

level of Congregational Finances as did the reporting congregations, the reported Congregational Finances figure of $214,939,212 was divided by 13.92% to yield an adjusted Congregational Finances figure of $1,544,543,517, an estimate of the Congregational Finances donated by the 1.2 million ABCUSA Total Full/Confirmed Members. By adding this adjusted Congregational Finances figure to the reported Total Benevolences figure of $38,078,517, which latter figure included donations from the total membership for some Benevolences categories, an adjusted Total Contributions figure was estimated as $1,582,622,034. When 2014 Overseas Missions Income of $12,977,000 was divided by the adjusted Total Contributions figure of $1,582,622,034, the resulting percent of Overseas Missions as a percent of Total Contributions was now 0.82%, rather than the 2014 percent figure of 5.1% presented in the table. A similar adjustment could be made to the ABCUSA figures for data years 2003 through 2013, and for subsequent years after 2014.

[15] Christian and Missionary Alliance: "Since both domestic and overseas works are budgeted through the same source (our 'Great Commission Fund'), the amount on lines 1 and 4 are actual amounts spent on overseas missions. Total Congregational Contributions no longer includes building fund income, as of Data Year 2012."

[16] Church of the Brethren (through Data Year 2011): "This amount is national denominational mission and service, i.e., direct staffing and mission support, and does not include other projects funded directly by congregations or districts, or independent missionaries sponsored by congregations and individuals that would not be part of the denominational effort."

[17] Churches of God General Conference: "[Data Year] 2008 line 2 represents a net loss in investment income included in line 1. By adding this net loss amount back, line 4 represents the amount received in contributions from donors."

[18] Conservative Congregational Christian Conference: "The structure of this communion limits the national office coordination of overseas ministries activity. By design, congregations are to conduct missions directly, through agencies of their choice. The national office does not survey congregations about these activities. The one common emphasis of affiliated congregations is a focus on Micronesia, represented by the reported numbers. Data Year 2010: The amount raised is down because we didn't have any missionary that we sent overseas."

[19] The Episcopal Church: "The Episcopal Church (aka, The Domestic and Foreign Missionary Society) does not specifically raise money to support our non-domestic ministries. Many of the activities included in our budget are, however, involved, directly or indirectly with providing worldwide mission...Many other expenditures (e.g., for ecumenical and interfaith relations; for federal chaplaincies; for management's participation in activities of the worldwide Anglican Communion) contain an overseas component; but we do not separately track or report domestic vs. overseas expenses in those categories."

[20] Evangelical Lutheran Church in America: "Some assumptions were made in arriving with the total income, and those remain consistent from year to year."

[21] Lutheran Church—Missouri Synod: "The Lutheran Church-Missouri Synod (LCMS) is a confessing, orthodox Lutheran church comprising nearly 6,000 congregations and approximately 600,000 households (1.98 million baptized individuals) across North America. LCMS witness and mercy work is carried out by two distinct offices: The Office of International Mission and the Office of National Mission. The majority of funding was supplied by voluntary charitable gifts from individuals, congregations, and organizations connected to the Synod.

In more recent years, the 35 districts (regional jurisdictions) of the LCMS, along with a growing number of congregations and Lutheran mission societies, began sponsoring various mission fields and projects directly. That support did not flow through the LCMS. More information regarding the international work of the 35 LCMS districts can be found at <www.lcmsdistricts.org> and the 75-plus members of Association of Lutheran Mission Agencies at <www.alma-online.org>. Therefore, millions of dollars of additional support from LCMS members is raised and spent for international ministry each year which are not part of this report. Since these funds are not sent through the LCMS national office—and thus are not part of Synod's annual auditing process—the total amount cannot be verified and incorporated into this report."

[22] Moravian Church in America, Northern Province: "Data provided by the Board of World Mission, an interprovincial agency of the North American Moravian Church. The Overseas Missions Income figure was estimated for the Northern Province by the Board of World Mission of the Moravian Church. The Northern Province is the only one of the three Moravian Provinces that reports Total Contributions to the *Yearbook of American and Canadian Churches series."*

[23] Orthodox Presbyterian Church: "These figures, as in past years, reflect only what was given through our denominational Committee on Foreign Missions. In addition, $66,751 [in 2015] was given through our Committee on Diaconal Ministries for diaconal and disaster relief ministries administered by our missionaries on various overseas fields. Local churches and individuals also give directly to a variety of overseas missions causes."

[24] Presbyterian Church (U.S.A.): For Data Year 2005: "Nos. 1 & 4 Year 2005: Higher for Asian Tsunami Relief."

[25] Primitive Methodist Church in the U.S.A. (through Data Year 2014): "This only includes monies passing through our Denominational Mission Board (International). Many churches send money directly to a mission field."

[26] Seventh-day Adventist, North American Division (NAD): "This estimate, prepared by the General Conference Treasury Department and NAD Stewardship Department, is for the U.S. portion of the total donated by congregations in Canada, the U.S., Bermuda, and Guam."

[27] Southern Baptist Convention (SBC): Data Year 2017: The SBC International Mission Board changed from a calendar year to an October 1-September 30 fiscal year in 2017; the FY 2017 IMB numbers include the note for the 2017 Fiscal Year of October 1, 2016 through September 30, 2017: "Oct. 1-Dec. 31, 2016 Quarter numbers are repeated from the 2016 Calendar Year."

[28] The United Methodist Church: "The above represents total income received by the General Board of Global Ministries of The United Methodist Church, Inc."

[29] See Table 26 for an individual denomination's endnote reference number.

[30] Charles H. Fahs, *Trends in Protestant Giving* (New York: Institute of Social and Religious Research, 1929), pp. 26, 29, 53. The eleven denominations included in the 1916-1927 figures are: Congregational; Methodist Episcopal; Methodist Episcopal, South; Northern Baptist Convention; Presbyterian Church in the U.S.; Presbyterian Church in the U.S.A.; Reformed Church in the United States; Reformed Church in America; Southern Baptist Convention; United Brethren; and United Presbyterian. For a more detailed discussion of the Fahs study, and a comparison of church member giving in the 1920s and 2003, see John and Sylvia Ronsvalle, *The State of Church Giving through 2003* (Champaign, IL: empty tomb, inc., 2005), pp. 55-60. The chapter is also available at <http://www.emptytomb.org/scg03missions.pdf>.

[31] Commission on World Mission and Evangelism of the World Council of Churches, "Mission and Evangelism—An Ecumenical Affirmation, *International Review of Mission*, vol. LXXI, no. 284 (October, 1982), p. 440.

[32] "Definitions: Unreached / Least Reached"; Joshua Project; n.d.; <http://www.joshuaproject.net/help/definitions>; p. 1 of 8/13/2017 1:45 PM printout.

[33] "Definitions: Unengaged"; Joshua Project; n.d.; <http://www.joshuaproject.net/help/definitions>; p. 1 of 8/13/2017 1:45 PM printout.

[34] Morris Chapman; "The Conversation is Changing"; published July 1, 2006; <http://www.morrischapman.com/article.asp?is=57>; p. 1 of 8/6/06 4:48 PM printout.

[35] Bob Rodgers, Southern Baptist Convention Executive Committee vice president for Cooperative Program &Stewardship; "Analysis: Are We Serious About Penetrating Lostness?"; Baptist Press; 5/28/2010; <http://www.bpnews.net/printer-friendly.asp?ID=33027>; p. 1 of 5/29/2010 10:54 AM printout.

[36] John Ronsvalle and Sylvia Ronsvalle, *The State of Church Giving through 2005: Abolition of the Institutional Enslavement of Overseas Missions* (Champaign, IL: empty tomb, inc., 2008), pp. 66-67.

[37] The historically Christian membership figure is an empty tomb, inc., calculation based on 44% of the mid-2021 U.S. population ("2021 World Population Data Sheet [Washington, DC: The Population Reference Bureau, August 2021]) and Gallup, 9/25/2022 printout, pp. 1, 6. Membership data for specific denominations is provided in Appendix B.

[38] The United Nations Inter-agency Group for Child Mortality Estimation (UN IGME) estimated there were 5,034,000 under-five deaths in 2021: UN IGME; *Levels & Trends in Child Mortality Report 2022*. Dividing that number by 365 days in 2021 yields the estimate of 13,790 children a day.

[39] Eric McDonald; Spectrem Group; email Subject: RE: 2021 Data Request[re: Market Insights 2022]; August 18, 2022 9:05 AM Central Daylight Time; pp. 1-2 of printout. Supplement to: "Market Insights 2022"; The Spectrem Group [spectrem.com]; 2022; Spectrem Group Market Insights 2022.pdf. To calculate the number of wealthy church member households at a given level, the total number of households in that category was multiplied by the 44% figure for self-identified church members (empty tomb estimate based on Gallup, 9/25/2022), that is 2,050,000 total households => $5 million net worth times 44% = 902,000 church member households; 14,600,000 total households => $1 million x 44% = 6,424,000; 21,560,000 households => $500,000 x 44% = 9,486,400).

[40] For a brief review of this topic, see John Ronsvalle and Sylvia Ronsvalle, *The State of Church Giving through 2002* (Champaign, IL: empty tomb, inc., 2004), pp. 65-66.

[41] The percent Catholic for each diocese was derived by dividing "Total Catholic Population" by "Total Population" as found in *The Official Catholic Directory*, P.J. Kenedy & Sons; NRP Direct; Athens, GA, 2022, subtitled, "Charitable Status of the Catholic Church as of January 1, 2022." The population data for the Archdioceses under consideration was

found in the *OCD* as follows: Baltimore, p. 61; Boston, p. 114; Chicago, p. 206; Detroit, p. 320; Galveston-Houston, p. 411; Los Angeles, p. 614; New York, p. 762; Newark, p. 730; Philadelphia, p. 878; and Washington, p. 1267.

The percent Catholic calculated for each diocese was used to obtain an estimate of U.S. BEA Personal Income for Catholics in each Archdiocesan county. An alternative approach would have been to employ data from Dale E. Jones et al., *Religious Congregations & Membership in the United States, 2000* (Nashville: Glenmary Research Center, 2002). The *RCMUS* provided "Total Adherents" as a "% of Total Pop." data for Catholics as well as other denominations and religions for each county. A cursory review in 2005 of this data for selected counties suggested that this latter approach using somewhat older data would have resulted in marginal differences. The *RCMUS* is part of a series that has been published decennially.

42 Total 2021 U.S. BEA Personal Income for Counties in Archdioceses ($s): County level U.S. BEA Personal Income data for 2021, was accessed on 7/16/2023 via <https://apps.bea.gov/iTable/?reqid=70&step=1&acrdn=6#eyJhcHBpZCI6NzAsInN0ZXBzIjpbMSwyNCwyOSwyNSwzMSwyNiwyNywzMF0sImRhdGEiOltbIlRhYmxlSWQiLCIyMCJdLFsiQ2xhc3NpZmljYXRpb24iLC JOb24tSW5kdXN0cnkiXSxbIk1ham9yX0FyZWEiLCI0Il0sWyJTdGF0ZSIsWyJYWCJdXSxbIkFyZWEiLFsiWFgiXV0sWyJTdGF0aXN0aWMiLFsiMSJdXSxbIlVuaXRfb2ZfbWVhc3VyZSIsIkxldmVscyJdLFsiWWVhciIsWyIyMDIxIl1dLFsiWWVhckJlZ2luIiwiLTEiXSxbIllllYXJfRW5kIiwiLTEiXV19>

Total Population 2021: United States Census Bureau: American Community Survey (ACS); <https://data.census.gov/table/ACSDT5YSPT2021.B01003?t=001:Populations%20and%20People&g=060XX00US2502338540,2502339450,2502372985&y=2021&moe=false&tp=true>

The Archdiocese of Boston was adjusted for Archdiocesan data "the towns of Marion, Mattapoisett and Wareham excepted" from Plymouth County, MA. This involved using the 2021 population of the five Archdiocesan counties and the aforementioned three excepted towns. Population for the five counties was derived from <https://apps.bea.gov/iTablecore/data/app/Downloads>. Population for the three towns in Plymouth County, MA, was obtained starting with https://data.census.gov via Advanced Search via Geography via County Subdivision via Massachusetts via Plymouth County via Marion, Mattapoisett, and Wareham towns: population total via Year via Total Population via Transpose via Print.

43 The original source for the estimate employed for current Catholic giving as 1.2% of income is as follows: " '...[W]e know that the national statistics are that Catholics give to the church about 1.2 percent of their income...' [Tim Dockery, director of development services for the Chicago archdiocese] said" (Cathleen Falsani, Religion Reporter, "Archdiocese May Ask for 10%: Cardinal George Considers Program That Includes Tithing," *Chicago Sun-Times*, Sunday, February 1, 2004, pp. 1A, and 6A).

A more recent citation of the figure is as follows: "The typical Catholic household contributes 1.1 to 1.2 percent of their income ..." in Charles E. Zech, Mary L. Gautier, Mark. M. Gray, Johnathon L. Wiggins, Thomas P. Gaunt, S.J., *Catholic Parishes of the 21st Century* (New York: Oxford University Press, 2017), p. 77.

44 John Ronsvalle and Sylvia Ronsvalle, "An Exploration of Roman Catholic Giving Patterns," *The State of Church Giving through 1993* (Champaign, Ill.: empty tomb, inc., 1995), pp. 59-78. The article is also available at: <http://www.emptytomb.org/cathgiv.html>.

45 A 2010 survey was conducted by the Center for Applied Research in the Apostolate (CARA), as a collaborative "work of five Catholic national ministerial organizations," (Mark M. Gray, Mary L. Gautier, and Melissa Cidade; "The Changing Face of U.S. Catholic Parishes"; National Association of May Ministry (Washington, D.C.); 2011; <www.emergingmodels.org/doc/Emerging Models Phase One report.pdf>; pp. 1, 2, 6 of 7/28/2011 printout). The survey found the "total average weekly offering in U.S. parishes" was $9,200. Multiplying that number by the 2010 number of parishes, 17,784, yielded a total annual offering calculation of $8,507,865,600. Using the *Official Catholic Directory* figure for membership, which was 68,503,456 in 2010, a per member total average weekly offering calculation of $124.20. The estimated 2010 U.S. per capita Disposable Person Income figure was $36,697. The $124.20 per member total average weekly offering amount represented 0.3% of 2010 income.

46 Littice Bacon-Blood; "No Saving Grace: Another Catholic School Closing"; The Time-Picayune; 5/21/2015; <http://www.nola.com/education/index.ssf/2015/05/no_saving_grace_another_cathol.html>; p. 5 of 8/13/2015 4:29 PM printout.

47 See for example: Zak Koeske; " 'I'm Sickened': Parents Scrambling After Word of Catholic School Closings"; Chicago Tribune; 01/18/2018; <https://www.chicagotribune.com/suburbs/ct-met-suburban-catholic-schools-close-20190118-story.html>; 8/15/2019 3:01 PM printout. Also: Megan McGibney; "With Schools Closing, Is Catholic Education Disappearing in Brooklyn?"; Bklyner.com; 6/21/2019; <https://bklyner.com/with-schools-closing-is-catholic-education-disappearing-in-brooklyn/>; 8/15/2019 3:07 PM printout. Also: Giulia McDonnell Nieto del Rio; "A Growing

Number of Catholic Schools Are Shutting Down Forever"; New York Times; 9/5/2020 and updated 10/27/2021; <https://www.nytimes.com/2020/09/05/us/catholic-school-closings.html>; 3/27/2024 8:15 PM printout.

[48] Nathan Glazer; "Catholic School Closures and the Decline of Urban Neighborhoods: What Is the Cause, and What the Effect?"; Education Next, Harvard University; Fall 2014; <https://www.educationnext.org/lost-classroom-lost-community-book-review>; p. 2 of 8/15/2019 3:09 PM printout.

[49] Tom Hoffarth; "Closure of Sister-run La Reina Catholic School near LA Sparks Organized Pushback"; National Catholic Reporter; 2/20/2024; <https://www.ncronline.org/news/closure-sister-run-la-reina-catholic-school-near-la-sparks-organized-pushback>; pp. 2, 3, 4, 7.

[50] Charles Zech, et al., *Catholic Parishes of the 21st Century*, pp. 16-17, 19.

[51] Charles Zech, et al., *Catholic Parishes of the 21st Century*, p. 15.

[52] Charles Zech, et al., *Catholic Parishes of the 21st Century*, pp. 79-80.

[53] Dom Cingoranelli; "Why Are Catholics Cheapskates Regarding Giving?"; Catholic Stand; 8/7/2016; <http://www.catholicstand.com/why-are-catholics-cheapskates-regarding-giving/>; p. 2 of 8/10/2016 12:24 PM printout.

[54] James Grant, *The State of the World's Children 1989* (New York: Oxford University Press, 1989), p. 82.

[55] "The Promise a Year Later," *First Call for Children*, UNICEF, No. 2 (n.d., approximately 1991), cover.; and James P. Grant, *The State of the World's Children 1995* (New York: UNICEF-Oxford University Press, 1995), pp. 10-11.

[56] World Health Organization; "Millennium Development Goals (MDGs)"; 2020; <https://www/who.int/topics/millennium_development_goals/about/en/>; p. 1 of 10/4/2020 1:49 PM printout.

[57] UNDP; "Background of the Sustainable Development Goals"; n.d.; <https://www.undp.org/content/undp/en/home/sustainable-development-goals/background/>; pp. 1, 3 of 10/4/2020 1:28 PM printout.

[58] As noted in endnote 5, a 2013 estimate of the additional cost to provide universal primary education was $26 billion (Fahad Al-Sulaiti, "Counting the Cost of Universal Primary Education," p. 2). A 2014 Brookings Institution article similarly cited a $26 billion need to expand "basic education" for all the children in low and middle income countries (Liesbet Steer; "Seven Facts About Global Education Financing"; Brookings Institution; 2/20/2014; <https://www.brookings.educ/blog/education-plus-development/2014/02/20/seven-facts-about-global-education-financing/>; p. 1 of 11/30/2020 12:28 PM printout). A UNESCO Policy Paper, dated July 2015, cited an annual $39 billion gap each year from 2015 to 2030 to fund both primary and secondary education ("Policy Paper 18: Pricing the Right to Education: The Cost of Reaching New Targets by 2030"; UNESCO; July 2015 Update; <https://unesdoc.unesco.org/ark:/48223/pf0000232197>; p. 1 of 11/30/2020 printout). For purposes of the present discussion, a figure of $26 billion will be used as the additional cost needed to provide universal primary education.

[59] Dana Vorisek and Shu Yu; "Policy Research Working Paper 9146: Understanding the Cost of Achieving the Sustainable Development Goals"; World Bank Group; February 2020; <http://documents1.worldbank.org/curated/en/744701582827333101/ped/Understanding-the-Cost-of-Achieving-the-Sustainable-Development-Goals.pdf>; p. 9 of 11/29/2020 4:11 PM printout. The amount of $11.8 billion is similar to an $11 billion figure found in: SDG Knowledge Hub; "Researchers Estimate Cost to Achieve SDG Target 2.1: End Hunger by 2030"; 10/18/2016; <http://sdg.iisd.org/news/researchers-estimate-cost-to-achieve-sdg-target-2-1-end-hunger-by-2030/>; p. 2 of 9/27/2020 5:16 PM printout.

[60] Guy Hutton and Mili Varughese; "The Costs of Meeting the 2030 Sustainable Development Goal Targets on Drinking Water, Sanitation, and Hygiene Summary Report"; World Bank Group; January 2016; <https://openknowledge.worldbank.org/bitstream/handle/10986/23681/K8632.pdf?sequence=4>; pp. 2, 3. This report was cited in Dana Vorisek and Shu Yu; "Policy Research Working Paper 9146: Understanding the Cost of Achieving the Sustainable Development Goals"; February 2020, p. 9.

[61] The $18,184,869,381 is an empty tomb estimate based on information in *The Index of Global Philanthropy and Remittances 2016*. The 2015 data was then updated to 2021 data by a percent increase based on the change in the U.S. GDP. Hudson Institute Center for Global Prosperity; Created 10/4/2016; Modified 2/6/2017; downloaded 5/8/2017; <https://s3.amazonaws.com/media.hudson.org/files/publications/201703IndexofGlobalPhilanthropyandRemittances2016.pdf>; pp. 9, 37 of 5/8/2017 printout.

chapter 7

Why and How Much Do Americans Give?

This chapter updates estimates of total charitable giving in the United States in order to explore both why people donate to charity, and how much Americans donate.

Why People Give

What makes people generous?

This is a complex question. For example, the question led to the founding of a center devoted to the Science of Generosity at the University of Notre Dame in Indiana. As the center's Web site notes, "Current studies of generosity come from many different and often disconnected disciplines and focus on various terms, such as philanthropy, volunteerism and altruism. The Science of Generosity initiative aims to bring together diverse approaches in order to create a field for the study of generosity in all its forms."[1]

The previous six chapters in this volume have focused on church member giving and membership in the United States from a numerical point of view. Placing religious giving in the broader context of total charitable giving may also provide insight into one aspect of Americans' motivation for participation in the practice of donating to charity.

A key source of available information is the United States Government Department of Labor Bureau of Labor Statistics (BLS) that takes a regular survey of Americans' spending patterns. In the Consumer Expenditure Survey (CE), the respondents are asked to categorize their "cash contributions" to four categories relevant to the present inquiry: (1) "charities and other organizations"; (2) "church, religious organizations"; (3) "educational institutions"; (4) "Gifts to non-CU [consumer unit] members of stocks, bonds, and mutual funds."

In 2021, the category of gifts to "church, religious organizations" represented 56 percent of the charitable donations reported by Americans.

This percentage differs from other sources that report a lower percent directed to the category of "religion." A major difference may be due to the fact that, in other surveys, the frame of reference has been defined by the professional practitioners interested in certain end-use categories, rather than either by the perception of the donors, or by the self-understanding and governance of the recipient organizations themselves.

Various well-known surveys of giving emphasize the end-use of the contributions. The amount of giving categorized as "church, religious organizations" by donors in the CE is therefore of interest, in that it may provide insight as to the motivation of donors. For example, while practitioner surveys might categorize a gift to Catholic Social Services or the Salvation Army under "human services," the donor may view the contribution as a gift to "church, religious organizations." Again, professional fundraiser surveys may label gifts to Lutheran World Relief and World Vision as "international" while donors might identify the gifts as being directed to "church, religious organizations." The net effect is that the category of "religion" is under reported in many surveys of charitable giving, thus making it more difficult to consider possible motivations of donors.

As can be seen from the analysis of CE data that follows, whether considering income groups, age brackets, or regions of the country, most donors identified gifts to "church, religious organizations" as the primary focus of their charitable activity.

If, as observed in earlier chapters of this volume, giving to church is weakening, over time the observed trends could have a negative impact on the entire charitable sector in the U.S. An accurate understanding of the role of religion in the practice of philanthropy in the U.S. could benefit academics, practitioners, and the general population in the U.S., as well.

An accurate understanding of the role of religion in the practice of philanthropy in the U.S. could benefit academics, practitioners, and the general population in the U.S., as well.

One suggestion for improving this categorization process is a revision of the nonprofit Form 990 reporting document. Before selecting one of the ten core definition categories, the reporting nonprofit organization could first indicate its form of governance as either "faith-based" or "secular." This suggestion about organizational self-definition is discussed in more detail below.

How Much Do Americans Give?

Various surveys provide different answers to the question of how much Americans give. The source that serves as a benchmark is the Consumer Expenditure Survey.

Overview of Estimates. **The Consumer Expenditure Survey.** The U.S. Government Bureau of Labor Statistics Consumer Expenditure Survey (CE) is a sophisticated research instrument that affects many aspects of American life through the Consumer Price Index.

The Consumer Expenditure Survey also serves as a benchmark for understanding charitable giving patterns. The data series provides information about Americans' giving patterns by age, region of residence, and income levels.

In 2021, the CE figure for charitable giving by living individuals was $1,476.12 per "consumer unit." Given that there were 133.595 million units in the U.S. in 2021, the aggregate amount of charitable giving from living individuals in 2021 was calculated to be $197.20 billion.

Other Sources of Giving Estimates. Another source of information about charitable giving is found in the U.S. Internal Revenue Service Form 990. The Form 990 series must be filled out by charitable organizations with at least $50,000 in income, and by foundations.

A third major source of philanthropic information is the *Giving USA* series. A key component of this series has been based on deductions claimed on IRS Individual Tax returns, as well as other economic variables. However, the estimating model has been adjusted to take into account effects of the Tax Cuts and Jobs Act passed by Congress at the end of 2017. The series is researched and written on behalf of professional fundraisers by a university-based philanthropy center.

Although estimates do not originate with the media, their reports disseminate giving estimates to the U.S. population as a whole. A review of Associated Press (AP) articles, and two from other media, for 2002 through 2023, found that the media routinely presented a more positive — or in some case more negative — change in giving from the previous year than resulted when the giving numbers were adjusted for changes in population and the economy.

The CE provides the U.S. Government data designed to measure Americans' charitable contributions.

Details of the Consumer Expenditure Survey, 2021. The U.S. Department of Labor, Bureau of Labor Statistics, Consumer Expenditure Survey (CE) provides a benchmark measure of Americans' charitable cash contributions. The CE provides the U.S. Government data designed to measure Americans' charitable contributions.

The CE presents data per "consumer unit." The definition reads:

> A consumer unit consists of any of the following: (1) All members of a particular household who are related by blood, marriage, adoption, or other legal arrangements; (2) a person living alone or sharing a household with others or living as a roomer in a private home or lodging house or in permanent living quarters in a hotel or motel, but who is financially independent; or (3) two or more persons living together who use their incomes to make joint expenditure decisions. Financial independence is determined by spending behavior with regard to the three major expense categories: Housing, food, and other living expenses. To be considered financially independent, the respondent must provide at least two of the three major expenditure categories, either entirely or in part.
>
> The terms consumer unit, family, and household are often used interchangeably for convenience. However, the proper technical term for purposes of the Consumer Expenditure Survey is consumer unit.[2]

The CE data for 2021 was aggregated, conflated, and analyzed by empty tomb, inc. The result found that Americans gave $197.20 billion in cash contributions to charitable causes in 2021, the latest year for which data was analyzed for this volume.

The CE categories include "Cash contributions to: charities and other organizations; church, religious organizations; and educational institutions" as well as "Gifts to non-

Table 32: U.S. Bureau of Labor Statistics, Consumer Expenditure Survey, Cash Contributions: Americans' Charitable Giving (Aggregated) 2021

Item	Average Annual Expenditures Multiplied by 133.595 Million Consumer Units: Aggregated (billions $)	Item as % of Total
Annual Expenditures		
Cash Contributions for Charitable Giving		
Cash contributions to:		
charities and other organizations	$66.83	33.9%
churches, religious organizations	$110.69	56.1%
educational institutions	$9.22	4.7%
Gifts to non-CU members of stocks, bonds, and mutual funds	$10.47	5.3%
Total	$197.20	100.0%

Details in table may not compute to numbers shown due to rounding. empty tomb, inc., 2024
Source: empty tomb, inc. analysis of U.S. BLS CE, 2021

CU [Consumer Unit] members of stocks, bonds, and mutual funds."[3] An analysis of the CE data resulted in the finding that Americans contributed 1.9% of their Disposable (after-tax) Personal Income (DPI) to charity in 2021, and of that amount, 1.05% to "church, religious organizations."

Further detail regarding this analysis of U.S. Department of Labor, Bureau of Labor Statistics, Consumer Expenditure Survey charitable giving data is presented in Table 32.[4]

Cash Contributions by Income Level, 2021

The CE measured Americans' cash contributions to charitable causes by income levels, as displayed in Tables 33 and 34.[5]

An analysis was conducted for nine income levels, ranging from Less than $15,000 up to both $150,000 to $199,999 and the highest category of $200,000 and more, with the average "Income after taxes" for the income levels ranging from $9,924 to $147,782 and $245,844, respectively.

Table 33: U.S. Bureau of Labor Statistics, Consumer Expenditure Survey, Cash Contributions for Charitable Giving by Income Level, 2021

Item	All consumer units	Less than $15,000	$15,000 to $29,999	$30,000 to $39,999	$40,000 to $49,999	$50,000 to $69,999
Number of consumer units (in thousands)	133,595	13,968	20,136	12,177	10,331	17,152
Consumer unit characteristics:						
Income after taxes	$78,743	$9,924	$25,410	$37,790	$46,593	$59,306
Average Annual Expenditures						
Cash Contributions for Charitable Giving						
Cash contributions to:						
charities and other organizations	$500.22	$197.56	$168.11	$179.94	$349.70	$220.46
churches, religious organizations	828.56	242.83	465.95	571.24	645.12	608.25
educational institutions	68.99	8.87	18.42	19.96	8.15	18.18
Gifts to non-CU members of stocks, bonds, and mutual funds	78.35	302.44	4.45	6.97	6.64	8.54
Total (calculated)	$1,476.12	$751.70	$656.93	$778.11	$1,009.61	$855.43
Calculated:						
% of Income after Taxes						
Cash contributions to:						
charities and other organizations	0.64%	1.99%	0.66%	0.48%	0.75%	0.37%
churches, religious organizations	1.05%	2.45%	1.83%	1.51%	1.38%	1.03%
educational institutions	0.09%	0.09%	0.07%	0.05%	0.02%	0.03%
Gifts to non-CU members of stocks, bonds, and mutual funds	0.10%	3.05%	0.02%	0.02%	0.01%	0.01%
Total	1.9%	7.6%	2.6%	2.1%	2.2%	1.4%

Details in table may not compute to numbers shown due to rounding. empty tomb, inc., 2024
Source: empty tomb, inc. analysis of U.S. BLS CE, 2021

A comparison of cash contributions among different income brackets may be of interest.

However, it should be noted that CE lower income brackets, which for purposes of this analysis ranged from Less than $15,000 through $49,999, reported higher expenses than income before taxes in 2021.[6] The CE observes:

> Data users may notice that average annual expenditures presented in the income tables sometimes exceed income before taxes for the lower income groups. The primary reason for that is believed to be the under reporting of income by respondents, a problem common to most household surveys...
>
> There are other reasons why expenditures exceed income for the lower income groups. Consumer units whose members experience a spell of unemployment may draw on their savings to maintain their expenditures. Self-employed consumers may experience business losses that result in low or even negative incomes, but are able to maintain their expenditures by borrowing or relying on savings. Students may get by on loans while they are in school, and retirees may rely on savings and investments.[7]

To the extent that income is proportionately under reported across all income levels, but is more evident in lower income brackets, then comparisons across income brackets may be informative on an exploratory basis.

Having noted this caveat, it is still of interest to observe that consumer units in the Less than $15,000 through the $40,000 to $49,999 income brackets reported charitable cash contributions that represented a higher portion of after-tax income in all but the $200,000 and above bracket.

Table 34: U.S. Bureau of Labor Statistics, Consumer Expenditure Survey, Cash Contributions for Charitable Giving by Higher Income Level, 2021

Item	All consumer units	$70,000 to $99,999	$100,000 to $149,999	$150,000 to $199,999	$200,000 and more
Number of consumer units (in thousands)	133,595	19,806	18,953	9,606	11,466
Consumer unit characteristics:					
Income after taxes	$78,743	$79,669	$110,501	$147,782	$245,844
Average Annual Expenditures					
Cash Contributions for Charitable Giving					
Cash contributions to:					
charities and other organizations	$500.22	$208.87	$396.27	$712.82	$2,843.50
churches, religious organizations	828.56	686.40	999.31	1,546.28	2,309.07
educational institutions	68.99	14.40	27.16	42.55	599.56
Gifts to non-CU members of stocks, bonds, and mutual funds	78.35	18.33	85.20	240.45	136.50
Total (calculated)	$1,476.12	$928.00	$1,507.94	$2,542.10	$5,888.63
Calculated:					
% of Income after Taxes					
Cash contributions to:					
charities and other organizations	0.64%	0.26%	0.36%	0.48%	1.16%
church, religious organizations	1.05%	0.86%	0.90%	1.05%	0.94%
educational institutions	0.09%	0.02%	0.02%	0.03%	0.24%
Gifts to non-CU members of stocks, bonds, and mutual funds	0.10%	0.02%	0.08%	0.16%	0.06%
Total	1.9%	1.2%	1.4%	1.7%	2.4%

Details in table may not compute to numbers shown due to rounding.
Source: empty tomb, inc. analysis of U.S. BLS CE, 2021

empty tomb, inc., 2024

It may be observed that 2021 giving as a percent of income after taxes to "church, religious organizations" was higher in each of the income levels, than to "charities and other organizations" or "educational institutions," with the exception of the $200,000 and more bracket.

Again, of the three categories of "charities and other organizations," "church, religious organizations, and "educational institutions," "charities and other organizations" was the highest recipient category in the $200,000 and more bracket, and the second largest recipient category in each of the other brackets.

The category of "Gifts to non-CU members of stocks, bonds, and mutual funds" posted a changed pattern from previous years. That is, the Less than $15,000 bracket reported "Gifts to non-CU members of stocks, bonds, and mutual funds" as receiving the largest portion of their charitable giving. The 3.05% of income reported was higher than that reported by any of the other income brackets.

In four of the nine income brackets, gifts to "educational institutions" were less than to "Gifts to non-CU members of stocks, bonds, and mutual funds."

This level of contribution to "church, religious organizations" suggests that the Under 25 years group first learned about giving in a religious context, and that religion serves as the seedbed of philanthropic giving in America.

In each income bracket, with the exception of the Less than $15,000 and $200,000 and more brackets, the dollars given to "church, religious organizations" equaled more than the sum of the dollars given to "charities and other organizations," "educational institutions," and "Gifts to non-CU members of stocks, bonds, and mutual funds," combined.

Cash Contributions by Age, 2021

The CE also measured Americans' cash contributions to charitable causes by age of contributor.[8] Table 35 presents the data in tabular form.

The seven age categories under consideration started with the "Under 25 years" grouping, proceeded with "25-34 years" as the first of five 10-year periods, and culminated with the "75 years and older" cohort.

The 75 years and older cohort had the lowest dollar income of any bracket. The 75 years and older bracket posted a 28% lower income than the 65-74 years group did. Yet the 75 years and older bracket reported the highest portion of after-tax income given to charity, and was the highest in the amount of total dollars donated.

The 75 years and older bracket also posted the highest amount given to "Gifts to non-CU members of stocks, bonds, and mutual funds."

In 2021, giving as a percent of income after taxes to "church, religious organizations" was the highest category in every age bracket with the exception of the 35-44 age bracket. The percent of income to this category increased from the previous bracket in each of the brackets.

Contributions to "charities, and other organizations" also grew as a portion of income in each age bracket with the exception of the 45-54 years bracket.

Donations to "educational institutions" were highest in the 55-64 years bracket.

Table 35: U.S. Bureau of Labor Statistics, Consumer Expenditure Survey, Cash Contributions for Charitable Giving by Age, 2021

Item	All consumer units	Under 25 years	25-34 years	35-44 years	45-54 years	55-64 years	65-74 years	75 years and older
Number of consumer units (in thousands)	133,595	6,608	21,024	22,921	22,276	24,751	21,479	14,537
Consumer unit characteristics:								
Income after taxes	$78,743	$44,389	$78,214	$97,916	$103,497	$85,573	$59,872	$43,217
Average Annual Expenditures								
Cash Contributions for Charitable Giving								
Cash contributions to:								
charities and other organizations	$500.22	$22.49	$101.92	$735.50	$390.38	$598.33	$577.69	$809.26
church, religious organizations	828.56	158.54	393.24	716.14	791.96	872.26	1,160.06	1,431.83
educational institutions	68.99	37.14	9.74	43.68	58.28	193.84	39.47	56.55
Gifts to non-CU members of stocks, bonds, and mutual funds	78.35	26.88	16.84	95.81	30.45	27.01	91.72	304.23
Total (calculated)	$1,476.12	$245.05	$521.74	$1,591.13	$1,271.07	$1,691.44	$1,868.94	$2,601.87
Calculated:								
% of Income after Taxes								
Cash contributions to:								
charities and other organizations	0.64%	0.05%	0.13%	0.75%	0.38%	0.70%	0.96%	1.87%
church, religious organizations	1.05%	0.36%	0.50%	0.73%	0.77%	1.02%	1.94%	3.31%
educational institutions	0.09%	0.08%	0.01%	0.04%	0.06%	0.23%	0.07%	0.13%
Gifts to non-CU members of stocks, bonds, and mutual funds	0.10%	0.06%	0.02%	0.10%	0.03%	0.03%	0.15%	0.70%
Total	1.9%	0.6%	0.7%	1.6%	1.2%	2.0%	3.1%	6.0%

Details in table may not compute to numbers shown due to rounding.
Source: empty tomb, inc. analysis of U.S. BLS CE, 2021

empty tomb, inc., 2024

In 2021, a pattern that had been evident in the years 2004 through 2015, and also in 2017 through 2020, was again observed. The Under 25 years cohort reported in CE Surveys that the majority of their donations went to "church, religious organizations." In 2021, the average portion of charitable giving to "church, religious organizations" was 65% of total charitable giving. The average for the years 2004 through 2015 and 2017 through 2020 was 84%.[9] This level of contribution to "church, religious organizations" suggests that the Under 25 years group first learned about giving in a religious context, and that religion serves as the seedbed of philanthropic giving in America.

Cash Contributions by Region, 2021

In addition, as shown in Table 36, the CE also measured Americans' cash contributions to charitable causes by region.[10]

The four region categories for which information was presented in the CE data were Northeast, Midwest, South, and West. Regional charitable giving data and regional income figures were available for the comparison.

Analysis of the 2021 data showed that contributions to charitable causes were highest in the Midwest, at 2.0% of income after taxes. The West followed at 1.9%. The South and the Northeast each measured 1.8%.

In the Midwest, South, and West, "church, religious organizations" received the highest amount of contributions, equaling more than the sum of contributions to "charities and other organizations" and "educational institutions." In the Northeast,

Table 36: U.S. Bureau of Labor Statistics, Consumer Expenditure Survey, Cash Contributions for Charitable Giving by Region of Residence, 2021

Item	All consumer units	Northeast	Midwest	South	West
Number of consumer units (in thousands)	133,595	23,152	28,230	51,808	30,406
Consumer unit characteristics:					
Income after taxes	$78,743	$87,948	$76,495	$72,248	$84,890
Average Annual Expenditures					
Cash Contributions for Charitable Giving					
Cash contributions to:					
charities and other organizations	$500.22	$1,033.02	$489.18	$331.33	$392.57
church, religious organizations	828.56	397.87	709.60	892.57	1,157.90
educational institutions	68.99	98.99	166.80	23.84	32.27
Gifts to non-CU members of stocks, bonds, and mutual funds	78.35	62.75	169.36	62.48	32.78
Total (calculated)	$1,476.12	$1,592.63	$1,534.94	$1,310.22	$1,615.52
Calculated:					
% of Income after Taxes					
Cash contributions to:					
charities and other organizations	0.64%	1.17%	0.64%	0.46%	0.46%
church, religious organizations	1.05%	0.45%	0.93%	1.24%	1.36%
educational institutions	0.09%	0.11%	0.22%	0.03%	0.04%
Gifts to non-CU members of stocks, bonds, and mutual funds	0.10%	0.07%	0.22%	0.09%	0.04%
Total	1.9%	1.8%	2.0%	1.8%	1.9%

Details in table may not compute to numbers shown due to rounding. empty tomb, inc., 2024
Source: empty tomb, inc. analysis of U.S. BLS CE, 2021

the largest recipient category was "charities and other organizations."

The differences in 2021 giving to "church, religious organizations" were significant at the 0.05 level between the Midwest and the Northeast, the Northeast and the South, and the Midwest and the South.[11]

Records by region were available back to 1987 from the Bureau of Labor Statistics Consumer Expenditure Survey.[12] The specific category of "Gifts to non-CU members of stocks, bonds, and mutual funds," however, was not available before the second quarter of 2001. Therefore, in the historical series for 1987-2021, comparing Charitable Giving as a portion of after-tax income, Charitable Giving included the three categories of "charities and other organizations," "church, religious organizations," and "educational institutions." Consequently, the 2021 numbers in Table 37, which does not include the category of "Gifts to non-CU members of stocks, bonds, and mutual funds," differ slightly from the figures in Table 35, which do include that category.

As can be seen in Table 37, the regional pattern indicates the South had the highest average percent of after-tax income in the "cash contributions for charitable giving" category in the 1987-2021 period. The West and the Midwest were next, and then the Northeast.

The South's overall average was 1.74% of income given to charity during the 1987-2021 period. The Northeast's 1.14% average for the 35-year period resulted from the Northeast posting the lowest portion of income donated for charitable purposes consistently throughout the 1987 through 2021 period, with the exceptions of 1994, when the Northeast was third and the West was the lowest in the comparison, and 2016, when the Northeast was the highest.

The Northeast region of the U.S. has traditionally measured lowest not only in charitable giving patterns, but also contained the five states measuring lowest in "overall religiosity," according a Pew Research study published in 2016. Pew's definition included "four common measures of religious observance: worship attendance, prayer frequency, belief in God and the self-described importance of religion in one's life." The five states with the lowest "religiosity" score were: New Hampshire, Massachusetts, Vermont, Maine, and Connecticut. These are five of the six states in the Census Bureau's "New England" subcategory within the "Northeast" section. The sixth state that makes up "New England" is Rhode Island, which measured 35th in the Pew study.[13] The relationship between religious commitment and charitable giving may merit further study.

Table 37: U.S. Bureau of Labor Statistics, Consumer Expenditure Survey, Expenditures for Charitable Giving by Region of Residence, 1987-2021

Year	All consumer units	Northeast	Midwest	South	West
1987	1.46%	0.86%	1.53%	1.76%	1.56%
1988	1.40%	0.83%	1.43%	1.68%	1.52%
1989	1.56%	1.04%	1.55%	2.01%	1.47%
1990	1.43%	1.03%	1.40%	1.69%	1.50%
1991	1.58%	1.11%	1.69%	1.74%	1.72%
1992	1.58%	1.26%	1.78%	1.78%	1.42%
1993	1.46%	0.98%	1.57%	1.57%	1.68%
1994	1.44%	1.30%	1.42%	1.73%	1.20%
1995	1.50%	1.06%	1.41%	1.66%	1.79%
1996	1.42%	0.93%	1.57%	1.75%	1.23%
1997	1.39%	0.88%	1.41%	1.70%	1.41%
1998	1.41%	0.89%	1.42%	1.68%	1.50%
1999	1.58%	1.03%	1.59%	1.83%	1.75%
2000	1.46%	0.95%	1.93%	1.42%	1.50%
2001	1.53%	1.14%	1.66%	1.72%	1.48%
2002	1.55%	1.14%	1.69%	1.64%	1.65%
2003	1.57%	0.99%	1.75%	1.82%	1.57%
2004	1.47%	0.84%	1.93%	1.53%	1.52%
2005	1.68%	1.13%	1.94%	1.99%	1.49%
2006	1.82%	1.19%	1.91%	1.81%	2.28%
2007	1.66%	1.02%	1.60%	1.67%	2.25%
2008	1.55%	1.00%	1.55%	1.71%	1.81%
2009	1.59%	0.99%	1.64%	1.80%	1.76%
2010	1.41%	0.95%	1.51%	1.61%	1.41%
2011	1.44%	1.10%	1.47%	1.61%	1.48%
2012	1.59%	1.29%	1.63%	1.73%	1.59%
2013	1.70%	1.18%	1.96%	1.90%	1.61%
2014	1.65%	1.26%	1.85%	1.77%	1.63%
2015	1.71%	1.19%	1.37%	2.05%	1.95%
2016	1.88%	2.66%	1.39%	1.75%	1.86%
2017	1.69%	1.09%	1.48%	1.91%	2.04%
2018	1.59%	1.05%	1.58%	1.73%	1.86%
2019	1.62%	0.98%	1.53%	1.66%	2.16%
2020	1.81%	1.72%	1.93%	1.76%	1.86%
2021	1.78%	1.74%	1.79%	1.73%	1.86%
Average for the 1987–2021 Period	1.57%	1.14%	1.62%	1.74%	1.67%

Details in table may not compute to numbers shown due to rounding. empty tomb, inc., 2024
Source: empty tomb analysis of U.S. BLS CE, series through 2021

The question may be asked whether regional differences in spending on other expenditures categories influence or limit charitable giving levels in the four regions. Specifically, does the cost of living in a region impact charitable giving levels? Table 38 presents CE expenditure data by region of residence for 2021.[14] The category of "Cash Contributions for Charitable Giving" was subtracted from the expenditures total. The reason for this adjustment was to calculate the portion of income remaining after expenditures other than those for charitable giving. The adjusted total expenditures figure was then divided by the region's after-tax income. The resulting percentage is shown in Table 38.

In 2021, in the four regions, the level of expenditures as a percent of after-tax income apart from charitable giving ranged from 81% in the Northeast to 85% in the West. Although the Northeast had the lowest percent of income spent on the named expenditures, it also posted the lowest percent of charitable giving. The West had the highest percent of income spent on the named expenditures, and also posted the second-highest percent of income given to charity. These findings suggests that there may be no clear pattern between regional expenses and charitable giving.

Table 38: U.S. Bureau of Labor Statistics, Consumer Expenditure Survey, Expenditures as a Percent of Income after Taxes, by Region of Residence, 2021

Item	All consumer units	Northeast	Midwest	South	West
Number of consumer units (in thousands)	133,595	23,152	28,230	51,808	30,406
Consumer unit characteristics:					
Income after taxes	$78,743	$87,948	$76,495	$72,248	$84,890
Average Annual Expenditures					
Seven Major Categories					
Food	$8,289.28	$9,333.80	$7,888.16	$7,638.70	$8,972.95
Housing	22,623.55	25,556.85	20,854.75	20,244.41	26,078.02
Apparel and services	1,754.39	2,068.55	1,749.09	1,489.43	1,966.61
Transportation	10,961.18	9,917.73	10,164.80	11,203.09	12,082.85
Health care	5,451.61	5,759.45	5,833.78	5,107.48	5,447.34
Entertainment	3,567.89	3,483.26	3,674.39	3,130.93	4,272.03
Personal insurance and pensions	7,873.19	9,209.29	7,906.83	6,876.18	8,523.39
Other Expenses*	6,406.74	7,348.93	6,470.45	5,782.53	6,689.70
Total Expenditures (published)	$66,927.83	$72,677.86	$64,542.26	$61,472.76	$74,032.90
Charitable Giving	$1,476.12	$1,592.63	$1,534.94	$1,310.22	$1,615.52
Total Expenditures Less Charitable Giving	$65,451.71	$71,085.23	$63,007.32	$60,162.54	$72,417.38
"Calculated: Average Annual Expenditures Less Charitable Giving as % Income after Taxes"	83%	81%	82%	83%	85%

Details in the above table may not compute to the numbers shown due to rounding.

*Other expenses include: "Alcoholic beverages; Personal care products and services; Reading; Education; Tobacco products and smoking supplies; Miscellaneous; Cash contributions." "Cash contributions" includes: "Support for college students; Alimony expenditures; Child support expenditures; 'Charitable giving' (Cash contributions to charities and other organizations; Cash contributions to church, religious organizations; Cash contributions to educational institutions; Gift to non-CU members of stocks, bonds, and mutual funds); Cash contribution to political organizations."

Source: empty tomb, inc. analysis of U.S. BLS CE, 2021 — empty tomb, inc., 2024

General Information regarding the Consumer Expenditure Survey

One benefit of the CE is its unbiased data. The Mission Statement of the U.S. Department of Labor, Bureau of Labor Statistics reads:

> The **Bureau of Labor Statistics (BLS)** is the principal fact-finding agency for the Federal Government in the broad field of labor economics and statistics. The BLS is an independent national statistical agency that collects, processes, analyzes, and disseminates essential statistical data to the American public, the U.S. Congress, other Federal agencies, State and local governments, business, and labor. The BLS also serves as a statistical resource to the Department of Labor.
>
> BLS data must satisfy a number of criteria, including relevance to current social and economic issues, timeliness in reflecting today's rapidly changing economic conditions, accuracy and consistently high statistical quality, and impartiality in both subject matter and presentation.[15]

The BLS, among its various activities, is the source for the following indexes:

> **Producer price index (PPI)**—This index, dating from 1890, is the oldest continuous statistical series published by BLS. It is designed to measure average changes in prices received by producers of all commodities, at all stages of processing, produced in the United States...
>
> **Consumer price indexes (CPI)**—The CPI is a measure of the average change in prices over time in a "market basket" of goods and services purchased either by urban wage earners and clerical workers or by all urban consumers. In 1919, BLS began to publish complete indexes at semiannual intervals, using a weighting

> structure based on data collected in the expenditure survey of wage-earner and clerical-worker families in 1917-19 (BLS Bulletin 357, 1924)...
>
> **International price indexes**—The BLS International Price Program produces export and import price indexes for nonmilitary goods traded between the United States and the rest of the world.[16]

Among the numerous applications of the BLS Consumer Expenditure Survey, the Survey is used for periodic revision of the Consumer Price Index (CPI). Following are excerpted comments from a "Brief Description of the Consumer Expenditure Survey."

> The current CE program was begun in 1980. Its principal objective is to collect information on the buying habits of U.S. consumers. Consumer expenditure data are used in a variety of research endeavors by government, business, labor, and academic analysts. In addition, the data are required for periodic revision of the CPI.
>
> The survey, which is conducted by the U.S. Census Bureau for the Bureau of Labor Statistics, consists of two components: A diary or recordkeeping, survey... and an interview survey, in which expenditures of consumer units are obtained in five interviews conducted at 3-month intervals...
>
> Each component of the survey queries an independent sample of consumer units that is representative of the U.S. population....[17]

The current CE program was begun in 1980. Its principal objective is to collect information on the buying habits of U.S. consumers.

A 2016 description of the CE "Sample Design" was as follows:

> The Interview survey is a rotating panel survey in which approximately 12,000 addresses are contacted each calendar quarter of the year of the survey. One-fourth of the addresses that are contacted each quarter are new to the survey. Usable interviews are obtained from approximately 6,900 households at those addresses each quarter of the year. After a housing unit has been in the sample for four consecutive quarters, it is dropped from the survey, and a new address is selected to replace it.[18]

The BLS, in commenting on the various functions of the Consumer Expenditure Survey, observed that, "Researchers use the data in a variety of studies, including those that focus on the spending behavior of different family types, trends in expenditures on various expenditure components including new types of goods and services, gift-giving behavior, consumption studies, and historical spending trends."[19]

Writing in the mid-1980s with reference to the then forthcoming Consumer Expenditure Survey-based revisions in the CPI, eminent business columnist Sylvia Porter remarked that the CPI is "the most closely watched, widely publicized and influential government statistic we have..."[20]

In addition to the fact that the "CPI is used to adjust federal tax brackets for inflation,"[21] a glimpse into the wide-ranging, Consumer Expenditure Survey-based network of CPI usage in American culture is gained from the following information:

> The CPI is the most widely used measure of inflation and is sometimes viewed as an indicator of the effectiveness of government economic policy. It provides information about price changes in the Nation's economy to government, business,

> labor, and private citizens and is used by them as a guide to making economic decisions. In addition, the President, Congress, and the Federal Reserve Board use trends in the CPI to aid in formulating fiscal and monetary policies …
>
> The CPI and its components are used to adjust other economic series for price changes and to translate these series into inflation-free dollars. Examples of series adjusted by the CPI include retail sales, hourly and weekly earnings, and components of the National Income and Product Accounts…
>
> The CPI is often used to adjust consumers' income payments (for example, Social Security), to adjust income eligibility levels for government assistance, and to automatically provide cost-of-living wage adjustments to millions of American workers. As a result of statutory action, the CPI affects the income of millions of Americans. Over 50 million Social Security beneficiaries, and military and Federal Civil Service retirees, have cost-of-living adjustments tied to the CPI.
>
> Another example of how dollar values may be adjusted is the use of the CPI to adjust the Federal income tax structure. These adjustments prevent inflation-induced increases in tax rates. In addition, eligibility criteria for millions of food stamp recipients, and children who eat lunch at school, are affected by changes in the CPI. Many collective bargaining agreements also tie wage increases to the CPI.[22]

"The CE survey can be used to address many economically crucial questions that no other U.S. survey can be used to address …"
— Economists from Northwestern Kellogg School of Management, The Wharton School University of Pennsylvania, and Johns Hopkins University

Three economists, from Northwestern University Kellogg School of Management, The Wharton School University of Pennsylvania, and Johns Hopkins University, prepared a paper on the value of the Consumer Expenditure Survey for a December 2011 National Bureau of Economic Research conference. Discussing the CE's panel studies, they wrote:

> Since the late 1970s, two characteristics have distinguished the U.S. consumer expenditure (CE) Survey from any other American household survey: Its goal is to obtain comprehensive spending data (not just data on a few spending categories and not just data over a brief time interval), and it has a panel structure (it reinterviews households so that it is possible to measure how their spending changes over time).
>
> These two features give the survey great value …
>
> The CE survey can be used to address many economically crucial questions that no other U.S. survey can be used to address …
>
> A re-interviewing process that yields true panel data on spending is critical to the core missions of the CE survey, such as the construction of group-specific price indices or improving the measurement of poverty. Panel data is even more important for the many research purposes to which the survey has been put, such as estimating the marginal propensity to consume out of economic stimulus payments.[23]

How Much Do Americans Give? An Estimate of Aggregate Giving to Religion, 1968-2021. An estimate of Americans' giving to religion was calculated for the 1968 to 2021 period. This estimate employed a 1974 benchmark estimate of $11.7 billion for giving to religion provided by the watershed Commission on Private

Philanthropy and Public Needs of the 1970s, commonly referred to as the Filer Commission.[24]

The amount of change from year to year, calculated for 1968 to 1973 and also 1975 to 2021, was the annual percent change in the composite denomination set analyzed in other chapters of this report.[25] This calculation yielded a total of $8.0 billion given to religion in 1968, and $69.2 billion in 2021. Table 39 presents this data both in aggregate form, and as adjusted for population and income.

A Comparison of Three Sources

Estimates of charitable giving vary by substantial margins. Three sources of information can be described and compared in an attempt to develop an overview of aggregate charitable giving patterns among Americans. In this comparison series, data was available for 1989 through 2019 for all three sources of charitable giving information.

Consumer Expenditure Survey, 2019. As noted earlier, the U.S. Government Bureau of Labor Statistics Consumer Expenditure Survey (CE) is a sophisticated research instrument that affects many aspects of American life. The CE is used to inform the Consumer Price Index which, in turn, is used, among other purposes, to adjust federal tax brackets, and determine cost-of-living adjustments for Social Security and military retirement benefits. The CE's figure for charitable giving serves as a benchmark for the level of philanthropy in the U.S.

As discussed earlier, the CE data included the categories of: "Cash contributions to charities and other organizations"; "Cash contributions to church, religious organizations"; "Cash contributions to educational institutions"; and "Gifts to non-CU [Consumer Unit] members of stocks, bonds, and mutual funds." The annual average expenditure for the four categories in 2019 was $1,189.62 per consumer unit. In 2019, there were 132.242 million consumer units in the United States. The average annual giving amount of $1,189.62 multiplied by the number of consumer units, resulted in a 2019 estimate of total charitable giving of $157.32 billion.

The CE charitable giving series is also available for the 1989-2018 period. As in the 1987-2021 series earlier in this chapter, the CE category of "Gifts to non-CU members of stocks, bonds, and mutual funds" was not available before

Table 39: **Giving to Religion, Based on the Commission on Private Philanthropy and Public Needs (Filer Commission) Benchmark Data for the Year of 1974, and Annual Changes in the Composite Denomination-Based Series, Aggregate Billions of Dollars and Per Capita Dollars as Percent of Disposable Personal Income, 1968-2021**

Denomination-Based Series Keyed to 1974 Filer Estimate		
Year	Billions, Dollars	Per Capita Dollars as % of Disposable Personal Income
1968	$8.04	1.25%
1969	$8.35	1.20%
1970	$8.68	1.14%
1971	$9.14	1.10%
1972	$9.79	1.09%
1973	$10.72	1.06%
1974	$11.70	1.06%
1975	$12.74	1.04%
1976	$13.85	1.04%
1977	$15.00	1.03%
1978	$16.37	1.00%
1979	$18.10	1.00%
1980	$20.04	0.99%
1981	$22.10	0.98%
1982	$23.95	0.98%
1983	$25.60	0.97%
1984	$27.71	0.95%
1985	$29.40	0.95%
1986	$31.11	0.94%
1987	$32.31	0.93%
1988	$33.55	0.89%
1989	$35.34	0.87%
1990	$36.81	0.85%
1991	$38.21	0.85%
1992	$39.27	0.82%
1993	$40.33	0.81%
1994	$43.25	0.82%
1995	$44.05	0.79%
1996	$47.55	0.81%
1997	$49.23	0.80%
1998	$52.11	0.79%
1999	$54.81	0.79%
2000	$59.00	0.80%
2001	$61.48	0.79%
2002	$63.47	0.78%
2003	$64.14	0.76%
2004	$66.45	0.74%
2005	$68.81	0.73%
2006	$71.64	0.71%
2007	$74.49	0.71%
2008	$74.30	0.68%
2009	$73.06	0.67%
2010	$70.29	0.62%
2011	$70.50	0.59%
2012	$69.45	0.56%
2013	$67.83	0.54%
2014	$67.21	0.51%
2015	$68.38	0.50%
2016	$68.07	0.48%
2017	$69.40	0.47%
2018	$69.77	0.45%
2019	$69.48	*0.42%*
2020	$67.50	*0.38%*
2021	$69.22	0.37%

Source: empty tomb analysis; Commission on Private Philanthropy and Public Needs; *YACC* adjusted series; U.S. BEA empty tomb, inc., 2024

Table 40: Living Individual Charitable Giving in the United States, Consumer Expenditure Survey, Not Including "Gifts of stocks bonds, and mutual funds," 2019

Item	Average Annual Expenditure: All Consumer Units	Average Annual Expenditures Multiplied by 132,242,000 Consumer Units Aggregated 000's of $	Item as Percent of Total
"Cash contributions to charities and other organizations"	$289.60	$38,297,283,200	24.9%
"Cash contributions to church, religious organizations"	$804.70	$106,415,137,400	69.3%
"Cash contributions to education institutions"	$67.21	$8,887,984,820	5.8%
Total	$1,161.51	$153,600,405,420	100.0%

Details in table may not compute to numbers shown due to rounding. empty tomb, inc., 2024
Source: empty tomb analysis of U.S. BLS CE, 2019

the year 2002. Also, both the Form 990 series and the *Giving USA* series were adjusted to remove noncash donations; that category includes gifts of stocks, bonds and mutual funds. Therefore, the CE series for 1989-2019 used in Table 43 below does not include the category of "Gifts to non-CU members of stocks, bonds, and mutual funds." When the 2019 CE figure was adjusted to exclude "Gifts to non-CU members of stocks, bonds, and mutual funds," the per capita gift amount decreased to $1,161.51, and the aggregate amount was $153.60 billion, the amounts used in the following comparison.

Table 40 presents CE data for the year 2019, excluding gifts of stocks, bonds, and mutual funds, in both "consumer unit" and aggregate values.[26]

Form 990 Series. A second source of information about charitable giving is found in the U.S. Internal Revenue Service Form 990 series. The Form 990 series must be filled out by tax exempt organizations, including political organizations and hospitals, with at least $50,000 in income, and by foundations. Form 990 data was obtained for the years 1989-2019, the latest year listed on the IRS Web site.[27]

The IRS changed the Form 990 category labels in 2008. Table 41 presents Form 990 data for the year 2019. The category of "All other contributions, gifts, etc." introduced in 2008 appears to be the equivalent of the previously used category of "Direct Public Support." As of the 2008 data, the categories of "Federated campaigns, "Fundraising events," and "Related organizations" appear to fall within the previous "Indirect Public Support" category that included receipts from parent charitable organizations or groups like the United Way. A third category introduced in the 2007 Form 990, support from Donor-Advised Funds, was not cited separately beginning in 2008. The sources of support detailed on the 2019 Form 990 totaled $324 billion. Organizations with at least $50,000 but less than $200,000 in gross receipts were able to use Form 990-EZ to report receipts of $4.9 billion in 2019 for a Form 990 and Form 990-EZ contributions total of $329 billion.

A figure of $43.26 billion was added to the Public Support figure to account for giving in 2019 to private foundations. Private foundations are required to file the IRS Form 990-PF. An adjusted total for giving to foundations was published in *Giving USA 2023*.[28]

Based on the Form 990 series data, the combined total of $372.4 billion is the amount that tax exempt organizations received in 2019.

Form 990 could, but does not, request data for cash contributions by living individuals. One recommendation to improve the usefulness of information in the Form 990 is that charitable organizations be required to report cash contributions from living individuals on a separate line of the form.

In order to compare the Form 990 series data with the CE data for cash contributions from living individuals for a 1989 to 2019 series, the Form 990 series information was adjusted. To obtain a figure for contributions from living individuals, estimates for giving by corporations and foundations, and receipts from bequests, were subtracted from the "Gifts to charities and foundations" figure in Table 41. Giving by Living Individuals was thus estimated to be $236.3 billion in 2019.

Table 41: Living Individual Charitable Giving in the United States, Form 990 Series, 2019

	000's of $
Form 990	
Federated campaigns	$1,913,023
Fundraising events	$9,220,752
Related Organizations	$30,123,507
All other contributions, gifts, etc.	+ $283,021,299
Subtotal from Form 990	$324,278,581
Form 990-EZ contributions, gifts, and grants	+ $4,860,632
Form 990 and 990-EZ contributions	$329,139,213
Gifts to foundations	+ $43,260,000
Gifts to charities and foundations	$372,399,213
Less gifts from other than Living Individuals	
Giving by Corporations	- $24,030,000
Giving by Foundations	- $74,000,000
Giving by Bequests	- $38,030,000
Giving by Living Individuals	$236,339,213
Less Individual "Other than cash contributions"	- $74,799,416
Living Individuals Giving in cash, not including giving to church	$161,539,797
Church: Individual Giving to church, adjusted for religious organizations included in Form 990	+ $95,773,624
Total Cash Giving by Living Donors	$257,313,421

Details in table may not compute to numbers shown due to rounding.
Source: empty tomb analysis of IRS Form 990 series data, 2019; U.S. BLS CE 2019; *Giving USA 2023*

empty tomb, inc., 2024

The Form 990 data also includes "Other than cash contributions." Therefore, the value of "Other than cash contributions" was subtracted from the Form 990 data to allow a comparison of charitable cash contributions. As shown in Table 41, the IRS estimated that Americans deducted $74.8 billion in "Other than cash contributions" in 2019.[29] This amount was subtracted from the Giving by Living Individuals figure, resulting in a subtotal of $161.5 billion in 2019.

To develop an estimate of Form 990 organizational receipts that could be compared with the CE figure of what people gave required one additional step. Churches are not required to file Form 990. The CE estimate, however, included a measure for charitable contributions to churches and religious organizations. The following procedure was followed to develop an estimate for church giving to be added to the Form 990 Living Individuals contributions figure. The CE figure for 2019 "Cash contributions to church, religious organizations" was $106.4 billion. The present analysis employs a working estimate that giving to church represents about 90% of giving to religion, based in part on the work of two publications in this area.[30] Charitable organizations that combine religion with international or human services activities would be expected to file Form 990, and therefore these figures would already be included in the 2019 Form 990 Living Individual figure of $236.3 billion. Subtracting 10% from the 2019 CE figure for "church, religious organizations" of $106.4 billion resulted in an estimate of $95.8 billion given to churches in 2019. When this "giving to church" estimate was added to the estimated 2019 Form 990 "Living Individual Giving in cash, not including giving to church" figure of $161.5

billion, Total Cash Giving by Living Donors was calculated to be $257.3 billion in 2019 based on the Form 990 series information.

Table 41 presents the procedure and results in tabular form for 2019. A similar procedure was followed to calculate the Form 990 series figures for 1989-2018[31] to compare with the CE series for those years.

Giving USA ***Series.*** A third source of charitable giving information, which is the most widely reported in the popular media, is from *Giving USA*, a series begun in the 1950s as an industry information compilation by a former vice president for public relations of a major professional fundraising firm.[32] The series has continued, and is currently prepared by a university-based program for the study of philanthropy, with active oversight by professional fundraisers.

The Methodology section in *Giving USA 2021* details efforts to improve the process of estimating the figures reported as national giving levels, particularly in light of changes in Federal tax procedures that went into effect in 2018.[33]

The publication has an Advisory Council on Methodology, made up of fundraising group representatives, as well as academics and end-user representatives. The involvement of the fundraising industry in the report series that is designed to measure the effectiveness of fundraising in the U.S. is reflected in the Editorial Review Board. Of the 22 individuals serving on the *Giving USA 2023* Editorial Review Board, 22 were principals or representatives of 20 fundraising firms, with these 20 included in the 68 entities that make up the Giving USA Institute Member Organizations.[34]

The strong presence of the fundraising industry on the Editorial Review Board suggests that *Giving USA* is a self-report of an industry dependent on a positive perception among the public that hires and supports the industry. Such an industry report, of course, is a perfectly legitimate activity. The question that may be raised, however, whether the numbers offered by an industry self-report should be cited uncritically as the most authoritative source of philanthropy information in the U.S., as *Giving USA* generally is. This topic is considered further in the section below titled, "Associated Press and Other Media Reports on Philanthropy."

In the present analysis, in order to compare a *Giving USA* estimate for individual giving with the CE data for the 1989-2019 period, the category of "Other than cash contributions" was subtracted from the *Giving USA* numbers. For the 2019 data, for example, the IRS $74.8 billion figure for "Other than cash contributions" that was subtracted from the Form 990 series data in the analysis above also was subtracted from the *Giving USA* figure. The *Giving USA* estimate for individual giving in 2019 was $300.9 billion. When the $74.8 billion figure for "Other than cash contributions" was subtracted from that number, the result was a Total Individual Cash Giving figure of $226.14 billion.

Table 42: Living Individual Charitable Cash Giving in the United States, *Giving USA*, 2019

Data Year 2019	000's of $
Giving by Individuals	$300,940,000
Less Individual "Other than cash contributions"	- $74,799,416
Total Individual Cash Giving	$226,140,584

Details in table may not compute to numbers shown due to rounding. empty tomb, inc., 2024
Source: empty tomb analysis of *Giving USA 2023*

Table 42 presents the development of the *Giving USA* figure for 2019 to be used in a comparison with the CE and Form 990 series data. A similar procedure was used to calculate comparable *Giving USA* figures for 1989 through 2018.

A Comparison of Three Charitable Giving Estimates, 1989-2019. As can be observed in Table 43, two of the sources of information on Total Charitable Giving in the U.S. differed from the CE by up to $104 billion in 2019 (CE and Form 990). The differences between the CE series and the Form 990 expanded over time. In 1989, the Form 990 adjusted aggregated total exceeded the CE total by 17%. In 2019, the Form 990 adjusted total exceeded the CE figure by 68%. The CE measurement for Total Individual Contributions in 2019 was calculated to be $153.6 billion dollars. Data from the Form 990 series reports filed by recipient organizations, with an estimate of giving to religion added and other-than-cash contributions subtracted, resulted in a calculation of $257.3 billion donated by living individuals in 2019. A line on the Form 990 requesting the amount of donations from living individuals might provide a number more readily available for comparison. Meanwhile, a *Giving USA* number for financial giving by living individuals in 2019, with other-than-cash contributions subtracted, was $226.1 billion, exceeding the benchmark CE figure by 47 percent.

Table 43: Living Individual Charitable Cash Giving in the Untied States, A Comparison of the Consumer Expenditure Survey, Form 990 Series, and *Giving USA*, 1989-2019

Year	U.S. BLS CE Survey (Calculated) millions of $	Form 990 Series (Adjusted) millions of $	*Giving USA* (Adjusted) millions of $
1989	$42,631	$49,875	$71,899
1990	$40,052	$52,558	$71,506
1991	$47,601	$55,614	$72,248
1992	$48,721	$56,842	$77,567
1993	$46,695	$57,680	$79,441
1994	$48,593	$56,032	$77,541
1995	$52,239	$77,101	$81,258
1996	$51,674	$75,578	$86,051
1997	$53,747	$70,895	$95,709
1998	$57,864	$89,257	$108,424
1999	$69,861	$92,333	$116,343
2000	$66,217	$85,463	$126,834
2001	$75,330	$103,946	$135,062
2002	$81,652	$101,287	$139,497
2003	$88,159	$116,523	$143,429
2004	$89,384	$120,709	$158,587
2005	$110,846	$142,889	$172,763
2006	$125,659	$171,845	$172,129
2007	$121,589	$175,752	$174,303
2008	$115,803	$170,698	$173,339
2009	$116,414	$187,306	$168,964
2010	$103,716	$159,101	$163,668
2011	$108,864	$172,693	$170,270
2012	$125,250	$198,427	$195,333
2013	$120,442	*$209,574*	$190,839
2014	$122,607	*$205,495*	$186,920
2015	$132,657	*$205,807*	$193,820
2016	$156,144	*$213,722*	$199,811
2017	$139,916	*$239,278*	*$214,728*
2018	$140,858	*$228,255*	*$219,299*
2019	$153,600	$257,313	$226,141

Source: empty tomb analysis; See Appendix B-6 — empty tomb, inc., 2024

The CE is a detailed U.S. BLS survey carried out on a quarterly basis, reflecting Americans' reports of their gifts to four categories: "charities and other organizations"; "church, religious organizations"; "educational institutions"; and "Gifts to non-CU members of stocks, bonds, and mutual funds."

The Form 990 series reports are completed by Federally tax-exempt organizations, including political organizations and nonprofit hospitals, and foundations, based on their accounting records. Because the Form 990 does not presently ask for cash contributions from living individuals, only a calculated estimate for cash contributions by living individuals can be developed. If for any reason the estimates for giving by corporations, foundations, or bequests — the categories that are used to calculate a "Form 990 cash donations from living individuals" figure — are not sound, that degree of error will impact the calculation. Historically, this has been a problem as evidenced in a 2007 *Akron Beacon Journal* article with the lead sentence: "Warning: Analyzing trends in corporate philanthropy is far from a perfect science." Citing The Foundation Center, the Committee Encouraging Corporate Philanthropy (CECP), and *Giving*

USA, the article noted corporate philanthropy in 2006 either increased 2.7% or 4.7%, or decreased 7.6%.[35]

This variation was still evident as of 2018. A January 2020 column on Forbes.com cited CECP survey figures that indicated corporate philanthropy had increased 11% from 2016 to 2018, reaching $25.7 billion in 2018.[36] Meanwhile, *Giving USA 2020* numbers indicated a 7% decline in corporate philanthropy from 2016 to 2018, with the 2018 total being $18.6 billion.[37]

The Methodology section in *Giving USA 2021* provides details of the attention given by the Lilly School of Philanthropy staff to improving philanthropy estimates in light of the Tax Cuts and Jobs Act passed by Congress that took effect in 2018. For example, the increase in the standard deduction decreased the number of itemizers. Itemized charitable giving by individuals was a key component of the model that developed the individual giving estimates through data year 2017. It was expected the increase in the standard deduction could have an impact on that category.[38]

It is not yet clear whether a decrease in itemizers on tax returns will help mitigate certain factors associated with using itemizer data in giving estimate models.

The valuation of noncash gifts to charity is a problem of long-standing.

For example, one factor in using Individual Income Tax Returns is that "75 percent of small businesses are organized in such a way that they pay personal income taxes on all business income."[39] That fact may have implications for what is, in fact, being measured by "individual" donations.

Another factor is the reliability of the reports. For example, in an IRS Oversight Board survey series, the percent of the population that admitted to thinking that tax cheating "A little here and there or As much as possible" was acceptable varied from 14% of the population in 2011 to 11% in 2014.[40]

A 2013 study by the U.S. Treasury Inspector General for Tax Administration report found that Americans overestimated the value of noncash gifts to charity by $3.8 billion in 2010. As a consequence, tax filers received $1.1 billion in undeserved tax refunds, according to the report.[41]

The valuation of noncash gifts to charity is a problem of long-standing. A discussion of issues with noncash contributions estimates was presented in some detail in a previous edition in *The State of Church Giving* series.[42] When he was Internal Revenue Service Commissioner, Mark W. Everson, in written testimony submitted to a Congressional hearing, in a section titled "Over-stated Deductions" wrote that, "A common problem occurs when a taxpayer takes an improper or overstated charitable contribution deduction. This happens most frequently when the donation is of something other than cash or readily marketable securities."[43] In a *Chronicle of Philanthropy* article, Mr. Everson was quoted as suggesting that noncash deductions may be overstated by as much as $15 to $18 billion a year.[44]

In an annual "Dirty Dozen" of Tax Scams for 2019, the IRS warned: "Taxpayers should watch for areas frequently targeted by unscrupulous tax preparers [including] overstating deductions such as charitable contributions ... Some taxpayers who prepare their own returns, as well as those who use unscrupulous preparers, may also pad their deductions and credits to inflate their refund or lower their tax bill."[45]

Again, it seems that these issues have been around for some time. Scott Burns, then business writer for *The Dallas Morning News* and Universal Press Syndicate columnist, considered the topic of "over-statement" of deductions in a 2006 column. A reader wrote in to say that a consultant had told the reader how he "can claim up to 10 percent of the total income as a write-off without proof or receipts." Pleased to be getting money back from the IRS, instead of paying taxes, he went on, "Our total income for 2005 was $101,083. My consultant has entered $9,224 for charities, $12,253 for job expenses and certain miscellaneous deductions, and $3,825 for meals and entertainment. I can tell you, those figures are exaggerated. But is it legal?"

Scott Burns began his reply with the comment, "Excuse me if I sound like a close relative of Goody Two Shoes, but do you really want to be a lying freeloader just because others are?" Burns also noted that, "The IRS has estimated unpaid taxes exceed $290 billion a year. The Treasury inspector general for tax administration thinks the IRS is low-balling the number." Burns advised the man to keep good records and deduct appropriately.[46]

These items illustrate some of the difficulties in estimating charitable giving from tax returns. Efforts to take all these factors into account and modify current models are laudable.

It may also be noted that the consistent methodology in the Consumer Expenditure Survey offers an information source that may circumvent factors that impact other sources.

The results of this comparison of three estimates of individual giving highlight differences that should be acknowledged in any discussion of philanthropy in the U.S., and suggest that the area of philanthropy measurement needs quality attention.

The results of this comparison of three estimates of individual giving highlight differences that should be acknowledged in any discussion of philanthropy in the U.S., and suggest that the area of philanthropy measurement needs quality attention.

Recommendations for Improving the Measurements. Past editions in *The State of Church Giving* series have presented recommendations for improving the measurement of philanthropy in the United States.[47]

Faith-based or Secular Governance Choice. An important refinement would provide a more complete picture of philanthropy in America. Before selecting one of the ten core definition categories, the nonprofit organization could first indicate its form of governance as either "faith-based" or "secular." This identification could provide valuable information to help clarify the role of religion in the area of giving. Form 990 could also require that the organization define itself, first by selecting either faith-based or secular as the category of governance, and then the specific activity described by one or more of the National Taxonomy of Exempt Organizations core codes.

The importance of being able to classify giving by both faith-based or secular categories, as well as by specific activity codes can be seen from an observation in *Giving USA 1990*'s discussion of "Giving to Religion." That issue of *Giving USA*, edited by Nathan Weber, noted, "Further, among many religious groups, giving to religion is considered identical with giving to human services, health care, etc., when such services are administered by organizations founded by the religious groups" (p. 187). An analysis of the CE data for 2021 found that donors identified 56% of their charitable donations as given to churches and religious organizations, a figure consistent with CE results from past surveys.

It is of interest that a 2013 survey found that, "73% of American giving goes to organizations that are explicitly religious ..."[48] Those figures compare to 40% for 2021 giving to religion as a percent of individual giving, using *Giving USA 2023* data.[49] The extent of this variation suggests that the definitions of what constitutes a religious organization differ broadly among the charitable giving estimate sources.

Further, the challenge to understand the role that faith-based giving fills in philanthropy activity was cited in *Giving USA 2022*. A paragraph in the "Giving to Religion" section reads: "If *Giving USA* were to include giving to all houses of worship and all religiously-oriented charities, up to 75 percent of all charitable giving could be considered religious in nature."[50]

In their book on the Unified Chart of Accounts, Russy D. Sumariwalla and Wilson C. Levis reproduced a graphic originally prepared by United Way of America that depicts how the account classification would appear in practical application.[51] For purposes of the present discussion, that graphic was adapted to include a statement about receipts classification, and to describe at what point the choice of faith-based or secular governance would be included in the accounting hierarchy (see Figure 19).

Form 990 Living Donor Category. With some adjustments, the Form 990 information could also provide a sound basis on which to answer the question of how much Americans give. The Form 990 would be improved by obtaining a measure of giving by living donors. As can be seen in Table 41, currently a variety of adjustments need to be made in order to obtain a working estimate of this number.

Figure 19: Account Classification Application with Faith-based/ Secular Governance Option Included

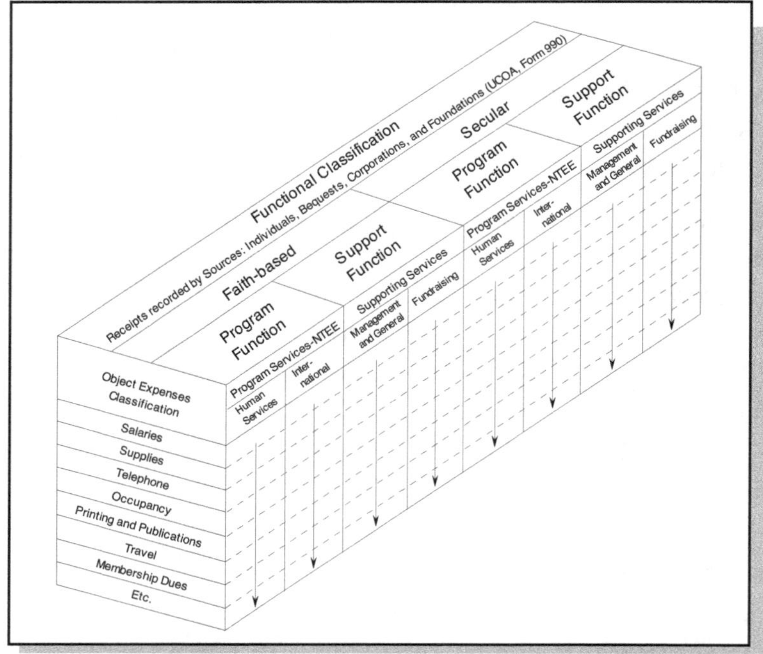

Source: Adaption of Graphic in Sumarwalla and Levis — empty tomb, inc. graphic 2001

Consumer Expenditure Survey as a Benchmark. Presently, the CE data has become an important source of information on the giving patterns of Americans. The CE, by presenting Americans' reports of cash contributions to four categories, avoids the problems inherent in using tax records, including cash and noncash deductions, and the types of organizations being considered. It is recommended that the U.S.

Department of Labor, Bureau of Labor Statistics, Consumer Expenditure Survey be utilized as the unbiased, broad-gauge benchmark of living Americans' aggregate cash giving to charity, until such time as the U.S. Internal Revenue Service makes summary Form 990 living individual giving data available on an annual basis.

Associated Press and Other Media Reports on Philanthropy. The power of the press in influencing the opinions of Americans was noted as a factor in a discussion of the "illusion of potential" in a 2010 book, *The Invisible Gorilla, And Other Ways Our Intuitions Deceive Us*. The authors, Christopher Chabris and Daniel Simons, state that the "*illusion of potential* leads us to think that vast reservoirs of untapped mental ability exists in our brains, just waiting to be accessed."[52] They give two examples of myths initially reported by the media that became quickly accepted by the general public enamored with the illusion of potential, observing: "The media gives tremendous weight and coverage to the *first* study published on a research question, and essentially ignores all of those that come later"[53] (emphases in original).

Consider that other researchers could not reproduce the initial finding that listening to certain types of music makes one more intelligent, popularly known as the "Mozart Effect." Media reported the initial research widely, but gave less attention to the follow-up studies that contradicted the initial findings. Chabris and Simons note, "Until we each had our first child, we didn't realize the extent to which the Mozart-for-babies myth has permeated the child-care industry. Intelligent, highly educated friends sent us toys that included—as a matter of routine, not a special feature—a 'Mozart' setting that played classical music."[54]

These examples indicate that the media's presentation of information to the public can have an important role in how the public views an issue.

Chabris and Simons also regard as a myth subliminal messages on movie screens impacting concessions purchases. They use as an example an "experiment" in the 1950s. The researcher reported that flashing subliminal messages in a movie theater increased popcorn and soft drink sales, helping to establish in the public's mind the idea of subliminal marketing. However, years later the "researcher" confessed that the "research" was fabricated as a way to increase business for his advertising firm. Yet a survey by Chabris and Simons found that 76 percent of respondents believed in subliminal marketing.[55]

In his book, *Thinking, Fast and Slow*, Nobel Prize winner Daniel Kahneman described the work of Cass Sunstein and Timur Kuran regarding what they term the "availability cascade." Kahneman offers the following description: "An availability cascade is a self-sustaining chain of events, which may start from media reports of a relatively minor event and lead up to public panic and large-scale government action." As media begin reporting on the public's emotional reaction, which now is a story in and of itself, "Scientists and others who try to dampen the increasing fear and revulsion attract little attention, most of it hostile ..."[56]

These examples indicate that the media's presentation of information to the public can have an important role in how the public views an issue. The examples also demonstrate the media's initial treatment of a topic may define that topic for the public, independent of relevant facts.

Media Reports and Basketball. In 2024, University of Iowa basketball senior guard Caitlin Clark was given much deserved attention in the media for the number of career points she scored. Clark eclipsed Pete Maravich's long-standing record for career points scored which he set in 1970 while attending Louisiana State University. However, an Associated Press writer, Brett Martel, raised the question of how Clark's record actually compares with Maravich's.

Martel points out, for example, that during 1967 to 1970, when Maravich was playing basketball, there was no shot clock, and no three-point line. In four games, Maravich scored more than 60 points, including 69 points on Feb. 7, 1970. Pete Maravich set his record of 3,667 in 88 games over three seasons.[57] Caitlin Clark broke Pete Maravich's record by scoring 3,685 points in 130 games. Gracious in success, Clark was quoted as saying, "Just to be in the same realm of all these players who have been so successful ... Hopefully somebody comes after me and breaks my records and I can be there supporting them."[58]

There is no doubt that what Caitlin Clark accomplished put her in the top echelons of college basketball. The broader set of circumstances of her feat, in comparison to Pete Maravich's record, does not lessen her achievement. The analysis provided in Martel's article does, however, give the reader a larger context in which to place her record.

> The impact of Associated Press (AP) news reports not only may be giving members of the public an inaccurate perception, but also be defining the standard for other media reporting on the topic.

Media Reports and Philanthropy. The discussion in this chapter considers whether the American public is being given an accurate understanding of charitable giving patterns through media reports. The impact of Associated Press (AP) news reports not only may be giving members of the public an inaccurate perception, but also be defining the standard for other media reporting on the topic.

The following analysis considers media reporting of the annual findings of the *Giving USA* series described above. The question being explored on the following pages is why annual media reports have generally focused on the estimates for aggregate amounts raised, in keeping with the *Giving USA* press releases, rather than serving the American public by putting the annual numbers in the context of changes of population and income.

A review of reporting on each edition of the annual *Giving USA* edition from 2002 through 2011, and again in 2014 through 2023, found the AP in all but two instances led its article with information about gross aggregate Total Giving. At least two issues are raised by the AP reporting of this number.

First, the aggregate *Giving USA* Total Giving figure to recipient organizations includes giving by four sources: individuals, the largest sector; corporate donations; bequests from dead people; and gifts from foundations. A problem with developing an estimate of Total Giving that includes both gifts from individuals to family foundations, and gifts from foundations to other entities, was articulated in *The Chronicle of Philanthropy*. The publication explained, in a description of how its own annual list of "America's most generous donors" was compiled: "Gifts that donors made from their family foundations were not counted to avoid including them twice: when the donor gave the money to the foundation and when he or she chose a beneficiary for the money."[59]

Second, significantly, AP reported the aggregate Total Giving figure, and did not take into account changes in either population or income from the previous year.

Rarely does the media provide numbers to the public without placing those numbers in a larger context of population and/or the economy. Consider that the press routinely reports the crime rate, the unemployment rate, the savings rate, the poverty rate, the on-time flight rate, the unpaid mortgage rate, and the Consumer Confidence Index. In each case, numbers are not reported as aggregates, but rather are put into context of the larger population so that the reader has some basis to evaluate the meaning.

Researchers considering the status of religion in the world offered another example of the importance of changes in population:

> An interesting overall comment is that virtually all activities of Christian churches, missions, denominations, and communions are growing numerically and expanding. This is usually interpreted as showing the success of church programs. In fact, however, everybody's programs are all expanding fast because since AD 1800 populations everywhere have been expanding rapidly and now stand at 372,000 births a day.
>
> In fact, the key to understanding religious trends is the ability to compare growth rates of religious variables with secular ones. This is the only way to know if a religion is growing faster or slower than the general population.[60]

Rarely does the media provide numbers to the public without placing those numbers in a larger context of population and/or the economy.

Good reporting seems to include the responsibility of placing numbers in the larger context so the reader will understand the importance of the figures being quoted.

Yet, when informing the public about charitable giving, the media has emphasized aggregate numbers that are independent of changes in either population or the economy.

For example, as noted in Tables 44 and 45, in the 22 report years under review, 2001 through 2022, the media presented data that averaged an increase of 2.3% annually in aggregate Total Giving.

When the Total Giving data for those same years was considered as a percent of Gross Domestic Product (GDP), the numbers actually averaged a decrease, measuring -1.3% a year. And individual giving, the largest component in charitable giving, when considered as a percent of Disposable (after-tax) Personal Income (DPI), measured an average of –1.4% for those 22 years.

A review of twenty AP articles, and two from other media, for 2002 through 2023, found that in 20 of 22 reports, the media led with the change in aggregate Total Giving, and one of the 22 reports with Individual Giving, from the previous year. When standard adjustments for population and the economy were applied to the giving numbers, the results were quite different than the media leads.

Consider 11 reports for data years 2001, 2002, 2003, 2004, 2005, 2006, 2010, 2012, 2016, 2020, and 2021. In each, the AP article led with a percent change that indicated an increase in aggregate Total Giving from the previous year. In contrast,

Table 44: Associated Press, 2002-2011 and 2014-23, and Other Media, 2012-2013, Reported Giving Changes; Calculated Changes from Previous Year's Base, Adjusted for U.S. Population and Economy, Using *Giving USA* 2002-2023 Editions' Individual and Total Giving Data, 2001-2022

Giving USA Edition	*Giving USA* Data Year Interval	Media: First Percent Change from Previous Year Listed in Media Story[63]	Per Capita Individual Giving as % of Per Capita DPI: % Change from Base Year[64]	Total Giving as % of GDP: % Change from Base Year[65]	Headline and First Mention of Giving Percent Change	Byline and Dateline
2002	2000-01	0.5%	-2.6%	-2.8%	"2001 Charitable Giving Same As 2000" "Total giving by individuals, corporations and other groups amounted to $212 billion, up 0.5 percent from 2000 before inflation is figured in…"	Helena Payne, Associated Press Writer, New York
2003	2001-02	1%	-4.7%	-2.5%	"Donations Held Steady in 2002" "Giving rose 1 percent last year to $240.92 billion from $238.46 billion in 2001…"	Mark Jewell, The Associated Press, Indianapolis
2004	2002-03	2.8%	-2.0%	-1.9%	"Charitable Giving Rises in 2003" "…the survey showed a 2.8 percent increase over 2002, when giving amounted to $234.1 billion"	Kendra Locke, The Associated Press, New York
2005	2003-04	5%	-1.6%	-1.6%	"Charitable Giving Among Americans Rises" "Americans increased donations to charity by 5 percent in 2004…"	Adam Geller, AP Business Writer, New York
2006	2004-05	6.1%	2.0%	-0.3%	"Charitable Giving in U.S. Nears Record Set at End of Tech Boom" "The report released Monday by the Giving USA foundation estimates that in 2005 Americans gave $260.28 billion, a rise of 6.1 percent…"	Vinnee Tong, AP Business Writer, New York
2007	2005-06	1%	-0.9%	-2.0%	"Americans Give Nearly $300 Billion to Charities in 2006, Set a New Record" "Donors contributed an estimated $295.02 billion in 2006, a 1 percent increase when adjusted for inflation, up from $283.05 billion in 2005."	Vinnee Tong, AP Business Writer, New York
2008	2006-07	"remained at…"	-2.8%	-1.0%	"Americans Are Steady in Donations to Charity" "Donations by Americans to charities remained at 2.2 percent of gross domestic product in 2007 …"	Vinnee Tong, AP Business Writer, New York
2009	2007-08	-2%	-7.0%	-5.2%	"Amid Meltdown, Charitable Gifts in US Fell in 2008" "Charitable giving by Americans fell by 2 percent in 2008 as the recession took root…"	David Crary, AP National Writer,[AP National Reporting Team: Family and Relationships], New York
2010	2008-09	-3.6%	-1.4%	-2.3%	"2009 Charitable Giving Falls 3.6 Percent in US" "Charitable giving fell by 3.6 percent last year as Americans continued to struggle with the recession…"	Caryn Rousseau, Associated Press Writer, Chicago
2011	2009-10	3.8%	-0.4%	-0.1%	"Charitable Giving in US Rebounds a Bit after Drop" "That represented growth of 3.8 percent in current dollars and 2.1 percent in inflation-adjusted dollars."	David Crary, AP National Writer, New York
2012	2010-11	4%	0.1%	0.1%	"U.S. Charitable Giving Approaches $300 Billion in 2011" "Giving by Americans increased 4 percent in 2011 compared with 2010…"	Michelle Nichols, Reuters, New York

Source: Associated Press; USBEA; *Giving USA*; empty tomb, inc. analysis

empty tomb, inc., 2024

Table 45: *Giving USA* Executive Statement or Foreword; Occasional Related Entity Presentations: First Mention of Percent Change and *Giving USA* Attribution from *Giving USA* 2002-2023 Editions

Giving USA Executive Statement, Foreword, or Section Presentation; Occasional Related Entity Presentation: First Mention of Total Giving Percent Change from Previous Year	*Giving USA* Attribution; Occasional Related Entity Attribution
"The 0.5 percent increase in giving for 2001 is more attributable to the economy than to crisis."	(Indianapolis, Ind.: AAFRC Trust for Philanthropy, 2002), p. 1 Executive Statements: Statement of Chair, AAFRC Trust for Philanthropy: Leo P. Arnoult, CFRE, Chair, AAFRC Trust for Philanthropy
"Giving in 2002 is estimated to be $240.92 billion, growing one percent over the new estimate for 2001 of $238.46 billion."	(Indianapolis, Ind.: AAFRC Trust for Philanthropy, 2003), p. ii Foreword: Leo P. Arnoult, CFRE, Chair, AAFRC Trust for Philanthropy John J. Glier, Chair, AAFRC Eugene R. Tempel, Ed.D., CFRE, Executive Director, The Center on Philanthropy at Indiana University
"Giving in 2003 grew 2.8 percent over the revised estimate for 2002 of $234.09 billion."	(Glenview, Ill.: AAFRC Trust for Philanthropy, 2004), p. ii Foreword: Henry (Hank) Goldstein, CFRE, Chair, Giving USA Foundation John J. Glier, Chair, AAFRC Eugene R. Tempel, Ed.D., CFRE, Executive Director, The Center on Philanthropy at Indiana University
"Giving grew at the highest rate since 2000, 5.0 percent over a revised estimate of $236.73 billion for 2003 (2.3 percent adjusted for inflation)."	(Glenview, Ill.: AAFRC Trust for Philanthropy, 2005), p. ii Foreword: Henry (Hank) Goldstein, CFRE, Chair, Giving USA Foundation™, President, The Oram Group, Inc., New York, New York C. Ray Clements, Chair, American Association of Fundraising Counsel, CEO and Managing Member, Clements Group, Salt Lake City, Utah Eugene R. Tempel, Ed.D., CFRE, Executive Director, The Center on Philanthropy at Indiana University, Indianapolis, Indiana
"The combined result is that charitable giving rose to $260.28 billion, showing growth of 6.1 percent (2.7 percent adjusted for inflation)."	(Glenview, Ill.: Giving USA Foundation, 2006), p. ii Foreword: Richard T. Jolly, Chair, Giving USA Foundation™, George C. Ruotolo, Jr., CFRE, Acting Chair, Giving Institute: Leading Consultants to Non-Profits Eugene R. Tempel, Ed.D., CFRE, Executive Director, The Center on Philanthropy at Indiana University
"In constant [*sic*] dollars, the increase was 4.2 percent over 2005; in inflation-adjusted numbers, the increase was 1.0 percent."	(Glenview, Ill.: Giving USA Foundation, 2007), p. ii Foreword: Richard T. Jolly, Chair, Giving USA Foundation™, George C. Ruotolo, Jr., CFRE, Chair, Giving Institute: Leading Consultants to Non-Profits Eugene R. Tempel, Ed.D., CFRE, Executive Director, The Center on Philanthropy at Indiana University
"The estimates for 2007 indicate that giving rose by 3.9 percent over the previous year (1 percent adjusted for inflation), to reach a record $306.39 billion."	(Glenview, Ill.: Giving USA Foundation, 2008), p. ii Foreword: Del Martin, CFRE, Chair, Giving USA Foundation™, George C. Ruotolo, Jr., CFRE, Chair, Giving Institute: Leading Consultants to Non-Profits Eugene R. Tempel, Ed.D., CFRE, Executive Director, The Center on Philanthropy at Indiana University
"This is a drop of 2 percent in current dollars (-5.7 percent adjusted for inflation), compared to 2007."	(Glenview, Ill.: Giving USA Foundation, 2009), p. ii Foreword: Del Martin, CFRE, Chair, Giving USA Foundation™, publisher of Giving USA Nancy L. Raybin, Chair, Giving Institute: Leading Consultants to Non-Profits Patrick M. Rooney, Ph.D., Executive Director, The Center on Philanthropy at Indiana University
"Total charitable giving fell 3.6 percent (-3.2 percent adjusted for inflation) in 2009, to an estimated $303.75 billion."	*Giving USA 2010;* Created: 6/8/10; published by Giving USA Foundation, Glenview, Ill.; <www.givingusa2010.org/downloads.php>; p. ii of 6/9/2010 printout. Foreword: Edith H. Falk, Chair, Giving USA Foundation Nancy L. Raybin, Chair, Giving Institute: Leading Consultants to Non-Profits Patrick M. Rooney, Ph.D., Executive Director, The Center on Philanthropy at Indiana University
"It is promising to see the 2010 inflation-adjusted increase of 2.1 percent after two years of such steep declines."	*Giving USA 2011*; Created: 6/20/11; published by Giving USA Foundation, Chicago, Ill.; <www.givingusareports.org/downloads.php>; p. i of 6/20/2011 printout. Foreword: Edith H. Falk, Chair, Giving USA Foundation Thomas W. Mesaros, CFRE, Chair, Giving Institute: Leading Consultants to Non-Profits Patrick M. Rooney, Ph.D., Executive Director, The Center on Philanthropy at Indiana University
"Total giving grew 4.0 percent in 2011."	*Giving USA 2012;* Created: 6/18/12; published by Giving USA Foundation, Chicago, Ill.; accessed via <storegivingusareports.org/Default.aspx>; p. 1 of 6/27/2012 printout. Foreword: James D. Yunker, Ed.D., Chair, Giving USA Foundation Thomas W. Mesaros, CFRE, Chair, Giving Institute Patrick M. Rooney, Ph.D., Executive Director, The Center on Philanthropy at Indiana University

Source: *Giving USA* series; empty tomb, inc. analysis

empty tomb, inc., 2024

Table 44: Associated Press, 2002-2011 and 2014-23, and Other Media, 2012-2013, Reported Giving Changes; Calculated Changes from Previous Year's Base, Adjusted for U.S. Population and Economy, Using *Giving USA* 2002-2023 Editions' Individual and Total Giving Data, 2001-2022 (continued)

Giving USA Edition	*Giving USA* Data Year Interval	Media: First Percent Change from Previous Year Listed in Media Story[63]	Per Capita Individual Giving as % of Per Capita DPI: % Change from Base Year[64]	Total Giving as % of GDP: % Change from Base Year[65]	Headline and First Mention of Giving Percent Change	Byline and Dateline
2013	2011–12	3.5%	0.6%	-0.5%	"Giving USA Report: 2012 Charitable Giving Grew Almost 4%, Corporate Donations Grew 12%" "Overall, U.S. donations to bolster the arts, health, religion and other activities totaled $316.2 billion in 2012, a 3.5 percent increase from the $305.5 billion donated in 2011…"	Susan Heavey, Reuters, Washington
2014	2012-13	3%	2.3%	1.0%	"Giving Increases for Some Sectors, Not for Others" "The Giving USA report, being released Tuesday, said Americans gave an estimated $335.17 billion to charity in 2013, up 3 percent from 2012 after adjustment for inflation."	David Crary, AP National Writer, New York
2015	2013-14	7.1%	1.8%	3.1%	"Charities Emerge from Recession with Record Donations" "Total giving increased by 7.1 percent from 2013 to 2014."	Donna Gordon Blankinship, The Associated Press, Seattle
2016	2014-15	4%	0.1%	0.6%	"US charitable giving rate tops more than $1 billion a day" "The total was up 4 percent from $359 billion in 2014."	David Crary, AP National Writer, New York
2017	2015-16	2.7%	-0.01%	-0.3%	"New report: Charitable giving in US rises slightly in 2016" "That was up 2.7 percent in current dollars (1.4 percent adjusted for inflation) from the estimate of $379.89 billion for 2015."	David Crary, AP National Writer, New York
2018	2016-17	5.2%	2.2%	1.1%	"Charitable giving in US tops $400 billion for first time" "The total was up 5.2 percent in current dollars (3 percent adjusted for inflation) from the estimate of $389.64 billion in 2016."	David Crary, AP National Writer, New York
2019	2017-18	-1.1%	-5.8%	-4.3%	"Charitable giving by individual Americans drops in 2018" "The Giving USA report, released Tuesday, said individual giving fell by 1.1%, from $295 billion in 2017 to $292 billion last year."	David Crary, AP, New York
2020	2018-19	2.4%	0.3%	0.1%	"Donations to fight virus, injustice could sustain charities" "The Giving USA report, released Tuesday, estimates nearly $450 billion was donated to charities in 2019, a 2.4% uptick from the previous year when adjusted for inflation."	Sally Ho, AP, Seattle
2021	2019-20	5.1%	-4.5%	7.6%	"Charitable giving in the U.S. reaches all-time high in 2020" "Faced with greater needs, estates and foundations also opened up their pocketbooks at increased levels — resulting in a 5.1% spike in total giving from the $448 billion recorded for 2019, or a 3.8% jump when adjusted for inflation."	Haleluya Hadero, AP, —
2022	2020-21	4%	-1.2%	-5.5%	" "US charitable giving hit record in 2021 but inflation looms." "The Giving USA report says donations in 2021 were 4% higher than the record-setting $466 billion contributed in 2020.""	Thalia Beaty and Glenn Gamboa, AP —
2023	2021-22	-3.4%	-6.3%	-11.5%	" "Charitable giving in 2022 drops for only the third time in 40 years: Giving USA report" "Total giving fell 3.4% in 2022 to $499.3 billion in current dollars, a drop of 10.5% when adjusted for inflation."	Glenn Gamboa, AP —

Source: Associated Press; USBEA; *Giving USA*; empty tomb, inc. analysis

empty tomb, inc., 2024

Table 45 *Giving USA* Executive Statement or Foreword; Occasional Related Entity Presentations: First Mention of Percent Change and *Giving USA* Attribution from *Giving USA* 2002-2023 Editions (continued)

Giving USA Executive Statement, Foreword, or Section Presentation; Occasional Related Entity Presentation: First Mention of Total Giving Percent Change from Previous Year	*Giving USA* Attribution; Occasional Related Entity Attribution
"Our data reveal that American households and individuals gave 3.9 percent more in 2012 than in 2011."	*Giving USA 2013;* Created: 6/18/13; published by Giving USA Foundation, Chicago, IL; accessed via <storegivingusareports.org>; p. 1 of 6/26/2013 printout. Foreword: L. Gregg Carlson, Chair, Giving USA Foundation David H. King, CFRE, Chair, The Giving Institute Gene Tempel, Ed.D., CFRE, Founding Dean, Indiana University Lilly Family School of Philanthropy
[The 2012 to 2013 percent change not presented.] "Donations in 2013 increased 4.4 percent (in current dollars) from the revised estimate of $320.97 billion for 2012."	*Giving USA 2014;* Created: 6/16/14; published by Giving USA Foundation, Chicago, IL; accessed via <storegivingusareports.org>; p. 1-3 of 6/18/2014 printout. Foreword: L. Gregg Carlson, Chair, Giving USA Foundation, David H. King, CFRE, Chair, The Giving Institute. Gene Tempel, Ed.D., CFRE, Founding Dean, Indiana University Lilly Family School of Philanthropy Indiana University–Purdue University Indianapolis, Lilly Family School of Philanthropy, School of Philanthropy News "Giving USA: Americans Gave $335.17 Billion to Charity in 2013; Total Approaches Pre-Recession Peak"; <http://www.philanthropy.iupui.edu/news/article/giving-usa-2014>; June 17, 2014; p. 1 of 6/24/2014 10:50 AM printout.
"Total estimated 2014 giving: $358.38 billion; a 7.1 percent increase (in current dollars) over the revised 2013 estimate of $334.50 billion"	(Chicago, IL.: Giving USA Foundation, 2015), p. 16 Giving USA Total Estimated 2014 Giving
"Total estimated charitable giving in the United States rose 4.1 percent between 2014 and 2015 (4.0 percent, adjusted for inflation), to $373.25 billion."	(Chicago, IL.: Giving USA Foundation, 2016), p. 22 Giving USA Key Findings
"Although economic and political uncertainty pervaded much of the year, Americans continued to be generous, giving a record $390.05 billion to U.S. charitable organizations, an increase of 2.7 percent over 2015."	(Chicago, IL.: Giving USA Foundation, 2017), p. 15 Foreword: Aggie Sweeney, Chair, Giving USA Foundation™, Jeffrey D. Byrne, Chair, The Giving Institute Amir Pasic, Eugene R. Tempel, Dean, Lilly Family School of Philanthropy, Indiana University
"Giving from individuals, bequests, foundations and corporations to U.S. charities surged to an estimated $410.02 billion, an increase of 5.2 percent over the previous year."	(Chicago, IL.: Giving USA Foundation, 2019), p. 17 Forward: Aggie Sweeney, Chair, Giving USA Foundation, Rachel Hutchisson, Chair, The Giving Institute, Amir Pasic, Eugene R. Tempel, Dean, Lilly Family School of Philanthropy, Indiana University
"Total estimated charitable giving in the United States rose 0.7 percent between 2017 and 2018 (a decline of 1.7 percent, adjusted for inflation), to $427.71 billion in contributions."	(Chicago, IL.: Giving USA Foundation, 2019), p. 25 Giving USA Key Findings
"Total estimated charitable giving in the United States rose 4.2 percent between 2018 and 2019 (2.4 percent, adjusted for inflation), to $449.64 billion in contributions."	(Chicago, IL.: Giving USA Foundation, 2020), p. 26 Giving USA Key Findings
"Total charitable giving grew 5.1 percent, substantial growth in any year and somewhat remarkable in such a tumultuous one."	*Giving USA: The Annual Report on Philanthropy for the Year 2020* (2021). Chicago: Giving USA Foundation, p. 14 Foreword: Laura MacDonald, CFRE, Chair, Giving USA Foundation, Ted Grossnickle, Chair, The Giving Institute Amir Pasic, Eugene R. Tempel, Dean, Lilly Family School of Philanthropy, Indiana University
"Thanks to a strong year for the stock market and GDP, giving increased by 4 percent."	*Giving USA: The Annual Report on Philanthropy for the Year 2021* (2022). Chicago: Giving USA Foundation, p. 13 Foreword: Laura MacDonald, Chair, Giving USA Foundation, Peter Fissinger, Chair, The Giving Institute Amir Pasic, Eugene R. Tempel Dean, Lilly Family School of Philanthropy, Indiana University"
"In 2022, Americans gave $499.33 billion to charity, a 3.4% decline compared to 2021."	*Giving USA: The Annual Report on Philanthropy for the Year 2022* (2023). Chicago: Giving USA Foundation, p. 22 Infographic: Total Estimated 2022 Giving"

Source: *Giving USA* series; empty tomb, inc. analysis

when a basic adjustment for changes in U.S. population and/or economic growth was made to the *Giving USA* aggregate numbers, Total Giving as a percent of U.S. GDP declined in 10 of the 11 years, and Individual giving as a percent of DPI declined in nine.

The 2008 *Giving USA* edition announced a 3.9% increase in aggregate Total Giving from 2006 to 2007. In her third AP report on new *Giving USA* editions, AP Business Writer Vinnee Tong, based in New York, broke with the tradition of reporting the *Giving USA* perspective. The 2008 article led with the announcement that aggregate donations were unchanged from 2006 to 2007 as a percent of GDP. While true at the first decimal, as presented in *Giving USA* table at the back of the 2008 *Giving USA* edition,[61] a calculation of the *Giving USA* Total Giving and GDP numbers in the same table allowed an analysis at the second decimal. That is, Total Giving as a percent of GDP was 2.24% in 2006, and 2.21% in 2007, resulting in a one percent decline from the 2006 base.

For the 2009 and 2010 coverage, the AP articles' focus was on aggregate decrease. In one year, 2010, AP announced a decline a decline of -3.6% from 2008 to 2009. However, when adjusted for GDP, the decline in Total Giving was actually -2.3%. Individual giving adjusted for DPI was -1.4%. Thus, the AP report was more alarmist than the facts merited due to a lack of adjustment for population and economy changes.

Figure 20: Associated Press, 2002-2011 and 2014-2023, and Other Media, 2012-2013, Reported Aggregate Changes; Calculated Changes from Previous Year's Base, Adjusted for U.S. Population and Economy, Using *Giving USA* 2002-2023 Editions' Individual and Total Giving Data, 2001-2022

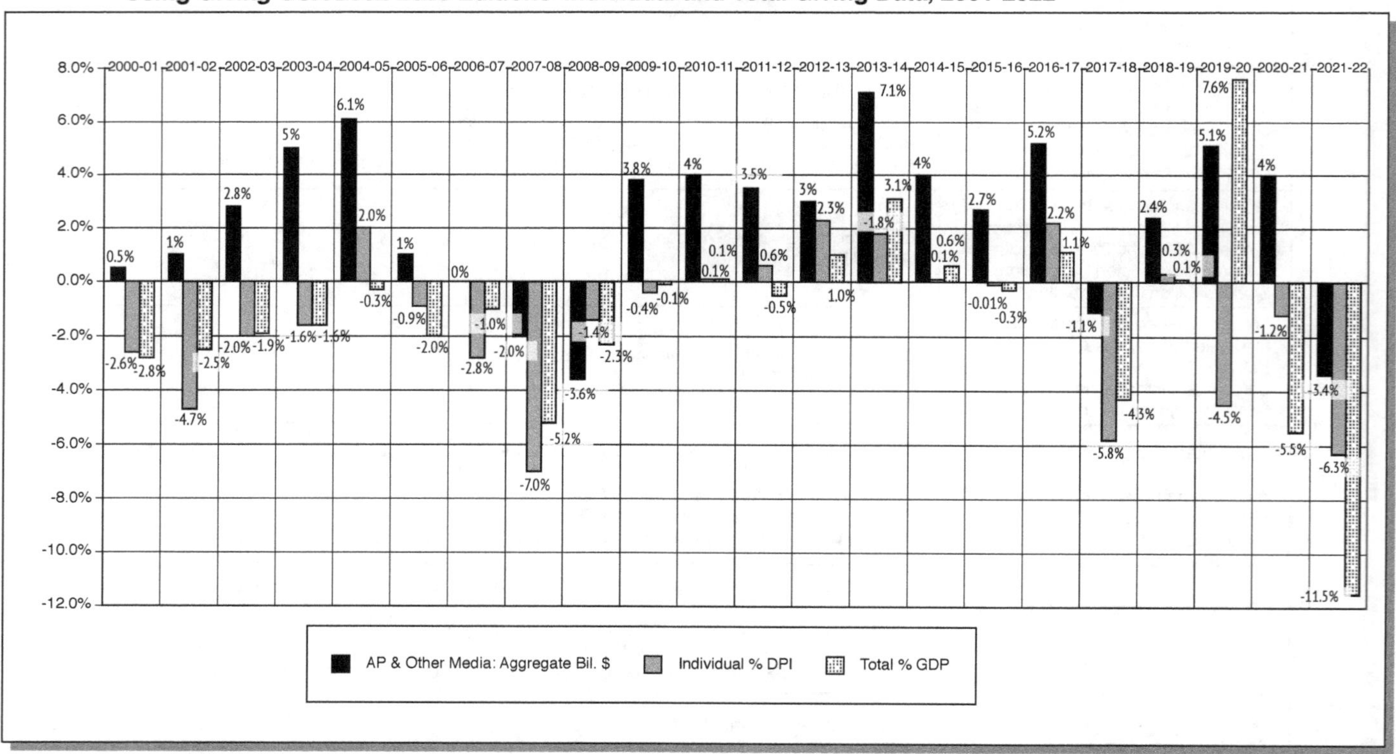

Source: Associated Press; US BEA; *Giving USA;* empty tomb analysis

empty tomb, inc., 2024

An Internet search indicated that AP apparently did not report on the release of *Giving USA 2012* or *Giving USA 2013*. A wire service that did publicize the findings of both editions was Reuters. The wire service's stories emphasized aggregate totals both years. The wire story's title in 2013 was, "Giving USA Report: 2012 Charitable Giving Grew Almost 4%, Corporate Donations Grew 12%." The first mention of the percent change from the previous year again referred to the aggregate total: "Overall, U.S. donations to bolster the arts, health, religion, and other activities totaled $316.2 billion in 2012, a 3.5 percent increase from the $305.5 billion donated in 2011..."[62] In contrast to the headline, when the aggregate total cited in the Reuters story was put in context of the total economy, considered as a percent of GDP, the total decreased from 2011 to 2012 by -0.5%.

This pattern of disparity between media reports on aggregate billions of dollars raised, and the complete picture of changes in charitable giving patterns, can be observed in Table 44, which includes the text from the related AP release. This AP text can be compared with the first mention of percent change mentioned in the related editions in the *Giving USA* series, or an occasional related entity, also presented in Table 45.

The titles and first number reference text in the Reuters articles on the release of *Giving USA 2012* and *2013* are also included in Table 44. For each edition in the *Giving USA* series, the media reporting can be compared to the statement from the *Giving USA* source in Table 45.

Figure 20 illustrates the disparity in the category of percent changes in aggregate total charitable giving reported by AP and Reuters and the cited Total Giving aggregate billions adjusted to a percent of GDP. In addition, the percent change from one year to the next for each *Giving USA* edition's individual giving figure is presented as a portion of DPI.

"You make some interesting points about how we might put these reports into better perspective for our readers."

—Mike Silverman

When correspondence was sent to then-Associated Press Vice President and Senior Managing Editor Mike Silverman, describing this topic, he responded in a May 8, 2008, letter: "You make some interesting points about how we might put these reports into better perspective for our readers." However, AP generally continued to emphasize the percent change in the aggregate Total Giving numbers, unadjusted for the standard categories of population and the economy, in subsequent reports.

A May 11, 2016, letter to Gary Pruitt, President and CEO, and Mary Junck, Board of Directors Chair, of The Associated Press, again pointed out AP's record of reporting aggregate Total Giving, not taking population and changes in the economy into account. The May 11, 2016, letter resulted in a phone call and email from the AP Standards Editor, who indicated the input would be forwarded to the appropriate news editor and writer. The 2016 article led with the change in aggregate Total Giving, but did include some adjustments to the data in the third and fourth paragraphs of the story.

The Associated Press often provides a service with its investigative analysis on topics in the news. For example, in a story about the spread of yellow fever in Africa, and mismanagement by agencies that aggravated the situation, the article authors referred to "internal U.N. emails and documents obtained by The Associated Press."[66]

However, in regard to charitable giving, the news reports generally take a "white-glove gala-event" approach, rather than a hard-news approach. The articles that appear through the Associated Press distribution network are not labeled as "sponsored content," and yet the articles do not bear the marks of hard news reporting, such as evident in the yellow fever investigation. In fact, in contacts with AP writers in 2005 and again in 2016, to discuss the value of placing the aggregate numbers in the context of changes in population and income, the AP writers responded in similar ways. In 2005, the writer said, "We have to report what they tell us." In 2016, the writer responded, "We need to report their numbers ... We're not going to do any calculations on their numbers." Neither writer explained why reporting the statistics had to be limited by the information in the *Giving USA* press release.

As a result of the leads in the annual reporting about charitable giving levels, the American people are currently functioning with a distortion in the lens that is supposed to help them see their world more clearly. The media is generally reporting a more positive level of charitable giving among Americans than is justified, once the numbers are placed in the context of population and economic changes.

... religion plays a vital role in the practice of philanthropy in the United States.

The nonprofit area constitutes a large enough sector of the American economy to merit quality reporting by the media. According to the Independent Sector, the nonprofit sector represented 5.6% of U.S. GDP in 2022.[67] The U.S. Bureau of Labor Statistics stated that in 2022 nonprofit jobs represented 6.5% of the U.S. workforce.[68] The public supporting nonprofits deserves the level of reporting applied to other economic sectors, including adjustment for population and income to provide information about changes in the rate of giving.

Yet reporting about philanthropy in the U.S. does not receive the same serious treatment that other economic categories do by putting the numbers into a context that the public can evaluate.

The American people have a right to know how their charitable giving rates are changing from year to year. As illustrated in earlier chapters in this volume, the measure that validly conveys that information is the category of individual giving as a percent of after-tax income, which adjusts the aggregate numbers for changes in both population and the economy.

Summary

Individuals give to charity for a variety of reasons. When given the opportunity to categorize their own donations in 2021, Americans indicated that 56% of their giving was to "churches, religious organizations." This finding suggests that religion plays a vital role in the practice of philanthropy in the United States.

The comparison of various estimates of giving in the U.S. suggests that the measurement of philanthropy could be improved. Currently, the U.S. Bureau of Labor Statistics Consumer Expenditure Survey serves as a benchmark in providing information about individual charitable giving levels in the United States.

Endnotes for Chapter 7

[1] "The Science of Generosity"; University of Notre Dame; 2020; <https://generosityresearch.nd.edu/>; pp. 2 of 10/8/2020 2:29 PM printout.

[2] U.S. Department of Labor Bureau of Labor Statistics; "Frequently Asked Questions"; n.d.; <http://www.bls.gov/cex/csxfaqs.htm>; p. 2 of 5/28/2005 10:32 AM printout.

[3] The estimate of $197.20 billion is likely a high measure of charitable giving insofar as it includes all of the $10.5 billion in the category, "Gift[s] to non-CU members of stocks, bonds, and mutual funds." This attribution thus assumes that all of the $10.5 billion given in this category went to charitable organizations, although the CE does not allocate the funds of this category between charitable and non-charitable recipients.

[4] Americans' charitable giving was calculated by multiplying the 133.59 million "Number of consumer units" by each of the average annual consumer unit contributions for 2021, the components of which were $500.22 ("charities and other organizations"), $828.56 ("church, religious organizations"), $68.99 ("educational institutions"), and $78.35 ("Gifts to non-CU members of stocks, bonds, and mutual funds"). The resultant sum of the components, $1,476.12, was aggregated to yield a total giving amount of $197.20 billion. The "Cash contributions to church, religious organizations" amount, therefore, was calculated by multiplying the number of consumer units by $828.56, yielding an amount of $110.69 billion for 2021. Religion as a percent of the total was calculated by dividing $110.69 billion by $197.20 billion, yielding 56%. "Cash contributions" items not included in the above calculations for charitable contributions were "Support for college students (Sec. 19); Alimony expenditures (Sec. 19); Child support expenditures (Sec. 19); Cash contribution to political organizations; Other cash gifts." Data source: U.S. Department of Labor, U.S. Bureau of Labor Statistics, "Table 1800. Region of residence: Average annual expenditures and characteristics, Consumer Expenditure Survey, 2021" [Item detail]; StTable1800Region2021.pdf; Created 9/1/2022 11:21 AM; unnumbered pp. 1, 17 & 21 of 4/11/2023 printout.

[5] Data sources: U.S. Department of Labor, U.S. Bureau of Labor Statistics, "Table 1203. Income before taxes: Average annual expenditures and characteristics, Consumer Expenditure Survey, 2021" [Item detail]; StTable1203Income2021.pdf; Created 9/1/2022 11:18 AM; unnumbered pp. 1, 20, & 25 of 4/11/2023 printout.

[6] U.S. Department of Labor, U.S. Bureau of Labor Statistics, Table 1203, p. 1.

[7] Consumer Expenditure Survey "Frequently Asked Questions"; U.S. Department of Labor, U.S. Bureau of Labor Statistics, Consumer Expenditure Surveys, Branch of Information and Analysis; Last Modified Date: March 17, 2005; <http://www.bls.gov/cex/csxfaqs.htm>; p. 7 of 5/28/05 10:32 AM printout.

[8] Data source: U.S. Department of Labor, U.S. Bureau of Labor Statistics, "Table 1300. Age of reference person: Average annual expenditures and characteristics, Consumer Expenditure Survey, 2021" [Item detail]; StTable1300Age2021.pdf; Created 9/1/2022 12:06 PM; unnumbered pp. 1,17 & 22 of 4/10/2023 printout.

[9] This analysis is based on information in chapter seven of 15 previous editions in *The State of Church Giving* series: *The State of Church Giving through 2004* through *The State of Church Giving through 2015*, and *The State of Church Giving through 2017* through *The State of Church Giving through 2020*.

[10] Data source: U.S. Department of Labor, U.S. Bureau of Labor Statistics, Table 1800, 2021; unnumbered pp. 1, 17 & 21 of 4/11/2023 printout.

[11] The significance levels noted in the text reflected a z statistic having an absolute value greater than 2 that indicates a difference significant at .05 level.

[12] 1987-2021: US Department of Labor, Bureau of Labor Statistics; "Table 1800. Region of residence: Average annual expenditures and, characteristics, Consumer Expenditure Survey, [Year]" [Item detail];

- 2021: StTable1800Region2021.pdf; unnumbered pp. 1, 17, & 21 of 4/11/2023 printout.
- 2020: StTable1800Region2020.pdf; Created 9/7/2021 12:57 PM; unnumbered pp. 1, 17, & 20 of 2/8/2022 printout.
- 2019: StTable1800Region2019.pdf; Created 8/19/2020 1:28 PM; unnumbered pp. 1, 17, & 21 of 8/4/2021 printout.
- 2018: StTable1800Region2018.pdf; Created 8/29/2019 10:38 AM; unnumbered pp. 1, 17, & 21 of 1/9/2020 printout.
- 2017: StTable1800Region2017.pdf; Created 9/7/2018 6:55 AM; unnumbered pp. 1, 17, & 21 of 2/15/2019 printout.

• 2016: StTable1800Region2016.pdf; Created 8/23/2017 11:36 AM; unnumbered pp. 1, 16, &21 of 1/29/2018 printout.

• 2015: StTable1800Region2015.pdf; Created 8/30/2016 9:12 AM; unnumbered pp. 1, 16, & 21 of 1/18/2017 printout.

• 2014: StTable1800Region2014.pdf; Created 8/26/2015 1:47 PM; unnumbered pp. 1, 16, & 20 of 1/12/2016 printout.

• 2013: StTable1800Region2013.pdf; Created 9/2/2014 1:14 PM; unnumbered pp. 1, 18, & 30 of 1/13/2015 printout.

• 2012: StTable1800Region2012.pdf; Created 8/13/2013 4:45 PM; unnumbered pp. 1, 17, & 28 of 1/28/2014 printout.

• 2011: StTable1800Region2011.pdf; Created 11/6/2012 12:39 PM; unnumbered pp. 1, 17, & 28 of 4/30/2013 printout.

• 2010: StTable1800Region2010.pdf; Created 9/29/2011 12:22 PM; unnumbered pp. 1, 17, & 28 of 2/28/2012 printout.

• 2009: StTable1800Region2009.pdf; Created 8/31/2010 7:04 AM; unnumbered pp. 1, 17, & 28 of 4/18/2011 printout.

• 2008: StTable1800Region2008.pdf; Created 9/1/2009 2:32 PM; unnumbered pp. 1, 17, & 29 of 4/23/2010 printout.

• 2007: StTable1800Region2007.pdf; Created 11/13/2008 9:12 PM; unnumbered pp. 1, 17, & 29 of 3/25/2009printout.

• 2006: StTable1800Region2006.pdf; Created 9/25/2007 2:27 PM; unnumbered pp. 1, 17, & 29 of 4/6/2008 printout.

• 2005: StTable1800Region2005.pdf; Created 10/16/2006 12:56 PM; unnumbered pp. 1, 17, & 29 of 7/12/2007 printout.

• 2004: region.pdf[2004.SH.1800]; Created 11/29/2005 8:13:52 AM; unnumbered pp. 1, 17, & 28 of 5/15/2006 printout.

• 2003: region.pdf[2003.Janini1800]; Created 12/2/2004 1:23:40 PM; unnumbered pp. 1, 17-18, & 30 of 5/25/2005 printout.

• 2002: Region.pdf.2002.Janini; Created 10/17/2003 2:11:39 PM; unnumbered pp. 1, 17-18, & 30 of 7/7/2004 printout.

• 2001: Region2001.pdf.Janini; Created 11/06/2002 10:12:32 AM; unnumbered pp. 1, 18, & 30 of 8/4/2003 download from email.

• 2000: StTable1800Region2000.pdf; Created 1/28/2002 11:53 AM; unnumbered pp. 1, 18, & 31 of 7/12/2007 printout.

• 1999: StTable1800Region1999.pdf; Created 1/28/2002 12:09 PM; unnumbered pp. 1, 18, & 30 of 7/12/2007 printout.

• 1998: StTable1800Region2005.pdf; Created 11/10/1999; unnumbered pp. 1, 18, & 30 of 7/12/2007 printout.

• 1997: 97Region.txt; Created 10/7/1998 [electronic 2/24/2004]; unnumbered pp. 1, 27, & 46 of 8/5/2007 printout.

• 1996: 96Region.txt; Created 8/6/1998 [electronic 2/26/2004]; unnumbered pp. 1, 27, & 46 of 8/5/2007 printout.

• 1995: 95Region.txt; Created 5/8/1997 [electronic 3/1/2004]; unnumbered pp. 1, 27, & 46 of 8/5/2007 printout.

• 1994: 94Region.txt; Created 12/23/1996 [electronic 3/3/2004]; unnumbered pp. 1, 26-27, & 45 of 8/5/2007 printout.

• 1993: 93Region.txt; Created 11/2/1994 [electronic 3/5/2004]; unnumbered pp. 1, 26, & 44 of 8/5/2007 printout.

• 1992: 92Region.txt; Created 10/20/1993 [electronic 3/9/2004]; unnumbered pp. 1, 26, & 44 of 8/5/2007 printout.

• 1991: 91Region.txt; Created 11/30/1992 [electronic 3/9/2004]; unnumbered pp. 1, 13, & 22 of 8/5/2007 printout.

• 1990: 90Region.txt; Created 12/29/1992 [electronic 3/8/2004]; unnumbered pp. 1, 13, & 22 of 8/5/2007 printout.

• 1989: 89Region.txt; Created 7/11/1991 [electronic 3/3/2004]; unnumbered pp. 1, 13, & 17 of 8/5/2007 printout.

• 1988: 88Region.txt; Created 7/11/1991 [electronic 3/2/2004]; unnumbered pp. 1, 13, & 17 of 8/5/2007 printout.

1987: US Department of Labor, Bureau of Labor Statistics, "Table 8. Region of residence: Average annual expenditures and characteristics, Consumer Expenditure Survey, 1987" [Item detail], 87Region.txt, Created 5/21/1992 [electronic 2/25/2004]; unnumbered pp. 1, 10, & 13 of 8/5/2007 printout.

[13] Michael Lipka; "How Religious Is Your State?"; PewResearchCenter; 2/29/2016; <http://www.pewresearch.org/fact-tank/2016/02/29/how-religious-is-your-state/?state=Alabama>; pp. 4-5 of 8/14/2016 12:37 PM printout.

[14] Data source: U.S. Department of Labor, Bureau of Labor Statistics CE, Table 1800, 2021, unnumbered pp. 1, 5-6, 10, 12-14, 16-17, & 21 of 4/11/2023 printout.

[15] "Mission Statement"; U.S. Department of Labor, Bureau of Labor Statistics; Last Modified Date: October 16, 2001; <http://www.bls.gov/bls/blsmissn.htm>; p. 1 of 8/15/05 4:59 PM printout.

[16] U.S. Census Bureau, *Statistical Abstract of the United States: 2006*, 125th edition; published 2005; <http://www.census.gov/prod/2005pubs/06statab/prices.pdf>; pp. 479, 481 of 5/31/06 printout.

[17] "Consumer Expenditures in 2004"; Report 992; U.S. Department of Labor, U.S. Bureau of Labor Statistics; April 2006; <http://www.bls.gov/cex/csxann04.pdf>; pp. 4-5 of 5/30/06 printout.

[18] "Consumer Expenditures and Income: Sample Design"; U.S. Department of Labor, U.S. Bureau of Labor Statistics; 2/25/2016; <https://www.bls.gov/opub/hom/cex/design.htm>; pp. 1-2 of 8/22/2018 printout.

[19] Consumer Expenditure Survey "Frequently Asked Questions"; U.S. Department of Labor, U.S. Bureau of Labor Statistics, Consumer Expenditure Surveys, Branch of Information and Analysis; Last Modified Date: March 17, 2005; <http://www.bls.gov/cex/csxfaqs.htm>; p. 2 of 5/28/05 10:32 AM printout.

[20] Sylvia Porter, "Out-of-Date Consumer Price Index to Be Revised in '87," a "Money's Worth" column appearing in *Champaign (Ill.) News-Gazette,* January 9, 1985, sec. D, p. 3.

[21] "Price Index Undergoes Statistical Adjustment," an Associated Press (Washington) article appearing in the *Champaign (Ill.) News-Gazette,* April 19, 1998, sec. C, p. 1.

[22] U.S. Bureau of Labor Statistics; "Consumer Price Index; Consumer Price Index Frequently Asked Questions"; Last Modified Date: March 25, 2020; <https://www.bls.gov/cpi/questions-and-answers.htm#Question_5>; p. 3 of 10/9/2020 3:49 PM printout.

[23] Jonathan A. Parker, Nicholas S. Souleles, and Christopher D. Carroll; "The Benefits of Panel Data in Consumer Expenditure Surveys"; 6/7/2012; <http://mitsloan.mit.edu/shared/oda/documents/?DocumentsID=4166>; pp. 2, 24 of 8/22/2018 printout.

[24] Gabriel Rudney, "The Scope of the Private Voluntary Charitable Sector," Research Papers Sponsored by The Commission on Private Philanthropy and Public Needs, Vol. 1, History, Trends, and Current Magnitudes, (Washington, DC: Department of the Treasury, 1977), p. 136. The nature of these numbers, specifically whether they are for giving to church only or combine giving to church and religious organizations, would benefit from a review in light of the relatively recent CE introduction of the "church, religious organizations" category.

[25] For this comparison, the composite data set of denominations was adjusted for missing data.

[26] Data Sources for the 1989-2019 Series: See endnote 12.

[27] See Appendix B-6 for sources of Form 990 series detail.

[28] *Giving USA: The Annual Report on Philanthropy for the Year 2022* (2023). Chicago: Giving USA Foundation. Page 301.

[29] "Table 2.1. Returns with Itemized Deductions: Sources of Income, Adjustments, Itemized Deductions by Type, Exemptions, and Tax Items, by Size of Adjusted Gross Income, Tax Year 2019"; IRS, Statistics of Income Division, Publication 1304, November 2021; download 19in21id.xls; <https://www.irs.gov/pub/irs-soi/19in21id.xls>; p. 8 of 1/10/2022 4:45 PM printout.

[30] "…church represents 90% of giving to religion…": Dean R. Hoge, Charles Zech, Patrick McNamara, Michael J. Donahue, *Money Matters: Personal Giving in American Churches* (Louisville: Westminster John Knox Press, 1996), p. 49; Jerry White, *The Church & the Parachurch* (Portland, OR: Multnomah Press, 1983), p. 104.

[31] See Appendix B-6 for the data used and sources.

[32] *Giving USA 1980 Annual Report* (New York: American Association of Fund-Raising Counsel, Inc., 1980), p. 9.

[33] *Giving USA: The Annual Report on Philanthropy for the Year 2020* (2021); Chicago: Giving USA Foundation. Pages 364-366.

[34] *Giving USA 2023*; pp. 353, 357.

[35] Paula Schleis; "Ups and Downs"; Akron Beacon Journal; posted 8/13/07; <http://www.ohio.com/business/9119806.html>; p. 1 of 8/15/07 11:45 AM printout.

[36] Timothy J. McClimon; "Corporate Giving By The Numbers"; forbes.com; 1/16/2020; <https://www.forbes.com/sites/timothyjmcclimon/2020/01/16/corporate-giving-by-the-numbers/#ce7e1b56c513>; p. 2 of 10/10/2020 12:16 PM printout.

[37] *Giving USA: The Annual Report on Philanthropy for the Year 2019* (2020); Chicago: Giving USA Foundation;, p. 332.

[38] *Giving USA 2021*, pp. 365.

[39] An Associated Press article appearing as "Madigan Urges Halving Corporate Tax," *The (Champaign, Ill.) News-Gazette*, January 31, 2014, p. A-3, col. 5-6.

[40] IRS Oversight Board; "IRS Oversight Board 2014 Taxpayer Attitude Survey"; December 2014; <http://www.treasury.gov/IRSOB/reports/Documents/IRSOB%20Taxpayer%20Attitude%20Survey%202014.pdf>; p. 5.

[41] Richard Rubin; "Donors Claim $1.1 Billion Skirting Tax Laws, Audit Says"; Bloomberg News; 1/15/2013; <http://www.bloomberg.com/news/articles/2013-01-15/donors-claim-1-1-billion-skirting-tax-laws-audit-says>; pp. 1-2 of 8/19/2015 2:49 PM printout.

[42] John Ronsvalle and Sylvia Ronsvalle, *The State of Church Giving through 2003* (Champaign, IL: empty tomb, inc., 2005), pp. 91-93. The chapter is also available at: <http://www.emptytomb.org/scg03chap7.pdf>.

[43] Mark W. Everson; "Written Statement of Mark W. Everson, Commissioner of Internal Revenue, Before The Committee on Finance, United States Senate, Hearing On Exempt Organizations: Enforcement Problems, Accomplishments, and Future Direction"; April 5, 2005; <http://finance.senate.gov/hearings/testimony/2005test/metest040505.pdf>; p. 9 of 4/27/05 printout.

[44] Brad Wolverton (Washington), "Taking Aim at Charity," *Chronicle of Philanthropy*, published by The Chronicle of Higher Education, Inc., Washington, D.C., April 14, 2005, p. 27.

[45] Internal Revenue Service; "IRS' 2019 'Dirty Dozen' Tax Scams List Highlights Inflating Deductions, Credits"; IRS; 3/12/2019; <https://www.irs.gov/ Newsroom/irs-2019-dirty-dozen-tax-scams-list-highlights-inflating-deductions-credits>; p. 1 of 8/21/2019 printout.

[46] Scott Burns, "No, It's Not OK to Lie on Return," *Champaign (Ill.) News-Gazette,* May 10, 2006, p. B-8.

[47] For the complete discussion of these recommendations, see Ronsvalle and Ronsvalle, *The State of Church Giving through 2003*, pp. 93-100. The chapter is also available at: <http://www.emptytomb.org/scg03chap7.pdf>.

[48] Melanie A. McKitrick, et al.; "Connected to Give: Faith Communities"; Jumpstart; 11/25/2013; <ConnectedToGive3_FaithCommunities_Jumpstart2013_v.1.0.pdf>; p. 6 of 6/24/2014 download from <faithcommunities.connectedtogive.org>.

[49] *Giving USA 2023*, pp. 312, 314. Calculated by attributing 100% of 2021 Religion, $136.43 billion, to 2021 Individuals, $340.97 billion.

[50] *Giving USA 2022*, p. 170.

[51] Russy D. Sumariwalla and Wilson C. Levis, Unified *Financial Reporting System for Not-for-Profit Organizations: A Comprehensive Guide to Unifying GAAP, IRS Form 990, and Other Financial Reports Using a Unified Chart of Accounts* (San Francisco: Jossey-Bass, 2000), p. 41.

[52] Christopher Chabris and Daniel Simons, *The Invisible Gorilla, And Other Ways Our Intuitions Deceive Us*, (New York, Crown, 2010), p. 186.

[53] Chabris and Simons, p. 190.

[54] Chabris and Simons, pp. 186-197, especially pp. 191, 194-195.

[55] Chabris and Simons, pp. 200-203.

[56] Daniel Kahneman, *Thinking, Fast and Slow* (New York: Farrar, Strauss and Giroux, 2013), p. 142.

[57] Brett Martel, Associated Press, "Her Place in History," *The (Champaign, Ill.) News-Gazette*, March 1, 2024, p. B-6, cols. 1-5.

[58] Eric Olson, Associated Press; "Iowa's Caitlin Clark Breaks Pete Maravich's NCAA Division 1 Scoring Record"; Associated Press; 3/3/2024; < https://apnews.com/article/caitlin-clark-iowa-ncaa-record-8d2a9bc33a9fdc59177a5ca4fe7221a9#:~:text=Clark%20entered%20the%20game%20in,to%203%2C685%20in%20130%20games>; pp. 2-3 of 3/30/2024 11:43 AM printout.

[59] Maria Di Mento, "How The Chronicle Compiled the Philanthropy 50 List," *The Chronicle of Philanthropy*, February 13, 2014, p. 28, col. 4.

[60] David B. Barrett, Todd M. Johnson, and Peter F. Crossing, "Missiometrics 2008: Reality checks for Christian World Communions," *International Bulletin of Missionary Research*, Vol. 32, No. 1, January 2008, p. 27.

[61] The Center on Philanthropy at Indiana University, *Giving USA 2008, The Annual Report on Philanthropy for the Year 2007* (Glenview, IL: Giving USA Foundation, 2008), p. 216.

[62] Susan Heavey, Reuters; "Giving USA Report: 2012 Charitable Giving Grew Almost 4%, Corporate Donations Grew 12%"; published June 18, 2013 12:00 AM EDT, updated 6/18/2013 10:00 AM EDT; <http://www.huffingtonpost.com/2013/06/18/giving-usa-report-_n_3457244.html>; p. 1 of 6/18/2013 9:08 AM printout.

[63] The references for the Associated Press stories listed are as follows:

- Helena Payne, Associated Press Writer; "2001 Charitable Giving Same As 2000"; published June 20, 2002, 12:20 PM; <http://www.washingtonpost.com/ac2/wp-dyn/A17534-2002Jun20?language=printer>; p. 1 of 6/27/02 9:09 PM printout.
- Mark Jewell, AP; "Donations Held Steady in 2002"; published June 23, 2003, 4:23 PM; <http://www.washingtonpost.com/ wp-dyn/A23604-2003Jun23.html>; p. 1 of 6/26/03 8:49 AM printout.
- Kendra Locke; "Charitable Giving Rises in 2003"; published June 21, 2004, 12:24 AM; <http://www.washingtonpost.com/wp-dyn/articles/A56830-2004Jun21.html>; p. 1 of 6/25/04 4:56 PM printout.
- Adam Geller, AP Business Writer; "Charitable Giving Among Americans Rises"; published June 14, 2005 10:16 AM; <http://www.guardian.co.uk/worldlateststory/0,1280,-5073041,00.html>; p. 1 of 6/15/2005 9:42 AM printout.
- Vinnee Tong, AP Business Writer; "Charitable Giving in U.S. Nears Record Set at End of Tech Boom"; The Associated Press, New York, published June 18, 2006 11:10 PM GMT; <http://web.lexis.com[...extended URL]>; p. 1 of 6/20/2006 8:51 AM printout.
- Vinnee Tong, AP Business Writer; "Americans Give Nearly $300 Billion to Charities in 2006, Set a New Record"; published June 25, 2007 4:58 GMT; <http://web.lexis.com...>; p. 1 of 6/25/07 5:01 PM printout.
- Vinee Tong, AP Business Writer; "Americans Are Steady in Donations to Charity"; published June 23, 2008; 11:43 AM GMT; <http://web.lexis.com...>; p. 1 of 6/23/2008 5:23 PM printout.
- David Crary, AP National Writer; "Amid Meltdown, Charitable Gifts in US Fell in 2008"; published June 10, 2010; 04:01 AM GMT; <http://web.lexis.com...>; p. 1 of 6/10/2010 5:11 PM printout.
- Caryn Rousseau, Associated Press Writer; "2010 Charitable Giving Falls 3.6 Percent in US"; published June 9, 2010; 04:01 AM GMT; <http://web.lexis.com...>; p. 1 of 6/9/2010 3:56 PM printout.
- David Crary, AP National Writer, New York; "Charitable Giving in US Rebounds a Bit After Drop"; published June 20 12:01 am ET [2011]; <http://news.yahoo.com/s/ap/20110620/ap_on_re_us/us_charitable_giving>; p. 1 of 6/22/2011 4:31 PM printout.
- Michelle Nichols, Reuters; "U.S. Charitable Giving Approaches $300 Billion in 2011"; published June 19, 2012 12:02 am EDT; <http://www.reuters.com/article/2012/06/19/us-usa-charity-idUSBRE85I05T20120619>; p. 1 of 6/19/2012 5:13 PM printout.
- Susan Heavey, Reuters, June 6/18/2013.
- David Crary, AP National Writer; "Giving Increases for Some Sectors, Not for Others"; June 17, 2014; <http://abcnews.go.com/US/wireStory/giving-increases-sectors-24168494?singlePage=true>; p. 1 of 6/17/2014 10:51 AM printout.
- Donna Gordon Blankinship; "Charities Emerge from Recession with Record Donations"; Associated Press; 6/16/2015; <http://bigstory.ap.org/a13b28e5c3624abab515eee2a797fcb/charities-emerge-recession-record-donations>; p. 2 of 6/16/2016 2:51 PM printout.
- David Crary, AP National Writer, New York; "U.S. Charitable Giving Tops More Than $1 Billion a Day"; 6/14/2016; <http://www.greenwichtime.com/news/article/US-charitable-giving-rate-topes-more-thant-1-8194357.php>; p. 1 of 6/14/2016 i:51 AM printout.
- David Crary, AP National Writer; "New Report: Charitable Giving in US Rises Slightly in 2016"; AP; 6/13/2017 12:01 AM; <http://hosted2.ap.org/ARLID/54828a5e8d9d48b7ba8b94ba38a9ef22/Article_2017-06-13-US--Charitable%20Giving/id-3d56da0176d7408b89fa3725e5b23443>; p. 1 of 6/13/2017 10:13 AM printout.

- David Crary, AP National Writer; "Charitable Giving in US Tops $400 Billion for First Time"; 6/13/2018; <https://www.jhnewsandguide.com/jackson_hole_daily/business/article_bd7e35e8-d53d-57d2-84f9-1100feffb0d5.html>; p. 2 of 6/28/2018 2:48 PM printout.
- David Crary, AP; "Charitable Giving by Individual Americans Drops in 2018"; 6/18/2019 11:43 AM; <https://www.washingtonpost.com/business/charitable-giving-by-individual-americans-drops-in-2018/2019/06/18/cc1ca18c-91df-11e9-956a-88c291ab5c38_story.html?utm_term=.69a6a93bf34e>; p. 1 of 6/18/2019 11:57 AM printout.
- Sally Ho; "Donations to Fight Virus, Injustice Could Sustain Charities"; 6/17/2020; <https://apnews.com/d5e9ac46ff2819f2215f9e473575c55a>; p. 2 of 8/10/2020 9:53 AM printout.
- Haleluya Hadero; "Charitable Giving in the U.S. Reaches All-Time High in 2020"; published 6/15/2021; <https://apnews.com/article/philanthropy-health-coronavirus-pandemic-business-94cac51d5caf18f48a7827de04e017c0>; p. 2 of 6/15/2021 4:56 PM printout.
- Thalia Beaty and Glenn Gamboa; "US charitable giving hit record in 2021 but inflation looms"; published 6/21/2022; <apnews.com/article/inflation-covid-health-united-states-2b036519257399ac12cd1fd7f6030569>; p. 2 of 6/21/2022 1:10 PM printout.
- Glenn Gamboa; Charitable Giving in 2022 Drops for Only the Third Time in 40 Years: Giving USA Report"; published 6/20/2023; <https://apnews.com/article/charitable-giving-decline-givingusa-report-becaca47cae4bc4f55063cc9f1c5865a>; p. 2 of 6/20/2023 9:57 AM printout.

[64] For the "Per Capita Individual Giving as % of Per Capita Disposable Personal Income: % Change from Base Year" calculations: See Appendix C for the source of Per capita Disposable Personal Income. The respective *Giving USA* editions for Individual Giving used in the calculations were as follows: 2000-2001, 2002, pp. 169, 177; 2001-2002, 2003, p. 194; 2002-2003, 2004, p. 218; 2003-2004, 2005, p. 194; 2004-2005, 2006, p. 204; 2005-2006, 2007, p. 212; 2006-2007, 2008, p. 210; 2007-2008, 2009, p. 210; 2008-2009, 2010, p. 50; 2009-2010, 2011, p. 53; 2010-2011, 2012, p. 264; 2011-2012, 2013, p. 248; 2012-2013, 2014, p. 204; 2013-2014, 2015, p. 238; 2014-2015, 2016, p. 320; 2015-2016, 2017, p. 352; 2016-2017, 2018, p. 372; and, 2017-2018, 2019, p. 342.

[65] For the "Total Giving as % of Gross Domestic Product: % Change from Base Year" calculations: See the previous endnote for the respective *Giving USA* editions. The source of Gross Domestic Product (GDP) data in current millions of dollars: U.S. Bureau of Economic Analysis; "Table 1.1.5. Gross Domestic Product"; Line 1: "Gross domestic product"; National Income and Product Accounts Tables; 1929-Present data published on March 28, 2019; 1929-2018: Tab "T10105-A" of "Section1All_xls_1.1.9_1.1.5.xlsx" downloaded as xlsx file "Section1All_xls.xlsx"; <https://apps.bea.gov/national/Release/XLS/Survey/Section1All_xls.xlsx>; downloaded 4/3/2019 [from <https://apps.www.bea.gov/iTable/iTable.cfm?ReqID-19&step=4&isuri=1&1921=flatfiles>].

[66] Maria Cheng and Krista Larson, an Associated Press article appearing as "Deadly Mistakes, Misplaced Vaccines, Agency Mismanagement Impeding Fight against Yellow Fever Outbreak," in *The (Champaign, Ill.) News-Gazette*, August 5, 2016, p. A-5, cols. 1-4.

[67] "Health of the U.S. Nonprofit Sector"; Independent Sector; 11/13/2023; <https://independentsector.org/resource/health-of-the-u-s-nonprofit-sector/>; 3/30/2024 12:24 PM printout.

[68] Claire McAnaw Gallagher; "For-Profit, Nonprofit, and Government Sector Jobs in 2022"; U.S. Bureau of Labor Statistics; October 2023; <https://www.bls.gov/spotlight/2023/for-profit-nonprofit-and-government-sector-jobs-in-2022/home.htm#:~:text=%E2%80%8B%20Click%20legend%20items%20to,U.S.%20Bureau%20of%20Labor%20Statistics.&text=In%202022%2C%2069.6%20percent%20of,percent%20worked%20in%20nonprofit%20organizations>; p. 2 of 3/30/2024 12:16 PM printout.

chapter 8

Intentional Miracles

"You can serve God or Money."
— Jesus in the Sermon on the Mount, Matthew 6:24

"I tell you the truth, anyone who has faith in me will do what I have been doing. He will do even greater things than these, because I am going to the Father."
— Jesus addressing the disciples in John 14:12

"Then Jesus told his disciples a parable to show them that they should always pray and not give up … 'However, when the Son of Man comes, will he find faith on earth?' "
— Jesus addressing the disciples in Luke 18:1, 8

This is an age of affluence.

Church members can make it an age of intentional miracles.

The implications of that statement are explored in the following topics in this chapter.

- What is an intentional miracle?
- How does pursuing intentional miracles prepare for the future?
- What makes this present time so special regarding intentional miracles?
- What would an intentional miracle look like?
- Are intentional miracles even possible?

What is an intentional miracle?

In this discussion, an intentional miracle is defined as a person choosing to take an action while following Jesus Christ's mandate and example, with the strong likelihood that the results of that action will have an intensely positive effect on a dire circumstance.

The word "miracle" has both a theologically influenced definition, and a more general definition, according to *Merriam Webster's 10th Collegiate Dictionary*. From a theological perspective, a miracle is "an extraordinary event manifesting divine intervention in human affairs." In the more general sense, a miracle is "an extremely outstanding or unusual event, thing, or accomplishment."[1]

In the discussion in this chapter, in line with the theologically influenced definition, an intentional miracle can result from a choice made to take a specific action, using available resources, because of faith in Jesus Christ. In a very real sense, church people choosing to take such action, functioning as Jesus' current body on earth, are providing a channel for divine intervention in human affairs.

... church people can pursue the functional equivalent of Jesus' miracle ministry because of the available resources God has entrusted to the current body of Christ.

When Jesus came to earth in a physical body, he himself was a miracle, in that he was a divine intervention at a specific point of human history. In addition, during three years of ministry recorded in the Gospels, Jesus also manifested specific miracles of divine intervention for people he encountered. Jesus states that the miracles were a result of Jesus doing what he "sees his Father doing, because whatever the Father does the Son also does" (John 5:19), and that what he was doing during these years was the work that the Father had given him to do (John 5:36).

In the present discussion, it is being proposed that Jesus wants to continue doing miracles by having the body of Christ, the church, step out in faith in order to provide a channel for divine intervention through intentional miracles.

That is, in the present discussion, it is being asserted that church people can pursue the functional equivalent of Jesus' miracle ministry because of the available resources God has entrusted to the current body of Christ. Church people can decide to take action to assist neighbors in need, in Jesus' name, with the full expectation that those actions will be supported by the Father, Son, and Holy Spirit, and that those actions will produce a desired result. When Jesus told the disciples that they would do greater things than he did (John 14:12-14), it can be argued that Jesus gave the disciples authorization to take action, in order to carry on the Father's work, as the continued presence of Christ's body in the world.

Just as Jesus, when on earth pre-resurrection, did miracles, so now too, Jesus' body, the church, can also manifest divine intervention in human affairs through intentional miracles that result from action taken in faith.

This idea is strengthened in Mark's recounting of the Great Commandment, when Jesus says, "Love the Lord your God with all your heart and with all your soul and with all your mind and with all your strength" (Mark 12:29-31). This inclusion of the *mind* suggests that Christians can think and plan how to address problems as the body of Christ, and then take intentional action to implement those solutions.

How does pursing intentional miracles prepare for the future?

A review of the past as a setting event for the present discussion: The Wesley Revival. In her book on what she terms "the Wesleyan Way," Mary Alice Tenney writes about John Wesley's conclusion that many of the church members and leaders of his time (1703-1791) were acting out of "practical atheism" which "denied the existence of spiritual things."[2] One observer's review of religion at the time Wesley lived concluded, "Every means had been adopted to temper the demands of Christianity to the infirmities of unregenerate human nature, and to promise the consolations of religion to the weakest of its professors."[3]

In response to these conditions observed by Wesley in the eighteenth century church, Wesley devoted himself to a study of early Christianity and concluded there was a reason that the early disciples were described as followers of "the Way" (e.g., Acts 9:2, 24:14, 22): they "had become a community which had accepted a distinctive way of life," empowered at Pentecost to act on Jesus' principles. Further, because of human nature, throughout the history of the church, this Way had to be rediscovered again and again; and when the Way was again recognized, revival followed.[4] Once Wesley identified the recurring theme in the early church and the later renewal movements of love God and love the neighbor, he emphasized practical love as a central tenet for the early Methodists. For example, the principle of not gambling was not a call to asceticism, but to choose to show love because to win at gambling meant that someone else was losing.[5]

Further, because of human nature, throughout the history of the church, this Way had to be rediscovered again and again; and when the Way was again recognized, revival followed.

Thus, Christians were to accept a life-changing love from God through Jesus Christ that led them to act in a distinct manner in the power of the Holy Spirit on behalf of their neighbors in need. The works of mercy that Wesley urged Methodists to follow had a major overflow impact on English society: "The great missionary enterprises were begun; Sunday schools spread throughout England [to provide basic education to children working in factories six days a week]; hospitals and children's homes were founded. Prison conditions were changed; factory laws improved working conditions; English trade in slaves came to an end."[6] The last letter that Wesley wrote was to William Wilberforce: "Go on, in the name of God and in the power of His might, till even American slavery (the vilest that ever saw the sun) shall vanish away before it."[7]

The future of the present-day church. The church is not all right. A Gallup finding about church membership in 2020 created a stir when released in 2021: "Americans' membership in houses of worship continued to decline last year, dropping below 50% for the first time in Gallup's eight-decade trend."[8] The article went on to point out that church membership in the U.S. was 73% in 1937, and continued near 70% until a decline became evident starting with the 21st century.[9]

The trend found by Gallup is not new. The first five chapters in this volume present data for church member giving and membership. These trends indicate that the church has been experiencing a slow decline for decades in both giving as a percent of income and membership as a percent of U.S. population. The declines in 2020 identified by Gallup were not a byproduct of the COVID pandemic, but began decades before that event, and even before the Great Recession of 2008. It is only the consequences of these quiet trends that were now becoming evident to the broader populace. Table 46 presents comments from several observers.

In their book, *The Great Dechurching*, authors Jim Davis and Michael Graham, with Ryan P. Burge, assert that the trend to leave church is not limited to specific characteristics. "No group of people is immune from the Great Dechurching." They point out that both men and women, all Christian traditions, Republicans, Democrats, and Independents are leaving in comparable numbers. Among age groups, baby boomers are leaving in higher numbers than younger age groups, but this "... is not a surprise as more baby boomers went to church in the first place, which gives them

Table 46: Leaders Comment on he Lukewarm Church in the U.S.
"As many as 30 percent of churches may close in the next 20 years, leaving philanthropy to confront questions about how much faith matters to its work — and how to fill the void it may leave." — Special report cover story in *The Chronicle of Philanthropy* titled "What's Lost When Religion Fades."[10]
"So many times we Christians act like we don't know what it's like to play to win ... We know what it's like to play not to lose, and there is a huge difference. Players who play not to lose, play scared. As opposed to those who play to win, who make an error and think, 'OK, on to the next thing.' " — "Father Mike" Schmitz, host of the top-rated "The Bible in a Year" and "The Catechism in a Year" podcasts[11]
"When the church becomes preoccupied with defending itself to the world, it eventually becomes incoherent. The only way to be a church is to speak the peculiar language of peace, of forgiveness, of repentance and resurrection ... The church today is at risk of merely reinstating the world's favored social outcomes and policies. It will continue spinning its wheels to advertise for and recruit people who hope for something like joining the board of a local nonprofit. Unless it remembers its task — to continue on with the worship of God — it will lose its identity entirely." — Kirsten Sanders, PhD, Adjunct Professor of Christian Thought, Gordon Conwell[12]
"But one lie is having a diabolical impact on the lives of modern Christians ... It is worth noting that this lie is not one that non-Christians tell. It's a lie we tell ourselves as Christians. This is the lie: Holiness is not possible ... "It is astounding that just one lie can neutralize the majority of Christians. That's right, neutralize. This lie takes us out of the game and turns us into mere spectators in the epic story of Christianity that continues to unfold in every generation. This one lie is largely, if not primarily, responsible for ushering in the post-Christian modern era throughout Western civilization." — Matthew Kelly, NY Times bestselling author[13]
"But even with our greater understanding, we still insult the King, going off instead to pursue our own priorities—our careers, our lifestyles, our social lives, and our happiness—even as the King beckons us. I have no doubt that our King is also enraged ... and heartbroken." — Richard Stearns, former president of World Vision, Inc., reflecting on the parable of the banquet in Matt. 22:1-14[14]
"In the United States, we are currently experiencing the largest and fastest religious shift in the history of our country, as tens of millions of formerly regular Christian worshipers nationwide have decided they no longer desire to attend church at all. These are what we now call the dechurched. About 40 million adults in America today used to go to church but no longer do, which accounts for around 16 percent of our adult population." — Jim Davis and Michael Graham with Ryan P. Burge, *The Great Dechurching*[15]

more opportunity to make this shift." Racial background also did not limit those who left the church, although Hispanic Americans were the least likely to leave.[16]

Accompanying these trends, the culture as a whole has changed its perspective on the church, as indicated in a March 2024 finding. "A new Pew Research Center survey finds that 80% of U.S. adults say religion's role in American life is shrinking — a percentage that's as high as it's ever been in our surveys."[17]

Data in chapter 5 of this volume, and projections based on that data, suggest the church will continue to be marginalized if current trends are uninterrupted.

Part of that marginalization is evident in how those with huge amounts of resources regard the church, and religion in general. An analysis of the *Chronicle of Philanthropy*'s survey of America's biggest donors in 2021 found four were from bequests. Of the 46 living donors, only five gave donations to organizations that could be identified as religious from the information provided. One donor gave to Mercy Ships; one to a Jewish foundation; one divided their gift between a private Catholic university and for Catholic education in the Archdiocese of Los Angeles; and two gave to "unspecified religious organizations."[18]

There is no basis to assume that those capable of making very large gifts are less religious, and therefore represent a smaller percentage of Christians than the population at large. Further, as shown in Table 47,[19] these wealthier people, as cited on the Forbes 400 list, for example, are located in all regions of the U.S., creating the possibility that those who attend religious services might do so in those same regions. Yet, a list of largest gifts indicates that religion is not offering a vision that attracts support from most of these individuals, on a scale with their abilities, and with global needs.

Table 47: Forbes 400 "Rich Listers," Region of Residence Summary, 2022

Region of U.S.	Northeast	Midwest	South	West	Unlisted, U.S. Area, or Outside U.S.	Total
Number of "Rich Listers"	91	45	134	116	14	400
Aggregate Wealth ($ Billions)	$750.70	$412.30	$ 1,299.90	$1,434.50	$107.50	$4,004.90

Source: Forbes; empty tomb analysis

empty tomb, inc., 2024

Further, a single denomination will not be able to withstand the larger trends of decline. For example, the Southern Baptist Convention continues global missions as a core priority. The SBC has faithfully provided data over many years. The SBC defined itself from its founding as existing to carry out mission in the whole world.[20] A primary designated giving opportunity in the SBC is the Lottie Moon Christmas Offering, with 100% of these donations supporting the SBC International Mission Board (IMB). Figure 21 presents contributions to the Lottie Moon Christmas Offering as a percent of income, and U.S. per capita DPI in inflation-adjusted dollars, from 1921 to 2021.[21]

Growing support for the Lottie Moon Offering was evident from the mid-1920s and peaked in 1965, at .0464% of Disposable Personal Income (DPI). However,

Figure 21: SBC Lottie Moon Christmas Offering, Per Member Giving as a Percent of Income, and U.S. Per Capita Disposable Personal Income, Inflation- Adjusted 2012 Dollars, 1921-2021

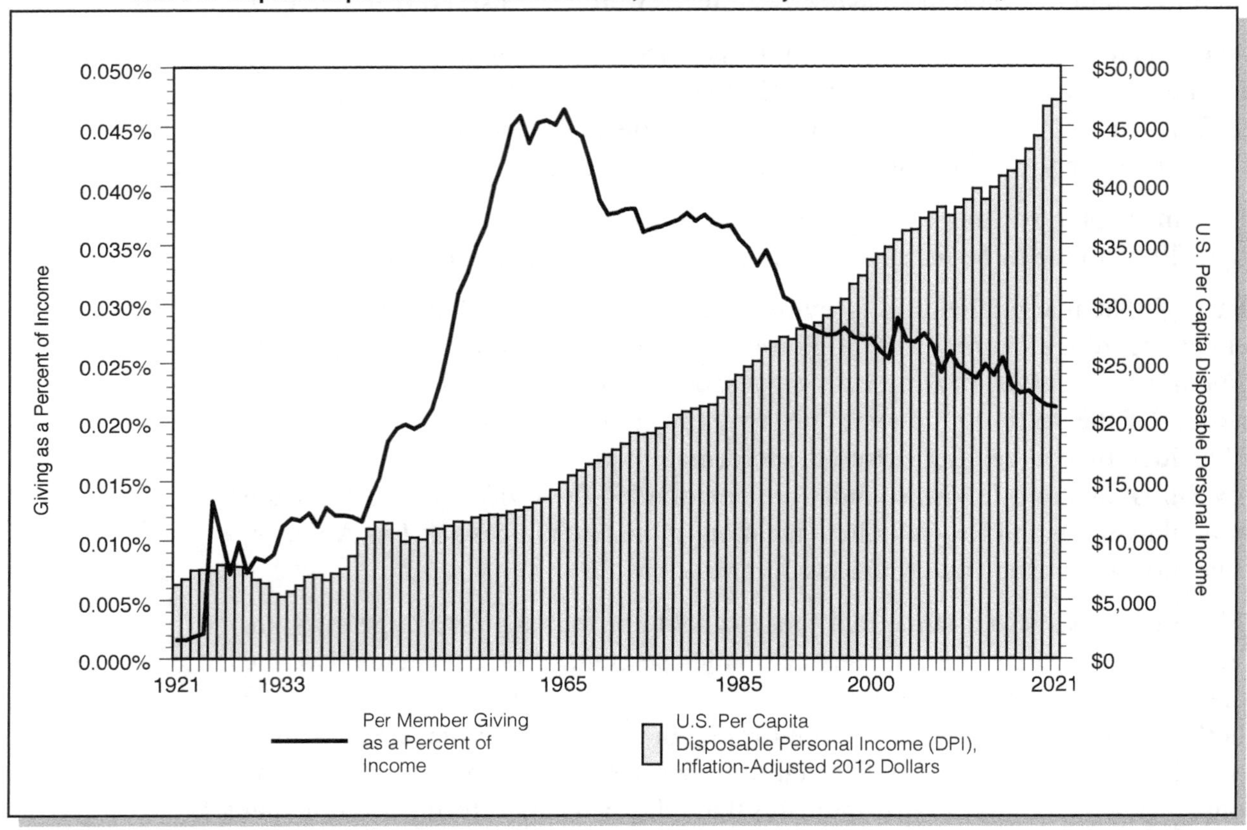

Source: SBC IMB; U.S. BEA; empty tomb, inc. analysis — empty tomb, inc., 2024

by 2021, giving as a portion of income to the Lottie Moon Christmas Offering had decreased 54%, to 0.0212% of DPI.

These and other findings suggest that the church in the U.S. is currently following a trajectory that is weakening its ability to present the Good News of Jesus Christ in a meaningful way. If John Wesley's observation is correct — that revival has happened throughout church history when the church recognized once again that the central tenet of Christianity is love for God and love for neighbor shown through works of mercy — then strengthening of the church is one reason, but likely not the main one, to pursue the idea of intentional miracles, and thereby perhaps impact the future trajectory of the church in the U.S. in a positive way.

For the future of world neighbors. Those in desperate need are not all right. While some countries experience affluence, many other global neighbors still struggle to survive. And those in a position to address the survival struggle are not insuring that their hurting neighbors' conditions will change.

For example, in July 2023, an update on achieving the Sustainable Development Goals (SDGs) had the headline, "Halfway to 2030, World 'Nowhere Near' Reaching Global Goals, UN Warns."[22]

In 2015, the SDGs succeeded the not-met Millennium Development Goals (MDGs), which were targets set by world leaders to improve global conditions by the year 2015.[23] A hopeful summary of the SDGs announced:

> The SDGs replace the Millennium Development Goals (MDGs), which started a global effort in 2000 to tackle the indignity of poverty. The MDGs established measurable, universally-agreed objectives for tackling extreme poverty and hunger, preventing deadly diseases, and expanding primary education to all children, among other development priorities …
>
> The SDGs are a bold commitment to finish what we started, and tackle some of the pressing challenges facing the world today. All 17 Goals interconnect, meaning success in one affects success for the others.[24]

The MDGs that were replaced by the SDGs were goals set in 2000 because a "promise" made by world leaders in 1990 — to reduce the rate of deaths among children under the age of 5 — did not meet those reduction goals by the year 2000. In 1990, James Grant, then Executive Director of UNICEF, organized a summit of "71 heads of State and Government — presidents, prime ministers, royal personages" as well as "senior representatives of 88 other countries" that convened in 1990, "the largest such gathering to that point in time."[25] These leaders agreed on 10 priorities, with most focused on child survival during 1990-2000. The first priority listed read: "A one-third reduction in 1990 under-five death rates (or to 70 per 1,000 live births, whichever is less)."[26]

Because these goals begun in 1990 have not been met, it is estimated that more than two children under the age of five continue to die each minute from treatable causes. The toll of this broken "promise" since 1990 amounts to the deaths of 44.3 million children through 2021. See Figure 22 on the next page.

The toll of this broken "promise" since 1990 amounts to the deaths of 44.3 million children through 2021.

The difference between the annual reduction goal in under-five child deaths and the actual annual rate of those deaths is referred to as the "Promise Gap" in this chapter.

Of the estimated 13,790 children under age five who die each day,[27] 7,000 are newborns less than one month old. Of the 13,790 daily deaths, it is estimated that 4,100 fall within the Promise Gap because reduction goals have not been met. "Each of these deaths is a tragedy, especially because the vast majority are preventable," according to a UN document.[28] Table 48 presents the consequences of the missed reduction-goals since 1990 in 40 countries with large rates of child deaths.

For each of the 40 countries, the table presents a calculation of the annual reduction rate the country needs to achieve, between the years 2000 and 2030, the Under-5 Mortality Rate (U5MR) target of 25 in 2030. Reported data for the years 2015 through 2021 is also presented. The reported data can be compared with the calculated rate, to see whether a country is closing the gap between the actual and target reduction rate.[29]

One of the major causes of death in children is malaria. A new drug has been developed that has the potential to save many children's lives. However, underfunding means only an inadequate supply is available. A Reuters article observed, "The limited international appetite to produce and distribute more Mosquirix stands in stark contrast to the record speed and funds with which wealthy countries secured vaccines for COVID-19, a disease that poses relatively little risk to children." In the

Figure 22: Children Under Age Five Who Died of Treatable Causes in the Promise Gap Between the Calculated Target Reduction Goal and the Actual Reported Numbers, 1990-2021

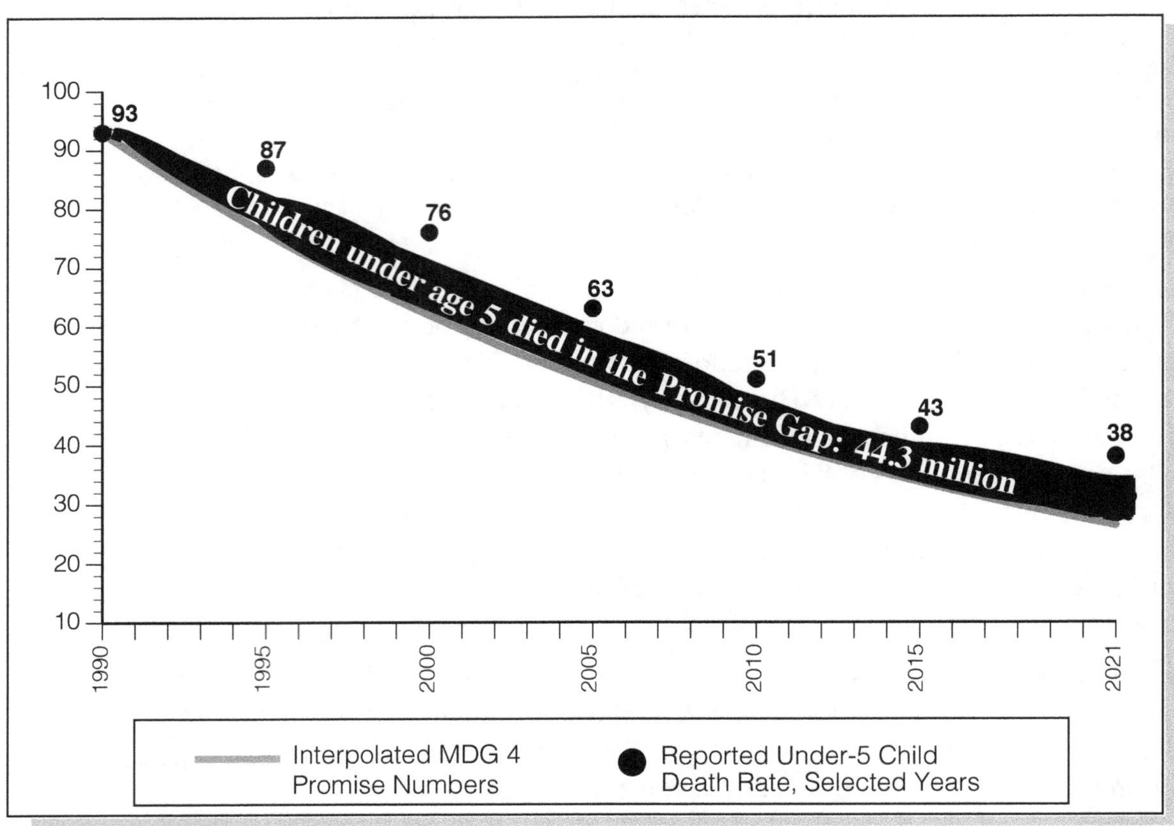

Source: UNICEF data; empty tomb, inc., analysis empty tomb, inc., 2024

same article, the chief executive of a nonprofit working with African governments to eliminate malaria commented, "This is a disease of the poor, so it's not been that appealing in terms of the market."[30]

Global neighbors face other challenges as well, such as food shortages, safe water and sanitation. In 2023, David Beasley, the retiring head of the U.N. World Food Program, warned that if the world does not "step up" to assist with global food needs, "you will have mass migration, and you will have destabilization nations and that will all be on top of starvation among children and people around the world."[31]

Paul Collier, a British development economist, asserts, "It is time to redefine the development problem as being about the countries of the bottom billion, the ones that are stuck in poverty."[32] Collier's studies have led him to conclude that specific actions can be taken to assist even the poorest countries to improve their circumstances. In looking at one problem, he wrote, "Because Africa is the epicenter of low income and slow growth, it has become the epicenter of coups. But, controlling for these risk factors, there is no 'Africa effect.' Africa does not have more coups because it is Africa; it has more coups because it is poor. That's also true of civil war; Africa became increasingly prone to civil war as its economic performance deteriorated, not because it was Africa."[33]

Table 48: U5MR Reduction Goal 2000-2030, with Reported Data 2015-2021, 40 Countries

Annual Actual And Reduction-Goal Rates of under-age 5 child deaths per 1,000 live births

Afghanistan		
2015 Missed Goal Child Deaths: 34,000		
Year	Actual	R-Goal
2000	137	137.0
2001		129.4
2002		122.3
2003		115.6
2004		109.2
2005		103.2
2006		97.5
2007		92.1
2008		87.0
2009		82.2
2010		77.7
2011		73.4
2012		69.4
2013		65.6
2014		61.9
2015	91	58.5
2016	70	55.3
2017	68	52.2
2018	62	49.4
2019	60	46.6
2020	58	44.1
2021	56	41.6
2022	2021 missed goal = 20,000 child deaths	39.4
2023		37.2
2024		35.1
2025		33.2
2026		31.4
2027		29.6
2028		28.0
2029		26.5
2030 Goal		25

Angola		
2015 Missed Goal Child Deaths: 90,000		
Year	Actual	R-Goal
2000	217	217.0
2001		201.9
2002		187.9
2003		174.8
2004		162.7
2005		151.4
2006		140.8
2007		131.1
2008		122.0
2009		113.5
2010		105.6
2011		98.3
2012		91.4
2013		85.1
2014		79.2
2015	157	73.7
2016	83	68.5
2017	81	63.8
2018	77	59.3
2019	75	55.2
2020	71	51.4
2021	69	47.8
2022	2021 missed goal = 28,000 child deaths	44.5
2023		41.4
2024		38.5
2025		35.8
2026		33.3
2027		31.0
2028		28.9
2029		26.9
2030 Goal		25

Benin		
2015 Missed Goal Child Deaths: 15,000		
Year	Actual	R-Goal
2000	145	145.0
2001		136.7
2002		129.0
2003		121.6
2004		114.7
2005		108.2
2006		102.0
2007		96.2
2008		90.7
2009		85.6
2010		80.7
2011		76.1
2012		71.8
2013		67.7
2014		63.8
2015	100	60.2
2016	98	56.8
2017	98	53.5
2018	93	50.5
2019	90	47.6
2020	86	44.9
2021	84	42.4
2022	2021 missed goal = 19,000 child deaths	40.0
2023		37.7
2024		35.5
2025		33.5
2026		31.6
2027		29.8
2028		28.1
2029		26.5
2030 Goal		25

Burkina Faso		
2015 Missed Goal Child Deaths: 14,000		
Year	Actual	R-Goal
2000	186	186.0
2001		174.0
2002		162.7
2003		152.2
2004		142.3
2005		133.1
2006		124.5
2007		116.5
2008		108.9
2009		101.9
2010		95.3
2011		89.1
2012		83.3
2013		78.0
2014		72.9
2015	89	68.2
2016	85	63.8
2017	81	59.7
2018	76	55.8
2019	88	52.2
2020	85	48.8
2021	83	45.6
2022	2021 missed goal = 28,000 child deaths	42.7
2023		39.9
2024		37.3
2025		34.9
2026		32.7
2027		30.6
2028		28.6
2029		26.7
2030 Goal		25

Annual Actual And Reduction-Goal Rates of under-age 5 child deaths per 1,000 live births

Burundi		
2015 Missed Goal Child Deaths: 9,000		
Year	Actual	R-Goal
2000	152	152.0
2001		143.1
2002		134.8
2003		126.9
2004		119.5
2005		112.5
2006		105.9
2007		99.8
2008		93.9
2009		88.4
2010		83.3
2011		78.4
2012		73.8
2013		69.5
2014		65.5
2015	82	61.6
2016	72	58.0
2017	61	54.7
2018	58	51.5
2019	56	48.5
2020	54	45.6
2021	53	43.0
2022	2021 missed goal = 4,000 child deaths	40.5
2023		38.1
2024		35.9
2025		33.8
2026		31.8
2027		29.9
2028		28.2
2029		26.6
2030 Goal		25

Cameroon		
2015 Missed Goal Child Deaths: 22,000		
Year	Actual	R-Goal
2000	150	150.0
2001		141.3
2002		133.1
2003		125.4
2004		118.1
2005		111.3
2006		104.8
2007		98.7
2008		93.0
2009		87.6
2010		82.5
2011		77.8
2012		73.3
2013		69.0
2014		65.0
2015	88	61.2
2016	80	57.7
2017	84	54.3
2018	76	51.2
2019	75	48.2
2020	72	45.4
2021	70	42.8
2022	2021 missed goal = 25,000 child deaths	40.3
2023		38.0
2024		35.8
2025		33.7
2026		31.7
2027		29.9
2028		28.2
2029		26.5
2030 Goal		25

Central African Republic		
2015 Missed Goal Child Deaths: 10,000		
Year	Actual	R-Goal
2000	175	175.0
2001		164.0
2002		153.7
2003		144.1
2004		135.0
2005		126.5
2006		118.6
2007		111.1
2008		104.2
2009		97.6
2010		91.5
2011		85.7
2012		80.4
2013		75.3
2014		70.6
2015	130	66.1
2016	124	62.0
2017	122	58.1
2018	116	54.4
2019	110	51.0
2020	103	47.8
2021	100	44.8
2022	2021 missed goal = 12,000 child deaths	42.0
2023		39.4
2024		36.9
2025		34.6
2026		32.4
2027		30.4
2028		28.5
2029		26.7
2030 Goal		25

Chad		
2015 Missed Goal Child Deaths: 42,000		
Year	Actual	R-Goal
2000	190	190.0
2001		177.6
2002		166.0
2003		155.1
2004		145.0
2005		135.5
2006		126.6
2007		118.4
2008		110.6
2009		103.4
2010		96.6
2011		90.3
2012		84.4
2013		78.9
2014		73.7
2015	139	68.9
2016	124	64.4
2017	123	60.2
2018	119	56.3
2019	114	52.6
2020	110	49.2
2021	107	45.9
2022	2021 missed goal = 43,000 child deaths	42.9
2023		40.1
2024		37.5
2025		35.1
2026		32.8
2027		30.6
2028		28.6
2029		26.7
2030 Goal		25

Source: UNICEF/IGME data; empty tomb, inc. analysis

empty tomb, inc., 2024

Table 48: U5MR Reduction Goal 2000-2030, with Reported Data 2015-2021, 40 Countries (continued)

Annual Actual And Reduction-Goal Rates of under-age 5 child deaths per 1,000 live births

Comoros		
2015 Missed Goal Child Deaths: 1,000		
Year	Actual	R-Goal
2000	**101**	**101.0**
2001		*96.4*
2002		*92.0*
2003		*87.8*
2004		*83.8*
2005		*80.0*
2006		*76.4*
2007		*72.9*
2008		*69.6*
2009		*66.4*
2010		*63.4*
2011		*60.5*
2012		*57.8*
2013		*55.2*
2014		*52.6*
2015	**74**	***50.2***
2016	**73**	*48.0*
2017	**69**	*45.8*
2018	**67**	*43.7*
2019	**63**	*41.7*
2020	**61**	*39.8*
2021	**50**	*38.0*
2022		*36.3*
2023		*34.6*
2024		*33.1*
2025		***31.6***
2026		*30.1*
2027		*28.7*
2028		*27.4*
2029		*26.2*
2030 Goal		**25**

2021 missed goal = 200 child deaths

Côte d'Ivoire		
2015 Missed Goal Child Deaths: 26,000		
Year	Actual	R-Goal
2000	**146**	**146.0**
2001		*137.7*
2002		*129.8*
2003		*122.4*
2004		*115.4*
2005		*108.8*
2006		*102.6*
2007		*96.7*
2008		*91.2*
2009		*86.0*
2010		*81.1*
2011		*76.4*
2012		*72.1*
2013		*68.0*
2014		*64.1*
2015	**93**	***60.4***
2016	**92**	*57.0*
2017	**89**	*53.7*
2018	**81**	*50.6*
2019	**79**	*47.7*
2020	**78**	*45.0*
2021	**75**	*42.4*
2022		*40.0*
2023		*37.7*
2024		*35.6*
2025		***33.5***
2026		*31.6*
2027		*29.8*
2028		*28.1*
2029		*26.5*
2030 Goal		**25**

2021 missed goal = 30,000 child deaths

Democratic Republic of the Congo		
2015 Missed Goal Child Deaths: 108,000		
Year	Actual	R-Goal
2000	**161**	**161.0**
2001		*151.3*
2002		*142.2*
2003		*133.6*
2004		*125.6*
2005		*118.0*
2006		*110.9*
2007		*104.3*
2008		*98.0*
2009		*92.1*
2010		*86.5*
2011		*81.3*
2012		*76.4*
2013		*71.8*
2014		*67.5*
2015	**98**	***63.4***
2016	**94**	*59.6*
2017	**91**	*56.0*
2018	**88**	*52.7*
2019	**85**	*49.5*
2020	**81**	*46.5*
2021	**79**	*43.7*
2022		*41.1*
2023		*38.6*
2024		*36.3*
2025		***34.1***
2026		*32.0*
2027		*30.1*
2028		*28.3*
2029		*26.6*
2030 Goal		**25**

2021 missed goal = 138,000 child deaths

Djibouti		
2015 Missed Goal Child Deaths: 200		
Year	Actual	R-Goal
2000	**101**	**101.0**
2001		*96.4*
2002		*92.0*
2003		*87.8*
2004		*83.8*
2005		*80.0*
2006		*76.4*
2007		*72.9*
2008		*69.6*
2009		*66.4*
2010		*63.4*
2011		*60.5*
2012		*57.8*
2013		*55.2*
2014		*52.6*
2015	**65**	***50.2***
2016	**64**	*48.0*
2017	**62**	*45.8*
2018	**59**	*43.7*
2019	**57**	*41.7*
2020	**56**	*39.8*
2021	**54**	*38.0*
2022		*36.3*
2023		*34.6*
2024		*33.1*
2025		***31.6***
2026		*30.1*
2027		*28.7*
2028		*27.4*
2029		*26.2*
2030 Goal		**25**

2021 missed goal = 300 child deaths

Annual Actual And Reduction-Goal Rates of under-age 5 child deaths per 1,000 live births

Equatorial Guinea		
2015 Missed Goal Child Deaths: 1,000		
Year	Actual	R-Goal
2000	**152**	**152.0**
2001		*143.1*
2002		*134.8*
2003		*126.9*
2004		*119.5*
2005		*112.5*
2006		*105.9*
2007		*99.8*
2008		*93.9*
2009		*88.4*
2010		*83.3*
2011		*78.4*
2012		*73.8*
2013		*69.5*
2014		*65.5*
2015	**94**	***61.6***
2016	**91**	*58.0*
2017	**90**	*54.7*
2018	**85**	*51.5*
2019	**82**	*48.5*
2020	**78**	*45.6*
2021	**77**	*43.0*
2022		*40.5*
2023		*38.1*
2024		*35.9*
2025		***33.8***
2026		*31.8*
2027		*29.9*
2028		*28.2*
2029		*26.6*
2030 Goal		**25**

2021 missed goal = 2,000 child deaths

Gabon		
2015 Missed Goal Child Deaths: 300		
Year	Actual	R-Goal
2000	**85**	**85.0**
2001		*81.6*
2002		*78.3*
2003		*75.2*
2004		*72.2*
2005		*69.3*
2006		*66.5*
2007		*63.9*
2008		*61.3*
2009		*58.9*
2010		*56.5*
2011		*54.3*
2012		*52.1*
2013		*50.0*
2014		*48.0*
2015	**51**	***46.1***
2016	**47**	*44.3*
2017	**48**	*42.5*
2018	**45**	*40.8*
2019	**42**	*39.2*
2020	**42**	*37.6*
2021	**40**	*36.1*
2022		*34.6*
2023		*33.3*
2024		*31.9*
2025		***30.7***
2026		*29.4*
2027		*28.3*
2028		*27.1*
2029		*26.0*
2030 Goal		**25**

2021 missed goal = 300 child deaths

Gambia		
2015 Missed Goal Child Deaths: 1,000		
Year	Actual	R-Goal
2000	**119**	**119.0**
2001		*113.0*
2002		*107.2*
2003		*101.8*
2004		*96.6*
2005		*91.8*
2006		*87.1*
2007		*82.7*
2008		*78.5*
2009		*74.5*
2010		*70.7*
2011		*67.2*
2012		*63.8*
2013		*60.5*
2014		*57.5*
2015	**69**	***54.5***
2016	**65**	*51.8*
2017	**64**	*49.2*
2018	**58**	*46.7*
2019	**52**	*44.3*
2020	**49**	*42.1*
2021	**48**	*39.9*
2022		*37.9*
2023		*36.0*
2024		*34.2*
2025		***32.4***
2026		*30.8*
2027		*29.2*
2028		*27.7*
2029		*26.3*
2030 Goal		**25**

2021 missed goal = 1,000 child deaths

Ghana		
2015 Missed Goal Child Deaths: 10,000		
Year	Actual	R-Goal
2000	**101**	**101.0**
2001		*96.4*
2002		*92.0*
2003		*87.8*
2004		*83.8*
2005		*80.0*
2006		*76.4*
2007		*72.9*
2008		*69.6*
2009		*66.4*
2010		*63.4*
2011		*60.5*
2012		*57.8*
2013		*55.2*
2014		*52.6*
2015	**62**	***50.2***
2016	**59**	*48.0*
2017	**49**	*45.8*
2018	**48**	*43.7*
2019	**46**	*41.7*
2020	**45**	*39.8*
2021	**44**	*38.0*
2022		*36.3*
2023		*34.6*
2024		*33.1*
2025		***31.6***
2026		*30.1*
2027		*28.7*
2028		*27.4*
2029		*26.2*
2030 Goal		**25**

2021 missed goal = 5,000 child deaths

Source: UNICEF/IGME data; empty tomb, inc. analysis

empty tomb, inc., 2024

Table 48: U5MR Reduction Goal 2000-2030, with Reported Data 2015-2021, 40 Countries (continued)

Annual Actual And Reduction-Goal Rates of under-age 5 child deaths per 1,000 live births

Guinea		
2015 Missed Goal Child Deaths: 13,000		
Year	Actual	R-Goal
2000	**170**	**170.0**
2001		159.5
2002		149.6
2003		140.3
2004		131.7
2005		123.5
2006		115.9
2007		108.7
2008		102.0
2009		95.7
2010		89.7
2011		84.2
2012		79.0
2013		74.1
2014		69.5
2015	**94**	**65.2**
2016	**89**	61.2
2017	**86**	57.4
2018	**101**	53.8
2019	**99**	50.5
2020	**96**	47.4
2021	**99**	44.4
2022		41.7
2023		39.1
2024		36.7
2025		**34.4**
2026		32.3
2027		30.3
2028		28.4
2029		26.6
2030 Goal		**25**

2021 missed goal = 25,000 child deaths

Guinea-Bissau		
2015 Missed Goal Child Deaths: 2,000		
Year	Actual	R-Goal
2000	**178**	**178.0**
2001		166.7
2002		156.2
2003		146.3
2004		137.0
2005		128.3
2006		120.2
2007		112.6
2008		105.5
2009		98.8
2010		92.5
2011		86.7
2012		81.2
2013		76.0
2014		71.2
2015	**93**	**66.7**
2016	**88**	62.5
2017	**84**	58.5
2018	**81**	54.8
2019	**78**	51.3
2020	**77**	48.1
2021	**74**	45.0
2022		42.2
2023		39.5
2024		37.0
2025		**34.7**
2026		32.5
2027		30.4
2028		28.5
2029		26.7
2030 Goal		**25**

2021 missed goal = 2,000 child deaths

Haiti		
2015 Missed Goal Child Deaths: 5,000		
Year	Actual	R-Goal
2000	**105**	**105.0**
2001		100.1
2002		95.4
2003		91.0
2004		86.7
2005		82.7
2006		78.8
2007		75.1
2008		71.6
2009		68.3
2010		65.1
2011		62.0
2012		59.1
2013		56.4
2014		53.7
2015	**69**	**51.2**
2016	**67**	48.8
2017	**72**	46.6
2018	**65**	44.4
2019	**63**	42.3
2020	**60**	40.3
2021	**59**	38.5
2022		36.7
2023		34.9
2024		33.3
2025		**31.8**
2026		30.3
2027		28.9
2028		27.5
2029		26.2
2030 Goal		**25**

2021 missed goal = 6,000 child deaths

India		
2015 Missed Goal Child Deaths: 8,000		
Year	Actual	R-Goal
2000	**91**	**91.0**
2001		87.2
2002		83.5
2003		80.0
2004		76.6
2005		73.4
2006		70.3
2007		67.3
2008		64.5
2009		61.8
2010		59.2
2011		56.7
2012		54.3
2013		52.0
2014		49.8
2015	**48**	**47.7**
2016	**43**	45.7
2017	**39**	43.8
2018	**37**	41.9
2019	**34**	40.1
2020	**33**	38.5
2021	**31**	36.8
2022		35.3
2023		33.8
2024		32.4
2025		**31.0**
2026		29.7
2027		28.4
2028		27.2
2029		26.1
2030 Goal		**25**

2021 missed goal = 0 child deaths

Annual Actual And Reduction-Goal Rates of under-age 5 child deaths per 1,000 live births

Lao People's Democratic Republic		
2015 Missed Goal Child Deaths: 2,000		
Year	Actual	R-Goal
2000	**118**	**118.0**
2001		112.1
2002		106.4
2003		101.0
2004		95.9
2005		91.1
2006		86.5
2007		82.2
2008		78.0
2009		74.1
2010		70.3
2011		66.8
2012		63.4
2013		60.2
2014		57.2
2015	**67**	**54.3**
2016	**64**	51.6
2017	**63**	49.0
2018	**47**	46.5
2019	**46**	44.2
2020	**44**	41.9
2021	**43**	39.8
2022		37.8
2023		35.9
2024		34.1
2025		**32.4**
2026		30.7
2027		29.2
2028		27.7
2029		26.3
2030 Goal		**25**

2021 missed goal = 500 child deaths

Lesotho		
2015 Missed Goal Child Deaths: 2,000		
Year	Actual	R-Goal
2000	**117**	**117.0**
2001		111.1
2002		105.6
2003		100.3
2004		95.2
2005		90.5
2006		85.9
2007		81.6
2008		77.5
2009		73.6
2010		69.9
2011		66.4
2012		63.1
2013		59.9
2014		56.9
2015	**90**	**54.1**
2016	**94**	51.4
2017	**86**	48.8
2018	**81**	46.3
2019	**86**	44.0
2020	**90**	41.8
2021	**73**	39.7
2022		37.7
2023		35.8
2024		34.0
2025		**32.3**
2026		30.7
2027		29.2
2028		27.7
2029		26.3
2030 Goal		**25**

2021 missed goal = 2,000 child deaths

Liberia		
2015 Missed Goal Child Deaths: 400		
Year	Actual	R-Goal
2000	**182**	**182.0**
2001		170.3
2002		159.4
2003		149.2
2004		139.7
2005		130.7
2006		122.4
2007		114.5
2008		107.2
2009		100.3
2010		93.9
2011		87.9
2012		82.3
2013		77.0
2014		72.1
2015	**70**	**67.5**
2016	**67**	63.1
2017	**75**	59.1
2018	**71**	55.3
2019	**85**	51.8
2020	**78**	48.5
2021	**76**	45.4
2022		42.4
2023		39.7
2024		37.2
2025		**34.8**
2026		32.6
2027		30.5
2028		28.5
2029		26.7
2030 Goal		**25**

2021 missed goal = 5,000 child deaths

Mali		
2015 Missed Goal Child Deaths: 29,000		
Year	Actual	R-Goal
2000	**220**	**220.0**
2001		204.6
2002		190.3
2003		177.0
2004		164.6
2005		153.1
2006		142.4
2007		132.4
2008		123.2
2009		114.6
2010		106.6
2011		99.1
2012		92.2
2013		85.7
2014		79.7
2015	**115**	**74.2**
2016	**111**	69.0
2017	**106**	64.2
2018	**98**	59.7
2019	**94**	55.5
2020	**91**	51.6
2021	**97**	48.0
2022		44.6
2023		41.5
2024		38.6
2025		**35.9**
2026		33.4
2027		31.1
2028		28.9
2029		26.9
2030 Goal		**25**

2021 missed goal = 43,000 child deaths

Source: UNICEF/IGME data; empty tomb, inc. analysis

empty tomb, inc., 2024

Table 48: U5MR Reduction Goal 2000-2030, with Reported Data 2015-2021, 40 Countries (continued)

Annual Actual And Reduction-Goal Rates of under-age 5 child deaths per 1,000 live births

Mauritania		
2015 Missed Goal Child Deaths: 4,000		
Year	**Actual**	**R-Goal**
2000	**114**	**114.0**
2001		*108.4*
2002		*103.0*
2003		*98.0*
2004		*93.1*
2005		*88.5*
2006		*84.2*
2007		*80.0*
2008		*76.1*
2009		*72.3*
2010		*68.7*
2011		*65.4*
2012		*62.1*
2013		*59.1*
2014		*56.2*
2015	**85**	***53.4***
2016	**81**	*50.8*
2017	**79**	*48.2*
2018	**76**	*45.9*
2019	**73**	*43.6*
2020	**71**	*41.5*
2021	**40**	*39.4*
2022		*37.5*
2023		*35.6*
2024		*33.9*
2025		***32.2***
2026		*30.6*
2027		*29.1*
2028		*27.7*
2029		*26.3*
2030 Goal		**25**

2021 missed goal = 100 child deaths

Mozambique		
2015 Missed Goal Child Deaths: 14,000		
Year	**Actual**	**R-Goal**
2000	**171**	**171.0**
2001		*160.4*
2002		*150.4*
2003		*141.1*
2004		*132.3*
2005		*124.1*
2006		*116.4*
2007		*109.2*
2008		*102.4*
2009		*96.0*
2010		*90.1*
2011		*84.5*
2012		*79.2*
2013		*74.3*
2014		*69.7*
2015	**79**	***65.4***
2016	**71**	*61.3*
2017	**72**	*57.5*
2018	**73**	*53.9*
2019	**74**	*50.6*
2020	**71**	*47.5*
2021	**70**	*44.5*
2022		*41.7*
2023		*39.2*
2024		*36.7*
2025		***34.4***
2026		*32.3*
2027		*30.3*
2028		*28.4*
2029		*26.7*
2030 Goal		**25**

2021 missed goal = 29,000 child deaths

Myanmar		
2015 Missed Goal Child Deaths: 4,000		
Year	**Actual**	**R-Goal**
2000	**82**	**82.0**
2001		*78.8*
2002		*75.8*
2003		*72.8*
2004		*70.0*
2005		*67.3*
2006		*64.7*
2007		*62.2*
2008		*59.7*
2009		*57.4*
2010		*55.2*
2011		*53.0*
2012		*51.0*
2013		*49.0*
2014		*47.1*
2015	**50**	***45.3***
2016	**51**	*43.5*
2017	**49**	*41.8*
2018	**46**	*40.2*
2019	**45**	*38.6*
2020	**44**	*37.1*
2021	**42**	*35.7*
2022		*34.3*
2023		*33.0*
2024		*31.7*
2025		***30.5***
2026		*29.3*
2027		*28.2*
2028		*27.1*
2029		*26.0*
2030 Goal		**25**

2021 missed goal = 6,000 child deaths

Niger		
2015 Missed Goal Child Deaths: 19,000		
Year	**Actual**	**R-Goal**
2000	**227**	**227.0**
2001		*210.9*
2002		*196.0*
2003		*182.1*
2004		*169.2*
2005		*157.2*
2006		*146.0*
2007		*135.7*
2008		*126.0*
2009		*117.1*
2010		*108.8*
2011		*101.1*
2012		*93.9*
2013		*87.3*
2014		*81.1*
2015	**96**	***75.3***
2016	**91**	*70.0*
2017	**85**	*65.0*
2018	**84**	*60.4*
2019	**80**	*56.1*
2020	**78**	*52.2*
2021	**115**	*48.5*
2022		*45.0*
2023		*41.8*
2024		*38.9*
2025		***36.1***
2026		*33.5*
2027		*31.2*
2028		*29.0*
2029		*26.9*
2030 Goal		**25**

2021 missed goal = 72,000 child deaths

Annual Actual And Reduction-Goal Rates of under-age 5 child deaths per 1,000 live births

Nigeria		
2015 Missed Goal Child Deaths: 280,000		
Year	**Actual**	**R-Goal**
2000	**187**	**187.0**
2001		*174.9*
2002		*163.5*
2003		*152.9*
2004		*143.0*
2005		*133.7*
2006		*125.0*
2007		*116.9*
2008		*109.3*
2009		*102.3*
2010		*95.6*
2011		*89.4*
2012		*83.6*
2013		*78.2*
2014		*73.1*
2015	**109**	***68.4***
2016	**104**	*63.9*
2017	**100**	*59.8*
2018	**120**	*55.9*
2019	**117**	*52.3*
2020	**114**	*48.9*
2021	**111**	*45.7*
2022		*42.8*
2023		*40.0*
2024		*37.4*
2025		***35.0***
2026		*32.7*
2027		*30.6*
2028		*28.6*
2029		*26.7*
2030 Goal		**25**

2021 missed goal = 501,000 child deaths

Pakistan		
2015 Missed Goal Child Deaths: 150,000		
Year	**Actual**	**R-Goal**
2000	**112**	**112.0**
2001		*106.5*
2002		*101.3*
2003		*96.4*
2004		*91.7*
2005		*87.2*
2006		*83.0*
2007		*78.9*
2008		*75.1*
2009		*71.4*
2010		*67.9*
2011		*64.6*
2012		*61.5*
2013		*58.5*
2014		*55.6*
2015	**81**	***52.9***
2016	**79**	*50.3*
2017	**75**	*47.9*
2018	**69**	*45.5*
2019	**67**	*43.3*
2020	**65**	*41.2*
2021	**63**	*39.2*
2022		*37.3*
2023		*35.5*
2024		*33.7*
2025		***32.1***
2026		*30.5*
2027		*29.0*
2028		*27.6*
2029		*26.3*
2030 Goal		**25**

2021 missed goal = 151,000 child deaths

Papua New Guinea		
2015 Missed Goal Child Deaths: 3,000		
Year	**Actual**	**R-Goal**
2000	**79**	**79.0**
2001		*76.0*
2002		*73.2*
2003		*70.4*
2004		*67.8*
2005		*65.2*
2006		*62.8*
2007		*60.4*
2008		*58.1*
2009		*55.9*
2010		*53.8*
2011		*51.8*
2012		*49.9*
2013		*48.0*
2014		*46.2*
2015	**57**	***44.4***
2016	**54**	*42.8*
2017	**53**	*41.2*
2018	**48**	*39.6*
2019	**45**	*38.1*
2020	**44**	*36.7*
2021	**43**	*35.3*
2022		*34.0*
2023		*32.7*
2024		*31.5*
2025		***30.3***
2026		*29.1*
2027		*28.0*
2028		*27.0*
2029		*26.0*
2030 Goal		**25**

2021 missed goal = 2,000 child deaths

Sierra Leone		
2015 Missed Goal Child Deaths: 9,000		
Year	**Actual**	**R-Goal**
2000	**236**	**236.0**
2001		*219.0*
2002		*203.2*
2003		*188.5*
2004		*175.0*
2005		*162.3*
2006		*150.6*
2007		*139.8*
2008		*129.7*
2009		*120.3*
2010		*111.7*
2011		*103.6*
2012		*96.1*
2013		*89.2*
2014		*82.8*
2015	**120**	***76.8***
2016	**114**	*71.3*
2017	**111**	*66.1*
2018	**105**	*61.4*
2019	**109**	*56.9*
2020	**108**	*52.8*
2021	**105**	*49.0*
2022		*45.5*
2023		*42.2*
2024		*39.2*
2025		***36.3***
2026		*33.7*
2027		*31.3*
2028		*29.0*
2029		*26.9*
2030 Goal		**25**

2021 missed goal = 14,000 child deaths

Source: UNICEF/IGME data; empty tomb, inc. analysis

empty tomb, inc., 2024

Table 48: U5MR Reduction Goal 2000-2030, with Reported Data 2015-2021, 40 Countries (continued)

Annual Actual And Reduction-Goal Rates of under-age 5 child deaths per 1,000 live births

Somalia		
2015 Missed Goal Child Deaths: 32,000		
Year	Actual	R-Goal
2000	174	174.0
2001		163.1
2002		152.9
2003		143.3
2004		134.3
2005		125.9
2006		118.0
2007		110.6
2008		103.7
2009		97.2
2010		91.1
2011		85.4
2012		80.1
2013		75.1
2014		70.4
2015	137	66.0
2016	133	61.8
2017	127	58.0
2018	122	54.3
2019	117	50.9
2020	115	47.7
2021	112	44.7
2022	2021 missed goal = 48,000 child deaths	41.9
2023		39.3
2024		36.9
2025		34.5
2026		32.4
2027		30.4
2028		28.5
2029		26.7
2030 Goal		25

South Sudan		
2015 Missed Goal Child Deaths: 11,000		
Year	Actual	R-Goal
2000	182	182.0
2001		170.3
2002		159.4
2003		149.2
2004		139.7
2005		130.7
2006		122.4
2007		114.5
2008		107.2
2009		100.3
2010		93.9
2011		87.9
2012		82.3
2013		77.0
2014		72.1
2015	93	67.5
2016	91	63.1
2017	96	59.1
2018	99	55.3
2019	96	51.8
2020	98	48.5
2021	99	45.4
2022	2021 missed goal = 17,000 child deaths	42.4
2023		39.7
2024		37.2
2025		34.8
2026		32.6
2027		30.5
2028		28.5
2029		26.7
2030 Goal		25

Sudan		
2015 Missed Goal Child Deaths: 24,000		
Year	Actual	R-Goal
2000	106	106.0
2001		101.0
2002		96.3
2003		91.7
2004		87.4
2005		83.3
2006		79.4
2007		75.7
2008		72.1
2009		68.7
2010		65.5
2011		62.4
2012		59.5
2013		56.7
2014		54.0
2015	70	51.5
2016	65	49.1
2017	63	46.8
2018	60	44.6
2019	58	42.5
2020	57	40.5
2021	55	38.6
2022	2021 missed goal = 25,000 child deaths	36.7
2023		35.0
2024		33.4
2025		31.8
2026		30.3
2027		28.9
2028		27.5
2029		26.2
2030 Goal		25

Swaziland: Eswatini		
2015 Missed Goal Child Deaths: 100		
Year	Actual	R-Goal
2000	128	128.0
2001		121.2
2002		114.8
2003		108.7
2004		103.0
2005		97.5
2006		92.3
2007		87.4
2008		82.8
2009		78.4
2010		74.3
2011		70.3
2012		66.6
2013		63.1
2014		59.7
2015	61	56.6
2016	70	53.6
2017	54	50.7
2018	54	48.0
2019	49	45.5
2020	47	43.1
2021	53	40.8
2022	2021 missed goal = 500 child deaths	38.6
2023		36.6
2024		34.7
2025		32.8
2026		31.1
2027		29.4
2028		27.9
2029		26.4
2030 Goal		25

Annual Actual And Reduction-Goal Rates of under-age 5 child deaths per 1,000 live births

Togo		
2015 Missed Goal Child Deaths: 6,000		
Year	Actual	R-Goal
2000	121	121.0
2001		114.8
2002		108.9
2003		103.3
2004		98.1
2005		93.0
2006		88.3
2007		83.8
2008		79.5
2009		75.4
2010		71.5
2011		67.9
2012		64.4
2013		61.1
2014		58.0
2015	78	55.0
2016	76	52.2
2017	73	49.5
2018	70	47.0
2019	67	44.6
2020	64	42.3
2021	63	40.1
2022	2021 missed goal = 6,000 child deaths	38.1
2023		36.1
2024		34.3
2025		32.5
2026		30.8
2027		29.3
2028		27.8
2029		26.3
2030 Goal		25

Turkmenistan		
2015 Missed Goal Child Deaths: 1,000		
Year	Actual	R-Goal
2000	82	82.0
2001		78.8
2002		75.8
2003		72.8
2004		70.0
2005		67.3
2006		64.7
2007		62.2
2008		59.7
2009		57.4
2010		55.2
2011		53.0
2012		51.0
2013		49.0
2014		47.1
2015	51	45.3
2016	51	43.5
2017	47	41.8
2018	46	40.2
2019	42	38.6
2020	42	37.1
2021	41	35.7
2022	2021 missed goal = 800 child deaths	34.3
2023		33.0
2024		31.7
2025		30.5
2026		29.3
2027		28.2
2028		27.1
2029		26.0
2030 Goal		25

Zambia		
2015 Missed Goal Child Deaths: 100		
Year	Actual	R-Goal
2000	163	163.0
2001		153.1
2002		143.8
2003		135.1
2004		126.9
2005		119.3
2006		112.0
2007		105.2
2008		98.9
2009		92.9
2010		87.3
2011		82.0
2012		77.0
2013		72.3
2014		68.0
2015	64	63.8
2016	63	60.0
2017	60	56.3
2018	58	52.9
2019	62	49.7
2020	61	46.7
2021	58	43.9
2022	2021 missed goal = 9,000 child deaths	41.2
2023		38.7
2024		36.4
2025		34.2
2026		32.1
2027		30.2
2028		28.3
2029		26.6
2030 Goal		25

Zimbabwe		
2015 Missed Goal Child Deaths: 10,000		
Year	Actual	R-Goal
2000	106	106.0
2001		101.0
2002		96.3
2003		91.7
2004		87.4
2005		83.3
2006		79.4
2007		75.7
2008		72.1
2009		68.7
2010		65.5
2011		62.4
2012		59.5
2013		56.7
2014		54.0
2015	71	51.5
2016	56	49.1
2017	50	46.8
2018	46	44.6
2019	55	42.5
2020	54	40.5
2021	50	38.6
2022	2021 missed goal = 5,000 child deaths	36.7
2023		35.0
2024		33.4
2025		31.8
2026		30.3
2027		28.9
2028		27.5
2029		26.2
2030 Goal		25

Source: UNICEF/IGME data; empty tomb, inc. analysis

empty tomb, inc., 2024

If Collier is correct, then nations in Africa and other poor countries elsewhere around the globe could respond positively to intentional miracles carried out by churches who have decided to follow Jesus' example of reaching out to those who are otherwise often overlooked. The church could provide leadership, in Jesus' name, for a mobilization on behalf of these neighbors who continue in desperate need.

For the future of the general good. Society is not all right. While global needs like clean water and sanitation challenge people in other countries, in the U.S., society is facing challenges of a different kind.

An Associated Press article was titled, "Retailers Try to Curb Theft While not Angering Shoppers." The article described the problem retailers face of making shelf products more secure from shoplifting, while other shoppers resent the extra effort it takes to find a store employee to get a product for them.[34]

A review of the problem in Investor's Business Daily found that some retailers are closing stores in certain areas or removing certain brands from their shelves because of the theft problem. The types of retail theft have changed as well: "In the 2023 survey of 117 retail brands, 88% reported shoplifters have grown more aggressive and violent than a year before."[35]

While global needs like clean water and sanitation challenge people in other countries, in the U.S., society is facing challenges of a different kind.

The issue of shoplifting highlights the confusion about the societal definition of "justice." An official of Walmart said that the stores with the highest theft rates are "in areas with the lowest prosecution rates for this type of crime." The article states that one reason for only 50% of retail crime being reported is that "Retailers' top reason for not reporting crime is because they believe police won't respond or investigate while prosecutors won't prosecute."[36]

Checks through the mail have also been the target of theft. An Associated Press article reported that "Banks issued roughly 680,000 reports of check fraud to the Financial Crimes Enforcement Network, also known as FinCen, last year. That's up from 350,000 reports in 2021. Meanwhile the U.S. Postal Inspection Service reported roughly 300,000 complaints of mail theft in 2021, more than double the prior year's total."[37]

As a result, people are using fewer checks as summarized in a *Washington Post* article, "Paper Checks Are Dead. Cash Is Dying. Who Still Uses Them?" The article states that in the year 2000, "... 6 out of every 10 noncash purchases, gifts and paid bills were handled with checks. A mere two decades later, just 1 in 20 are." Further, the article includes a chart showing that in January of 2017, more than 30% of transactions were paid with cash, while by January of 2022, it was about 18%, cash having been displaced by credit cards and debit cards.[38]

With echoes of the mark of the beast in Revelation 13, other experts suggest that the move to electronic transactions sets the scene for human chipping, perhaps in 50 years, according to a USA Today article titled, "You Will Get Chipped — Eventually." The article notes that,

> "In the aftermath of a Wisconsin firm embedding microchips in employees last week to ditch company badges and corporate logons, the Internet has entered into full-throated debate.

"Religious activists are so appalled, they've been penning nasty 1-star reviews of the company ... on Google, Glassdoor and social media."[39]

The shift to electronic financial systems can raise a question about the future of privacy in more than religious circles. An Associated Press article included the summary, "Governments worldwide asked their citizens to share data and use high-tech tools to help stop COVID-19's spread. Now, those governments are using the data and tools for surveillance and social control purposes unrelated to the coronavirus." John Scott-Railton of Citizen Lab was quoted in the article: "What COVID did was accelerate state use of these tools and that data and normalize it, so it fit a narrative about there being a public benefit ... Now the question is, are we going to be capable of having a reckoning around the use of this data, or is this the new normal?"[40]

In addition to these macro issues, society appears to be changing some longstanding patterns. In his book, *Democracy in America* (Vol. 1, 1835 and Vol. 2, 1840), Alexander de Tocqueville observed, "Americans of all ages constantly unite. Not only do they have commercial and industrial associations, in which all take part, but they also have a thousand other kinds: religious, moral, grave, futile, very general and very particular, immense and very small."[41]

The shift to electronic financial systems can raise a question about the future of privacy in more than religious circles.

In their seminal book from the 1980s, *Habits of the Heart: Individualism and Commitment in American Life*, Robert Bellah and his coauthors review Alexander de Tocqueville's observations about early American life, and the implications for contemporary American values. They note: "And so Tocqueville is particularly interested in all those countervailing tendencies that pull people back from their isolation into social communion. Immersion in private economic pursuits undermines the person as citizen ... The habits and practices of religion and democratic participation educate the citizen to a larger view than his purely private world would allow."[42]

Current trends stand in contrast to Tocqueville's observation about the ethos of early America. *The Chronicle of Philanthropy* covers the nonprofit world. The publication highlighted an Associated Press article titled, "Nonprofits Scramble for Help Amid Dearth of Volunteers."[43] Stories by *The Chronicle of Philanthropy* staff highlight other issues:

- "The Giving Crisis"[44]
- "What Happened to Local Corporate Philanthropy?"[45]
- "Nonprofits Find Ways to Manage a Staffing Crisis with No End in Sight"[46]

These changes in social behaviors previously practiced for the common good are accompanied by changes in the conditions of individual Americans.

As one example, the U.S. National Institutes of Health is concerned about the level of obesity in the U.S.: "Nearly 3 in 4 adults age 20 or older in the United States have either overweight or obesity. Nearly 1 in 5 children and teens ages 2 to 19 years have obesity. Overweight and obesity can lead to serious health issues for people of all ages."[47]

A development with more immediate consequences is the increase in "deaths of despair." The Economist described this trend: "... in 2022 more than 200,000 people died from alcohol, drugs or suicide, equivalent to a Boeing 747 falling out of the sky every day with no survivors."[48]

Interestingly, a 2023 study circulated by the National Bureau of Economic Research and reported by marketwatch.com looked at the relationship between "deaths of despair" from suicide and alcohol, and decreased religious participation. "The decline in religiosity matches mortality trends in all these characteristics" among middle-aged White Americans, the study authors state. The relationship seems to be with "actual formal religious participation, rather than belief or personal activities like prayer. 'These results underscore the importance of cultural institutions such as religious establishments in promoting well-being.' " The study discounted the opioid crisis as a major contributing factor since the trends identified predate the broad availability of opioids.[49]

These social changes have occurred during the decades when church participation has declined. There may be no causal effect, although the study of the relationship between deaths of despair and lack of religious participation suggests a possible connection. In any case, even as a faith statement, an agenda of at-scale intentional miracles in the church might be worth a try as a counterforce to these deteriorating social conditions.

There may be no causal effect, although the study of the relationship between deaths of despair and lack of religious participation suggests a possible connection.

For the future of the youth. The kids are not all right. Washington Post advice columnist Carolyn Hax responded to a reader concerned that both her children were on medication for diagnosed mental problems. Hax responded, "Stop. You did not 'screw up.' Kids everywhere are having an extraordinarily difficult time right now."[50]

There is documentation for Hax's statement. In December 2021, the Surgeon General of the U.S., Dr. Vivk Murthy, released a report on a "youth mental health crisis" in the U.S. "Even before the pandemic, an alarming number of young people struggled with feelings of helplessness, depression, and thoughts of suicide — and rates have increased over the past decade," according to the Surgeon General. "Between 2007 and 2018, suicide rates among youth ages 10-24 in the U.S. increased by 57%, and early estimates show more than 6,600 suicide deaths."[51]

A study published in the American Psychological Association's *Journal of Personality and Social Psychology* in the year 2000 found that, "Anxiety is so high now that normal samples of children from the 1980s outscore psychiatric populations from the 1950s." A main solution, according to Jean Twenge, the study's author, is to increase social connectedness. "However, social connectedness has not improved very much."[52]

Improving social connectedness for youth may be difficult given the amount of time young people are spending in front of screens. The Academy of Child and Adolescent Psychiatry estimated that in 2020 "On average, children ages 8-12 in the United States spend 4-6 hours a day watching or using screens, and teens spend up to 9 hours." The Academy defines "screens" as "smartphones, tablets, gaming consoles, TVs, and computers."[53]

Research by Common Sense media found that, in their survey of young people and their smartphone use, "over half of the participants received 237 or more notifications per day. The barrage of notifications, along with smartphone use during school days and nighttime, combines to create a powerful yet complicated relationship between teens and their phone." The study also found that many teens reported checking their phones an average of 100 times per day. Further, "... over two-thirds of 11 to 17-year-old participants said they 'sometimes' or 'often' find it difficult to stop using technology and use it to get relief from negative feelings."[54]

This preoccupation with screen time does not advance the socialization that would be necessary to lessen anxiety in children and youth, as prescribed in the American Psychological Association's article. A Pew Research survey found that 42% of teens "say smartphones make learning good social skills harder," while 30% thought smartphones made it easier and about 30% said it neither helps nor hurts.[55]

While society has traditionally protected youth, the area of social media has challenged that idea. In fact, a study led by the Harvard T.H. Chan School of Public Health found that social media views children as a profit center. A news release on the study noted: "The platforms collectively generated nearly $11 billion in ad revenue from these users: $2.1 billion from users ages 12 and under and $8.6 billion from users ages 13-17."[56]

"But since 2006-2010 ... happiness among the young (aged 15-24) has fallen sharply in North America — to a point where the young are less happy than the old."
— 2024 World Happiness Report

It would be one thing, if these developments were making young people happy. However, the 2024 World Happiness Report found a decline in the happiness level of youth in North America. "In the West, the received wisdom was that the young are the happiest and that happiness thereafter declines until middle age, followed by substantial recovery. But since 2006-2010 ... happiness among the young (aged 15-24) has fallen sharply in North America — to a point where the young are less happy than the old."[57]

A contributing factor to the decrease in happiness among youth may be the fact that young people in the U.S. have to worry about the consequences of gun violence. According to an article in the American Academy of Pediatrics *Pediatrics* journal, "In 2019, gun injury became the leading cause of death among children aged birth to 19 years, surpassing vehicle-related deaths for the first time." [58]

A crime committed by a group of juveniles led to an editorial in a central Illinois newspaper with the title, "Kids with Guns, without Conscience Raise Unsolvable Questions." The editorial reflected on a shoot-out during the school day by an elementary school, involving five youths. One, age 15, was arrested and charged. But an 11-year old was found to be carrying a variety of guns in his backpack for some of those involved. The editorial notes, "But an 11-year-old? He's not even eligible under Illinois law to be held in the juvenile detention center ..."[59]

In an article about young men at risk, a pastor, Gil Monrose of Brooklyn, talked about a young rapper killed in his Hollywood Hills home because he posted a picture on social media of a stack of money in his house, and another photo that revealed his address. Five young men came to get the money and killed him. The article summarized Monrose's conclusion: "These killers lacked connection to the deeper culture within our society. They held no faith in God or any higher power, and they scoffed at the American principles of honor, hard work and respect. With no larger purpose to live for, they were nihilists who valued the most shallow and materialist aspects of society — to the point of killing for it."[60]

Not all young people are taking a violent route to disengage from the culture at large. "Quiet quitting" has become a phenomenon. A TikTok post that went viral provided this definition: "... where you're not outright quitting your job but you're quitting the idea of going above and beyond." This attitude, according to a thoughtful piece in *The New Yorker*, particularly impacts the youngest workers, with the author suggesting it may even be a positive trend: "Figuring out how work fits into a life well lived is hard, but it's an evolution that has to happen. Quiet quitting is the messy starting gun of a new generation embarking on this challenge."[61] Yet, the fact that a Gallup survey found that, " 'Quiet quitters' make up at least 50% of the U.S. workforce — and probably more" suggests the problem is not limited to young people. Even so, a negative trend has been noticeable among young people, according to Gallup: "The percentage of engaged employees under the age of 35 dropped by four percentage points from 2019 to 2022."[62]

If young people in general share the perspective that causes, rather than institutions, are important, then churches pursuing intentional miracles at-scale with the global need, may speak volumes to isolated young people being lost to anxiety, violence, and confusion about their larger purpose.

Young people struggling with the above variety of challenges need to be given an agenda other than self and immediate gratification, two options that have produced little satisfaction so far. *The Chronicle of Philanthropy*'s review of the 50 biggest gifts in 2023 reported a shift among the younger mega-wealthy donors. The younger mega-donors favored specific causes, rather than institutions such as universities and hospitals, because "They want to create tangible change in the world."[63]

If young people in general share the perspective that causes, rather than institutions, are important, then churches pursuing intentional miracles at-scale with the global need, may speak volumes to isolated young people being lost to anxiety, violence, and confusion about their larger purpose.

For the future of each individual church member. Many church members are not all right, as shown by the increased number that are leaving the church. Can a church member be all right if the church is not providing a bigger vision? The downward trend in church membership would suggest the answer is no. In the same way that one denomination cannot maintain a strong commitment to missions in the face of competing societal forces, as shown in the analysis of Southern Baptist missions giving above, so also an individual will find it difficult to resist the pressure to focus on self rather than God when confronted by the overwhelming tsunami of affluence flooding the U.S.

John Wesley felt that it was very hard for Christians to be all right if they had access to great resources: "... from the time that riches and honour poured in upon them that feared and loved God, their hearts began to be estranged from him, and to cleave to the present world." As a defense against this repeating and debilitating pattern, Wesley's formula was the famous, "Gain all you can, Save all you can, Give all you can."[64]

Peter Brown has written two books, *Through the Eye of the Needle: Wealth, the Fall of Rome, and the Making of Christianity in the West, 350-550 AD* ,[65] and *The*

Ransom of the Soul: Afterlife and Wealth in Early Western Christianity,[66] that provide great insight into the attitudes of the early church toward "treasure in heaven," a key concept from Matthew 6:20. Brown writes that Christians in the early centuries of the church "... retained the great images of the transfer of treasure from earth to heaven and of the preparation of heavenly mansions through regular almsgiving." Brown refers to Gary Anderson's book *Charity*, summarizing Anderson's point that, "Almsgiving triggered the ultimate hope of a world ruled by a Creator who would reward mercy with mercy." Brown continues:

> "Furthermore, on a more subliminal level, the notion of treasure in heaven gripped the imagination because it seemed to join apparent incommensurables. To transfer money to heaven was not simply to store it there. It was to bring together two zones of the imagination that common sense held apart. In an almost magical imaginative implosion, the untarnished and eternal heavens were joined to earth through 'unrighteous mammon ...' "[67]

A focus on "storing treasure in heaven" can feel uncomfortable because the idea of rewards for the Christian has been discounted since the Protestant Reformation of the 1500s. The concept of rewards has also been distorted in some circles with the idea of the "prosperity gospel," a result of a materialistic society that promotes a focus on self rather than the other. For example, a 2023 Lifeway Research survey found that "... 52% of American Protestant churchgoers say their church teaches God will bless them if they give more money to their church and charities ..."[68] This theory may be shrouding a deeper truth.

> The apostle Paul, the church's eloquent champion of grace, did not divorce grace from the idea that there will also be rewards.

The apostle Paul, the church's eloquent champion of grace, did not divorce grace from the idea that there will also be rewards. In 1 Cor. 3:10-15, Paul describes each person's workmanship to be "revealed through the fire, and the fire will test the quality of each man's work. If what he has built survives, he will receive his reward. If it is burned up, he will suffer loss; he himself will be saved, but only as one escaping through the flames."

Both Martin Luther and John Calvin made it clear that it is by faith that one is saved. Yet, both Luther and Calvin expected actions to result from that faith. For example, Luther wrote,

> "Look for the poor, sick and all kinds of needy, help them and let your life's energy appear in this, so that they may enjoy your kindness, helping wherever your help is needed, as much as you possibly can with your life, property and honor. Know that to serve God is nothing else than to serve your neighbor in love, whether he be enemy or friend, or whether you can help in temporal or spiritual matters. This is serving God and doing good works."[69]

John Calvin commented, "Conversion, or turning unto God, is joined with repentance... And because repentance is an inward thing, and placed in the affection of the heart, Paul requireth, in the second place, such works as may make the same known, according to that exhortation of John the Baptist: 'Bring forth fruits meet for repentance' (Matth. iii. 8)."[70]

Paul's famous faith verses in Ephesians 2:8 and 9 are following immediately in verse 10 by a call to action.

> "(8) For it is by grace you have been saved, through faith — and this not from yourselves, it is the gift of God — (9) not by works, so that no one can boast. (10) For we are God's workmanship, created in Christ Jesus to do good works which God prepared in advance for us to do."

Jesus himself states in Matthew 16:27, "For the Son of Man is going to come in his Father's glory with his angels, and then he will reward each person according to what he has done."

Hugh Magers, when he was the Stewardship Director for The Episcopal Church, thought that the problem of stewardship is not a matter of how to pay the bills, but rather how to help people to understand what Jesus is actually talking about:

> " 'Lay up for yourself treasure in heaven.' *We* human beings are the treasure. We can use our resources to nurture folk into heaven. We have an opportunity to establish a deep appropriation of the faith. Instead of being in a world with starving babies, we have the opportunity to help there be well babies and to support a friend for eternity."[71]

The fact that Christians in the U.S. could tap as much as $474 billion more a year to address, in Jesus' name, global needs has not been conceptualized let alone explored by church leaders.

Tenney summarizes Wesley's view of materialists as "disbelievers in the eternal."[72] If churches are not yet ready to discount that there is an afterlife, then church leadership has a responsibility to help each church member change priorities from materialism to God, from the immediate to the eternal. In this way, leaders can help the individual church member be prepared for their long-term future by understanding that current actions have an impact now and also forever. In that context, one way to make preparations for the long-term future is to carry out the good works that God has prepared in advance. Deciding to create intentional miracles now is a good step for the future as well.

What makes this present time so special regarding intentional miracles?

The answer to that question can be summed up in one word: Scale.

The church has the potential to respond, in Jesus' name, to global needs at a scale never seen before.

Although the declines in church membership and giving documented in the first five chapters have become generally recognized, the findings of chapter 6 have been largely ignored and undiscussed. The fact that Christians in the U.S. could tap as much as $474 billion more a year to address, in Jesus' name, global needs has not been conceptualized let alone explored by church leaders.

Church leaders and members are thus out of step with those of the faith who have gone before. Historically, Christians have responded within the context of the times in which they found themselves.

Early Christians lived in a brutal pagan culture. Rodney Stark looked at the growth of Christianity from a sociological point of view. He claims, for instance, that Christians freed from a fear of death helped others during plagues that spread in the Roman world in 165 and 251 AD. Christians exhibited what one observer viewed as "a contempt for death." Christians saw the plagues as "... 'schooling and testing.' Thus, at a time when all other faiths were called to question, Christianity offered explanation and comfort. Even more important, Christian doctrine provided a *prescription for action*. That is, the Christian way appeared to work"[73] (emphasis in original).

At other points in church history, renewal movements appeared. Francis of Assisi (c. 1181-1226) founded the Franciscan movement which was seeking a more pure experience of God. Tom Holland describes the ministry of Francis: "His genius for taking Christ's teachings literally, for dramatizing their paradoxes and complexities, for combining simplicity and profundity in a single memorable gesture would never leave him. He served lepers; preached to birds; rescued lambs from butchers."[74] There was a reform element as well. Pope Innocent III approved Francis' request to form an order after meeting with him and realizing that Francis was the man in a dream Innocent had had. Innocent had seen "... the Lateran basilica was almost ready to fall down. A little poor man, small and scorned, was propping it up with his own back bent so that it would not fall. 'I'm sure,' he said, 'he is the one who will hold up Christ's Church by what he does and what he teaches.' "[75]

It is being argued here that the current body of Christ has a unique opportunity to further this story in a previously unimaginable way.

As mentioned above, the Wesleyan revival addressed needs present at that time, and had an impact on slavery, prisons, schools, and factory conditions through the "works of mercy" that Wesley emphasized. Sundays were transformed from a day of dissipation to a Sabbath rest. Mary Alice Tenney quotes Daniel Defoe, author of *Robinson Crusoe*, to describe Sundays among the lower classes in England in 1729 and the inconsistencies practiced in enforcing the Sunday Law by the upper classes:

> "Defoe in 1729 comments upon the strict enforcement of the law against meatsellers, which results in the loss of valuable food, and the utter failure to regulate public-houses, where the common people observe Sunday as a day of debauchery, becoming so drunken that 'they cannot work for a day or two following.' He complains that 'Instead of a day of rest, we make it a day of labour, by toiling in the Devil's vineyard; and but too many surfeit themselves with the fruits of gluttony, drunkenness and uncleanness.' "[76]

Evidence for the impact of the widespread changes in English society brought about by the Wesleyan revival receives further support from an unexpected source. Regarding Sundays being widely regarded as the Sabbath, by the time Jane Austen's novel, *Persuasion*, was published in 1817, the heroine, Anne Elliot, had reason to question the character of her cousin, Mr. Elliot, because, among other things, she surmises that "Sunday travelling (*sic*) had been a common thing."[77]

Other generations in the history of the church have responded to the particular circumstances of their times, and wrote their chapter in the unfolding story of the body of Christ. It is being argued here that the current body of Christ has a unique opportunity to further this story in a previously unimaginable way.

Specifically, the church can respond to global need at a scale never before possible. This at-scale mobilization could enable goals not only to be set but also to be met, in Jesus' name, on behalf of neighbors in need.

One factor is the unprecedented affluence flooding the church for the past two hundred years. Figure 23 presents two lines of selected points from an analysis by British economist Angus Maddison. He calculated per capita (per person) Gross Domestic Product (GDP) from the Year 0 through 1998. Maddison adjusted for inflation using 1990 dollars so that the amounts would be comparable over the centuries. In this chart, Maddison's data for the world and for the U.S. (which appears in the 1500s in his series) are presented. His analysis indicates that U.S. per capita GDP increased from $400 in the 1500s to $27,331 in 1998.[78]

The 2022 figures added to Angus Maddison's data are estimates calculated based on the percent increase, in constant 2015 dollars, between 1998 and 2022 for the U.S. per capita GDP.[79]

The effective altruism movement echoes Biblically-based ideas without reference to the Bible. The movement may indicate a hunger among the general populace for the truths that Jesus presented and the early church promoted about the choice that had to be made between God and money.

The figure is a graphic depiction of the affluence that has flooded the U.S. in recent centuries It is proposed here that church leaders have not had a positive agenda for this affluence. An effort to set goals and achieve them on behalf of global neighbors' needs is well within the possibilities for Christians in the U.S. What is needed is an at-scale vision for calling church members to solve, rather than cope with — or worse, ignore — global needs. And as is pointed out in chapter 6 of this volume, the amount of affluence available to church members in the U.S. can also provide the resources to address needs within the U.S. The situation is both/and rather than either/or.

While church leaders have ignored the reality of this affluence, a group working through Longview Philanthropy has reviewed these financial resources. One article, using a calculator developed by the group, suggested that a surprising number of Americans would find themselves in the richest 1% of the world's population.[80] Another movement is "effective altruism" that was featured in a TIME magazine cover story.[81] Founded by a Scottish philosopher, William Macaskill, the movement is attracting a variety of young people. According to the article, "In encouraging a norm where people give 10% of their income — significantly more than the 2% of disposable income the average American gives — to causes that are unrelated to their immediate emotional satisfaction, effective altruism is asking more of people than to simply 'try to make things better,' says Alexander Berger, the co-CEO of Open Philanthropy."[82]

The effective altruism movement echoes Biblically-based ideas without reference to the Bible. The movement may indicate a hunger among the general populace for the truths that Jesus presented and the early church promoted about the choice that had to be made between God and money. What is clear is that without such a choice being presented to church members by their leaders, church members have found other channels for the affluence spreading through U.S. society. Joining other Americans, average spending per person includes:

Figure 23: Gross Domestic Product, Per Capita, 1990 Dollars, the World and the U.S.,Year 0 - 1998 AD, U.S. GDP Updated through 2022

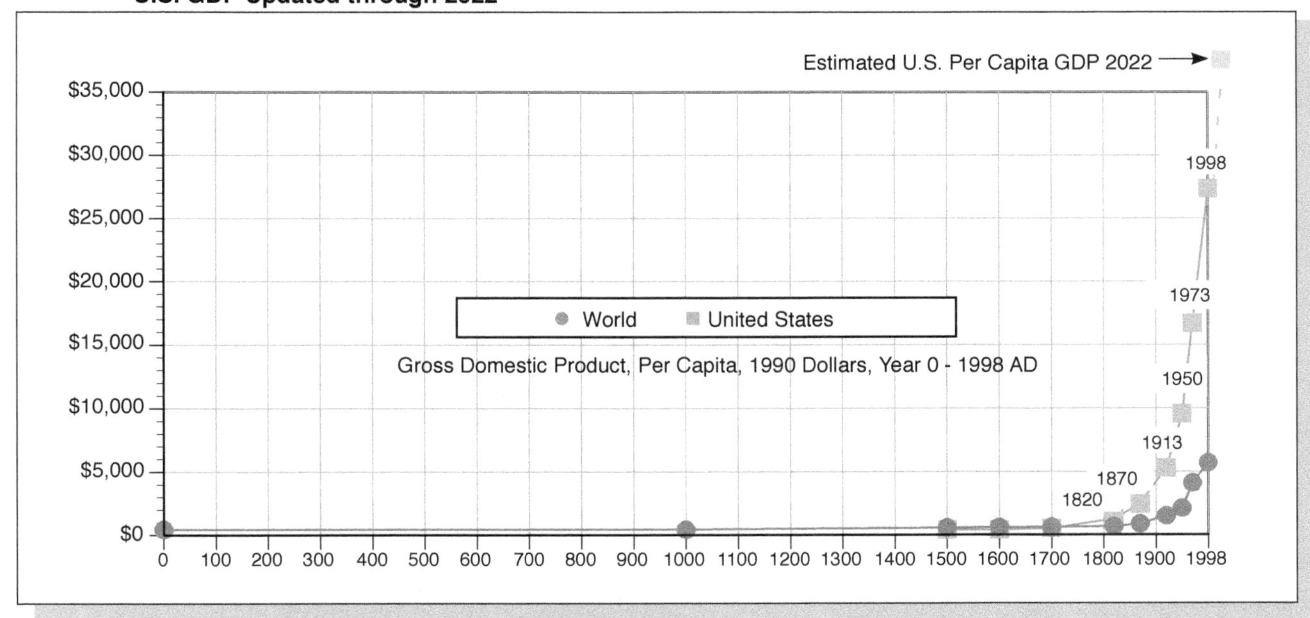

Source for Chart Dollars: Angus Maddison, *The World Economy: A Millennial Perspective* (Year 0-1998) empty tomb, inc. 2024
Through 2022: World Bank data; empty tomb, inc. analysis

- $144.90 on chocolate[83]: That's a total of $48 billion in 2021.
- $1,341 on soft drinks: That's $447.38 billion in 2022.[84]
- $172 on professional sporting events: That's $56 billion in 12 months in 2016-2017, and includes tickets, transportation, food, and drinks.[85]
- $44.78 on Super Bowl parties: For those not spending on tickets for the special day, that's $14.8 billion in 2019 on parties for that one day.[86]
- $170 on jewelry: That's $56 billion in 2020.[87]
- $292.78 on video gaming, which totals $97.67 billion in 2022.[88]
- $2,887 on leisure travel in 2022, which totals $963 billion.[89]

While Americans annually spent almost one trillion dollars on leisure travel, the church has not been able to spark church members' imaginations to direct an additional $16 billion a year to help prevent annually more than one million under-age five child deaths from treatable causes. For perspective, that $16 billion needed to prevent these child deaths from treatable causes is about the amount that was legally wagered in just one state during 2022.[90]

Even though Jesus talked about the topic of money frequently, the church has been largely silent on addressing the topic. The result in this age of affluence is that the church's voice has been replaced by "influencers" guiding people as to how they prioritize their use of money.

Consider that a Gallup poll found that "Clergy" had slipped eight points, between 2019-2023, in a survey asking about ethics ratings of various professions. In response to a request to rate "the honesty and ethical standards of people in these different fields," 40% ranked Clergy "Very high/High" in 2019 while 32% did in 2023. Other categories in the 30% response range in the 2023 survey were Chiropractors at 33%, and Psychiatrists at 36%.[91]

Meanwhile, social media "influencers" are on the ascendency.

The Influencer Marketing Hub provides this explanation of the term: "Influencers in social media are people who have built a reputation for their knowledge and expertise on a specific topic. They make regular posts about that topic on their preferred social media channels and generate large followings of enthusiastic, engaged people who pay close attention to their views." These people might be bloggers, YouTubers, Podcasters, or provide social posts only.[92]

The relationship between influencers and social media users is hauntingly similar to the relationship people have traditionally have had with church. An article provided an overview of the effect of influencers on marketing products:

The relationship between influencers and social media users is hauntingly similar to the relationship people have traditionally have had with church.

- "To understand the impact of influencer marketing on consumer behavior, it's crucial to consider the role of trust and authenticity."
- "Influencers, having built a loyal following by sharing their personal experiences and recommendations, are trusted by their followers."
- "... 61% of consumers are more likely to trust influencers' recommendations — compare it with brand-produced content (38%)."
- "Influencers sway consumer behavior by leveraging the halo effect, where credibility in one area leads to trusted opinions in other areas. However, influence extends beyond trust. The desire to conform to social norms and be part of a group also drives engagement with influencers."
- "Authenticity is crucial as consumers can usually tell when an endorsement isn't genuine."[93]

The presence of social media influencers indicates that people can be guided in their choices of how to spend their money. With 47% of the U.S. population still claiming membership in churches, pastors could choose to influence these members to take on a positive agenda for the affluence that is now being directed into so many other channels. The Bible provides a great resource for developing a compelling view of the role of money in members' priorities.

Another factor that makes this time special in regard to meeting global needs is the medical advances available. The estimated 1.5 million children that are slated to die in the Promise Gap during 2024 are dying from *treatable conditions*. The medical knowledge exists to stop these needs. The problem is that the parents of the children do not have access to these solutions.

Also, although weakened, the church structures in the U.S. still have a broad network throughout the globe, with on-the-ground contacts through whom the churches can work. As the church in the U.S. weakens, these networks are bound to be affected. Therefore, the sooner a decision is made to take action, the more of these networks will be available.

John Wesley saw that money was a force that competed for people's hearts. He struggled with the fact that, as people became committed to following Jesus, it was hard not also to act responsibly and, as a consequence, become richer. And once rich, it was too easy to become indifferent. Wesley reflected, late in his life, on the three rules he had set forth: Earn all you can; Save all you can; and Give all you can. However, he observed, "And yet nothing can be more plain, than that all who observe the two first rules without the third, will be twofold more the children of hell than ever they were before." [94]

Wesley had developed a strategy that would help richer Methodists keep their feet when flooded with affluence, even the comparatively small affluence of the early years of the industrial revolution. Tenney observes that Wesley saw the works of mercy as a key defense against being consumed by materialism. "So long as they remain responsive to the world's need Christianity continues to spread."[95] When richer Methodists suggested paying for a doctor to visit a sick person, instead of going themselves, Wesley responded:

> "...a doctor 'cannot do them more good to their souls ... And if he could, this would not excuse *you*: his going would not fulfil *your* duty.' "[96] (emphasis in original)

"And yet nothing can be more plain, than that all who observe the two first rules without the third, will be twofold more the children of hell than ever they were before."
— John Wesley reflecting on his formula of Earn all you can; Save all you can; Give all you can.

If Wesley is correct, then this current time of great affluence, even while the church is weakening, is the perfect time to recover the Christian heritage of loving God and loving neighbors through a priority of pursuing a positive agenda of intentional miracles.

What would an intentional miracle look like?

Figure 24 has been repeated in the last several editions of *The State of Church Giving* series. The numbers in the accompanying chart have been updated through 2021. However, the two photos are repeated because it is difficult to find a more clear illustration of the potential to carry out intentional miracles. These two Associated Press photos are of the same child, 12 days apart. His mother was able to travel from Somalia to a clinic in Kenya. The visible change in the same child in only a few days testifies to the difference that timely medical intervention can make.

Table 49 and Table 50 present the 40 countries and the treatable causes of death among children under five in each of those countries.

Tables 49 and 50 develop a model to estimate the cost to address various causes of death impacting children around the globe. This information provides the large parameters within which many churches can choose to carry out, in Jesus' name, intentional miracles, one medical intervention project at a time.

The results presented in Tables 49 and 50 provide dollar-cost estimates, based on the total estimate of $16 billion, for the causes of under-5 deaths in each of the 40 countries included in the tables. The model suggests the type of information that can be developed to foster initiatives to eliminate conditions that result in needless child deaths. A description of the related methodology is included in the endnotes.[97]

This model, a first approximation for estimating country-specific costs to prevent child deaths, was based on the assumption that the cost of the disease or other cause of death remedies was equal for each disease. A second working assumption was that the cost of a package of remedies per child was the same across the different countries. While this model could be refined by disease (or other cause of death)-specific information, this early approximation may be useful for exploring how to address, and mobilize for meeting, specific country goals and the increased church giving needed to accomplish the task.

In Table 49 a summed dollar figure for all Neonatal causes is presented in addition to 12 specific causes of death in children under age five.

Table 50 presents the Neonatal detail for the ten subcategories within the Neonatal cause.

Overall, the global Under-5 Mortality Rate (U5MR) was declining from 1990 to 2020, from 93 per 1,000 live births in 1990 to 38 in 2021. However, the rate of progress in reaching the target reduction rate was slowing. That statement is based on a comparison between a calculated U5MR reduction goal for a particular year and the actual U5MR for that year. For example, in order to reach a global U5MR of 15 deaths per thousand live births in 2035, the U5MR should have dropped from 93 in 1990 to the U5MR reduction goal target of 62 in 2000. In fact, the actual U5MR in 2000 was 76. The difference between 76 and 62, as a percent of the U5MR reduction goal base of 62, equals 22.6%. Looking at the years 1990 through 2015, in 5-year increments, the difference between the actual U5MR and the U5MR reduction goal as a percent of the U5MR reduction goal base increased from 1990 to 2005 suggesting the rate of progress in reducing child deaths was slowing. The difference decreased between 2005 and 2010. However, it increased again between 2010 and 2015. By 2021, the difference between the actual U5MR and the U5MR reduction goal as a percent of the U5MR reduction goal base was 43.6%, the largest difference in the 1990 to 2021 period.

Again, Jesus includes "with all your mind" in the Great Commandment in Mark 12:29-31. Applying one's mind, as well as heart, soul, and strength, could be a key element in defining what an intentional miracle looks like on behalf of these dying children.

Again, Jesus includes "with all your mind" in the Great Commandment in Mark 12:29-31. Applying one's mind, as well as heart, soul, and strength, could be a key element in defining what an intentional miracle looks like on behalf of these dying children.

The group publishing *The State of Church Giving* series has thought long and hard about how to effectively mobilize churches to pursue intentional miracles. Their practical efforts began in the late 1980s, with a structure that might be described as a "Weight Watcher's®" program for church budgets. The structure worked, to the surprise of church leaders who withdrew when they found members would respond with more money if that money were to be directed to mission. As one church leader explained, "We didn't think they would give more money."

Figure 24: Exponential Interpolation Of MDG 4 Under-5 Child Deaths Per 1,000 Live Births, Based on Reported 1990 Data and 2035 Goal; Reported Data, 1995, 2000, 2010, 2015, and 2021; Projected 2024 Data

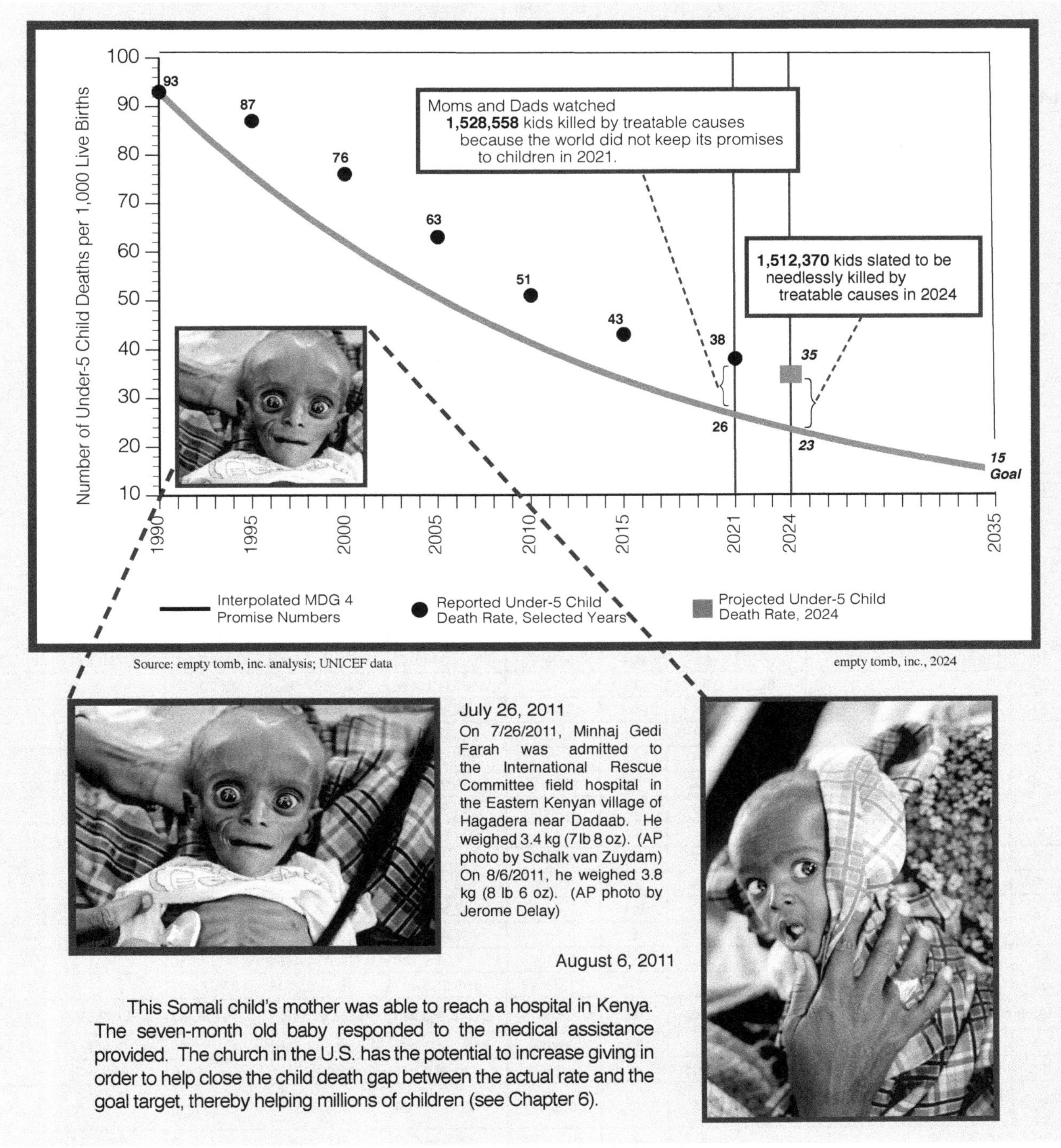

July 26, 2011
On 7/26/2011, Minhaj Gedi Farah was admitted to the International Rescue Committee field hospital in the Eastern Kenyan village of Hagadera near Dadaab. He weighed 3.4 kg (7 lb 8 oz). (AP photo by Schalk van Zuydam) On 8/6/2011, he weighed 3.8 kg (8 lb 6 oz). (AP photo by Jerome Delay)

August 6, 2011

This Somali child's mother was able to reach a hospital in Kenya. The seven-month old baby responded to the medical assistance provided. The church in the U.S. has the potential to increase giving in order to help close the child death gap between the actual rate and the goal target, thereby helping millions of children (see Chapter 6).

The next iteration was a project that would match congregation's special mission giving offerings for projects named by the congregations in their applications. From 2002 through 2016, this effort provided $222,000 in 124 matching contributions to 112 church mission projects (in some cases, more than one church worked on the same project). The churches often oversubscribed the match amount, and so over

Table 49: Country-Specific Dollar-Cost Estimates for Causes of Under-5 Child Deaths, 40 Countries

Nation		Under-5 Mortality Rank	Annual no. of Under-5 Deaths (000s) 2015	Missed Goal Deaths 2015	Country Total as % of Total Annual No. of Missed Goal Under-5 Deaths	Country Total$ Need, Based on $16 Billion Total Estimate 2015	Pneumonia: $2,180,658,541 2017	AIDS $289,225,598 2017	Measles: $324,246,257 2017	Meningitis: $343,233,684 2017
Areas and Countries			**(000s)**	**(000s)**	**2015**	**($s)**	**($s)**	**($s)**	**($s)**	**($s)**
Africa: 32 Nations			**3,027.3**	**804**	**80%**	**$12,744,111,028**	**$1,845,429,963**	**$286,812,398**	**$310,104,981**	**$308,004,750**
1	Angola	1	169	90	8.88%	$1,421,536,406	$199,015,097	$42,646,092	$14,215,364	$28,430,728
2	Benin	8	37	15	1.46%	233,285,144	27,994,217	2,332,851	0	4,665,703
3	Burkina Faso	18	60	14	1.39%	222,281,674	26,673,801	0	2,222,817	4,445,633
4	Burundi	21	37	9	0.91%	145,534,722	17,464,167	1,455,347	0	2,910,694
5	Cameroon	19	71	22	2.14%	342,133,668	41,056,040	10,264,010	0	3,421,337
6	Central African Republic	4	21	10	1.02%	163,443,791	19,613,255	3,268,876	4,903,314	4,903,314
7	Chad	2	83	42	4.14%	663,048,307	139,240,144	6,630,483	0	26,521,932
8	Comoros	25	2	1	0.06%	10,170,974	1,423,936	0	0	203,419
9	Côte d'Ivoire	13	75	26	2.60%	416,372,724	45,801,000	12,491,182	4,163,727	4,163,727
10	Democratic Republic of the Congo	9	305	108	10.65%	1,704,121,295	187,453,343	17,041,213	102,247,278	34,082,426
11	Djibouti	32	1	0.2	0.02%	3,595,723	395,530	107,872	0	35,957
12	Equatorial Guinea	11	3	1	0.10%	16,361,972	1,963,437	981,718	327,239	163,620
13	Gabon	42	3	0.3	0.03%	4,569,180	411,226	182,767	365,534	45,692
14	Gambia	29	6	1	0.12%	19,918,324	1,991,832	398,366	0	199,183
15	Ghana	35	54	10	1.01%	162,163,167	12,973,053	8,108,158	0	1,621,632
16	Guinea	11	42	13	1.27%	203,949,891	30,592,484	2,039,499	6,118,497	6,118,497
17	Guinea-Bissau	13	6	2	0.17%	26,876,699	2,956,437	1,075,068	268,767	537,534
18	Lesotho	17	6	2	0.24%	37,939,783	3,414,580	4,173,376	0	379,398
19	Liberia	27	11	0.4	0.04%	6,340,092	634,009	63,401	760,811	126,802
20	Mali	6	83	29	2.92%	467,018,595	65,382,603	4,670,186	0	9,340,372
21	Mauritania	20	11	4	0.41%	64,826,245	7,779,149	0	648,262	648,262
22	Mozambique	23	82	14	1.40%	223,945,352	22,394,535	17,915,628	0	2,239,454
23	Niger	10	88	19	1.88%	300,183,396	39,023,841	0	0	6,003,668
24	Nigeria	7	750	280	27.68%	4,429,231,994	752,969,439	132,876,960	88,584,640	132,876,960
25	Sierra Leone	5	26	9	0.93%	148,268,859	16,309,575	1,482,689	0	1,482,689
26	Somalia	3	61	32	3.13%	501,227,576	85,208,688	0	75,184,136	20,049,103
27	South Sudan	13	39	11	1.06%	169,745,852	28,856,795	5,092,376	1,697,459	5,092,376
28	Sudan	27	89	24	2.33%	373,134,674	41,044,814	0	7,462,693	3,731,347
29	Swaziland	36	2	0.1	0.01%	2,302,163	253,238	322,303	0	23,022
30	Togo	24	20	6	0.58%	93,444,238	8,409,981	2,803,327	934,442	1,868,885
31	Zambia	33	39	0.1	0.01%	1,586,138	174,475	111,030	0	15,861
32	Zimbabwe	26	38	10	1.03%	165,552,407	16,555,241	8,277,620	0	1,655,524
Asia: 6 Nations			**2,500**	**198**	**20%**	**$3,140,563,223**	**$317,821,462**	**$106,684**	**$13,722,336**	**$32,607,041**
33	Afghanistan	16	94	34	3.32%	$531,551,052	$53,155,105	$0	$10,631,021	$5,315,511
34	India	48	1,201	8	0.75%	120,140,911	13,215,500	0	2,402,818	2,402,818
35	Lao People's Democratic Republic	31	12	2	0.23%	36,001,764	4,680,229	0	0	360,018
36	Myanmar	44	46	4	0.43%	68,849,676	8,261,961	0	688,497	688,497
37	Pakistan	22	432	150	14.83%	2,373,351,408	237,335,141	0	0	23,733,514
38	Turkmenistan	42	6	1	0.07%	10,668,411	1,173,525	106,684	0	106,684
Latin America/Caribbean: 1 Nation										
39	Haiti	29	18	5	0.46%	73,431,760	$13,217,717	$1,468,635	$0	$2,202,953
Oceania: 1 Nation										
40	Papua New Guinea	38	12	3	0.26%	$41,893,989	$4,189,399	$837,880	$418,940	$418,940

Source: UNICEF data; empty tomb, inc. analysis

Malaria: $1,314,967,882 2017	Preterm: $173,330,311 2017	Intrapartum: $199,152,366 2017	Congenital: $424,103,737 2017	NCDs: $613,518,029 2017	Injuries: $845,577,877 2017	Other $1,411,319,334 2017	Diarrhoea $1,428,812,720 2017	Neonatal $6,322,175,296 2017
($s)	($s)	($s)	($s)	($s)	($s)	($s)	($s)	($s)
$1,309,940,604	**$167,524,701**	**$195,733,351**	**$357,197,270**	**$466,562,409**	**$682,354,900**	**$1,198,488,030**	**$1,196,987,522**	**$4,290,493,187**
$99,507,548	$28,430,728	$28,430,728	$56,861,456	$56,861,456	$85,292,184	$142,153,641	$127,938,277	$511,753,106
37,325,623	4,665,703	2,332,851	6,998,554	11,664,257	11,664,257	23,328,514	20,995,663	81,649,800
46,679,152	2,222,817	2,222,817	4,445,633	8,891,267	13,336,900	26,673,801	17,782,534	66,684,502
14,553,472	2,910,694	1,455,347	2,910,694	7,276,736	10,187,431	18,919,514	11,642,778	53,847,847
44,477,377	6,842,673	3,421,337	10,264,010	17,106,683	20,528,020	34,213,367	30,792,030	116,325,447
27,785,444	1,634,438	1,634,438	3,268,876	4,903,314	6,537,752	11,441,065	14,709,941	60,474,203
53,043,865	13,260,966	13,260,966	19,891,449	19,891,449	39,782,898	59,674,348	79,565,797	212,175,458
0	203,419	101,710	305,129	406,839	610,258	1,118,807	813,678	4,882,068
29,146,091	8,327,454	4,163,727	12,491,182	16,654,909	24,982,363	41,637,272	37,473,545	179,040,271
238,576,981	17,041,213	17,041,213	34,082,426	68,164,852	85,206,065	170,412,130	153,370,917	545,318,815
0	71,914	35,957	107,872	143,829	215,743	359,572	251,701	1,905,733
2,617,916	163,620	163,620	490,859	490,859	654,479	1,145,338	1,145,338	6,217,549
274,151	45,692	45,692	137,075	137,075	182,767	319,843	228,459	2,238,898
597,550	199,183	199,183	597,550	597,550	1,195,099	1,792,649	1,394,283	10,955,078
11,351,422	1,621,632	1,621,632	4,864,895	4,864,895	8,108,158	12,973,053	9,729,790	82,703,215
30,592,484	2,039,499	2,039,499	4,078,998	6,118,497	10,197,495	18,355,490	16,315,991	63,224,466
1,075,068	0	268,767	806,301	806,301	1,612,602	2,418,903	2,150,136	12,094,515
0	758,796	379,398	1,138,193	1,517,591	1,896,989	3,414,580	2,655,785	18,590,493
507,207	63,401	63,401	190,203	190,203	317,005	507,207	443,806	2,536,037
65,382,603	4,670,186	4,670,186	14,010,558	18,680,744	23,350,930	46,701,860	46,701,860	163,456,508
2,593,050	1,296,525	648,262	1,944,787	2,593,050	3,889,575	7,130,887	5,834,362	29,171,810
26,873,442	2,239,454	2,239,454	6,718,361	6,718,361	11,197,268	17,915,628	15,676,175	91,817,594
57,034,845	6,003,668	3,001,834	0	12,007,336	18,011,004	30,018,340	27,016,506	93,056,853
442,923,199	44,292,320	88,584,640	132,876,960	132,876,960	221,461,600	398,630,879	442,923,199	1,328,769,598
34,101,838	0	2,965,377	4,448,066	7,413,443	7,413,443	14,826,886	13,344,197	41,515,281
0	5,012,276	5,012,276	10,024,552	15,036,827	25,061,379	45,110,482	55,135,033	155,380,549
11,882,210	1,697,459	1,697,459	3,394,917	5,092,376	8,487,293	11,882,210	15,277,127	66,200,882
3,731,347	7,462,693	3,731,347	11,194,040	29,850,774	26,119,427	33,582,121	29,850,774	175,373,297
0	69,065	23,022	115,108	115,108	138,130	230,216	161,151	851,800
20,557,732	934,442	934,442	1,868,885	2,803,327	4,672,212	6,541,097	5,606,654	35,508,810
126,891	31,723	31,723	47,584	63,446	111,030	158,614	126,891	618,594
6,622,096	3,311,048	3,311,048	6,622,096	6,622,096	9,933,144	14,899,717	9,933,144	76,154,107
$0	**$3,918,034**	**$1,950,379**	**$63,131,317**	**$140,139,637**	**$156,722,372**	**$205,177,441**	**$222,702,700**	**$1,981,362,410**
$0	$0	$0	$10,631,021	$31,893,063	$26,577,553	$26,577,553	$37,208,574	$329,561,652
0	2,402,818	0	2,402,818	3,604,227	3,604,227	4,805,636	9,611,273	74,487,365
0	720,035	360,018	720,035	3,240,159	2,520,124	2,520,124	3,600,176	17,280,847
0	688,497	1,376,994	1,376,994	5,507,974	4,819,477	4,819,477	5,507,974	35,113,335
0	0	0	47,467,028	94,934,056	118,667,570	166,134,599	166,134,599	1,518,944,901
0	106,684	213,368	533,421	960,157	533,421	320,052	640,105	5,974,310
$0	$1,468,635	$1,468,635	$2,937,270	$5,140,223	$4,405,906	$5,140,223	$6,608,858	$29,372,704
$5,027,279	$418,940	$0	$837,880	$1,675,760	$2,094,699	$2,513,639	$2,513,639	$20,946,994

empty tomb, inc., 2024

Table 50: Country-Specific Dollar-Cost Estimates Detail for Causes of Neonatal Deaths, 40 Countries

	Nation	Total Neonatal $6,322,175,296 2017	Neonatal Diarrhoea $29,049,025 2017	Neonatal Tetanus $125,384,228 2017	Neonatal Preterm $2,032,706,655 2017	Neonatal Intrapartum-related event $1,799,540,924 2017
Africa: 32 Nations		**$4,290,493,187**	**$0**	**$66,926,161**	**$1,347,443,964**	**$1,338,425,536**
1	Angola	$511,753,106	$0	$0	$142,153,641	$170,584,369
2	Benin	81,649,800	0	0	27,994,217	20,995,663
3	Burkina Faso	66,684,502	0	0	20,005,351	17,782,534
4	Burundi	53,847,847	0	0	16,008,819	16,008,819
5	Cameroon	116,325,447	0	0	34,213,367	37,634,704
6	Central African Republic	60,474,203	0	1,634,438	17,978,817	17,978,817
7	Chad	212,175,458	0	6,630,483	53,043,865	66,304,831
8	Comoros	4,882,068	0	101,710	1,830,775	1,118,807
9	Côte d'Ivoire	179,040,271	0	0	54,128,454	49,964,727
10	Democratic Republic of the Congo	545,318,815	0	0	187,453,343	170,412,130
11	Djibouti	1,905,733	0	35,957	683,187	467,444
12	Equatorial Guinea	6,217,549	0	163,620	1,963,437	1,799,817
13	Gabon	2,238,898	0	0	776,761	548,302
14	Gambia	10,955,078	0	0	2,788,565	3,186,932
15	Ghana	82,703,215	0	0	24,324,475	22,702,843
16	Guinea	63,224,466	0	0	16,315,991	20,394,989
17	Guinea-Bissau	12,094,515	0	268,767	3,225,204	3,762,738
18	Lesotho	18,590,493	0	379,398	6,829,161	5,311,570
19	Liberia	2,536,037	0	0	697,410	697,410
20	Mali	163,456,508	0	0	51,372,046	46,701,860
21	Mauritania	29,171,810	0	0	11,020,462	6,482,625
22	Mozambique	91,817,594	0	0	26,873,442	24,633,989
23	Niger	93,056,853	0	0	30,018,340	24,014,672
24	Nigeria	1,328,769,598	0	44,292,320	442,923,199	442,923,199
25	Sierra Leone	41,515,281	0	0	11,861,509	13,344,197
26	Somalia	155,380,549	0	10,024,552	35,085,930	60,147,309
27	South Sudan	66,200,882	0	3,394,917	18,672,044	22,066,961
28	Sudan	175,373,297	0	0	70,895,588	37,313,467
29	Swaziland	851,800	0	0	299,281	230,216
30	Togo	35,508,810	0	0	9,344,424	11,213,309
31	Zambia	618,594	0	0	174,475	174,475
32	Zimbabwe	76,154,107	0	0	26,488,385	21,521,813
Asia: 6 Nations		**$1,981,362,410**	**$29,049,025**	**$58,458,067**	**$669,432,463**	**$447,907,054**
33	Afghanistan	$329,561,652	$5,315,511	$10,631,021	$95,679,189	$85,048,168
34	India	74,487,365	0	0	33,639,455	14,416,909
35	Lao People's Democratic Republic	17,280,847	0	360,018	5,040,247	5,040,247
36	Myanmar	35,113,335	0	0	11,015,948	9,638,955
37	Pakistan	1,518,944,901	23,733,514	47,467,028	522,137,310	332,269,197
38	Turkmenistan	5,974,310	0	0	1,920,314	1,493,578
Latin America/Caribbean: 1 Nation						
39	Haiti	$29,372,704	$0	$0	$9,546,129	$7,343,176
Oceania: 1 Nation						
40	Papua New Guinea	$20,946,994	$0	$0	$6,284,098	$5,865,158

Source: UNICEF data; empty tomb, inc. analysis

Neonatal Sepsis $979,383,689 2017	Neonatal Congenital $444,000,000 2017	Neonatal Injuries $56,912,203 2017	Neonatal Meningitis $95,335,301 2017	Neonatal Other $327,721,494 2017	Neonatal Pneumonia $432,141,778 2017
$669,172,806	**$302,996,333**	**$1,821,209**	**$35,977,311**	**$222,313,785**	**$305,416,084**
$85,292,184	$42,646,092	$0	$0	$28,430,728	$42,646,092
16,329,960	4,665,703	0	2,332,851	4,665,703	4,665,703
13,336,900	4,445,633	0	2,222,817	4,445,633	4,445,633
8,732,083	4,366,042	0	1,455,347	2,910,694	4,366,042
17,106,683	10,264,010	0	0	6,842,673	10,264,010
9,806,627	3,268,876	0	1,634,438	3,268,876	4,903,314
33,152,415	13,260,966	0	6,630,483	13,260,966	19,891,449
711,968	406,839	0	101,710	305,129	305,129
37,473,545	12,491,182	0	4,163,727	8,327,454	12,491,182
85,206,065	34,082,426	0	0	34,082,426	34,082,426
251,701	179,786	35,957	35,957	107,872	107,872
654,479	490,859	163,620	0	490,859	490,859
319,843	274,151	0	0	182,767	137,075
2,191,016	995,916	0	199,183	796,733	796,733
14,594,685	8,108,158	1,621,632	1,621,632	4,864,895	4,864,895
12,236,993	4,078,998	0	2,039,499	4,078,998	4,078,998
2,150,136	806,301	0	268,767	806,301	806,301
2,655,785	1,138,193	0	0	1,138,193	1,138,193
507,207	190,203	0	63,401	190,203	190,203
32,691,302	9,340,372	0	4,670,186	9,340,372	9,340,372
5,834,362	1,944,787	0	648,262	1,296,525	1,944,787
17,915,628	6,718,361	0	2,239,454	6,718,361	6,718,361
18,011,004	6,003,668	0	3,001,834	6,003,668	6,003,668
177,169,280	88,584,640	0	0	44,292,320	88,584,640
7,413,443	2,965,377	0	0	2,965,377	2,965,377
15,036,827	10,024,552	0	0	10,024,552	15,036,827
6,789,834	5,092,376	0	1,697,459	3,394,917	5,092,376
29,850,774	14,925,387	0	0	11,194,040	11,194,040
115,108	92,087	0	0	69,065	46,043
5,606,654	2,803,327	0	934,442	2,803,327	2,803,327
95,168	63,446	0	15,861	47,584	47,584
9,933,144	8,277,620	0	0	4,966,572	4,966,572
$302,872,398	**$136,706,014**	**$53,937,737**	**$58,204,733**	**$101,528,997**	**$123,265,921**
$47,839,595	$26,577,553	$5,315,511	$10,631,021	$21,262,042	$21,262,042
9,611,273	8,409,864	0	0	4,805,636	3,604,227
2,520,124	1,800,088	360,018	0	1,080,053	1,080,053
4,819,477	4,130,981	688,497	0	2,753,987	2,065,490
237,335,141	94,934,056	47,467,028	47,467,028	71,200,542	94,934,056
746,789	853,473	106,684	106,684	426,736	320,052
$4,405,906	$2,202,953	$734,318	$734,318	$2,202,953	$2,202,953
$2,932,579	$2,094,699	$418,940	$418,940	$1,675,760	$1,256,820

empty tomb, inc., 2024

$444,000, combining the matching contribution and the money raised by the church, was directed to these congregations' mission activities. The projects were mostly international and there were also some domestic projects. Many involved mission trips that the congregation was taking.

In 2016, the focus of the matching effort changed for at least two reasons. First, data became available that indicated the Millennium Development Goals (MDGs) had not been met by 2015. The target reduction goal for reducing under-age 5 child deaths, for example, left what the matching effort termed the "Promise Gap": The difference between the child-death reduction goals set in 1990 and again in 2000, and the actual rate of death in 2015. It became clear that this ongoing tragedy of these young children dying from treatable causes would need intentional intervention if the reduction goals were to be met.

Another issue that surfaced was that donors helping to provide the matching funds expressed concern about not knowing precisely what their donations would accomplish. There was not a clear focus nor was there an overview goal that their donations were trying to achieve during the project years of 2002 to 2016.

Using the churches' own distribution networks, churches can apply for a matching contribution for a medical mission project, to be carried out in Jesus' name, in one of 40 countries ...

At that point, the matching group began to focus solely on church mission medical projects that would address one or more of the preventable causes of death facing children and their parents. Using the churches' own distribution networks, churches can apply for a matching contribution for a medical mission project, to be carried out in Jesus' name, in one of 40 countries where the large majority of the under-five child deaths are occurring. The project, empty tomb®'s Mission Match®, offers these funds to churches at missionmatch.org.

And here is where the challenge to imaginations occurs. The goal behind this project is not to build a big organization. It is to mobilize the power for good of most of the 300,000+ historically Christians churches at a level that will impact at-scale the tragedy of these needless child deaths.

The largest relief and development organization in the U.S. is World Vision, a group that has established itself as an important parachurch outreach. According to World Vision's Form 990, for the year beginning 2019 (the latest year easily accessible), the organization's contributions totaled $1.226 billion. Of this, $408 million, or 33%, was in-kind (non-cash) donations, indicating that cash contributions totaled about $819 million that year.[98] Similarly, Samaritan's Purse was the second largest group on a list of 45 relief and development groups published by Ministry Watch.[99] Samaritan's Purse Form 990 2019 provided information that about one-third of its reported contributions was from in-kind sources.[100] The latest data available for Compassion International was 2018. With contributions of $947,571,184 that year, only about $2 million came from in-kind donations.[101] Catholic Relief Services is not required to file Form 990 because of its affiliation with the Catholic Church; however the group voluntarily presents a copy of Form 990 2018 on its Web site, indicating that of the $936,869,875 received in contributions, $211,271,822, or 23%, were via in-kind contributions.[102]

Thus these four largest groups — with contributions equal to a third of the total contributions of the 45 relief and development groups on the Ministry Watch list —reported cash donations of $3.0 billion in 2018 or 2019.

The work of these organizations has likely made very important contributions to the decline in the number of child deaths that has occurred over the years. However, as noted above, the data indicates the rate of reduction is slowing down. The level of activity to date has not closed the Promise Gap, resulting in 44.3 million children under age five dying from treatable causes from 1990 through 2021. It is the extra effort needed that empty tomb's Mission Match is designed to challenge churches to undertake. Churches, working independently in a parallel fashion, through their own selected channels, yet pursuing a common goal, can accomplish what has eluded the efforts of world leaders and vital organizations to date. This matching project is an at-scale strategy to end an ongoing tragedy as soon as possible.

Focusing on one issue first, such as meeting the child death reduction goal, has a practical value. Bjorn Lomborg, president of a Danish think tank, was quoted in an interview as arguing "that global efforts to do good are often hampered by wanting to achieve too much at once. 'Saying everything is a priority means nothing is a priority,' he says."[103]

Bestselling author Matthew Kelly asserts that Christians acting together is a powerful force. If Christians acted together to address an agreed-on problem, he says, Christians could change that problem. "In the process we could completely change the image of Christianity in this country and around the world. We would no longer be seen as a massively divided people who mostly *talk about* doing good things; we would be seen as modern leaders committed to changing the world one problem at a time"[104] (emphasis in original).

If Christians acted together to address an agreed-on problem, he says, Christians could change that problem. "In the process we could completely change the image of Christianity in this country and around the world ..."
— Matthew Kelly

Other groups can continue their ongoing, very important efforts. What is being described here is an *additional* effort conducted at-scale with both the problem facing the little children and their parents, as well as the resources available to church members that are now being spent in so many other ways. The goal of $16 billion a year is impossible for one congregation. Yet, anything short of that amount will not be at-scale with the need. The solution is many congregations, agreeing to move independently in the same general direction, with a shared goal of closing, in Jesus' name, the Promise Gap by the year 2030.

The goal is to solve this problem not in church members' lifetimes, but in the children's lifetimes.

Are intentional miracles even possible?

Jesus said all things are possible for the person who believes (Mark 9:23).

Jesus also asked whether anyone would have faith when the Son of Man returns (Luke 18:8).

The question of whether intentional miracles are possible seems to come down to whether church members will choose to believe.

There is a certain irony about people having a hard time having faith in what Jesus says about the impossible being possible, given that humans live surrounded by seeming impossibilities and accept their surroundings on faith. For example, although scientists are trying, no one can figure out infinity, time with no end, as well as explain what happened in the centillions of earth-year equivalents, one centillion being a digit with 303 zeroes, a widely recognized "large" number,

...1,000,000,000,000,000,000,000,000,000,000,000,000,000,000,000,000,000,
000,000,000,000,000,000,000,000,000,000,000,000,000,000,000,000,000,
000,000,000,000,000,000,000,000,000,000,000,000,000,000,000,000,000,
000,000,000,000,000,000,000,000,000,000,000,000,000,000,000,000,000,
000,000,000,000,000,000,000,000,000,000,000,000,000,000,000,000,000,
000,000,000,000,000,000,000,000,000,000,000,000...

before the earth was formed, and what will happen in all those centillions,

...1,000,000,000,000,000,000,000,000,000,000,000,000,000,000,000,000,000,
000,000,000,000,000,000,000,000,000,000,000,000,000,000,000,000,000,
000,000,000,000,000,000,000,000,000,000,000,000,000,000,000,000,000,
000,000,000,000,000,000,000,000,000,000,000,000,000,000,000,000,000,
000,000,000,000,000,000,000,000,000,000,000,000,000,000,000,000,000,
000,000,000,000,000,000,000,000,000,000,000,000...

after.

> There is a certain irony about people having a hard time having faith in what Jesus says about the impossible being possible, given that humans live surrounded by seeming impossibilities and accept their surroundings on faith.

Also, although scientists keep trying, it's becoming more, not less, difficult to understand how the universe functions. The more scientists explore, apparently, the more questions develop. A 2024 article highlighted a recent finding that two different telescopes, the James Webb and the Hubble, have confirmed the existence of "... one of the most troubling conundrums in all of physics — that the universe appears to be expanding at bafflingly different speeds depending on where we look." This problem is called the "Hubble tension," and "has the potential to alter or even upend cosmology altogether."[105]

Then there is "dark energy" and "dark matter." For millennia, people thought the space between stars was ... well, space, empty space. That view has been recently changing with new findings from, again, the Hubble telescope. "It turns out that roughly 68% of the Universe is dark energy. Dark matter makes up about 27%. The rest — everything on Earth, everything ever observed with all our instruments, all normal matter — adds up to less than 5% of the Universe," according to NASA.[106]

And that's to say nothing about how scientists strive to understand how anything began, and how as a result anything came to exist, including, for example, the paper on which this book is printed.

Closer to home, an international team of researchers reviewed "1,500 papers to evaluate the size and number of 400 cell types, including muscle, nerve, and immune cells. Their conclusion: The average adult male has 36 trillion cells, while the average adult female has 28 trillion cells."[107]

Yet, these reports, as potentially disturbing as they are with their unexplained impossibilities and overwhelming information, generally do not disrupt people's daily routines. At some level, all humans proceed in faith that the universe will continue to expand and dark energy will do whatever dark energy does, and the trillions of cells in their bodies will continue to coordinate while people exist in the midst of this who-knows-where-it-initially-came-from physical environment that surrounds them, even as the world continues as it has.

And if humans can take all those impossibilities in faith, then why not also believe Jesus when he says that nothing is impossible with God (Matt. 19:26)? If church members trust Jesus with their eternal salvation, why not also trust him with the idea that intentional miracles are possible?

Part of the problem, of course, is the temptation to believe that intentional miracles are impossible so humans are then free to pursue other priorities. The comic strip, *Pearls Before Swine* by Stephan Pastis, has a character list built on animals with human traits. Rat is the cynical, acerbic counterpoint to, for example, the optimistic, naïve Pig and the reading, intellectual Goat. One day, in panel 1, Rat climbs the hill on which a bearded, plump donkey with glasses, the "Wise Ass On The Hill," sits, dispensing insight and knowledge. Having arrived at the top in panel 2, Rat asks, "Oh, Great Wise Ass, why are we put on earth?" to which the reply is, "To love one another." In panel 3, Rat then asks, "Where does acquiring as much loot as we can come in?" to which the reply is, "It doesn't." At the bottom of the hill in panel 4, Rat muses, "One of us has been badly misinformed."[108]

The question is not actually whether intentional miracles are possible, but rather, within the Christian worldview, whether church members in an age of affluence will choose to make them happen.

The struggle to set priorities, especially in this age of affluence, is very real. Jesus described that challenge as choosing either God or Money as the master to be served, and this at a time when few people had much money, as presented in the Figure 23 of Angus Maddison's Year 0-1998 analysis. As "Jesus Christ is the same yesterday and today and forever" (Hebrews 13:8), his words to those in the first century remain just as true for those of us in the twenty-first.

A good description of the struggle for those living in this age of affluence was included in a column by George Will. Will quoted economist John Maynard Keynes' reflection on the choice before those who would be living in the unfolding age of prosperity. Economic growth "would mean that 'for the first time since his creation man will be faced with his real, his permanent problem — how to use his freedom from pressing economic cares ... to live wisely and agreeably and well.' "[109]

The apostle Peter presented not a problem but a solution: "Live as free men, but do not use your freedom as a cover-up for evil; live as servants of God." (1 Peter 2:16).

The question is not actually whether intentional miracles are possible, but rather, within the Christian worldview, whether church members in an age of affluence will choose to make them happen.

Tenney writes:

> "The design of the Wesleyan way subordinated all of life to spiritual principles even more effectively and comprehensively than had the mediaeval church, in that it placed upon each individual the responsibility for the total welfare of the world. It relegated neither special religious experience nor special religious duties to the chosen few. It expected the utmost in both personal attainment and social responsibility of every man and woman."[110]

These early Methodists did not break under the pressure. Rather, Tenney recounts, they "laughed at impossibilities." One verse of a Methodist hymn of that time reads:

"All things are possible to God,
To Christ, the power of God in man,
To me, when I am all renewed,
When I in Christ am formed again,
And witness, from all sin set free,
All things are possible to me."[111]

In the power of that faith, historians conclude those Methodists changed their world.

Such great things can happen through intentional miracles undertaken by Christians using more of the amazing amount of resources presently available even as they apply their minds as well as their hearts to the needs of their neighbors.

Today, Christians from a variety of traditions continue to serve God with their money, and great things continue to happen. A key point being made in this chapter is that church members have the power for good to expand those good works, at-scale with the global needs and the resources still available to church members, to a level not seen before in history.

An example of the consequences of Christians taking their faith seriously was reported in a Wycliffe Associates newsletter. An interview with a new Christian in Togo, one of the 40 countries listed in Table 48, recounts how the only water her village had to drink was polluted water from the river, and she had to walk a distance to get that. When she heard a new well had been built locally, she went with her container. A pastor was "talking about Jesus Christ, who I'd never heard of in my life. He shared with us that this water was being given by God through Christians who are living in the United States ..." The young mother of three was so impressed, she decided to become a Christian. Soon, her husband and her whole family "decided to follow Christ and join the church." She concludes, "I continue talking to other women about the God who loves us and how He gave water through people who do not know us."[112]

This woman experienced the potential for good that is being acted on in the church, and that could be scaled up to heal more people than Jesus did while on earth. Perhaps such broad action through the current body of Christ, the church, is one of the "greater things" that Jesus promised in John 14:12. Such great things can happen through intentional miracles undertaken by Christians using more of the amazing amount of resources presently available even as they apply their minds as well as their hearts to the needs of their neighbors.

In an excerpt from their book, *Resident Aliens*, Stanley Hauerwas and William Willimon, describing what they see as the true, not traditional, content of Jesus' Sermon on the Mount, reflect on this alternative reality in contrast to what is going on in the world. They write, "The old debate about whether or not Christian ethics should emphasize the personal or the social, individual conversion or social transformation, was misguided." They continue,

> "The function of the text is not the cultivation of a subjective attitude but rather the formation of a visible people of God. Our ethics do involve individual transformation, not as some subjective, inner, personal experience, but rather as the work of a transformed people who have adopted us, supported us, disciplined us, enabled us to be different. The most interesting, creative, political solutions we Christians have to offer our troubled society are not new laws or increased funds for social programs — although we may find ourselves supporting such national efforts. The most creative social strategy to offer is the church. Here we show the world a manner of life that the world can never achieve through social coercion or governmental action. We serve the world by showing it something that it is not, namely a place where God is forming a family out of strangers."[113]

The woman in Africa was open to the God who loves her and gave her water through people who did not know her. The miracle is twofold: that her village received water, and that Christians decided to act.

The woman in Africa was open to the God who loves her and gave her water through people who did not know her. The miracle is twofold: that her village received water, and that Christians decided to act.

This is an age of affluence. Church members can make it an age of intentional miracles at a scale never before possible. Is that realistic? Let Christians in the U.S. hope so.

The context for Jesus' statement that all things are possible with God (Matt. 19:26) is as a response to the disciples' shock that Jesus had just said, "I tell you the truth, it is hard for a rich man to enter the kingdom of heaven" (Matt. 19:23).

Those who are rich in this world's goods have a special challenge to navigate life's opportunities in a wise way. To whom much is given, Jesus said, much will be demanded (Luke 12:48).

The apostle Paul was aware of the huge grace given him, in light of his pre-Christian persecution of Jesus and the church (Acts 9:4-5, 26:10). Yet God used Paul to spread the news about the Father's divine intervention through Jesus Christ far and wide. Knowing his own background, Paul's honest assessment was that God is able to "do immeasurably more than all we ask or imagine, according to his power that is at work within us" (Eph. 3:20).

May the church in the U.S., in this age of affluence, have the courage to ask largely, to imagine wonderful things not yet seen, and then to step out in faith to do them in Jesus' name. If that occurs, it will be fun to see what happens next.

Endnotes for Chapter 8

[1] "Miracle." *Merriam-Webster Collegiate Dictionary, Tenth Edition* (Springfield, MA: Merriam-Webster, Incorporated, 1994), p. 742.

[2] Mary Alice Tenney, *Blueprint for a Christian World: An Analysis of the Wesleyan Way* (Wilmore, KY: First Fruits Press, 2016), p. 25.

[3] Tenney, p. 31.

[4] Tenney, pp. 101, 102.

[5] Tenney, p. 165.

[6] Tenney, p. 259.

[7] Tenney, p. 245.

[8] Jeffrey M. Jones; "U.S. church Membership Falls Below Majority for first Time"; Gallup; 3/29/2021; <https://news.gallup.com/poll/341963/church-membership-falls-below-majority-first-time.aspx>; p. 2 of 3/21/2024 6:08 PM printout.

[9] Jones, p. 3.

[10] Drew Lindsay, "What's Lost When Religion Fades," *The Chronicle of Philanthropy*, December 2023, pp. 6-7.

[11] "Podcaster Urges Catholics to 'Get Back in the Game', " *The (Peoria, Ill.) Catholic Post*, 9/3/2023, p. 9.

[12] Kirsten Sanders, "Why Church? (Is the Wrong Question)," *Christianity Today*, March 2023, p. 71.

[13] Matthew Kelly, *The Biggest Lie in the History of Christianity* (North Palm Beach, FL: Blue Sparrow Books, 2018), pp. 32, 33.

[14] Richard Stearns, *Unfinished* (Nashville: Thomas Nelson, 2013), p. 86.

[15] Jim Davis and Michael Graham with Ryan P. Burge, *The Great Dechurching* (Grand Rapids, MI: Zondervan Reflective, 2023), p. 3.

[16] Davis and Graham, pp. 22-24.

[17] Michael Rotolo, Gregory A. Smith, and Jonathan Evans; "8 in 10 Americans Say Religion Is Losing Influence in Public Life"; Pew Research Center; 3/15/2024; <https://www.pewresearch.org/religion/2024/03/15/8-in-10-americans-say-religion-is-losing-influence-in-public-life/>; p. 2 of 3/18/2024 9:17 AM printout.

[18] Maria Di Mento and Ben Gose, "Fresh Faces: Our Annual Survey of America's Biggest Donors, Philanthropy 50," *The Chronicle of Philanthropy*, February 2022, pp. 16-18, 20, 22-23, 25-27.

[19] "The Forbes 400: The Definitive Ranking Of The Wealthiest Americans In 2022"; forbes.com; published September 27, 2022; 1-400; https://www.forbes.com/forbes-400/; pp. 2-14 of 1-200 of 6/26/2023 10:24 AM printout and pp. 2-14 of 201-400 of 6/26/2023 10:25 AM printout.

[20] "About Us"; Southern Baptist Convention; 2019; < http://www.sbc.net/aboutus/>; p. 1 of 9/6/2019 8:19 PM printout.

[21] Sources for Figure 21 and Table 50, Southern Baptist Convention Lottie Moon Offerings, 1921-2021, and Membership, 1921-1967. See Appendix B-1 for 1968-2021 membership.

• 1921-2021 Lottie Moon Offering Amounts: "Lottie Moon Christmas Offering from its Beginning in 1888"; International Mission Board, SBC; LMCO Historical Campaign Year.XLS' attachment to e-mail from David Steverson, IMB; June 9, 2010 6:54 AM; p. 1 of 6/9/2010 11:53 AM printout. 2010: "Lottie Moon Christmas Offering," *SBC Life*, Dec. 2011-Feb. 2012, p. 2. 2011: Don Graham; "IMB int'l missions offering: $146.8M in 2011, up $1.1M"; Baptist Press; 6/11/2012; <http://www.bpnews.net/38020>; p. 1 of 6/13/2012 12:15 PM printout; 2012: Erich Bridges; "Lottie Moon Missions gifts grow to $149.3M, third-largest ever"; Baptist Press; 6/6/2013; http://www.bpnews.net/40461>; p. 1 of 6/7/2013 3:44 PM printout. 2013: Erich Bridges; "Lottie Moon Offering Hits Record $154 Million"; Baptist Press; 6/5/2014; <http://www.bpnews.net/42717>; p. 1 of 6/6/2014 8:53 AM printout. 2014: Erich Bridges; "Lottie Moon Mission Gifts Top $153 million"; Baptist Press; 6/8/2015; <http://www.bpnews.net/44895/lottie-moon-mission-gifts-top-153-million>; p. 1 of 6/9/2015 7:40 AM printout. 2015: "Lottie Moon Christmas Offering", SBC Life, vol. 25, no. 2, Winter 2016, p. 1. 2016: David Roach; "Lottie Moon offering nears $153 million"; Baptist Press; 6/7/2017; <http://www.bpnews.net/49001/lottie-moon-offering-nears-153-million>; p. 1 of 6/8/2017 8:09 AM printout; 2017: The SBC International Mission Board changed from a fiscal year to a calendar year in 2017; the FY 2017 Lottie Moon numbers were obtained on a form signed on 7/1/2019, from the IMB Vice President, Support Services and Treasurer, and include the following note for the 2017 Fiscal Year of October 1, 2016 through September 30, 2017: "Oct. 1-Dec. 31, 2016 Quarter numbers are repeated from the 2016 Calendar Year."; 2018 and 2019: Price Jett, VP, Logistics, Finance,

Travel, & Technology and Treasurer, IMB, SBC, 7/10/2020; Price Jett, VP and Treasurer, IMB, SBC, 7/11/2022; ; FY 2020-21 and 2021-2022: Price Jett, VP, Logistics, Finance, Travel & Technology and Treasurer, IMB, SBC, 7/26/2023.

• 1921-1952 SBC Membership: Historical Statistics of the United States: Colonial Times to 1970, Bicentennial Edition, Part 1 (Washington Bureau of the Census, 1975), series H 805, pp. 391-392. 1953-1967: YACC series. 1968-2021: See Appendix B-1.

Table 51: SBC Lottie Moon Christmas Offerings, 1921– 2021, and SBC Membership, 1921–1967

Year	Lottie Moon Christmas Offering $	SBC Membership	Year	Lottie Moon Christmas Offering $	SBC Membership	Year	Lottie Moon Christmas Offering $
1921	28,615.78	3,220,000	1955	4,628,691.03	7,517,653	1989	80,197,870.78
1922	29,583.67	3,366,000	1956	5,240,745.39	7,725,486	1990	79,358,610.87
1923	42,206.37	3,494,000	1957	6,121,585.14	7,952,397	1991	81,358,723.00
1924	48,677.00	3,575,000	1958	6,762,448.63	8,221,384	1992	80,980,881.11
1925	306,376.21	3,649,000	1959	7,706,847.29	8,413,859	1993	82,899,291.40
1926	246,152.84	3,617,000	1960	8,238,471.07	8,631,627	1994	85,932,597.88
1927	172,457.36	3,674,000	1961	9,315,754.78	9,978,139	1995	89,019,719.75
1928	235,274.31	3,706,000	1962	10,323,591.69	10,192,451	1996	93,089,179.27
1929	190,130.81	3,771,000	1963	10,949,857.35	10,395,264	1997	100,064,318.10
1930	200,799.84	3,850,000	1964	11,870,649.35	10,601,935	1998	101,713,066.69
1931	170,724.87	3,945,000	1965	13,194,357.32	10,770,573	1999	105,443,786.95
1932	143,331.24	4,066,000	1966	13,760,146.80	10,947,389	2000	113,175,191.96
1933	172,512.86	4,174,000	1967	14,664,679.30	11,140,486	2001	113,709,471.17
1934	213,925.81	4,277,000	1968	15,159,206.92		2002	115,015,216.49
1935	240,455.12	4,389,000	1969	15,297,558.63		2003	136,204,648.17
1936	292,401.57	4,482,000	1970	16,220,104.99		2004	133,886,221.58
1937	290,219.74	4,596,000	1971	17,833,810.22		2005	137,939,677.59
1938	315,000.40	4,770,000	1972	19,664,972.53		2006	150,178,098.06
1939	330,424.70	4,949,000	1973	22,232,757.09		2007	150,409,653.86
1940	363,746.30	5,104,000	1974	23,234,093.89		2008	141,315,110.24
1941	449,162.48	5,238,000	1975	26,169,421.12		2009	148,984,819.41
1942	562,609.30	5,367,000	1976	28,763,809.71		2010	145,662,925.00
1943	761,269.79	5,493,000	1977	31,938,553.04		2011	146,828,116.05
1944	949,844.17	5,668,000	1978	35,919,605.40		2012	149,276,303.72
1945	1,201,962.24	5,866,000	1979	40,597,113.02		2013	154,057,852.36
1946	1,381,048.76	6,079,000	1980	44,700,339.76		2014	153,002,394.13
1947	1,503,010.12	6,271,000	1981	50,784,173.38		2015	165,798,102.86
1948	1,669,683.38	6,489,000	1982	54,077,464.49		2016	152,982,560.94
1949	1,745,682.81	6,761,000	1983	58,025,336.79		2017	152,308,802.00
1950	2,110,019.07	7,080,000	1984	64,775,763.83		2018	158,865,136.53
1951	2,668,051.30	7,373,000	1985	66,862,113.65		2019	157,306,798.24
1952	3,280,372.79	7,634,000	1986	69,412,195.09		2020	159,453,598.29
1953	3,602,554.86	6,999,275	1987	69,912,637.50		2021	162,759,879.00
1954	3,957,821.00	7,246,233	1988	78,787,726.26			

Source: SBC IMB. See endnote 21.

empty tomb, inc., 2024

[22] "Halfway to 2030, World 'Nowhere Near' Reaching Global Goals, UN Warns"; UN News; 7/17/2023; <https://news.un.org/en/story/2023/07/1138777>; p. 1 of 9/18/2023 10:16 AM printout.

[23] For information on the Millennium Development Goals, see: Secretary General of the United Nations; "Road Map Towards the Implementation of the United Nations Millennium Declaration"; United Nations; 9/6/2001; <http://www.un.org/documents/ga/docs/56/a56326.pdf>; 7/5/2008 printout, and, "About the MDGs: Basics"; United Nations Development Programme; <http://www.undp.org/mdg/basics.shtml>; 7/4/2008 5:28 PM printout.

[24] UNDP; "Background of the Sustainable Development Goals"; n.d.; <https://www.undp.org/content/undp/en/home/sustainable-development-goals/background/>; pp. 1, 3 of 10/4/2020 1:28 PM printout.

[25] "The Promise a Year Later," *First Call for Children*, UNICEF, No. 2 (n.d., approximately 1991.

[26] James P. Grant, *The State of the World's Children 1995* (New York: Oxford University Press, 1995), p. 10.

[27] The United Nations Inter-agency Group for Child Mortality Estimation (UN IGME) estimated there were 5,034,000 under-five deaths in 2021: UN IGME; *Levels & Trends in Child Mortality Report 2022*. Dividing that number by 365 days in 2021 yields the estimate of 13,790 children a day.

[28] "Every Child Alive: The Urgent Need to End Newborn Deaths"; UNICEF; February 2018; <unicef.org/media/48096/file/Every_Child_Alive_The_urgent_need_to_end_newborn_deaths-ENG.pdf>; p. 1 of 5/11/2023 printout.

[29] The 2015 Missed Goal in the number of annual under-five child deaths for 40 nations, which is a key metric used in the present analysis of the 40 countries, was derived and calculated as follows.

The two main information sources were: "Table 10. The Rate of Progress," *The State of The World's Children 2016* (New York: UNICEF, June 2016), pp. 118-121; and Jennifer Requejo, Cesar Victora, and Jennifer Bryce; Countdown to 2015: Maternal, Newborn & Child Survival; UNICEF and World Health Organization; created 11/25/2015 and modified 11/30/2015; <http://www.countdown2015mnch.org/documents/2015Report/Countdown_to_2015_final–report.pdf>; downloaded 8/3/2016.

1. Of the 75 "Countdown to 2015: Maternal, Newborn & Child Survival" [Countdown 2015, 2016] countries, 40 nations each had an actual 2015 Under-5 Mortality Rate (U5MR) that was larger than the 2015 Reduction Goal U5MR calculated for each nation. These 40 nations may be considered Slower Progress countries.

2. The 2015 U5MR Reduction Goal was calculated by using an exponential interpolation between the Start date of 2000 and the 2030 Goal date. The Start date of 2000 used *The State of the World's Children 2016* Actual reported data. The 2030 Goal date used the United Nations Sustainable Goal 3 Target 3.2, "with all countries aiming to reduce … under-5 mortality to at least as low as 25 per 1,000 live births" [Sustainable Development Knowledge Platform: Goal 3 Targets; n.d.; <https://sustainabledevelopment.un.org/sdg3>; p. 1 of 12/30/2015 printout]. This portion of Goal 3 Target 3.2 was used, in part, inasmuch as it provides historical consistency with the earlier Under-5 Mortality Rate goals set for both 2000 and 2015, the latter of which was Millennium Development Goal 4. [Secretary General of the United Nations; "Road Map Towards the Implementation of the United Nations Millennium Declaration"; United Nations; 9/6/2001; <http://www.un.org/documents/ga/docs/56/a56326.pdf>; p. 56 of 7/5/2008 printout.] It may also be noted that neonatal mortality is reflected in, and an integral part of, under-5 mortality.

3. The ratio of Actual to Goal U5MR for 2015 was applied to the 2015 Actual annual number of under-5 deaths (thousands) in order to calculate the Reduction Goal number of under-5 child deaths that occurred in 2015 due to the Reduction Goal U5MR not having been successfully reached. Thus, the Reduction Goal-related number of under-5 child deaths calculation for 2015 is based on the following relationship among four variables: (1) Actual U5MR is to (2) Goal U5MR as (3) Actual number of under-5 child deaths is to (4) Reduction Goal-related number of under-5 child deaths, leading to the following equation for 2015:

Reduction Goal-related number of under-5 child deaths = Actual number of under-5 child deaths x (Reduction Goal U5MR/Actual U5MR).

4. Subtracting the calculated Reduction Goal-related number of under-5 child deaths for 2015 from the Actual number of under-5 child deaths in 2015 provides the Missed Goal number of under-5 child deaths that occurred in 2015 due to the U5MR Goal not having been successfully reached.

5. The 2016 Reported data is found in: "Table 1. Basic Indicators," *The State of The World's Children 2017* (New York: UNICEF, December 2017), pp. 154-157.

6. The 2017 Reported data is found in: UN IGME; *Levels & Trends in Child Mortality Report 2018*, pp. 30-38.

7. The 2018 Reported data is found in: "Table 2. Child Mortality," *The State of the World's Children 2019* (New York: UNICEF, 2019), pp. 190-191.

8. The 2019 Reported data is found in: "Statistical Table: Country, Regional and Global Estimates of Mortality among Children, Adolescents and Youth Under Age 25"; UN IGME; *Levels & Trends in Child Mortality Report 2020*; <UN-IGME-child-mortality-report-2020.pdf>; pp. 40-56 of 1/4/2021 printout.

9. The 2020 Reported data is found in: United Nations Inter-agency Group for Child Mortality Estimation (UN IGME); *Levels & Trends in Child Mortality Report 2021*; UNICEF (New York: UNICEF, 2021); <https://www.unicef.org/wp-content/uploads/2021/12/Levels-and-trends-in- child-mortality-IGME-English_2021.pdf>; pp. 42-52 of 12/20/2021 printout.

[30] Jennifer Rigby, Natalie Grover and Maggie Fick; "Why World's First Malaria Shot Won't Reach Millions of Children Who Need It"; Reuters; 7/13/2022; <https:www.reuters.com/business/healthcare-pharmaceuticals/why-worlds-first-malaria-shot-wont-reach-millions-children-who-need-it-2022-07-13/>; pp. 1, 3 of 7/13/2022 9:34 AM printout.

[31] "Billions Needed to Avert Unrest and Starvation, U.N. Food Chief Says"; Associated Press; 4/1/2023; <https:///www.nbcnews.com/news/world/billios-needed-avert-unrest=starvation-un-food-chief-says-rcna77757>; p. 3 of 4/1/2023 11:26 AM printout.

[32] Paul Collier, *The Bottom Billion: Why the Poorest Countries Are Failing and What Can Be Done About It* (New York: Oxford University Press, 2007), pp. 189-190.

[33] Paul Collier, *The Bottom Billion*, p. 36.

[34] "Retailers Try to Curb Theft While Not Angering Shoppers," an Associated Press article appearing in *The (Champaign, Ill.) News-Gazette*, February 7, 2023, p. B-4, cols. 1-5.

[35] Harrison Miller; "Retail Theft Losses Mount from Shoplifting, Flash Mobs — And Organized Crime"; Investor's Business Daily; 10/6/2023; <https://www.investors.com/news/retail-theft-losses-mount-from-shoplifting-flash-mobs-organized-crime/>; unnumbered pp. 1, 2 of 4/3/2024 printout.

[36] Harrison Miller, ibid., pp. 3, 5.

[37] "Check Fraud Back in a Big Way Nationwide," Associated Press, appearing in *The (Champaign, Ill.) News-Gazette*, 6/14/2023, p. B-4, cols. 4-5.

[38] Andrew Van Dam; "Paper Checks Are Dead. Cash Is Dying. Who Still Uses them?"; The Washington Post; 9/18/2023; <https://.www.washingtonpost.com/business/2023/09/15/paper-checks-who-uses/>; pp. 1, 3 of 4/5/2024 3:17 PM printout.

[39] Jefferson Graham; "You Will Get Chipped — Eventually"; USA Today; 8/9/2017; <https://www.usatoday.com/story/tech/2017/08/09/you-get-chipped-eventually/547336001/>; p. 1 of 8/10/2017 8:57 AM printout.

[40] Garance Burke, et al., "Data Privacy: Big Brother Is Watching," an Associated Press article appearing in *The (Champaign, Ill.) News-Gazette*, 12/24/2022, p. C-4, cols. 1-4, and p. C-5, col. 5.

[41] "Tocqueville: A View from Outside"; Library of Congress; n.d.; <https://www.loc.gov/exhibitions/join-in-voluntary-associations-in-america/about-this-exhibition/tocqueville-a-view-from-outside/>; p. 1 of 4/5/2024 printout.

[42] Robert N. Bellah, Richard Madsen, William M. Sullivan, Ann Swidler, and Steven M. Tipton, *Habits of the Heart: Individualism and Commitment in American Life* (New York: Harper & Row Publishers, 1985), p. 38.

[43] Thalia Beaty and Glenn Gamboa, Associated Press; "Nonprofits Scramble for Help Amid Dearth of Volunteers"; Chronicle of Philanthropy; 4/20/2023; < https://www.philanthropy.com/article/nonprofits-scramble-for-help-amid-dearth-of-volunteers?sra=true>; p. 1 of 4/24/2023 9:54 AM printout.

[44] Drew Lindsay, Cover title with internal title, "The Generosity Cure," *The Chronicle of Philanthropy*, July 2022, cover and pp. 7-8.

[45] Eden Stiffman, Cover title with internal title, "Corporate Philanthropy at a Crossroads," *The Chronicle of Philanthropy*, October 2023, Cover and p. 6.

[46] Jim Rendon, "Nonprofits Find Ways to Manage a Staffing Crisis With No End in Sight," *The Chronicle of Philanthropy*, January 2024, p. 27.

[47] "What Are Overweight and Obesity?"; National Institutes of Health; last update 3/34/2022; <https://www.nhlbi.nih.gov/health/overweight-and-obesity>; p. 1 of 4/6/2024 10:44 AM.

[48] "The Deaths-of-Despair Narrative Is Out of Date"; The Economist; 12/23/2023; <https://www.economist.com/united-states/2023/12/23/the-deaths-of-despair-narrative-is-out-of-date#:~:text=This%20 "deaths%2Dfrom%2Ddespair,every%20day%20with%20no%20survivors.>; p. 2 of 4/6/2024 11:06 AM printout.

[49] Steve Goldstein; "Rise in Middle-Aged White 'Deaths of Despair' May Be Fueled by Loss of Religion, New Research Paper Argues"; marketwatch.com; 1/17/2023; <https://www.marketwatch.com/story/deaths-of-despair-may-be-driven-by-loss-of-religion-paper-argues-11673876749>; pp. 1-3 of 1/17/2023 12:55 PM printout.

[50] Carolyn Hax, "Mom Feels Like Failure as Teens Struggle with Mental Health," appearing in *The (Champaign, Ill.) News-Gazette*, 2/27/2024, p. B-6, col. 1.

[51] "U.S. Surgeon General Issues Advisory on Youth Mental Health Crisis Further exposed by COVID-19 Pandemic"; HHS.gov; 12/7/2021; <https://www.hhs.gov/about/news/2021/12/07/us-surgeon-general-issues-advisory-on-youth-mental-health-crisis-further-exposed-by-covid-19-pandemic.html>; p. 1, 2 of 12/30/2021 3:41 PM printout.

[52] Jean M. Twenge; "The Age of Anxiety? Birth Cohort Change in Anxiety and Neuroticism, 1952-1993"; Journal of Personality and Social Psychology, American Psychological Association, Inc.; 2000, Vol. 79, No. 6, 1007-1021; <https:..www.apa.org/pubs/journals/releases/psp7961007.pdf>; p. 1021 of 3/16/2024 12:35 PM printout.

[53] "Screen Time and Children"; American Academy of Child & Adolescent Psychiatry; No. 54, updated February 2020; <https://www.aacap.org/AACAP/Families_and_Youth/Facts_for_Families/FFF-Guide/Children-And-Watching-TV-054.aspx>; p. 1 of 4/6/2024 printout.

[54] "Teens Are Bombarded with Hundreds of Notifications a Day on Their Smartphones, New Report Reveals"; Common Sense Media; 9/26/2023; https://www.commonsensemedia.org/press-releases/teens-are-bombarded-with-hundreds-of-notifications-a-day>; p. 1 of 4/6/2023 12:44 PM printout.

[55] Monica Anderson, Michelle Faverio, and Eugenie Park; "How Teens and Parents Approach Screen Time"; Pew Research Center; 3/11/2024; <https://www.pewresearch.org/internet/2024/03/11/how-teens-and-parents-approach-screen-time/>; p. 8 of 4/6/1014 12:27 PM printout.

[56] Maya Brownstein; "Harvard Study Is First to Estimate Annual Ad Revenue Attributable to Young Users of These Platforms"; Harvard Chan School Communications; 1/2/2024; <https://news.harvard.edu/gazette/story/2024/01/social-media-platforms-make-11b-in-ad-revenue-from-u-s-teens/>; p. 3 of 4/6/2024 printout.

[57] "Happiness and Age: Summary, The World Happiness Report"; The World Happiness Report; 3/20/2024; <https://worldhappiness.report/ed/2024/happiness-and-age-summary/>; p. 2 of 3/23/2024 11:36 AM printout.

[58] Luke J. Rapa, *et al.*; "School Shootings in the United States: 1997-2022"; American Academy of Pediatrics *Pediatrics*; 3/4/2024; <https://publications.aap.org/pediatrics/article/153/4/e2023064311/196816/School-Shootings-in-the-United-States-1997-2022?autologincheck=redirected>; p. 1 of 4/14/2024 2:37 PM printout.

[59] "Kids with Guns, without Conscience Raise Unsolvable Questions," *The (Champaign, Ill.) News-Gazette*, 11/3/2023, p. D-1, cols. 1-4.

[60] Eli Steele; "Rooftop Revelations: Pastors Discuss How Nihilism Is Destroying A Generation"; Fox News; 12/28/2021; <https://www.foxnews.com/opinion/rooftop-revelations-pastors-nihilism-destroying-generation.print>; p. 1 of 12/28/2021 9:30 AM printout.

[61] Cal Newport; "The Year in Quiet Quitting"; The New Yorker; 12/29/2022; <https://www.newyorker.com/culture/2022-in-review/the-year-in-quiet-quitting>; pp. 2, 7 of 4/6/2024 4:32 PM printout.

[62] Jim Harter; "Is Quiet Quitting Real?" Gallup; 9/6/2022, updated 5/17/2023; <https://www.gallup.com/workplace/398306/quiet-quitting-real.aspx>; pp. 3, 5 of 4/6/2024 4:11 PM printout.

[63] Maria Di Mento and Jim Rendon, "Power Shift," *The Chronicle of Philanthropy*, March 2024, p. 7.

[64] Tenney, pp. 222, 223.

[65] Peter Brown, *Through the Eye of the Needle: Wealth, the Fall of Rome, and the Making of Christianity in the West, 350-550 AD* (Princeton, NJ: Princeton University Press, 2012).

[66] Peter Brown, *The Ransom of the Soul: Afterlife and Wealth in Early Western Christianity* (Cambridge, MA: Harvard University Press, 2015).

[67] Brown, *The Ransom of the Soul*, pp. 30, 31.

[68] Marissa Postell Sullivan; "Prosperity Gospel on the Rise Among Protestant Churchgoers"; Lifeway Research; 8/22/2023; <https://news.lifeway.com/2023/08/22/prosperity-gospel-beliefs-on-the-rise-among-churchgoers/>; p. 1 of 4/12/2024 11:26 AM printout.

[69] John Sander, ed., *Devotional Readings from Luther's Works for Every Day of the Year* (Rock Island, IL: Augustana Book Concern, 1915), 439-440.

[70] John Calvin, *Commentary Upon the Acts of the Apostles*, Henry Beveridge, ed. (Edinburgh, Scotland: T. & T. Clark, 1859), 322.

[71] John Ronsvalle and Sylvia Ronsvalle, *Behind the Stained Glass Windows: Money Dynamics in the Church* (Grand Rapids, MI: Baker Books, 1996), pp. 184-185.

[72] Tenney, p. 122.

[73] Rodney Stark, *The Rise of Christianity: How the Obscure, Marginal Jesus Movement Became the Dominant Religious Force in the Western World in a Few Centuries* (New York: HarperOne, 1996), p. 82.

[74] Tom Holland, *Dominion: How the Christian Revolution Remade the World* (New York: Basic Books, 2019), p. 251.

[75] Donald R. McClarey; "St. Francis and Pope Innocent III"; The American Catholic; 10/4/2011; <https://the-american-catholic.com/2011/10/04/saint-francis-of-assisi-and-innocent-iii/>; p. 2 of 3/4/2023 5:14 PM printout.

[76] Tenney, p. 150.

77 Jane Austen, *Persuasion* (New York: Penguin Books, 2003), p. 151.

78 Angus Maddison; *The World Economy: A Millennial Perspective*; Organisation for Economic Co-operation and Development; 2001; < https://www.oecd-ilibrary.org>, p. 264.

79 "GDP Per Capita (constant 2015 US$) – United States, World"; World Bank; <https://data.worldbank.org/indicator/NY.GDP.PCAP.KD?locations=US-1W>; accessed 4/7/2024. To calculate an estimate for 2022 to extend the chart data beyond 1998, the following procedure was used, since a 1990 $ deflator was not located to convert 2022 dollars to 1990 $. The GDP per capita percent change between 1990 and 2022 was calculated as follows. For the U.S.: In 2015 constant dollars, per capita GDP was $45,715.70 in 1998, and $62,789.00 in 2022, a 37% increase. To obtain an estimate for 2022 per capita GDP for the chart, the 1998 per capita GDP for the U.S. in 1990 $ of $27,331.00 was multiplied by 37%, yielding an estimate of $37,538.22 per capita GDP in 2022. For the World: In 2015 $ constant dollars, per capita GDP was $7,483.50 in 1998, and $11,318.70 in 2022, a 51% increase. To obtain an estimate for 2022 per capita GDP for the figure, the 1998 per capita GDP for the World in 1990 $ figure of $5,709 was multiplied by 51%, yielding an estimate of $8,634.79 per capita GDP in 2022.

80 Sigal Samuel; "Lots of Americans Are in the Global 1%. A Tenth of Their Income Could Transform the World"; Vox; 9/15/2023; <https://www.vox.com/future-perfect/2023/9/15/23874111/chahrity-philanthropy-americans-global-rich>; p. 2 of 10/9/2023 12:06 PM printout.

81 Naina Bajerkal, "How to Do More Good," TIME magazine, August 22/August 29, 2022, pp. 69-75.

82 Bajerkal, p. 74.

83 "31 Current Chocolate Statistics (Market Data 2023)"; Damecacao; n.d.; <https://damecaco.com/chocolate-statistics/#9>; p. 11 of 6/20/2023 10:24 AM printout. The $48 billion total was calculated by multiplying the average spending figure of $144.90 by 2021 U.S. population of 332,351,000.

84 Chris Kolmar; "15+ U.S. Beverage Industry Statistics [2023]: Refreshing Trends, Facts, and Stats"; Zippia.com; 3/6/2023; <https://www.zippia.com/advice/us-beverage-industry-statistics>; p. 1 of 6/20/2023 10:17 AM printout. The statistic refers to "non-alcoholic drink revenue in the U.S." The average was calculated by dividing the total market figure of $447.38 billion by 2022 U.S. population of 333,595,000.

85 Sarah O'Brien; "Americans Spend $56 Billion on Sporting Events"; 9/12/2017; <https://cnbc.com/2017/09/11/americans-spend-56-billion-on-sporting-events.html>; p. 3 of 6/21/2023 9:43 AM printout. The $172 is calculated by dividing the total figure of $56 billion by 2016 U.S. population of 324,609,000. The article cites a figure of $710 per American adult who actually spends on this activity.

86 Jennifer Farrington; "Planning to Host a Super Bowl Party? Here's How Much It Could Cost"; Market Realist; 2/6/2023; < https://marketrealist.com/consumer/cost-of-hosting-super-bowl-party/>; p. 1 of 6/10/2023 11:26 AM printout. The $44.78 figure was calculated by dividing the total figure of $14.8 billion by 2019 U.S. population of 330,513,000. The article notes that there were 44 million Super Bowl Parties in 2019. That calculates to a figure of $336 per party.

87 Grandview Research; "Jewelry Market Size, Share & Trends Analysis Report By Product Type (Necklace, Ring, Earring, Bracelet, Others), By Material (Gold, Platinum, Diamond, Others), By Region, And segment Forecasts, 2023-2030"; n.d.; <https://grandviewmarketingresearch.com/industry-analysis/jewelry-market>; p. 1 of 9/4/2023 printout. The $170 figure was calculated by dividing the 2020 U.S. total market of $56.5 billion by 2020 U.S. population of 331,768,000.

88 J. Clement; "Market Size of the Video Games Industry in the United States from 2013 to 2023 (in billion U.S. dollars"; Statistica; 3/20/2024; <https://www.statista.com/statistics/246892/value-of-the-video-game-market-in-the-us/#:~:text=In%202022%2C%20the%20video%20game,new%20all%2Dtime%20industry%20record.>; p. 2 of 4/8/2024 11:43 AM printout.

89 U.S. Travel Association; "The State of the Travel Industry"; April 2023; <https://www.ustravel.org/sites/default/files/2023-04/answersheet_2023_final.pdf>; pp. 2 and 5 of 9/3/2023 printout. The following calculations yield the $963 billion estimate of leisure travel by Americans. Domestic leisure travel is 71% of the entire $1.2 trillion in direct travel spending in 2022 (p. 2). Domestic leisure travel spending was $837 billion in 2022 (p. 7). To calculate a figure for international leisure travel spending (not provided in the document), the following formula was used. Domestic travel spending, both leisure and other, was 91% of the 2022 total travel spending. The 71% of leisure spending divided by the total domestic travel spending figure of 91% resulted in a figure of 78% domestic leisure travel spending as a percent of total domestic travel spending. Therefore, it was assumed, for purposes of this estimate, that 78% of the international

travel total was also leisure travel. Multiplying the total international travel spending figure by Americans of $161 billion (p. 5) by 78% resulted in a figure of $126 billion for leisure international travel spending. Adding the $837 billion figure for domestic leisure travel to the $126 billion calculation for international leisure travel spending resulted in the estimate of $963 billion spending on leisure travel, both domestic and international, by Americans in 2022.

[90] Jenna Ross; "Mapped: Legal Sports Betting Totals by State"; Visual Capitalist; 3/13/2023; <https://www.visualcapitalist.com/legal-sports-betting-totals-by-state/>; p. 3 of 4/8/2024 printout. New York had the highest 2022 total of legal wagering, at $16.3 billion. The total for the U.S. that year was $93 billion.

[91] Megan Brenan and Jeffrey M. Jones; "Ethics Ratings of Nearly All Professions Down in U.S."; Gallup; 1/22/2024; <https://gallup.com/poll/608903/ethics-ratings-nearly-prefessions-down.aspx>; 1/26/2024 1:59 PM.

[92] Werner Geyser; "What Is An Influencer? — Social Media Influencers Defined [Updated 2024]"; Influencer Marketing Hub; 2/14/2024; <https://influencermarketinghub.com/what-is-an-influencer/>; pp. 3, 8, 9.

[93] Julia Shandrokha; "How Influencer Marketing Impacts Consumer Behavior and Purchase Decisions"; Famesters; 12/21/2023; <https://famesters.com/blog/how-influencer-marketing-impacts-consumer-behavior-and-purchase-decisions>; pp. 5, 6, 7, 9.

[94] John Wesley; "Causes of the Inefficacy of Christianity"; Wesley's Sermons – Sermon 116; Http://www.godrules.net/library/wsermons/wsermons116.htm>; pp. 4, 3 of 10/29/2019, 10:28 AM printout.

[95] Tenney, p. 267.

[96] Tenney, p. 233.

[97] **Monetization by 40 Countries and by Causes of Under-5 Deaths: Missed Goal: within Country**

Monetization by Country

For each country of the above 40 Slower Progress countries, the country's percent of the total annual number of Missed Goals under-5 child deaths was calculated by dividing (1) the annual number of Missed Goal under-5 child deaths for each country by (2) the above 40 countries' total of 1,009.8 thousand Missed Goal under-5 child deaths for DY 2015. The suggested, at least initial, total additional cost for churches in the U.S. of helping to close the Promise Gap globally of the under-5 child deaths by providing funds in Jesus' name for the 40 Slower Progress countries was estimated at $16 billion [see discussion of this figure in chapter 6, Potential Giving at 10% of Income in 2020 section]. The cost per Slower Progress country to reduce Missed Goal under-5 child deaths then was calculated by multiplying each country's percent of the 40 Slower Progress countries' Missed Goal total annual number of under-5 child deaths by $16 billion.

Monetization by Causes, Data Year 2017, of Missed Goal Under-5 Deaths within Slower Progress Country

The cost, to reduce Missed Goal under-5 child deaths, per Slower Progress country by cause of under-5 deaths was calculated by multiplying (1) the cost per country for any given country for all causes of under-5 child deaths, by (2) the list of the percentage by cause of under-5 deaths within that country. The possible 12 causes of under-5 deaths categories listed in the Countdown 2030 for Data Year 2017, in addition to the summary category of "Neonatal," were: Pneumonia, AIDS, [Pertussis category removed in 2017 data set], Measles, Meningitis, Malaria, Preterm, Intrapartum, Congenital, Non-Communicable Diseases (NCDs), Injuries, Other, and Diarrhoea. The calculation was carried out for the 40 countries for which a percentage by cause of under-5 deaths within any given country was available.

Monetization by Causes, Data Year 2017, Detail for the Summary Category of Neonatal Deaths

The explanation for the monetization of the 10 causes of death within the Neonatal summary category is parallel to that for the 12 causes of death, in addition to the "Neonatal" summary, calculations above. The cost to reduce neonatal deaths per country, by cause of neonatal deaths, was calculated by multiplying (1) the cost per country, for any given country, for all causes of under-five deaths as calculated above, by (2) the list of the percentage by cause of neonatal deaths within that country. The possible 10 causes of neonatal deaths categorized in the Countdown 2030 report for Data Year 2017 were: Neonatal Diarrhoea, Neonatal Tetanus, Neonatal Preterm, Neonatal Intrapartum-related events, Neonatal Sepsis, Neonatal Congenital, Neonatal Injuries, Neonatal Meningitis [category added in 2017 data set], Neonatal Other, Neonatal Pneumonia. This calculation was carried out for the 40 Missed Goal countries for which percentage data was available by cause of neonatal deaths within any given country.

[98] World Vision Form 990 2019; IRS; <https://apps.irs.gov/pub/epostcard/cor/951922279_202009_990_2021051118085927.pdf>; p. 9, accessed 4/9/2024.

[99] Warren Cole Smith; "Largest Christian Ministries in The U.S."; Ministry Watch; 11/1/2023; < https://ministrywatch.com/largest-christian-ministries-in-the-u-s-2/>; p. 4.

[100] Samaritan's Purse Form 990 2019; IRS; < https://apps.irs.gov/pub/epostcard/cor/581437002_201912_990_2020101417372188.pdf>; p. 9, accessed 4/9/2024.

[101] Compassion International Form 990 2018; Compassion International; < https://www.compassion.com/multimedia/2018-2019-form990-compassion-international.pdf>; p. 11, accessed 4/9/2024.

[102] Catholic Relief Services Form 1990 2018; Catholic Relief Services; < https://www.crs.org/sites/default/files/fy2019_2018_form_990_web_version.pdf>; accessed 4/9/2024.

[103] Eden Stiffman; "It's Halftime for the Sustainable Development Goals. Are They Achievable?"; The Chronicle of Philanthropy; 9/8/2023; < https://www.philanthropy.com/article/its-halftime-for-the-sustainable-development-goals-are-they-achievable?sra=true>; p. 3 of 9/28/2023 3:55 PM printout.

[104] Kelley, p. 59.

[105] Ben Turner; "James Webb Telescope Confirms There Is Something Seriously Wrong with Our Understanding of the Universe"; LiveScience; 3/14/2024; <https://www.livescience.com/space/cosmology/james-webb-telescope-confirms-there-is-something-seriously-wrong-with-our-understanding-of-the-universe>; p. 2 of 3/15/2024 3:21 PM printout.

[106] "Dark Energy, Dark Matter"; NASA; n.d.; <http://science.nasa.gov/astrophysics/focus-areas/what-is-dark-energy/>; pp. 1, 2 of 4/27/2016 2:54 PM printout.

[107] Heather Frank, "And the Number of Human Cells Is …" *World* magazine, 10/21/2023, p. 68.

[108] Stephan Pastis, *Pearls Before Swine*, distributed by Andrews McMeel Syndication, appearing in *The (Champaign, Ill.) News-Gazette*, 4/8/2022, p. C-6, col. 1.

[109] George Will, "Why Toxic Politics Thrives in an Age of Plenty," Washington Post Writers Group appearing in *The (Champaign, Ill.) News-Gazette*, 11/26-27/2022, p. C-5, col. 1.

[110] Tenney, p. 264.

[111] Tenney, p. 109.

[112] "Another Woman Encounters Jesus at the Well"; Wycliffe Associates *Involved*, June 2022, p. 8.

[113] Stanley Hauerwas and William H. Willimon, "Peculiar People," Christianity Today; 3/5/1990; <https://www.christianitytoday.com/ct/1990/march-5/book-expert-peculair-people.html>; pp. 8, 9 of 3/31/2024 7:27 PM printout.

APPENDIXES

APPENDIX A: *List of Denominations*

Church Member Giving, 1968–2021 Composite Set

American Baptist Churches in the U.S.A.
The American Lutheran Church (through 1986)
Associate Reformed Presbyterian Church (General Synod)
Brethren in Christ Church
Christian Church (Disciples of Christ)
Church of God (Anderson, Ind.) (through 1997)
Church of God General Conference (McDonough, Ga.; formerly of Oregon, Ill., and Morrow, Ga.)
Church of the Brethren
Church of the Nazarene
Conservative Congregational Christian Conference
Cumberland Presbyterian Church
Evangelical Congregational Church
Evangelical Covenant Church (through 2007)
Evangelical Lutheran Church in America
  The American Lutheran Church (merged 1987)
  Lutheran Church in America (merged 1987)
Evangelical Lutheran Synod
Fellowship of Evangelical Bible Churches (through 2012)
Fellowship of Evangelical Churches (formerly Evangelical Mennonite Church)
Free Methodist Church-USA (formerly of North America)
Friends United Meeting (through 1990)
General Association of General Baptists
Lutheran Church in America (through 1986)
Lutheran Church-Missouri Synod
Mennonite Church USA (1999)
  Mennonite Church (merged 1999)
  Mennonite Church, General Conference (merged 1999)
Moravian Church in America, Northern Province
North American Baptist Conference (through 2006)
The Orthodox Presbyterian Church
Presbyterian Church (U.S.A.)
Reformed Church in America
Seventh-day Adventist Church, North American Division of
Southern Baptist Convention
United Church of Christ
Wisconsin Evangelical Lutheran Synod

Church Member Giving, 2020–2021

The Composite Set Denominations included in the 1968–2021 analysis with data available for both years, plus the following:
Allegheny Wesleyan Methodist Connection
Brethren Church (Ashland, OH)
Christian and Missionary Alliance
Church of Christ (Holiness) U.S.A.
Church of the Lutheran Brethren of America
Church of the Lutheran Confession
Churches of God General Conference
The Episcopal Church
The Missionary Church
Presbyterian Church in America
The United Methodist Church
The Wesleyan Church

By Organizational Affiliation: NAE, 1968–1985–2002–2021

Brethren in Christ Church
Church of the Nazarene
Conservative Congregational Christian Conference
Evangelical Congregational Church
Fellowship of Evangelical Churches
Free Methodist Church-USA
General Association of General Baptists

By Organizational Affiliation: NCC, 1968–1985–2002–2021

American Baptist Churches in the U.S.A.
Christian Church (Disciples of Christ)
Church of the Brethren
Evangelical Lutheran Church in America
Moravian Church in America, Northern Province
Presbyterian Church (U.S.A.)
Reformed Church in America
United Church of Christ

11 Denominations, 1921–2021

American Baptist (Northern)
Christian Church (Disciples of Christ)
Church of the Brethren
The Episcopal Church
Evangelical Lutheran Church in America
  The American Lutheran Church
    American Lutheran Church
    The Evangelical Lutheran Church
    United Evangelical Lutheran Church
    Lutheran Free Church
  Evangelical Lutheran Churches, Assn. of
  Lutheran Church in America
    United Lutheran Church
      General Council Evangelical Lutheran Ch.
      General Synod of Evangelical Lutheran Ch.
      United Synod Evangelical Lutheran South
    American Evangelical Lutheran Church
    Augustana Lutheran Church
    Finnish Lutheran Church (Suomi Synod)
Moravian Church in America, Northern Province
Presbyterian Church (U.S.A.)
  United Presbyterian Church in the U.S.A.
    Presbyterian Church in the U.S.A.
    United Presbyterian Church in North America
  Presbyterian Church in the U.S.
Reformed Church in America
Southern Baptist Convention
United Church of Christ
  Congregational Christian
    Congregational
  Evangelical and Reformed
    Evangelical Synod of North America/German
    Reformed Church in the U.S.
The United Methodist Church
  The Evangelical United Brethren
  The Methodist Church
    Methodist Episcopal Church
    Methodist Episcopal Church South
    Methodist Protestant Church

Trends in Membership, 10 Mainline Protestant Denominations, 1968–2021

American Baptist Churches in the U.S.A.
Christian Church (Disciples of Christ)
Church of the Brethren
The Episcopal Church
Evangelical Lutheran Church in America
Moravian Church in America, Northern Province
Presbyterian Church (U.S.A.)
Reformed Church in America
United Church of Christ
The United Methodist Church

Trends in Membership, 14 Evangelical Denominations, 1968–2021

Assemblies of God
Brethren in Christ Church
Christian and Missionary Alliance
Church of God (Cleveland, Tenn.)
Church of the Nazarene
Conservative Congregational Christian Conference
Converge Worldwide (formerly Baptist General Conference)
Evangelical Congregational Church
Fellowship of Evangelical Churches
Free Methodist Church-USA (formerly of North America)
General Association of General Baptists
Lutheran Church-Missouri Synod
Salvation Army
Southern Baptist Convention

Trends in Membership, 34 Protestant Denominations and the Roman Catholic Church, 1968–2021

10 Mainline Protestant Denominations (above)
14 Evangelical Denominations (above)
The Roman Catholic Church
Additional Composite Denominations:
Associate Reformed Presbyterian Church (General Synod)
Church of God (Anderson, Ind.)
Church of God General Conference (McDonough, Ga.)
Cumberland Presbyterian Church
Evangelical Covenant Church
Evangelical Lutheran Synod
Mennonite Church USA
The Orthodox Presbyterian Church
Seventh-day Adventist Church, North American Division of
Wisconsin Evangelical Lutheran Synod

APPENDIX B SERIES: *Denominational Data Tables*

Introduction

Unless otherwise noted, the data in the following tables is from the *Yearbook of American and Canadian Churches* (*YACC*) series; from 1933 to 1972, that series title was *Yearbook of American Churches* (*YAC*). Financial data is presented in current dollars.

Data in italics indicates a change from the previous edition in *The State of Church Giving* (SCG) series.

The Appendix B tables are described below.

Appendix B-1, Church Member Giving, 1968–2021: This table presents aggregate data for the denominations which comprise the data set analyzed for the 1968 through 2021 period.

Elements of this data are also used for the analyses in chapters two through seven.

• Data for the American Baptist Churches in the U.S.A. has been obtained directly from the denominational office as follows. In discussions with the American Baptist Churches Office of Planning Resources, it became apparent that there had been no distinction made between the membership of congregations reporting financial data, and total membership for the denomination, when reporting data to the *YACC*. Records were obtained from the denomination for a smaller membership figure that reflected only those congregations reporting financial data. While this revised membership data provided a more useful per member giving figure for Congregational Finances, the total Benevolences figure reported to the *YACC*, while included in the present data set, does reflect contributions to some Benevolences categories from 100% of the American Baptist membership. The membership reported in Appendix B-1 for the American Baptist Churches is the membership for congregations reporting financial data, rather than the total membership figure provided in editions of the *YACC*. However, in the sections that consider membership as a percentage of population, the Total Membership figure for the American Baptist Churches, shown in Appendix B-4, is used.

• The Church of God General Conference (McDonough, GA) was previously the Church of God General Conference (Oregon, IL and Morrow, GA).

• Also in Appendix B-1, data for the Evangelical Lutheran Church in America (ELCA) appears beginning in 1987. Before that, the two major component communions that merged into the ELCA—the American Lutheran Church and the Lutheran Church in America—are listed as individual denominations from 1968 through 1986.

• In the Appendix B series, the denomination listed as the Fellowship of Evangelical Bible Churches was named the Evangelical Mennonite Brethren Church prior to July 1987.

• The Free Methodist Church–USA was previously the Free Methodist Church of North America.

• For 1999, the Mennonite Church (Elkhart, IN) provided information for the Mennonite Church USA. The latter communion is the result of a merger passed at a national convention in July 2001 between the Mennonite Church and the Mennonite Church, General Conference. The Mennonite Church, General Conference 1968–1998 data has been added to the composite set series. The Mennonite Church USA dollar figures for 1999, and membership through 2001, combine available data for the two predecessor communions.

• In Appendix B-1, the data for the Presbyterian Church (U.S.A.) combined data for the United Presbyterian Church in the U.S.A. and the Presbyterian Church in the United States for the period 1968 through 1982. These two communions merged to become the Presbyterian Church (U.S.A.) in 1983, data for which is presented for 1983 through 2021.

• Southern Baptist Convention, 1968-2021: Beginning with *The State of Church Giving through 2020*, a decision was made to revise the Southern Baptist Convention (SBC) series in *The State of Church Giving* series. empty tomb staff concluded that a "carried-forward" data factor in the published SBC data had not been accounted for in the annual adjustments to the SBC data heretofore used in *The State of Church Giving* series. After reviewing the SBC Annuals and other documents in some depth, it seemed that the best approach was to revise the SBC series in *The State of Church Giving* series, removing previous adjustments to published SBC data for DY 1999 through DY 2019 that were intended to account for missing data. The data sources used in the revised series, now extended through Data Year 2021, are either the *Yearbook of American and Canadian Churches* (YACC), which published data for the SBC through 2010, or the SBC *Annuals*, with the exception of three years. In three data years, 1996, 2002, and 2003, SBC staff provided corrections to the SBC *Annual* membership figures, as well as 1996 Benevolences, and those corrections have been retained in the revised series.

Appendix B-2, Church Member Giving for 36 Denominations, 2020–2021: Appendix B-2 presents the Full or Confirmed Membership, Congregational Finances and Benevolences data for the 12 additional denominations included in the 2020–2021 comparison.

Appendix B-3, Church Member Giving for 11 Denominations, In Current Dollars, 1921–2021: This appendix presents additional data that is not included in Appendix B-1 for the 11 Denominations.

The data from 1921 through 1928 in Appendix B-3.1 is taken from summary information contained in the *YAC*, 1949 Edition, George F. Ketcham, ed. (Lebanon, PA: Sowers Printing Company, 1949, p. 162). The summary membership data provided is for Inclusive Membership. Therefore, giving as a percentage of income for the years 1921 through 1928 may have been somewhat higher had Full or Confirmed Membership been used. The list of denominations that are summarized for this period is presented in the *YAC*, 1953 Edition, Benson Y. Landis, ed. (New York: National Council of the Churches of Christ in the U.S.A., 1953, p. 274).

The data from 1929 through 1952 is taken from summary information presented in the *YAC*, Edition for 1955, Benson Y. Landis, ed. (New York: National Council of the Churches of Christ in the U.S.A., 1954, pp. 286-287). A description of the list of denominations included in the 1929 through 1952 data summary on page 275 of the *YAC* Edition for 1955 indicated that the Moravian Church, Northern Province is not included in the 1929 through 1952 data.

The data in Appendix B-3.2 for 1953 through 1964 was obtained for the indicated denominations from the relevant edition of the *YAC* series. Giving as a percentage of income was derived for these years by dividing the published Total Contributions figure by the published Per Capita figure to produce a membership figure for each denomination. The Total Contributions figures for the denominations were added to produce an aggregated Total Contributions figure. The calculated membership figures were also added to produce an aggregated membership figure. The aggregated Total Contributions figure was then divided by the aggregated membership figure to yield a per member giving figure which was used in calculating giving as a percentage of income.

Data for the years 1965 through 1967 was not available in a form that could be readily analyzed for the present purposes, and therefore data for these three years was estimated by dividing the change in per capita Total Contributions from 1964 to 1968 by four, the number of years in this interval, and cumulatively adding the result to the base year of 1964 and the succeeding years of 1965 and 1966 to obtain estimates for the years 1965 through 1967.

In most cases, this procedure was also applied to individual denominations to avoid an artificially low total due to missing data: If data was not available for a specific year, the otherwise blank entry was filled in with a calculation based on surrounding years for the denomination. For example, this procedure was used for the American Baptist Churches for the years 1955 and 1956; the Christian Church (Disciples of Christ) for the years 1955 and 1959; and the Evangelical United Brethren, later to merge into The United Methodist Church, for the years 1957, 1958 and 1959. Data for the Methodist Church was changed for 1957 in a similar manner.

Available Total Contributions and Full or Confirmed Members data for The Episcopal Church and The United Methodist Church for 1968 through 2021 is presented in Appendix B-3.3. These two communions are included in the 11 Denominations. The United Methodist Church was created in 1968 when the Methodist Church and the Evangelical United Brethren Church merged. While the Methodist Church filed summary data for the year 1968, the Evangelical United Brethren Church did not. Data for these denominations was calculated as noted in the appendix. However, since the 1968 data for The Methodist Church would not have been comparable to the 1985 and 2021 data for The United Methodist Church, this communion was not included in the more focused 1968–2021 composite analysis. The United Methodist Church Connectional Clergy Support 1969–2008 data used in Chapter 5 was obtained directly from the denominational source and is also presented in this appendix.

Appendix B-4, Membership for Seven Denominations, 1968–2021: This appendix presents denominational membership data used in the membership analyses presented in chapter five that is not available in the other appendixes. Unless otherwise indicated, the data is from the *YACC* series. Converge Worldwide was previously the Baptist General Conference. The Inclusive Membership series is used for The Salvation Army as it was consistently available for the period.

Appendix B-5, Overseas Missions Income, 2003 through 2021: This appendix presents numbers provided on the four lines of the Overseas Missions Income form completed by the respective denominations. Also provided is Overseas Missions Income for denominations that are not otherwise included in one or more years of the analyses (see chapter 6, note 13).

Appendix B-6, Estimates of Giving: This appendix provides the data used in the comparison of the Consumer Expenditure Survey, the Form 990 series, and the *Giving USA* series, for 1989–2019, presented in chapter 7.

APPENDIX B-1: *Church Member Giving, 1968-2021*

Key to Denominational Abbreviations: Data Years 1968–2021

Abbreviation	Denomination
abc	American Baptist Churches in the U.S.A.
alc	The American Lutheran Church
arp	Associate Reformed Presbyterian Church (General Synod)
bcc	Brethren in Christ Church
ccd	Christian Church (Disciples of Christ)
cga	Church of God (Anderson, IN)
cgg	Church of God General Conference (McDonough, GA; formerly of Oregon, IL and Morrow, GA)
chb	Church of the Brethren
chn	Church of the Nazarene
cccc	Conservative Congregational Christian Conference
cpc	Cumberland Presbyterian Church
ecc	Evangelical Congregational Church
ecv	Evangelical Covenant Church
elc	Evangelical Lutheran Church in America
els	Evangelical Lutheran Synod
emc	Evangelical Mennonite Church
feb	Fellowship of Evangelical Bible Churches
fec	Fellowship of Evangelical Churches
fmc	Free Methodist Church-USA (formerly of North America)
fum	Friends United Meeting
ggb	General Association of General Baptists
lca	Lutheran Church in America
lms	Lutheran Church-Missouri Synod
mch	Mennonite Church
mgc	Mennonite Church, General Conference
mus	Mennonite Church USA
mca	Moravian Church in America, Northern Province
nab	North American Baptist Conference
opc	The Orthodox Presbyterian Church
pch	Presbyterian Church (U.S.A.)
rca	Reformed Church in America
sda	Seventh-day Adventist, North American Division of
sbc	Southern Baptist Convention
ucc	United Church of Christ
wel	Wisconsin Evangelical Lutheran Synod

Appendix B-1: Church Member Giving, in Current Dollars, 1968–2021

	Data Year 1968			Data Year 1969			Data Year 1970		
	Full/Confirmed Members	Congregational Finances	Benevolences	Full/Confirmed Members	Congregational Finances	Benevolences	Full/Confirmed Members	Congregational Finances	Benevolences
abc	1,179,848 [a]	95,878,267 [a]	21,674,924 [a]	1,153,785 [a]	104,084,322	21,111,333	1,231,944 [a]	112,668,310	19,655,391
alc	1,767,618	137,260,390	32,862,410	1,771,999	143,917,440	34,394,570	1,775,573	146,268,320	30,750,030
arp	28,312 [a]	2,211,002 [a]	898,430 [a]	28,273	2,436,936 [a]	824,628 [a]	28,427 [a]	2,585,974 [a]	806,071 [a]
bcc	8,954	1,645,256	633,200 [a]	9,145	1,795,859	817,445	9,300 [a]	2,037,330 [a]	771,940 [a]
ccd	994,683	105,803,222	21,703,947	936,931	91,169,842	18,946,815	911,964	98,671,692	17,386,032
cga	146,807	23,310,682	4,168,580	147,752	24,828,448	4,531,678	150,198	26,962,037	4,886,223
cgg	6,600	805,000	103,000	6,700	805,000	104,000	6,800	810,000	107,000
chb	187,957	12,975,829	4,889,727	185,198	13,964,158	4,921,991	182,614	14,327,896	4,891,618
chn	364,789	59,943,750 [a]	14,163,761 [a]	372,943	64,487,669 [a]	15,220,339 [a]	383,284	68,877,922 [a]	16,221,123 [a]
cccc	15,127	1,867,978	753,686	16,219	1,382,195	801,534	17,328	1,736,818	779,696
cpc	87,044 [a]	6,247,447 [a]	901,974 [a]	86,435 [a]	7,724,405 [a]	926,317 [a]	86,683 [a]	7,735,906 [a]	1,011,911 [a]
ecc	29,582 [a]	3,369,308 [a]	627,731 [a]	29,652 [a]	3,521,074 [a]	646,187 [a]	29,437 [a]	3,786,288 [a]	692,428 [a]
ecv	66,021	14,374,162 [a]	3,072,848	67,522	14,952,302 [a]	3,312,306	67,441	15,874,265 [a]	3,578,876
elc	ALC & LCA	ALC & LCA	ALC & LCA	ALC & LCA	ALC & LCA	ALC & LCA	ALC & LCA	ALC & LCA	ALC & LCA
els	10,886 [a]	844,235 [a]	241,949 [a]	11,079	1,003,746	315,325	11,030	969,625	242,831 [a]
emc	2,870 [a]	447,397	232,331	NA	NA	NA	NA	NA	NA
feb	1,712 [a]	156,789 [a]	129,818 [a]	3,324	389,000	328,000	3,698	381,877	706,398
fec	see EMC	see EMC	see EMC	see EMC	see EMC	see EMC	see EMC	see EMC	see EMC
fmc	47,831 [a]	12,032,016 [a]	2,269,677 [a]	47,954 [a]	13,187,506 [a]	2,438,351 [a]	64,901	9,641,202	7,985,264
fum	55,469	3,564,793	1,256,192	55,257	3,509,509	1,289,026	53,970	3,973,802	1,167,183
ggb	65,000	4,303,183 [a]	269,921 [a]	NA	NA	NA	NA	NA	NA
lca	2,279,383	166,337,149	39,981,858	2,193,321	161,958,669	46,902,225	2,187,015	169,795,380	42,118,870
lms	1,877,799	178,042,762	47,415,800	1,900,708	185,827,626	49,402,590	1,922,569	193,352,322	47,810,664
mch	85,682 [a]	7,078,164 [a]	5,576,305 [a]	85,343	7,398,182	6,038,730	83,747 [a]	7,980,917 [a]	6,519,476 [a]
mgc	36,337 [a]	2,859,340 [a]	2,668,138 [a]	35,613	2,860,555 [a]	2,587,079 [a]	35,536	3,091,670	2,550,208
mus	MCH & MGC	MCH & MGC	MCH & MGC	MCH & MGC	MCH & MGC	MCH & MGC	MCH & MGC	MCH & MGC	MCH & MGC
mca	27,772	2,583,354	444,910	27,617	2,642,529	456,182	27,173	2,704,105	463,219
nab	42,371 [a]	5,176,669 [a]	1,383,964 [a]	55,100	6,681,410	2,111,588	55,080	6,586,929	2,368,288
opc	9,197	1,638,437	418,102	9,276	1,761,242	464,660	9,401 [a]	1,853,627 [a]	503,572 [a]
pch	4,180,093	375,248,474	102,622,450	4,118,664	388,268,169	97,897,522	4,041,813	401,785,731	93,927,852
rca	226,819 [b]	25,410,489 [b]	9,197,642 [b]	224,992 [b]	27,139,579 [b]	9,173,312 [b]	223,353 [b]	29,421,849 [b]	9,479,503 [b]
sda	395,159 [a]	36,976,280	95,178,335	407,766	40,378,426	102,730,594	420,419	45,280,059	109,569,241
sbc	11,332,229 [a]	666,924,020 [a]	128,023,731 [a]	11,487,708	709,246,590	133,203,885	11,628,032	753,510,973	138,480,329
ucc	2,032,648 [a]	152,301,536	18,869,136	1,997,898	152,791,512	27,338,543	1,960,608	155,248,767	26,934,289
wel	259,649 [a]	18,982,244 [a]	6,572,250 [a]	264,710 [a]	20,761,838 [a]	6,414,099 [a]	270,073 [a]	22,525,244 [a]	6,781,600 [a]
Total	27,852,248	2,126,599,624	569,206,727	27,738,884	2,200,875,738	595,650,854	27,879,411	2,310,446,837	599,147,126

[a] Data obtained from denominational source.
[b] empty tomb review of RCA directory data.

Appendix B-1: Church Member Giving, in Current Dollars, 1968–2021(continued)

	Data Year 1971			Data Year 1972			Data Year 1973		
	Full/Confirmed Members	Congregational Finances	Benevolences	Full/Confirmed Members	Congregational Finances	Benevolences	Full/Confirmed Members	Congregational Finances	Benevolences
abc	1,223,735 [a]	114,673,805	18,878,769	1,176,092 [a]	118,446,573	18,993,440	1,190,455 [a]	139,357,611	20,537,388
alc	1,775,774	146,324,460	28,321,740	1,773,414	154,786,570	30,133,850	1,770,119	168,194,730	35,211,440
arp	28,443 [a]	2,942,577 [a]	814,703 [a]	28,711 [a]	3,329,446 [a]	847,665 [a]	28,763 [a]	3,742,773 [a]	750,387 [a]
bcc	9,550	2,357,786	851,725	9,730	2,440,400	978,957	9,877 [a]	2,894,622 [a]	1,089,879 [a]
ccd	884,929	94,091,862	17,770,799	881,467	105,763,511	18,323,685	868,895	112,526,538	19,800,843
cga	152,787	28,343,604	5,062,282	155,920	31,580,751	5,550,487	157,828	34,649,592	6,349,695
cgg	7,200	860,000	120,000	7,400	900,000	120,000	7,440	940,000	120,000
chb	181,183	14,535,274	5,184,768	179,641	14,622,319 [c]	5,337,277 [c]	179,333	16,474,758	6,868,927
chn	394,197	75,107,918 [a]	17,859,332 [a]	404,732	82,891,903 [a]	20,119,679 [a]	417,200	91,318,469 [a]	22,661,140 [a]
cccc	19,279 [a]	1,875,010 [a]	930,485 [a]	20,081 [a]	1,950,865 [a]	994,453 [a]	20,712 [a]	2,080,038 [a]	1,057,869 [a]
cpc	86,945 [a]	7,729,131 [a]	1,009,657 [a]	88,200 [a]	8,387,762 [a]	1,064,831 [a]	88,203 [a]	9,611,201 [a]	1,220,768 [a]
ecc	29,682 [a]	4,076,576 [a]	742,293 [a]	29,434 [a]	4,303,406 [a]	798,968 [a]	29,331 [a]	4,913,214 [a]	943,619 [a]
ecv	68,428	17,066,051 [a]	3,841,887	69,815	18,021,767 [a]	4,169,053	69,922	18,948,864 [a]	4,259,950
elc	ALC & LCA	ALC & LCA	ALC & LCA	ALC & LCA	ALC & LCA	ALC & LCA	ALC & LCA	ALC & LCA	ALC & LCA
els	11,426 [a]	1,067,650 [a]	314,335 [a]	11,532	1,138,953	295,941 [a]	12,525	1,296,326	330,052 [a]
emc	NA	NA	NA	NA	NA	NA	3,131	593,070	408,440
feb	NA	NA	NA	NA	NA	NA	NA	NA	NA
fec	see EMC	see EMC	see EMC	see EMC	see EMC	see EMC	see EMC	see EMC	see EMC
fmc	47,933 [a]	13,116,414 [a]	2,960,525 [a]	48,400 [a]	14,311,395 [a]	3,287,000 [a]	48,763 [a]	15,768,216 [a]	3,474,555 [a]
fum	54,522	3,888,064	1,208,062	54,927	4,515,463	1,297,088	57,690	5,037,848	1,327,439
ggb	NA	NA	NA	NA	NA	NA	NA	NA	NA
lca	2,175,378	179,570,467	43,599,913	2,165,591	188,387,949	45,587,481	2,169,341	200,278,486	34,627,978
lms	1,945,889	203,619,804	48,891,368	1,963,262	216,756,345	50,777,670	1,983,114	230,435,598	54,438,074
mch	88,522	8,171,316	7,035,750	89,505	9,913,176	7,168,664	90,967	9,072,858	6,159,740
mgc	36,314	3,368,100	2,833,491	36,129	3,378,372	3,219,439	36,483	3,635,418	3,392,844
mus	MCH & MGC	MCH & MGC	MCH & MGC	MCH & MGC	MCH & MGC	MCH & MGC	MCH & MGC	MCH & MGC	MCH & MGC
mca	26,101	2,576,172	459,447	25,500	2,909,252	465,316	25,468	3,020,667	512,424
nab	54,997	7,114,457	2,293,692	54,441	7,519,558	2,253,158	41,516	6,030,352	1,712,092
opc	9,536 [a]	2,054,448 [a]	533,324 [a]	9,741 [a]	2,248,969 [a]	602,328 [a]	9,940 [a]	2,364,079 [a]	658,534 [a]
pch	3,963,665	420,865,807	93,164,548	3,855,494	436,042,890	92,691,469	3,730,312 [d]	480,735,088 [d]	95,462,247 [d]
rca	219,915 [b]	32,217,319 [b]	9,449,655 [b]	217,583 [b]	34,569,874 [b]	9,508,818 [b]	212,906 [b]	39,524,443 [b]	10,388,619 [b]
sda	433,906	49,208,043	119,913,879	449,188	54,988,781	132,411,980	464,276	60,643,602	149,994,942
sbc	11,824,676	814,406,626	160,510,775	12,065,333	896,427,208	174,711,648	12,295,400	1,011,467,569	193,511,983
ucc	1,928,674	158,924,956	26,409,521	1,895,016	165,556,364	27,793,561	1,867,810	168,602,602	28,471,058
wel	274,635 [a]	24,315,801 [a]	7,456,829 [a]	277,628 [a]	26,585,530 [a]	8,204,262 [a]	282,355 [a]	29,377,447 [a]	8,623,460 [a]
Total	27,958,221	2,434,469,498	628,423,554	28,043,907	2,612,675,352	667,708,168	28,170,075	2,873,536,079	714,366,386

[a] Data obtained from denominational source.

[b] empty tomb review of RCA directory data.

[c] *YACC* Church of the Brethren figures reported for 15 months due to fiscal year change: adjusted here to 12/15ths.

[d] The Presbyterian Church (USA) data for 1973 combines United Presbyterian Church in the U.S.A. data for 1973 (see *YACC* 1975) and an average of Presbyterian Church in the United States data for 1972 and 1974, since 1973 data was not reported in the *YACC* series.

Appendix B-1: Church Member Giving, in Current Dollars, 1968–2021 (continued)

	Data Year 1974			Data Year 1975			Data Year 1976		
	Full/Confirmed Members	Congregational Finances	Benevolences	Full/Confirmed Members	Congregational Finances	Benevolences	Full/Confirmed Members	Congregational Finances	Benevolences
abc	1,176,989 [a]	147,022,280	21,847,285	1,180,793 [a]	153,697,091	23,638,372	1,142,773 [a]	163,134,092	25,792,357
alc	1,764,186	173,318,574	38,921,546	1,764,810	198,863,519	75,666,809	1,768,758	215,527,544	76,478,278
arp	28,570	3,935,533 [a]	868,284 [a]	28,589	4,820,846 [a]	929,880 [a]	28,581	5,034,270 [a]	1,018,913 [a]
bcc	10,255	3,002,218	1,078,576	10,784	3,495,152	955,845	11,375	4,088,492	1,038,484
ccd	854,844	119,434,435	20,818,434	859,885	126,553,931	22,126,459	845,058	135,008,269	23,812,274
cga	161,401	39,189,287	7,343,123	166,259	42,077,029	7,880,559	170,285	47,191,302	8,854,295
cgg	7,455	975,000	105,000	7,485	990,000	105,000	7,620	1,100,000	105,000
chb	179,387	18,609,614	7,281,551	179,336	20,338,351	7,842,819	178,157	22,133,858	8,032,293
chn	430,128	104,774,391	25,534,267 [a]	441,093	115,400,881	28,186,392 [a]	448,658	128,294,499	32,278,187 [a]
cccc	21,661 [a]	2,452,254 [a]	1,181,655 [a]	22,065 [a]	2,639,472 [a]	1,750,364 [a]	21,703 [a]	3,073,413 [a]	1,494,355 [a]
cpc	87,875 [a]	9,830,198 [a]	1,336,847 [a]	86,903 [a]	11,268,297 [a]	1,445,793 [a]	85,541 [a]	10,735,854 [a]	1,540,692 [a]
ecc	29,636 [a]	4,901,100 [a]	1,009,726 [a]	28,886 [a]	5,503,484 [a]	1,068,134 [a]	28,840 [a]	6,006,621 [a]	1,139,209 [a]
ecv	69,960	21,235,204 [a]	5,131,124	71,808	23,440,265 [a]	6,353,422	73,458	25,686,916 [a]	6,898,871
elc	ALC & LCA	ALC & LCA	ALC & LCA	ALC & LCA	ALC & LCA	ALC & LCA	ALC & LCA	ALC & LCA	ALC & LCA
els	13,097	1,519,749	411,732 [a]	13,489 [a]	1,739,255	438,875 [a]	14,504	2,114,998	521,018 [a]
emc	3,123	644,548	548,000	NA	NA	NA	3,350	800,000	628,944
feb	NA	NA	NA	NA	NA	NA	NA	NA	NA
fec	see EMC	see EMC	see EMC	see EMC	see EMC	see EMC	see EMC	see EMC	see EMC
fmc	49,314 [a]	17,487,246 [a]	3,945,535 [a]	50,632	19,203,781 [a]	4,389,757 [a]	51,565	21,130,066 [a]	4,977,546 [a]
fum	NA	NA	NA	56,605	6,428,458	1,551,036	51,032	6,749,045	1,691,190
ggb	NA	NA	NA	NA	NA	NA	NA	NA	NA
lca	2,166,615	228,081,405	44,531,126	2,183,131	222,637,156	55,646,303	2,187,995	243,449,466	58,761,005
lms	2,010,456	249,150,470	55,076,955	2,018,530	266,546,758	55,896,061	2,026,336	287,098,403	56,831,860
mch	92,930 [a]	13,792,266	9,887,051	94,209	15,332,908	11,860,385	96,092 [a]	17,215,234	12,259,924
mgc	35,534	4,071,002 [a]	4,179,003 [a]	35,673 [a]	3,715,279 [a]	3,391,943 [a]	36,397	4,980,967	4,796,037 [a]
mus	MCH & MGC	MCH & MGC	MCH & MGC	MCH & MGC	MCH & MGC	MCH & MGC	MCH & MGC	MCH & MGC	MCH & MGC
mca	25,583	3,304,388	513,685	25,512	3,567,406	552,512	24,938	4,088,195	573,619
nab	41,437	6,604,693	2,142,148	42,122	7,781,298	2,470,317	42,277	8,902,540	3,302,348
opc	10,186 [a]	2,627,818 [a]	703,653 [a]	10,129 [a]	2,930,128 [a]	768,075 [a]	10,372	3,288,612 [a]	817,589 [a]
pch	3,619,768	502,237,350	100,966,089	3,535,825	529,327,006	111,027,318	3,484,985	563,106,353	125,035,379
rca	210,866 [b]	41,053,364 [b]	11,470,631 [b]	212,349 [b]	44,681,053 [b]	11,994,379 [b]	211,628 [b]	49,083,734 [b]	13,163,739 [b]
sda	479,799	67,241,956	166,166,766	495,699	72,060,121	184,689,250	509,792	81,577,130	184,648,454
sbc	12,513,378	1,123,264,849	219,214,770	12,733,124	1,237,594,037	237,452,055	12,917,992	1,382,794,494	262,144,889
ucc	1,841,312	184,292,017	30,243,223	1,818,762	193,524,114	32,125,332	1,801,241	207,486,324	33,862,658
wel	286,083 [a]	32,596,319 [a]	9,974,758 [a]	292,431 [a]	35,807,415 [a]	11,173,226 [a]	297,037 [a]	39,932,827 [a]	11,260,203 [a]
Total	28,221,828	3,126,649,528	792,432,543	28,466,918	3,371,964,491	903,376,672	28,578,340	3,690,813,518	963,759,610

[a] Data obtained from denominational source.

[b] empty tomb review of RCA directory data.

Appendix B-1: Church Member Giving, in Current Dollars, 1968–2021 (continued)

	Data Year 1977			Data Year 1978			Data Year 1979		
	Full/Confirmed Members	Congregational Finances	Benevolences	Full/Confirmed Members	Congregational Finances	Benevolences	Full/Confirmed Members	Congregational Finances	Benevolences
abc	1,146,084 [a]	172,710,063	27,765,800	1,008,495 [a]	184,716,172	31,937,862	1,036,054 [a]	195,986,995	34,992,300
alc	1,772,227	231,960,304	54,085,201	1,773,179	256,371,804	57,145,861	1,768,071	284,019,905	63,903,906
arp	28,371 [a]	5,705,295 [a]	1,061,285 [a]	28,644	6,209,447 [a]	1,031,469 [a]	28,513	6,544,759 [a]	1,125,562 [a]
bcc	11,915 [a]	4,633,334 [a]	957,239 [a]	12,430 [a]	4,913,311 [a]	1,089,346 [a]	12,923	5,519,037	1,312,046
ccd	817,288	148,880,340	25,698,856	791,633	166,249,455	25,790,367	773,765	172,270,978	27,335,440
cga	171,947	51,969,150	10,001,062	173,753	57,630,848	11,214,530	175,113	65,974,517	12,434,621
cgg	7,595	1,130,000	110,000	7,550	1,135,000	110,000	7,620	1,170,000	105,000
chb	177,534	23,722,817	8,228,903	175,335	25,397,531	9,476,220	172,115	28,422,684	10,161,266
chn	455,100	141,807,024	34,895,751 [a]	462,124	153,943,138	38,300,431 [a]	473,726	170,515,940 [a]	42,087,862 [a]
cccc	21,897 [a]	3,916,248 [a]	1,554,143 [a]	22,364 [a]	4,271,435 [a]	1,630,565 [a]	23,481 [a]	4,969,610 [a]	1,871,754 [a]
cpc	85,227 [a]	11,384,825 [a]	1,760,117 [a]	84,956 [a]	13,359,375 [a]	1,995,388 [a]	85,932 [a]	13,928,957 [a]	2,192,562 [a]
ecc	28,712 [a]	6,356,730 [a]	1,271,310 [a]	28,459 [a]	6,890,381 [a]	1,454,826 [a]	27,995 [a]	7,552,495 [a]	1,547,857 [a]
ecv	74,060	28,758,357 [a]	7,240,548	74,678	32,606,550 [a]	8,017,623	76,092	37,118,906 [a]	9,400,074
elc	ALC & LCA	ALC & LCA	ALC & LCA	ALC & LCA	ALC & LCA	ALC & LCA	ALC & LCA	ALC & LCA	ALC & LCA
els	14,652	2,290,697	546,899 [a]	14,833	2,629,719	833,543 [a]	15,081	2,750,703	904,774 [a]
emc	NA	NA	NA	3,634	1,281,761	794,896	3,704	1,380,806	828,264
feb	NA	NA	NA	3,956	970,960	745,059	NA	NA	NA
fec	see EMC	see EMC	see EMC	see EMC	see EMC	see EMC	see EMC	see EMC	see EMC
fmc	52,563	23,303,722 [a]	5,505,538 [a]	52,698 [a]	25,505,294 [a]	5,869,970 [a]	52,900 [a]	27,516,302 [a]	6,614,732 [a]
fum	52,599	6,943,990	1,895,984	53,390	8,172,337	1,968,884	51,426	6,662,787	2,131,108
ggb	72,030	9,854,533	747,842	NA	NA	NA	73,046	13,131,345	1,218,763
lca	2,191,942	251,083,883	62,076,894	2,183,666	277,186,563	72,426,148	2,177,231	301,605,382	71,325,097
lms	1,991,408	301,064,630	57,077,162	1,969,279	329,134,237	59,030,753	1,965,422	360,989,735	63,530,596
mch	96,609	18,540,237	12,980,502	97,142	22,922,417	14,124,757 [a]	98,027	24,505,346	15,116,762
mgc	35,575 [a]	5,051,708 [a]	4,619,590 [a]	36,775 [a]	5,421,568 [a]	5,062,489 [a]	36,736 [a]	6,254,850 [a]	5,660,477 [a]
mus	MCH & MGC	MCH & MGC	MCH & MGC	MCH & MGC	MCH & MGC	MCH & MGC	MCH & MGC	MCH & MGC	MCH & MGC
mca	25,323	4,583,616	581,200	24,854	4,441,750	625,536	24,782	4,600,331	689,070
nab	42,724	10,332,556	3,554,204	42,499	11,629,309	3,559,983	42,779	13,415,024	3,564,339
opc	10,683 [a]	3,514,172	931,935	10,939	4,107,705	1,135,388	11,306 [a]	4,683,302	1,147,191
pch	3,430,927	633,187,916	130,252,348	3,382,783	692,872,811	128,194,954	3,321,787	776,049,247	148,528,993
rca	210,637 [b]	53,999,791 [b]	14,210,966 [b]	211,778 [b]	60,138,720 [b]	15,494,816 [b]	210,700 [b]	62,997,526 [b]	16,750,408 [b]
sda	522,317	98,468,365	216,202,975	535,705	104,044,989	226,692,736	553,089	118,711,906	255,936,372
sbc	13,078,239	1,506,877,921	289,179,711	13,191,394	1,668,120,760	316,462,385	13,372,757	1,864,213,869	355,885,769
ucc	1,785,652	219,878,772	35,522,221	1,769,104	232,593,033	37,789,958	1,745,533	249,443,032	41,100,583
wel	301,125 [a]	44,378,032 [a]	11,600,902 [a]	303,134 [a]	50,123,714 [a]	12,907,953 [a]	305,454 [a]	54,789,339 [a]	14,178,008 [a]
Total	28,712,962	4,026,289,028	1,022,117,088	28,531,163	4,414,992,094	1,092,914,696	28,723,160	4,887,695,615	1,213,581,556

[a] Data obtained from denominational source.

[b] empty tomb review of RCA directory data.

Appendix B-1: Church Member Giving, in Current Dollars, 1968–2021(continued)

	Data Year 1980			Data Year 1981			Data Year 1982		
	Full/Confirmed Members	Congregational Finances	Benevolences	Full/Confirmed Members	Congregational Finances	Benevolences	Full/Confirmed Members	Congregational Finances	Benevolences
abc	1,008,700 [a]	213,560,656	37,133,159	989,322 [a]	227,931,461	40,046,261	983,580 [a]	242,750,027	41,457,745
alc	1,763,067	312,592,610	65,235,739	1,758,452	330,155,588	96,102,638	1,758,239	359,848,865	77,010,444
arp	28,166 [a]	6,868,650 [a]	1,054,229 [a]	28,334 [a]	7,863,221 [a]	1,497,838 [a]	29,087 [a]	8,580,311 [a]	1,807,572 [a]
bcc	13,578 [a]	6,011,465 [a]	1,490,334 [a]	13,993	6,781,857	1,740,711	14,413 [a]	7,228,612 [a]	1,594,797 [a]
ccd	788,394	189,176,399	30,991,519	772,466	211,828,751	31,067,142	770,227	227,178,861	34,307,638
cga	176,429	67,367,485	13,414,112	178,581	78,322,907	14,907,277	184,685	84,896,806	17,171,600
cgg	NA	NA	NA	5,981	1,788,298	403,000	5,781 [a]	1,864,735 [a]	418,000 [a]
chb	170,839	29,813,265	11,663,976	170,267	31,641,019	12,929,076	168,844	35,064,568	12,844,415
chn	483,101	191,536,556	45,786,446 [a]	490,852	203,145,992	50,084,163 [a]	497,261	221,947,940	53,232,461 [a]
cccc	24,410 [a]	6,017,539 [a]	2,169,298 [a]	25,044 [a]	8,465,804	2,415,233	26,008	9,230,111	2,574,569
cpc	86,941 [a]	15,973,738 [a]	2,444,677 [a]	87,493 [a]	16,876,846 [a]	2,531,539 [a]	88,121 [a]	17,967,709 [a]	2,706,361 [a]
ecc	27,567 [a]	8,037,564 [a]	1,630,993 [a]	27,287 [a]	8,573,057 [a]	1,758,025 [a]	27,203 [a]	9,119,278 [a]	1,891,936 [a]
ecv	77,737	41,888,556 [a]	10,031,072	79,523	45,206,565 [a]	8,689,918	81,324	50,209,520 [a]	8,830,793
elc	ALC & LCA	ALC & LCA	ALC & LCA	ALC & LCA	ALC & LCA	ALC & LCA	ALC & LCA	ALC & LCA	ALC & LCA
els	14,968	3,154,804	876,929 [a]	14,904	3,461,387	716,624	15,165	3,767,977	804,822
emc	3,782	1,527,945	1,041,447	3,753	1,515,975	908,342	3,832	1,985,890	731,510
feb	4,329	1,250,466	627,536	NA	NA	NA	2,047	696,660	1,020,972
fec	see EMC	see EMC	see EMC	see EMC	see EMC	see EMC	see EMC	see EMC	see EMC
fmc	54,145 [a]	30,525,352 [a]	6,648,248 [a]	54,764 [a]	32,853,491 [a]	7,555,713 [a]	54,198	35,056,434	8,051,593
fum	51,691	9,437,724	2,328,137	51,248	9,551,765	2,449,731	50,601	10,334,180	2,597,215
ggb	74,159	14,967,312	1,547,038	75,028	15,816,060	1,473,070	NA	NA	NA
lca	2,176,991	371,981,816	87,439,137	2,173,558	404,300,509	82,862,299	2,176,265	435,564,519	83,217,264
lms	1,973,958	390,756,268	66,626,364	1,983,198	429,910,406	86,341,102	1,961,260	468,468,156	75,457,846
mch	99,511	28,846,931	16,437,738	99,651	31,304,278	17,448,024	101,501	33,583,338	17,981,274
mgc	36,644 [a]	6,796,330 [a]	5,976,652 [a]	36,609 [a]	7,857,792 [a]	7,203,240 [a]	37,007 [a]	8,438,680 [a]	7,705,419 [a]
mus	MCH & MGC	MCH & MGC	MCH & MGC	MCH & MGC	MCH & MGC	MCH & MGC	MCH & MGC	MCH & MGC	MCH & MGC
mca	24,863	5,178,444	860,399	24,500	5,675,495	831,177	24,669	6,049,857	812,015
nab	43,041	12,453,858	3,972,485	43,146	15,513,286	4,420,403	42,735	17,302,952	4,597,515
opc	11,553 [a]	5,235,294	1,235,849	11,884 [a]	5,939,983	1,382,451	11,956 [a]	6,512,125 [a]	1,430,061 [a]
pch	3,262,086	820,218,732	176,172,729	3,202,392	896,641,430	188,576,382	3,157,372	970,223,947	199,331,832
rca	210,762	70,733,297	17,313,239 [b]	210,312	77,044,709	18,193,793 [b]	211,168	82,656,050	19,418,165 [b]
sda	571,141	121,484,768	275,783,385	588,536	133,088,131	297,838,046	606,310	136,877,455	299,437,917
sbc	13,600,126	2,080,375,258	400,976,072	13,782,644	2,336,062,506	443,931,179	13,991,709	2,628,272,553	486,402,607
ucc	1,736,244	278,546,571	44,042,186	1,726,535	300,730,591	48,329,399	1,708,847	323,725,191	52,738,069
wel	307,810 [a]	60,458,213 [a]	15,989,577 [a]	310,553 [a]	67,830,319 [a]	18,198,804 [a]	311,364 [a]	71,611,865 [a]	18,608,914 [a]
Total	28,906,733	5,402,773,866	1,348,940,701	29,020,810	5,953,679,479	1,492,832,600	29,102,779	6,517,015,172	1,536,193,341

[a] Data obtained from denominational source.
[b] empty tomb review of RCA directory data.

Appendix B-1: Church Member Giving, in Current Dollars, 1968–2021(continued)

	Data Year 1983			Data Year 1984			Data Year 1985		
	Full/Confirmed Members	Congregational Finances	Benevolences	Full/Confirmed Members	Congregational Finances	Benevolences	Full/Confirmed Members	Congregational Finances	Benevolences
abc	965,117 [a]	254,716,036	43,683,021	953,945 [a]	267,556,088	46,232,040	894,732 [a]	267,694,684	47,201,119
alc	1,756,420	375,500,188	84,633,617	1,756,558	413,876,101	86,601,067	1,751,649	428,861,660	87,152,699
arp	31,738	10,640,050 [a]	2,180,230 [a]	31,355	11,221,526 [a]	3,019,456 [a]	32,051	12,092,868 [a]	3,106,994 [a]
bcc	14,782	7,638,413	1,858,632	15,128	8,160,359	2,586,843	15,535 [a]	8,504,354 [a]	2,979,046 [a]
ccd	761,629	241,934,972	35,809,331	755,233	263,694,210	38,402,791	743,486	274,072,301	40,992,053
cga	182,190	81,309,323	13,896,753	185,404	86,611,269	14,347,570	185,593	91,078,512	15,308,954
cgg	5,759	1,981,300	412,000	4,711	2,211,800	504,200	4,575	2,428,730	582,411
chb	164,680	39,726,743	14,488,192	161,824	37,743,527	15,136,600	159,184	40,658,904	16,509,718
chn	506,439	237,220,642	57,267,073 [a]	514,937	253,566,280	60,909,810 [a]	520,741	267,134,078	65,627,515 [a]
cccc	26,691 [a]	9,189,221 [a]	2,980,636	28,383	10,018,982	3,051,425	28,624	11,729,365	3,350,021
cpc	87,186 [a]	19,252,942 [a]	3,028,953 [a]	86,995 [a]	20,998,768 [a]	3,331,065 [a]	85,346 [a]	22,361,332 [a]	3,227,932 [a]
ecc	26,769 [a]	9,505,479 [a]	2,019,373 [a]	26,375 [a]	10,302,554 [a]	2,220,852 [a]	26,016	8,134,641 [a]	1,777,172
ecv	82,943	53,279,350 [a]	10,615,909	84,185	60,295,634 [a]	11,243,908	85,150	63,590,735 [a]	13,828,030
elc	ALC & LCA	ALC & LCA	ALC & LCA	ALC & LCA	ALC & LCA	ALC & LCA	ALC & LCA	ALC & LCA	ALC & LCA
els	15,576	3,842,625	838,788	15,396	4,647,714	931,677 [a]	15,012	4,725,783	791,586
emc	3,857	1,930,689	738,194	3,908	2,017,565	862,350	3,813	2,128,019	1,058,040
feb	2,094	622,467	1,466,399	NA	NA	NA	2,107 [a]	1,069,851 [a]	402,611 [a]
fec	see EMC	see EMC	see EMC	see EMC	see EMC	see EMC	see EMC	see EMC	see EMC
fmc	56,442 [a]	36,402,355 [a]	8,334,248 [a]	56,667 [a]	39,766,087 [a]	8,788,189 [a]	56,242	42,046,626 [a]	9,461,369 [a]
fum	49,441	11,723,240	2,886,931	48,713	11,549,163	2,875,370	48,812	12,601,820	3,012,658
ggb	75,133	17,283,259	1,733,755	75,028	17,599,169	1,729,228	73,040	18,516,252	1,683,130
lca	2,176,772	457,239,780	88,909,363	2,168,594	496,228,216	99,833,067	2,161,216	539,142,069	103,534,375
lms	1,984,199	499,220,552	76,991,991 [a]	1,986,392	539,346,935	81,742,006 [a]	1,982,753	566,507,516	83,117,011 [a]
mch	103,350 [a]	34,153,628	17,581,878	90,347	37,333,306	16,944,094	91,167	34,015,200	25,593,500
mgc	36,318 [a]	8,702,849 [a]	7,661,415 [a]	35,951 [a]	9,197,458 [a]	7,795,680 [a]	35,356 [a]	9,217,964 [a]	7,070,700 [a]
mus	MCH & MGC	MCH & MGC	MCH & MGC	MCH & MGC	MCH & MGC	MCH & MGC	MCH & MGC	MCH & MGC	MCH & MGC
mca	24,913	6,618,339	911,787	24,269	7,723,611	1,183,741	24,396	8,698,949	1,170,349
nab	43,286	18,010,853	5,132,672	43,215	19,322,720	5,724,552	42,863	20,246,236	5,766,686
opc	12,045	6,874,722	1,755,169	12,278 [a]	7,555,006	2,079,924	12,593 [a]	8,291,483	2,204,998
pch	3,122,213	1,047,756,995	197,981,080	3,092,151	1,132,098,779	218,412,639	3,057,226 [a]	1,252,885,684 [a]	232,487,569 [a]
rca	211,660	92,071,986	20,632,574	209,968 [b]	100,378,778	21,794,880	209,395	103,428,950	22,233,299
sda	623,563	143,636,140	323,461,439	638,929	155,257,063	319,664,449	651,594	155,077,180	346,251,406
sbc	14,178,051	2,838,573,815	528,781,000	14,341,822	3,094,913,877	567,467,188	14,477,364	3,272,276,486	609,868,694
ucc	1,701,513	332,613,396	55,716,557	1,696,107	385,786,198	58,679,094	1,683,777	409,543,989	62,169,679 [a]
wel	312,974 [a]	75,825,104 [a]	24,037,480 [a]	314,559 [a]	82,507,020 [a]	22,845,856 [a]	315,374 [a]	86,879,662 [a]	22,275,822 [a]
Total	29,345,743	6,974,997,453	1,638,426,440	29,459,327	7,589,485,763	1,726,941,611	29,476,782	8,045,641,883	1,841,797,146

[a] Data obtained from denominational source.

[b] empty tomb review of RCA directory data.

Appendix B-1: Church Member Giving, in Current Dollars, 1968–2021 (continued)

	Data Year 1986			Data Year 1987			Data Year 1988		
	Full/Confirmed Members	Congregational Finances	Benevolences	Full/Confirmed Members	Congregational Finances	Benevolences	Full/Confirmed Members	Congregational Finances	Benevolences
abc	862,582 [a]	287,020,378 [a]	49,070,083 [a]	868,189 [a]	291,606,418 [a]	55,613,855	825,102 [a]	296,569,316 [a]	55,876,771
alc	1,740,439	434,641,736	96,147,129	See ELCA	See ELCA	See ELCA	See ELCA	See ELCA	See ELCA
arp	32,438 [a]	12,336,321 [a]	3,434,408 [a]	32,289	13,553,176 [a]	3,927,030 [a]	31,922	13,657,776 [a]	5,063,036 [a]
bcc	15,911	10,533,883	2,463,558	16,136	11,203,321	3,139,949	16,578 [a]	13,522,101 [a]	4,346,690 [a]
ccd	732,466	288,277,386	42,027,504	718,522	287,464,332	42,728,826	707,985	297,187,996	42,226,128
cga	188,662	91,768,855	16,136,647	198,552	124,376,413	20,261,687	198,842	132,384,232	19,781,941
cgg	NA	NA	NA	4,348	2,437,778	738,818	4,394 [a]	2,420,600 [a]	644,000 [a]
chb	155,967	43,531,293	17,859,101	154,067	45,201,732	19,342,402	151,169	48,008,657	19,701,942 [a]
chn	529,192	283,189,977	68,438,998 [a]	541,878	294,160,356	73,033,568 [a]	550,700	309,478,442	74,737,057 [a]
cccc	28,948	15,559,846 [a]	3,961,037	29,429	15,409,349 [a]	3,740,688	29,015	13,853,547	4,120,974
cpc	84,579 [a]	22,338,090 [a]	3,646,356 [a]	85,781	22,857,711	3,727,681	85,304	23,366,911 [e]	3,722,607
ecc	25,625	10,977,813 [a]	2,422,879 [a]	25,300	14,281,140 [a]	2,575,415 [a]	24,980	12,115,762	2,856,766 [a]
ecv	86,079	67,889,353 [a]	14,374,707	86,741	73,498,123 [a]	14,636,000	87,750	77,504,445 [a]	14,471,178
elc	ALC & LCA	ALC & LCA	ALC & LCA	3,952,663	1,083,293,684	169,685,942	3,931,878	1,150,483,034	169,580,472
els	15,083 [a]	4,996,111 [a]	1,050,715 [a]	15,892	5,298,882	1,082,198	15,518 [a]	5,713,773 [a]	1,043,612 [a]
emc	NA	NA	NA	3,841	2,332,216	1,326,711	3,879	2,522,533	1,438,459
feb	NA	NA	NA	NA	NA	NA	NA	NA	NA
fec	see EMC	see EMC	see EMC	see EMC	see EMC	see EMC	see EMC	see EMC	see EMC
fmc	56,243	46,150,881	9,446,120	57,262	47,743,298	9,938,096	57,432	48,788,041	9,952,103
fum	48,143	12,790,909	2,916,870	47,173	13,768,272	3,631,353	48,325	14,127,491	3,719,125
ggb	72,263	19,743,265	1,883,826	73,515	20,850,827	1,789,578	74,086	21,218,051	1,731,299
lca	2,157,701	569,250,519	111,871,174	See ELCA	See ELCA	See ELCA	See ELCA	See ELCA	See ELCA
lms	1,974,798	605,768,688	87,803,646 [a]	1,973,347	620,271,274	86,938,723 [a]	1,962,674	659,288,332	88,587,175 [a]
mch	91,467 [a]	40,097,500 [a]	24,404,200 [a]	92,673 [a]	43,295,100	25,033,600	92,682	47,771,200	27,043,900
mgc	35,170	10,101,306 [a]	7,717,998 [a]	34,889	11,560,998	8,478,414	34,693	11,399,995	9,638,417
mus	MCH & MGC	MCH & MGC	MCH & MGC	MCH & MGC	MCH & MGC	MCH & MGC	MCH & MGC	MCH & MGC	MCH & MGC
mca	24,260	8,133,127	1,155,350	24,440	9,590,658	1,174,593	23,526	9,221,646	1,210,476
nab	42,084	20,961,799	5,982,391	42,150 [a]	23,773,844 [a]	7,873,096 [a]	42,629	24,597,288	6,611,840
opc	12,919 [a]	9,333,328 [a]	2,347,928 [a]	13,013 [a]	9,884,288	2,425,480	13,108 [a]	10,797,786 [a]	2,648,375 [a]
pch	3,007,322	1,318,440,264	249,033,881	2,967,781	1,395,501,073	247,234,439	2,929,608	1,439,655,217	284,989,138
rca	207,993	114,231,429	22,954,596	203,581	114,652,192 [b]	24,043,270	200,631	127,409,263	25,496,802 [b]
sda	666,199	166,692,974	361,316,753	675,702	166,939,355	374,830,065	687,200	178,768,967	395,849,223
sbc	14,613,638	3,481,124,471	635,196,984	14,722,617	3,629,842,643	662,455,177	14,812,844	3,706,652,161	689,366,904
ucc	1,676,105	429,340,239	63,808,091	1,662,568	451,700,210	66,870,922	1,644,787	470,747,740	65,734,348
wel	315,510 [a]	92,309,279 [a]	22,354,781 [a]	316,393 [a]	97,179,349 [a]	22,112,031 [a]	316,098 [a]	101,545,536 [a]	22,323,451 [a]
Total	29,499,786	8,517,531,020	1,931,227,711	29,640,732	8,943,528,012	1,960,389,607	29,605,339	9,270,777,839	2,054,514,209

[a] Data obtained from denominational source.

[b] empty tomb review of RCA directory data.

[e] A *YACC* prepublication data table listed 23,366,911 for Congregational Finances which, added to Benevolences, equals the published Total of 27,089,518.

Appendix B-1: Church Member Giving, in Current Dollars, 1968–2021(continued)

	Data Year 1989			Data Year 1990			Data Year 1991		
	Full/Confirmed Members	Congregational Finances	Benevolences	Full/Confirmed Members	Congregational Finances	Benevolences	Full/Confirmed Members	Congregational Finances	Benevolences
abc	789,730 [a]	305,212,094 [a]	55,951,539	764,890 [a]	315,777,005 [a]	54,740,278	773,838 [a]	318,150,548 [a]	52,330,924
alc	See ELCA	See ELCA	See ELCA	See ELCA	See ELCA	See ELCA	See ELCA	See ELCA	See ELCA
arp	32,600	16,053,762 [a]	4,367,314 [a]	32,817 [a]	17,313,355 [a]	5,031,504 [a]	33,494 [a]	17,585,273 [a]	5,254,738 [a]
bcc	16,842	12,840,038	3,370,306	17,277	13,327,414	3,336,580	17,456 [a]	14,491,918 [a]	3,294,169 [a]
ccd	690,115	310,043,826	42,015,246	678,750	321,569,909	42,607,007	663,336	331,629,009	43,339,307
cga	199,786	134,918,052	20,215,075	205,884	141,375,027	21,087,504	214,743 [a]	146,249,447 [a]	21,801,570 [a]
cgg	4,415	3,367,000	686,000	4,399	3,106,729	690,000	4,375	2,756,651	662,500
chb	149,681	51,921,820	19,737,714 [a]	148,253	54,832,226	18,384,483 [a]	147,954 [a]	55,035,355 [a]	19,694,919 [a]
chn	558,664	322,924,598	76,625,913 [a]	563,756 [a]	333,397,255 [a]	77,991,665 [a]	572,153	352,654,251	82,276,097 [a]
cccc	28,413	18,199,823	4,064,111	28,355	16,964,128	4,174,133	28,035	17,760,290	4,304,052
cpc	84,994 [a]	25,867,112 [a]	4,086,994 [a]	85,025 [a]	27,027,650 [a]	4,139,967 [a]	84,706 [a]	28,069,681 [a]	5,740,846 [a]
ecc	24,606	13,274,756 [a]	2,703,095 [a]	24,437	12,947,150 [a]	2,858,077 [a]	24,124 [a]	13,100,036 [a]	3,074,660 [a]
ecv	89,014	80,621,293 [a]	15,206,265	89,735	84,263,236 [a]	15,601,475	89,648	87,321,563 [a]	16,598,656
elc	3,909,302	1,239,433,257	182,386,940	3,898,478	1,318,884,279	184,174,554	3,890,947	1,375,439,787	186,016,168
els	15,740	6,186,648	1,342,321	16,181	6,527,076	1,193,789	16,004	6,657,338	1,030,445
emc	3,888	2,712,843	1,567,728	4,026	2,991,485	1,800,593	3,958	3,394,563	1,790,115
feb	NA	NA	NA	NA	NA	NA	2,008 [a]	1,398,968 [a]	500,092 [a]
fec	see EMC	see EMC	see EMC	see EMC	see EMC	see EMC	see EMC	see EMC	see EMC
fmc	59,418 [a]	50,114,090 [a]	10,311,535 [a]	58,084	55,229,181	10,118,505	57,794	57,880,464	9,876,739
fum	47,228	16,288,644	4,055,624	45,691	10,036,083	2,511,063	50,803 [f]	NA	NA
ggb	73,738	23,127,835	1,768,804	74,156	23,127,835	1,737,011	71,119 [a]	22,362,874 [a]	1,408,262 [a]
lca	See ELCA	See ELCA	See ELCA	See ELCA	See ELCA	See ELCA	See ELCA	See ELCA	See ELCA
lms	1,961,114	701,701,168 [a]	90,974,340 [a]	1,954,350	712,235,204	96,308,765 [a]	1,952,845	741,823,412	94,094,637 [a]
mch	92,517	55,353,313	27,873,241	92,448 [a]	65,709,827	28,397,083	93,114 [a]	68,926,324	28,464,199
mgc	33,982	12,096,435	9,054,682	33,535	13,669,288	8,449,395	33,937 [a]	13,556,484 [a]	8,645,993 [a]
mus	MCH & MGC	MCH & MGC	MCH & MGC	MCH & MGC	MCH & MGC	MCH & MGC	MCH & MGC	MCH & MGC	MCH & MGC
mca	23,802	10,415,640	1,284,233	23,526	10,105,037	1,337,616	22,887	10,095,337	1,205,335
nab	42,629	28,076,077	3,890,017	44,493	31,103,672	7,700,119	43,187 [a]	27,335,239 [a]	7,792,876 [a]
opc	12,573 [a]	11,062,590 [a]	2,789,427 [a]	12,177 [a]	10,631,166 [a]	2,738,295 [a]	12,265	11,700,000	2,700,000
pch	2,886,482	1,528,450,805	295,365,032	2,847,437	1,530,341,707	294,990,441	2,805,548	1,636,407,042	311,905,934 [a]
rca	198,832	136,796,188 [b]	29,456,132 [b]	197,154	144,357,953 [b]	27,705,029 [b]	193,531 [b]	147,532,382 [b]	26,821,721 [b]
sda	701,781	196,204,538	415,752,350	717,446	195,054,218	433,035,080	733,026	201,411,183	456,242,995
sbc	14,907,826	3,873,300,782	712,738,838	15,038,409	4,146,285,561	718,174,874	15,232,347	4,283,283,059	731,812,766
ucc	1,625,969	496,825,160	72,300,698	1,599,212	527,378,397	71,984,897	1,583,830	543,803,752	73,149,887
wel	316,163 [a]	110,112,151 [a]	22,717,491 [a]	315,840 [a]	115,806,027 [a]	23,983,079 [a]	315,853 [a]	121,159,792 [a]	24,160,350 [a]
Total	29,581,844	9,793,502,338	2,134,659,005	29,616,221	29,261,375,080	2,166,982,861	29,718,062	10,658,972,022	2,225,990,952

[a] Data obtained from denominational source.

[b] empty tomb review of RCA directory data.

[f] Membership obtained from the denomination and used only in Chapter 5 analysis; not included in the Total sum on this page.

Appendix B-1: Church Member Giving, in Current Dollars, 1968–2021(continued)

	Data Year 1992			Data Year 1993			Data Year 1994		
	Full/Confirmed Members	Congregational Finances	Benevolences	Full/Confirmed Members	Congregational Finances	Benevolences	Full/Confirmed Members	Congregational Finances	Benevolences
abc	730,009 [a]	310,307,040 [a]	52,764,005	764,657 [a]	346,658,047 [a]	53,562,811	697,379 [a]	337,185,885 [a]	51,553,256 [a]
alc	See ELCA	See ELCA	See ELCA	See ELCA	See ELCA	See ELCA	See ELCA	See ELCA	See ELCA
arp	33,550	18,175,957 [a]	5,684,008 [a]	33,662 [a]	20,212,390 [a]	5,822,845 [a]	33,636	22,618,802 [a]	6,727,857
bcc	17,646 [a]	15,981,118 [a]	3,159,717 [a]	17,986	13,786,394	4,515,730 [a]	18,152	14,844,672	5,622,005
ccd	655,652	333,629,412	46,440,333	619,028	328,219,027	44,790,415	605,996	342,352,080	43,165,285
cga	214,743	150,115,497	23,500,213	216,117	158,454,703	23,620,177	221,346 [a]	160,694,760 [a]	26,262,049 [a]
cgg	4,085	2,648,085	509,398	4,239	2,793,000	587,705	3,996	2,934,843	475,799
chb	147,912	57,954,895	21,748,320	146,713	56,818,998	23,278,848	144,282	57,210,682	24,155,595
chn	582,804 [a]	361,555,793 [a]	84,118,580 [a]	589,398	369,896,767	87,416,378 [a]	595,303	387,385,034	89,721,860
cccc	30,387	22,979,946	4,311,234	36,864	24,997,736 [a]	5,272,184	37,996 [a]	23,758,101 [a]	5,240,805 [a]
cpc	85,080 [a]	27,813,626 [a]	4,339,933 [a]	84,336 [a]	27,462,623 [a]	4,574,550 [a]	83,733 [a]	29,212,802 [a]	4,547,149 [a]
ecc	24,150	13,451,827 [a]	3,120,351 [a]	23,889	13,546,159 [a]	3,258,595 [a]	23,504	13,931,409	3,269,986
ecv	90,985 [a]	93,071,869 [a]	16,732,701 [a]	89,511	93,765,006 [a]	16,482,315	90,919 [a]	101,746,341 [a]	17,874,955 [a]
elc	3,878,055	1,399,419,800	189,605,837	3,861,418	1,452,000,815	188,393,158	3,849,692	1,502,746,601	187,145,886
els	15,929 [a]	6,944,522 [a]	1,271,058 [a]	15,780	6,759,222 [a]	1,100,660	15,960	7,288,521	1,195,698
emc	4,059	3,839,838 [a]	1,403,001 [a]	4,130 [a]	4,260,307 [a]	1,406,682 [a]	4,225 [a]	4,597,730 [a]	1,533,157 [a]
feb	1,872 [a]	1,343,225 [a]	397,553 [a]	1,866 [a]	1,294,646 [a]	429,023 [a]	1,898 [a]	1,537,041 [a]	395,719 [a]
fec	see EMC	see EMC	see EMC	see EMC	see EMC	see EMC	see EMC	see EMC	see EMC
fmc	58,220	60,584,079	10,591,064	59,156	62,478,294	10,513,187	59,354 [a]	65,357,788 [a]	10,708,854 [a]
fum	50,005 [f]	NA	NA	45,542 [f]	NA	NA	44,711 [f]	NA	NA
ggb	72,388 [a]	21,561,432 [a]	1,402,330 [a]	73,129 [a]	22,376,970 [a]	1,440,342 [a]	71,140 [a]	19,651,624 [a]	2,052,409 [a]
lca	See ELCA	See ELCA	See ELCA	See ELCA	See ELCA	See ELCA	See ELCA	See ELCA	See ELCA
lms	1,953,248	777,467,488	97,275,934 [a]	1,945,077	789,821,559	96,355,945 [a]	1,944,905	817,412,113	96,048,560 [a]
mch	94,222 [a]	68,118,222	28,835,719	95,634	71,385,271	27,973,380	87,911 [a]	64,651,639	24,830,192
mgc	34,040	14,721,813 [a]	8,265,700	33,629	14,412,556	7,951,676	32,782	16,093,551 [a]	8,557,126 [a]
mus	MCH & MGC	MCH & MGC	MCH & MGC	MCH & MGC	MCH & MGC	MCH & MGC	MCH & MGC	MCH & MGC	MCH & MGC
mca	22,533	10,150,953	1,208,372	22,223	9,675,502	1,191,131	21,448	9,753,010	1,182,778
nab	43,446	28,375,947	7,327,594	43,045	30,676,902	7,454,087	43,236	32,800,560	7,515,707
opc	12,580 [a]	12,466,266 [a]	3,025,824 [a]	12,924 [a]	13,158,089 [a]	3,039,676 [a]	13,970	14,393,880	3,120,454
pch	2,780,406	1,696,092,968	309,069,530	2,742,192	1,700,918,712	310,375,024	2,698,262	1,800,008,292	307,158,749
rca	190,322 [b]	147,181,320 [b]	28,457,900 [b]	188,551 [b]	159,715,941 [b]	26,009,853 [b]	185,242	153,107,408	27,906,830
sda	748,687	191,362,737	476,902,779	761,703	209,524,570	473,769,831	775,349	229,596,444	503,347,816
sbc	15,358,866	4,462,915,112	751,366,698	15,398,642	4,621,157,751	761,298,249	15,614,060	5,263,421,764	815,360,696
ucc	1,555,382	521,190,413	73,906,372	1,530,178	550,847,702	71,046,517	1,501,310	556,540,722	67,269,762
wel	315,062 [a]	127,139,400 [a]	26,239,464 [a]	314,757 [a]	136,405,994 [a]	24,403,323 [a]	314,141 [a]	142,238,820 [a]	23,825,002 [a]
Total	29,756,320	10,958,560,600	2,282,981,522	29,730,434	11,313,481,653	2,287,334,297	29,791,127	12,195,072,919	2,367,771,996

[a] Data obtained from denominational source.
[b] empty tomb review of RCA directory data.
[f] Membership obtained from the denomination and used only in Chapter 5 analysis; not included in the Total sum on this page.

Appendix B-1: Church Member Giving, in Current Dollars, 1968–2021 (continued)

	Data Year 1995			Data Year 1996			Data Year 1997		
	Full/Confirmed Members	Congregational Finances	Benevolences	Full/Confirmed Members	Congregational Finances	Benevolences	Full/Confirmed Members	Congregational Finances	Benevolences
abc	726,452 [a]	365,873,197 [a]	57,052,333 [a]	670,363 [a]	351,362,401	55,982,392 [a]	658,731 [a]	312,860,507 [a]	54,236,977 [a]
alc	See ELCA	See ELCA	See ELCA	See ELCA	See ELCA	See ELCA	See ELCA	See ELCA	See ELCA
arp	33,513	23,399,372 [a]	5,711,882 [a]	34,117	23,419,989 [a]	5,571,337 [a]	34,344	25,241,384	6,606,829
bcc	18,529	16,032,149	5,480,828	18,424	16,892,154	4,748,871	19,016 [a]	17,456,379 [a]	5,934,414 [a]
ccd	601,237	357,895,652	42,887,958	586,131	370,210,746	42,877,144	568,921	381,463,761	43,009,412
cga	224,061	160,897,147	26,192,559	229,240	180,581,111	26,983,385	229,302	194,438,623	29,054,047
cgg	3,877	2,722,766	486,661	3,920	2,926,516	491,348	3,877	2,987,337	515,247
chb	143,121	60,242,418	22,599,214	141,811	60,524,557 [a]	19,683,035 [a]	141,400	60,923,817 [a]	19,611,047 [a]
chn	598,946	396,698,137	93,440,095	608,008	419,450,850	95,358,352	615,632	433,821,462	99,075,440
cccc	38,853 [a]	24,250,819 [a]	5,483,659 [a]	38,469 [a]	25,834,363 [a]	4,989,062 [a]	38,956	28,204,355	5,167,644
cpc	81,094 [a]	31,072,697 [a]	4,711,934 [a]	80,122 [a]	31,875,061 [a]	5,035,451 [a]	79,576 [a]	32,152,971 [a]	5,152,129 [a]
ecc	23,422	14,830,454	3,301,060	23,091	14,692,608	3,273,685	22,957	15,658,454	3,460,999
ecv	91,458	109,776,363 [a]	17,565,085 [a]	91,823 [a]	115,693,329 [a]	18,726,756 [a]	93,414	127,642,950	20,462,435
elc	3,845,063	1,551,842,465	188,107,066	3,838,750	1,629,909,672	191,476,141	3,844,169	1,731,806,133	201,115,441
els	16,543	7,712,358 [a]	1,084,136	16,511	8,136,195	1,104,996	16,444	8,937,103	1,150,419
emc	4,284 [a]	5,321,079 [a]	1,603,548 [a]	4,201	5,361,912 [a]	1,793,267 [a]	4,348 [a]	7,017,588 [a]	2,039,740 [a]
feb	1,856 [a]	1,412,281 [a]	447,544 [a]	1,751 [a]	1,198,120 [a]	507,656 [a]	1,763 [a]	1,120,222 [a]	518,777 [a]
fec	see EMC	see EMC	see EMC	see EMC	see EMC	see EMC	see EMC	see EMC	see EMC
fmc	59,060	67,687,955	11,114,804	59,343 [a]	70,262,626	11,651,462	62,191 [a]	74,139,941 [a]	12,139,144 [a]
fum	43,440 [f]	NA	NA	42,918 [f]	NA	NA	41,040 [f]	NA	NA
ggb	70,886 [a]	24,385,956 [a]	1,722,662 [a]	70,562 [a]	27,763,966 [a]	1,832,909 [a]	72,326	28,093,944	1,780,851
lca	See ELCA	See ELCA	See ELCA	See ELCA	See ELCA	See ELCA	See ELCA	See ELCA	See ELCA
lms	1,943,281	832,701,255	98,139,835 [a]	1,951,730	855,461,015	104,076,876 [a]	1,951,391	887,928,255	110,520,917
mch	90,139 [a]	71,641,773	26,832,240	90,959	76,669,365	27,812,549	92,161 [a]	76,087,609 [a]	25,637,872 [a]
mgc	35,852	15,774,961 [a]	7,587,049 [a]	35,333	18,282,833	7,969,999	34,731	14,690,904	6,514,761
mus	MCH & MGC	MCH & MGC	MCH & MGC	MCH & MGC	MCH & MGC	MCH & MGC	MCH & MGC	MCH & MGC	MCH & MGC
mca	21,409	10,996,031	1,167,513	21,140	11,798,536	1,237,349	21,108	12,555,760	1,148,478
nab	43,928	37,078,473	7,480,331	43,744 [a]	37,172,560 [a]	7,957,860 [a]	43,850	37,401,175	7,986,099
opc	14,355	16,017,003	3,376,691	15,072 [a]	17,883,915 [a]	3,467,207 [a]	15,072	20,090,259	3,967,490
pch	2,665,276	1,855,684,719	309,978,224	2,631,466	1,930,179,808	322,336,258	2,609,191	2,064,789,378	344,757,186
rca	183,255	164,250,624	29,995,068	182,342	183,975,696 [a]	31,271,007	180,980 [a]	181,977,101 [a]	32,130,943 [a]
sda	790,731	240,565,576	503,334,129	809,159	242,316,834	524,977,061	825,654	249,591,109	552,633,569
sbc	15,663,296	5,209,748,503	858,635,435	15,691,249 [a]	5,987,033,115	891,149,403 [a]	15,891,514	6,098,933,137	930,176,909
ucc	1,472,213	578,042,965	67,806,448	1,452,565	615,727,028	69,013,791	1,438,181	651,176,773	70,180,193
wel	312,898 [a]	150,060,963 [a]	33,096,069 [a]	313,446 [a]	156,363,694 [a]	47,334,098 [a]	314,038 [a]	163,568,990 [a]	52,241,401 [a]
Total	29,818,888	12,404,616,111	2,436,422,060	29,754,842	13,488,960,575	2,530,690,707	29,925,238	13,942,757,381	2,648,926,810

[a] Data obtained from denominational source.

[f] Membership obtained from the denomination and used only in Chapter 5 analysis; not included in the Total sum on this page.

Appendix B-1: Church Member Giving, in Current Dollars, 1968–2021 (continued)

	Data Year 1998			Data Year 1999			Data Year 2000		
	Full/Confirmed Members	Congregational Finances	Benevolences	Full/Confirmed Members	Congregational Finances	Benevolences	Full/Confirmed Members	Congregational Finances	Benevolences
abc	621,232 [a]	326,046,153 [a]	53,866,448 [a]	603,014 [a]	331,513,521 [a]	58,675,160	593,113 [a]	359,484,902 [a]	63,042,002 [a]
alc	See ELCA	See ELCA	See ELCA	See ELCA	See ELCA	See ELCA	See ELCA	See ELCA	See ELCA
arp	34,642 [a]	28,831,982 [a]	7,378,121 [a]	35,643 [a]	33,862,219 [a]	7,973,285 [a]	35,022 [a]	33,004,995 [a]	8,048,586 [a]
bcc	19,577	24,116,889	5,274,612	20,010	22,654,566	5,913,551	20,587	25,148,637	5,703,506
ccd	547,875 [a]	395,699,954 [a]	45,576,436 [a]	535,893	410,583,119	47,795,574	527,363	433,965,354	48,726,390
cga	234,311 [f]	NA	NA	235,849 [f]	NA	NA	238,891 [f]	NA	NA
cgg	3,824	3,087,000	689,756	4,083	3,357,300	503,365	4,037	3,232,160	610,113
chb	140,011 [a]	57,605,960 [a]	22,283,498 [a]	138,304 [a]	63,774,756 [a]	21,852,687 [a]	135,978	67,285,361	25,251,272 [a]
chn	623,028	460,776,715	104,925,922	626,033 [a]	487,437,668 [a]	110,818,743 [a]	633,264	516,708,125	122,284,083
cccc	38,996	28,976,122	5,194,733	40,414	31,165,218	5,931,456	40,974 [a]	33,537,589 [a]	6,360,912 [a]
cpc	80,829 [a]	33,623,232 [a]	5,412,917 [a]	79,452 [a]	36,303,752 [a]	5,879,014 [a]	86,519	39,533,829	6,591,617
ecc	22,868	15,956,209	3,599,440	22,349	16,574,783	3,587,877	21,939	17,656,789	1,982,328
ecv	96,552	140,823,872	20,134,436	98,526 [a]	161,361,490 [a]	23,237,513 [a]	101,317 [a]	181,127,526 [a]	25,983,315 [a]
elc	3,840,136	1,822,915,831	208,853,359	3,825,228	1,972,950,623	220,647,251	3,810,785	2,067,208,285	231,219,316
els	16,897	9,363,126	1,120,386	16,734	10,062,900	1,129,969	16,569	10,910,109	949,421
emc	4,646 [a]	6,472,868 [a]	1,854,222 [a]	4,511 [a]	7,528,256 [a]	1,982,985 [a]	4,929	8,289,743 [a]	2,085,475 [a]
feb	1,828 [a]	1,433,305 [a]	502,839 [a]	1,936 [a]	1,496,949 [a]	534,203 [a]	1,764 [a]	1,360,133 [a]	373,057 [a]
fec	see EMC	see EMC	see EMC	see EMC	see EMC	see EMC	see EMC	see EMC	see EMC
fmc	62,176	88,286,727 [a]	12,850,607	62,368 [a]	81,560,638 [a]	12,646,064 [a]	62,453	92,051,401 [a]	13,425,940 [a]
fum	33,908 [f]	NA	NA	34,863 [f]	NA	NA	41,297 [f]	NA	NA
ggb	67,314 [a]	28,533,439 [a]	2,594,098 [a]	55,549 [a]	22,857,097 [a]	2,331,087 [a]	66,296 [a]	30,470,298 [a]	2,950,915 [a]
lca	See ELCA	See ELCA	See ELCA	See ELCA	See ELCA	See ELCA	See ELCA	See ELCA	See ELCA
lms	1,952,020	975,113,229	121,536,226	1,945,846	986,295,136	123,632,549	1,934,057	1,101,690,594	127,554,235
mch	92,002 [a]	75,796,469 [a]	26,452,444 [a]	See MUS	See MUS	See MUS	See MUS	See MUS	See MUS
mgc	36,600	14,786,936 [a]	5,853,292 [a]	See MUS	See MUS	See MUS	See MUS	See MUS	See MUS
mus	MCH & MGC	MCH & MGC	MCH & MGC	123,404 [a]	95,843,112 [a]	34,821,702 [a]	120,381 [f]	NA	NA
mca	20,764	13,082,671	1,131,742	20,400	11,527,684	849,837	20,925 [a]	13,224,765 [a]	1,014,314 [a]
nab	43,844 [a]	41,939,978 [a]	7,731,550 [a]	45,738	47,207,867	9,055,128	47,097	54,866,431	9,845,352
opc	15,936	22,362,292	4,438,333	17,279 [a]	24,878,935	4,920,310	17,914	28,120,325	5,978,474
pch	2,587,674	2,173,483,227	355,628,625	2,560,201	2,326,583,688	384,445,608	2,525,330	2,517,278,130	398,602,204
rca	179,085	189,390,759	33,890,048	178,260 [a]	216,305,458 [a]	36,158,625 [a]	177,281	226,555,821	37,221,041
sda	839,915	269,679,595	588,227,010	861,860	301,221,572	629,944,965	880,921	316,562,375	675,000,508
sbc	15,729,356 [a]	6,498,607,390 [a]	953,491,003 [a]	15,851,756 [a]	6,977,245,645 [a]	795,207,316 [a]	15,960,308 [a]	7,500,657,552 [a]	936,520,388 [a]
ucc	1,421,088	678,251,694	74,861,463	1,401,682	700,645,114	76,550,398	1,377,320	744,991,925	78,525,195
wel	314,265 [a]	177,633,393 [a]	44,584,079 [a]	314,217 [a]	181,513,283 [a]	49,143,360 [a]	314,941 [a]	193,625,639 [a]	52,918,434 [a]
Total	29,454,980	14,602,677,017	2,719,937,645	29,490,690	15,564,312,349	2,676,169,582	29,419,003	16,618,548,793	2,888,768,393

[a] Data obtained from denominational source.

[f] Membership obtained from the denomination and used only in Chapter 5 analysis; not included in the Total sum on this page.

Appendix B-1: Church Member Giving, in Current Dollars, 1968–2021(continued)

	Data Year 2001			Data Year 2002			Data Year 2003		
	Full/Confirmed Members	Congregational Finances	Benevolences	Full/Confirmed Members	Congregational Finances	Benevolences	Full/Confirmed Members	Congregational Finances	Benevolences
abc	631,771 [a]	381,080,930 [a]	74,228,212 [a]	617,034 [a]	396,380,200 [a]	65,103,943 [a]	572,218 [a]	391,456,166 [a]	60,965,853 [a]
alc	See ELCA	See ELCA	See ELCA	See ELCA	See ELCA	See ELCA	See ELCA	See ELCA	See ELCA
arp	35,181	36,976,653	7,707,456	35,556	37,394,125	8,091,930	35,418	36,664,331	7,615,661
bcc	20,739	29,566,287	6,864,936	20,579 [a]	29,069,369 [a]	5,619,911 [a]	21,538 [a]	30,219,066 [a]	6,090,287 [a]
ccd	518,434	437,447,942	48,609,107	504,118	438,378,385	46,708,737	491,085 [a]	456,513,192 [a]	45,243,300 [a]
cga	237,222 [l]	NA	NA	247,007 [k]	NA	NA	250,052 [l]	NA	NA
cgg	4,155	3,436,200	477,457	3,860 [k]	NA	NA	3,694 [a]	3,786,000 [a]	511,394 [a]
chb	134,828	68,790,933	22,869,690	134,844	70,524,998	22,730,417	132,481	73,120,173	20,756,646
chn	639,296 [a]	557,589,101 [a]	121,203,179 [a]	639,330	587,027,991	132,183,078	616,069	595,552,079	133,379,908
cccc	40,857	34,483,917	6,754,192	40,041	36,747,983	8,190,510	42,032 [a]	46,340,288 [a]	6,232,465 [a]
cpc	85,427	41,216,632	6,744,757	84,417	42,570,586	6,876,097	83,742	41,950,671	7,218,214
ecc	21,463	17,932,202	2,011,619	21,208	18,195,387	2,002,028	20,743	17,648,320	1,980,327
ecv	103,549 [a]	198,202,551 [a]	25,137,813 [a]	105,956 [a]	211,733,299 [a]	22,644,569 [a]	108,594 [a]	222,653,578 [a]	24,786,692 [a]
elc	3,791,986 [a]	2,166,061,437 [a]	239,796,502 [a]	3,757,723	2,238,773,875	233,875,597	3,724,321	2,285,110,767 [a]	231,916,904 [a]
els	16,815	11,361,255	1,246,189	16,849	11,787,432	1,010,416	16,674	12,018,180	995,710
emc	5,278 [a]	10,563,872 [a]	2,335,880 [a]	see FEC	see FEC	see FEC	see FEC	see FEC	see FEC
feb	1,271 [a]	1,086,582 [a]	246,296 [a]	1,896 [a]	1,651,056 [a]	512,269 [a]	1,861 [a]	1,723,143 [a]	673,694 [a]
fec	see EMC	see EMC	see EMC	5,686 [a]	10,457,231 [a]	1,811,985 [a]	5,780 [a]	11,862,813 [a]	2,275,726 [a]
fmc	61,202	104,337,169 [a]	14,595,290	62,742 [a]	104,764,295 [a]	12,575,713 [a]	63,538 [a]	109,648,283 [a]	13,075,586 [a]
fum	40,197 [f]	NA	NA	38,764 [f]	NA	NA	37,863 [f]	NA	NA
ggb	66,636 [a]	30,152,750 [a]	3,091,252 [a]	67,231	31,000,633	2,922,004	62,377 [a]	32,581,954 [a]	2,846,173 [a]
lca	See ELCA	See ELCA	See ELCA	See ELCA	See ELCA	See ELCA	See ELCA	See ELCA	See ELCA
lms	1,920,949	1,092,453,907	124,703,387	1,907,923	1,086,223,370	117,110,167	1,894,822	1,131,212,373 [a]	125,169,844
mch	See MUS	See MUS	See MUS	See MUS	See MUS	See MUS	See MUS	See MUS	See MUS
mgc	See MUS	See MUS	See MUS	See MUS	See MUS	See MUS	See MUS	See MUS	See MUS
mus	113,972 [f]	NA	NA	112,688 [g]	NA	NA	111,031 [f]	NA	NA
mca	21,319 [a]	13,237,006 [a]	1,054,515 [a]	20,583 [a]	13,037,136 [a]	971,527 [a]	19,456	16,939,268	925,302
nab	49,017	50,871,441	9,742,646	47,692	56,813,620	8,952,067	47,812 [a]	55,566,213 [a]	9,602,812 [a]
opc	18,414	30,012,219	6,077,752	18,746	29,251,600	5,216,600	19,725	30,972,500	5,671,600
pch	2,493,781	2,526,681,144	409,319,291	2,451,969	2,509,677,412	392,953,913	2,405,311	2,361,944,688	381,693,067
rca	173,463	228,677,098	39,313,564	171,361	229,560,092	39,393,056	168,801	235,422,160	39,932,078
sda	900,985	329,285,946	707,593,100	918,882	346,825,034	725,180,278	935,428	348,219,525	740,463,422
sbc	16,052,920	7,954,789,416	980,224,243	16,137,736 [a]	8,432,952,589	1,028,650,682	16,205,050 [a]	8,546,166,798	1,102,363,842
ucc	1,359,105	772,191,485	80,464,673	1,330,985	789,083,286	78,157,356	1,296,652	802,327,537	76,647,374
wel	314,360 [a]	203,334,779 [a]	53,455,670 [a]	313,690 [a]	211,121,810 [a]	49,035,869 [a]	313,330 [a]	227,521,597 [a]	50,687,438 [a]
Total	29,483,201	17,331,820,854	2,995,868,668	29,434,777	17,971,002,794	3,018,480,719	29,308,552	18,125,141,663	3,099,721,319

[a] Data obtained from denominational source.

[f] Membership obtained from the denomination and used only in Chapter 5 analysis; not included in the Total sum on this page.

g Data available in *YACC* series used only in Chapter 5 analysis; not included in Total sum on this page

Appendix B-1: Church Member Giving, in Current Dollars, 1968–2021 (continued)

	Data Year 2004			Data Year 2005			Data Year 2006		
	Full/Confirmed Members	Congregational Finances	Benevolences	Full/Confirmed Members	Congregational Finances	Benevolences	Full/Confirmed Members	Congregational Finances	Benevolences
abc	498,407 [a]	372,241,219 [a]	60,493,722 [a]	375,917 [a]	277,122,001 [a]	59,772,842	343,301 [a]	261,159,450	51,325,563
alc	See ELCA	See ELCA	See ELCA	See ELCA	See ELCA	See ELCA	See ELCA	See ELCA	See ELCA
arp	35,640 [a]	43,324,132 [a]	5,965,950 [a]	35,209 [a]	41,256,621 [a]	9,664,612 [a]	34,939 [a]	40,305,680 [a]	8,286,494 [a]
bcc	22,818 [a]	27,218,450 [a]	5,016,990 [a]	23,498 [a]	34,920,636 [a]	4,879,420 [a]	22,168 [a]	37,146,168 [a]	5,211,550 [a]
ccd	479,075 [a]	447,535,858 [a]	45,841,497 [a]	431,365 [a]	453,623,467 [a]	49,421,931 [a]	450,057 [a]	489,840,866 [a]	49,271,591 [a]
cga	252,419 [k]	NA	NA	255,771 [f]	NA	NA	249,845 [k]	NA	NA
cgg	3,267 [a]	3,966,000 [a]	479,000 [a]	3,200 [a]	4,115,400 [a]	381,422 [a]	3,080 [a]	4,030,000 [a]	391,793 [a]
chb	131,201	71,402,128	19,038,122	128,820	73,982,601	23,958,373	126,994 [a]	72,676,903	20,157,405
chn	623,774	610,902,447	132,624,279	630,159	622,257,466	143,177,276	633,154	655,937,953	136,893,238
cccc	42,725	51,335,963	8,459,095	42,838 [j]	50,845,153 [j]	8,501,074 [j]	42,862 [a]	55,997,723 [a]	9,419,501 [a]
cpc	83,007 [a]	42,431,192	7,368,979	81,464 [a]	45,769,458 [a]	8,379,379 [a]	81,034	46,396,330	8,331,581
ecc	20,745 [a]	19,402,040 [h]	3,429,948 [h]	20,169 [a]	17,880,135 [a]	3,528,552 [a]	19,166 [a]	18,741,363 [a]	3,432,641 [a]
ecv	113,002 [a]	244,040,438 [a]	23,226,589	114,283 [a]	266,614,225 [a]	25,232,786 [a]	120,030 [a]	290,965,669 [a]	22,805,559 [a]
elc	3,685,987	2,329,793,744	238,220,062	3,636,948	2,348,010,569 [a]	256,787,436 [a]	3,580,402	2,413,738,345 [a]	250,408,865
els	16,407	11,808,028	1,118,456	15,917	12,581,651	1,250,120 [a]	65,782	127,710,053	15,087,052
emc	See FEC	See FEC	See FEC	See FEC	See FEC	See FEC	See FEC	See FEC	See FEC
feb	1,844 [a]	2,023,545 [a]	511,470 [a]	1,664 [a]	2,043,940 [a]	595,313 [a]	1,434 [a]	2,265,710 [a]	427,685 [a]
fec	6,496	13,855,056 [a]	2,670,733	6,694 [a]	15,751,410 [a]	2,675,422 [a]	6,786 [a]	16,301,682 [a]	2,729,537 [a]
fmc	65,272	117,524,393 [a]	14,052,134 [a]	65,907 [a]	122,795,812 [a]	15,824,150 [a]	65,782 [a]	127,710,053 [a]	15,087,052 [a]
fum	34,323 [f]	NA	NA	38,121 [f]	NA	NA	43,612 [f]	NA	NA
ggb	78,863 [a]	30,631,505 [a]	3,140,132 [a]	60,559 [a]	36,990,479 [a]	3,156,104 [a]	52,279 [a]	32,918,373 [a]	2,987,587 [a]
lca	See ELCA	See ELCA	See ELCA	See ELCA	See ELCA	See ELCA	See ELCA	See ELCA	See ELCA
lms	1,880,213	1,186,000,747	121,763,263	1,870,659	1,176,649,592	120,169,146	1,856,783	1,229,305,441 [a]	126,153,117 [a]
mch	See MUS	See MUS	See MUS	See MUS	See MUS	See MUS	See MUS	See MUS	See MUS
mgc	See MUS	See MUS	See MUS	See MUS	See MUS	See MUS	See MUS	See MUS	See MUS
mus	110,420 [i]	NA	NA	109,808 [f]	NA	NA	109,385 [f]	NA	NA
mca	19,021	17,545,228	969,697	18,529	16,738,701	1,096,554	17,955	16,729,153 [a]	1,051,451
nab	46,995 [a]	59,832,412 [a]	10,342,080 [a]	46,671 [f]	NA	NA	47,150	62,175,197	10,104,273
opc	19,993 [a]	32,760,800 [a]	5,899,500 [a]	19,965	34,520,600	6,215,800	20,850	38,642,300	7,241,000
pch	2,362,136	2,387,317,945	387,589,903	2,313,662	2,425,999,953	388,271,070	2,267,118	2,459,679,132	395,040,718
rca	166,761	256,915,687	39,941,147	164,697	267,082,267	43,827,424	163,160	286,075,445	42,718,072
sda	948,787 [a]	347,797,864 [a]	773,751,848 [a]	964,811	427,285,012	846,114,329	980,551	426,686,109	863,635,364
sbc	16,267,494	8,971,390,824	1,199,806,224	16,270,315 [a]	9,487,900,433	1,233,644,135	16,306,246	10,086,992,362	1,285,616,031
ucc	1,266,129 [a]	822,172,566	73,481,544	1,224,297	827,237,883	81,488,911	1,218,541	846,482,513 [a]	73,611,594 [a]
wel	313,088 [a]	245,098,070 [a]	51,692,943 [a]	311,950 [a]	244,718,123 [a]	54,606,362 [a]	310,338 [a]	250,589,183 [a]	63,427,503 [a]
Total	29,199,147	18,766,268,281	3,236,895,307	28,833,496	19,334,693,588	3,392,619,943	28,788,479	20,284,594,905	3,457,073,243

[a] Data obtained from denominational source.
[f] Membership obtained from the denomination and used only in Chapter 5 analysis; not included in the Total sum on this page.
[h] Data obtained from the denomination included the following note: "2004 figures differ substantially due to change in accounting procedures."
[i] 2004 membership data is an average of 2003 and 2005 data obtained from the denomination; used only in Chapter 5 analysis; not included in Total sum on this page.
[j] The denomination stated that the data appearing in *YACC* 2007 as 2004 data was actually for 2005
[k] Data available in *YACC* series used only in Chapter 5 analysis; not included in Total sum on this page.

Appendix B-1: Church Member Giving, in Current Dollars, 1968–2021 (continued)

	Data Year 2007			Data Year 2008			Data Year 2009		
	Full/Confirmed Members	Congregational Finances	Benevolences	Full/Confirmed Members	Congregational Finances	Benevolences	Full/Confirmed Members	Congregational Finances	Benevolences
abc	345,588 [a]	272,304,732 [a]	53,636,473	331,262 [a]	268,264,419 [a]	49,073,811	305,486 [a]	241,316,884	47,522,456
alc	See ELCA	See ELCA	See ELCA	See ELCA	See ELCA	See ELCA	See ELCA	See ELCA	See ELCA
arp	34,954 [a]	40,442,600 [a]	8,981,600 [a]	34,911	32,784,800 [a]	14,163,289 [a]	34,977 [a]	43,677,370 [a]	11,123,351 [a]
bcc	22,732 [a]	38,797,921 [a]	5,138,646 [a]	22,967 [a]	39,993,609 [a]	4,678,366 [a]	23,014 [a]	35,229,064 [a]	5,141,733 [a]
ccd	447,340	473,677,625	45,405,339	434,008	479,485,251	44,728,431	417,068	453,043,802	42,944,443
cga	252,905 [k]	NA	NA	251,429 [f]	NA	NA	250,202 [k]	NA	NA
cgg	3,039 [a]	4,066,200 [a]	312,545 [a]	3,122 [a]	3,655,813 [a]	400,946 [a]	3,010	3,568,750	445,000
chb	125,418	68,434,534	20,233,969	123,855	69,331,885	18,163,083	121,781	72,679,289	16,952,618
chn	635,526	677,586,886	140,135,344	636,923	690,867,740	138,934,121	639,182	690,753,074	133,162,454
cccc	41,772	64,471,078	9,996,077	42,149	62,792,643	9,885,002	42,296	60,595,568	9,900,687
cpc	78,451	49,306,468	8,460,302	78,074	49,052,918	8,593,296	77,811 [a]	48,174,829 [a]	8,208,372
ecc	19,339	15,731,559 [a]	1,449,196 [a]	18,710	16,658,718	2,077,928	17,834	17,551,723	2,042,520
ecv	123,150 [a]	301,961,227 [a]	21,955,749 [a]	NA	NA	NA	NA	NA	NA
elc	3,533,956	2,470,777,573 [a]	254,571,455 [a]	3,483,336	2,507,117,689	256,892,032	3,444,041	2,474,851,188	241,234,666
els	15,734	14,738,808	1,365,828	15,672	14,565,105	1,070,176	15,672	14,271,293	1,648,567
emc	See FEC	See FEC	See FEC	See FEC	See FEC	See FEC	See FEC	See FEC	See FEC
feb	1,248 [a]	2,261,292 [a]	400,589 [a]	1,799 [a]	3,361,033 [a]	544,127 [a]	1,721 [a]	2,794,938 [a]	653,235 [a]
fec	6,834 [a]	17,646,038 [a]	2,300,708 [a]	6,933	22,705,650	1,741,233	7,137	22,451,650	1,871,850
fmc	64,309 [a]	129,238,283 [a]	15,419,527 [a]	63,210 [a]	123,884,296 [a]	18,954,534 [a]	64,465 [a]	129,048,512 [a]	17,354,830 [a]
fum	43,647 [f]	NA	NA	35,302 [a]	NA	NA	35,302 [a]	NA	NA
ggb	46,242 [a]	27,179,045 [a]	4,206,088 [a]	45,721 [a]	29,433,584 [a]	4,087,132 [a]	54,088 [a]	34,438,595 [a]	3,822,657 [a]
lca	See ELCA	See ELCA	See ELCA	See ELCA	See ELCA	See ELCA	See ELCA	See ELCA	See ELCA
lms	1,835,064	1,278,836,855	120,937,847	1,803,900	1,223,607,882	119,478,393	1,784,139	1,234,616,467	126,921,340
mch	See MUS	See MUS	See MUS	See MUS	See MUS	See MUS	See MUS	See MUS	See MUS
mgc	See MUS	See MUS	See MUS	See MUS	See MUS	See MUS	See MUS	See MUS	See MUS
mus	108,651 [f]	NA	NA	106,617 [f]	NA	NA	105,768 [f]	NA	NA
mca	17,554	17,869,301	1,152,271	16,733	17,264,555	1,003,550	16,352	17,198,636	1,043,314
nab	NA	NA	NA	NA	NA	NA	NA	NA	NA
opc	21,031	38,486,700	7,243,700	21,243	39,118,505	6,917,483	21,608	39,785,674	6,790,182
pch	2,209,546	2,518,402,119	398,386,295	2,140,165	2,542,921,235	378,650,258	2,077,138	2,414,721,917	358,621,774
rca	162,182	294,008,651	44,438,226	157,570	283,598,231	46,305,818	154,977	258,802,017	43,036,743
sda	1,000,472	368,356,521	890,924,215	1,021,777	321,184,421	874,235,374	1,043,606	413,465,740 [a]	862,030,314
sbc	16,266,920	10,779,240,776	1,327,856,082	16,228,438	10,762,418,889	1,358,802,036	16,160,088	10,578,021,610	1,334,157,703
ucc	1,145,281	859,744,628	77,117,434	1,111,691	869,869,656	71,683,884	1,080,199	861,387,225	67,251,700
wel	309,658 [a]	255,887,929 [a]	67,194,722 [a]	307,452 [a]	251,506,951 [a]	68,481,343 [a]	306,881 [a]	255,254,310 [a]	59,728,209 [a]
Total	28,513,340	21,079,455,349	3,529,220,227	28,151,621	20,725,445,478	3,499,545,646	27,914,571	20,417,700,125	3,403,610,718

[a] Data obtained from denominational source.

[f] Membership obtained from the denomination and used only in Chapter 5 analysis; not included in the Total sum on this page.

[k] Data available in *YACC* series used only in Chapter 5 analysis; not included in Total sum on this page.

Appendix B-1: Church Member Giving, in Current Dollars, 1968–2021 (continued)

	Data Year 2010			Data Year 2011			Data Year 2012		
	Full/Confirmed Members	Congregational Finances	Benevolences	Full/Confirmed Members	Congregational Finances	Benevolences	Full/Confirmed Members	Congregational Finances	Benevolences
abc	292,392 [a]	241,463,947	47,881,389	291,363 [a]	263,321,076	46,646,045	216,216 [a]	276,410,133 [a]	46,121,511 [a]
alc	See ELCA	See ELCA	See ELCA	See ELCA	See ELCA	See ELCA	See ELCA	See ELCA	See ELCA
arp	34,328 [a]	46,085,018 [a]	8,144,620 [a]	35,911 [a]	55,171,267 [a]	11,602,822 [a]	34,960 [a]	54,283,587 [a]	9,569,463 [a]
bcc	22,739 [a]	34,079,545 [a]	5,352,723 [a]	22,120 [a]	40,105,642 [a]	5,154,219 [a]	22,431 [a]	34,929,183 [a]	4,897,007 [a]
ccd	405,338 [a]	443,712,948	45,652,854	393,677	433,042,420	40,680,609	374,266 [a]	454,891,666 [a]	42,039,102 [a]
cga	249,521 [k]	NA	NA	248,722 [k]	NA	NA	241,282 [f]	NA	NA
cgg	3,121	3,692,900	465,343	3,089	3,636,000	466,502	2,979 [a]	3,540,000 [a]	455,565 [a]
chb	120,041	72,339,775	19,930,435	118,315	68,648,156	17,713,217	116,151 [a]	68,123,197 [a]	17,553,028 [a]
chn	640,966	648,769,174	126,057,895	641,989	628,476,287	119,449,511	637,099 [a]	608,172,024 [a]	117,889,099 [a]
cccc	33,146 [a]	40,777,835 [a]	7,294,704 [a]	29,462 [a]	45,130,561 [a]	6,348,168 [a]	43,715 [a]	45,328,173 [a]	9,909,439 [a]
cpc	71,809	43,118,256	9,412,929	67,076 [a]	39,636,506 [a]	9,599,579 [a]	65,703 [a]	37,620,056 [a]	9,207,211 [a]
ecc	17,557	18,183,077	2,037,928	16,779	16,012,255 [a]	2,050,297	14,072 [a]	15,078,389 [a]	1,513,352 [a]
ecv	NA	NA	NA	NA	NA	NA	NA	NA	NA
elc	3,259,371 [a]	2,007,197,248 [a]	219,215,741 [a]	3,107,925	1,954,879,486	212,890,820	3,002,270 [a]	1,939,908,516 [a]	208,706,514 [a]
els	15,301	13,842,672	1,118,086	15,041	14,200,085	1,199,216	14,775 [a]	13,679,788 [a]	1,157,335 [a]
emc	See FEC	See FEC	See FEC	See FEC	See FEC	See FEC	See FEC	See FEC	See FEC
feb	1,720 [l]	NA	NA	1,718	NA	NA	1,923 [f]	NA	NA
fec	7,754	22,776,188	1,831,350	7,316	22,076,775	1,818,550	6,711 [a]	22,066,220 [a]	1,190,926 [a]
fmc	64,252 [a]	128,468,416 [a]	18,144,976 [a]	63,522 [a]	119,258,697 [a]	26,822,704 [a]	63,511 [a]	130,622,603 [a]	20,139,554 [a]
fum	34,472 [f]	NA	NA	35,500 [f]	NA	NA	34,900 [f]	NA	NA
ggb	46,367 [a]	31,980,744 [a]	3,476,780 [a]	52,920 [a]	41,051,396 [a]	3,267,122 [a]	55,420 [a]	41,345,045 [a]	3,807,511 [a]
lca	See ELCA	See ELCA	See ELCA	See ELCA	See ELCA	See ELCA	See ELCA	See ELCA	See ELCA
lms	1,764,024	1,254,192,118	121,592,097	1,731,522	1,255,443,938 [a]	120,711,376	1,707,509 [a]	1,295,271,716 [a]	128,071,113 [a]
mch	See MUS	See MUS	See MUS	See MUS	See MUS	See MUS	See MUS	See MUS	See MUS
mgc	See MUS	See MUS	See MUS	See MUS	See MUS	See MUS	See MUS	See MUS	See MUS
mus	104,687 [f]	NA	NA	103,529 [f]	NA	NA	98,696 [f]	NA	NA
mca	16,220	17,312,747	907,935	16,180 [a]	15,341,244 [a]	413,610 [a]	15,641 [a]	15,848,892 [a]	573,107 [a]
nab	NA	NA	NA	NA	NA	NA	NA	NA	NA
opc	22,134	41,396,760	6,959,769	22,451	42,261,333	7,102,231	22,791 [a]	43,806,839 [a]	7,184,214 [a]
pch	2,016,091	2,254,593,261	359,879,672	1,952,287	2,277,643,836	343,294,225	1,849,496 [a]	2,162,203,279 [a]	325,996,119 [a]
rca	152,134	257,415,342	44,746,699	148,534	265,645,282	44,875,336	147,184 [a]	289,926,467 [a]	46,981,071 [a]
sda	1,060,386	400,622,149	867,960,056	1,074,418	401,345,082	895,724,988	1,097,497 [a]	420,929,749 [a]	902,505,902 [a]
sbc	16,136,044	10,418,340,666	1,302,479,654	15,978,112 [a]	10,476,354,833 [a]	1,328,672,872 [a]	15,872,404 [a]	10,206,543,408 [a]	1,314,875,376 [a]
ucc	1,058,423	867,668,652	70,331,870	1,028,324	867,082,244	67,741,866	998,906 [a]	851,918,612 [a]	60,886,340 [a]
wel	303,786 [a]	256,398,621 [a]	58,567,749 [a]	301,300 [a]	257,407,217 [a]	53,606,109 [a]	298,832 [a]	268,265,588 [a]	57,969,017 [a]
Total	27,563,744	19,564,428,059	3,349,443,254	27,119,633	19,613,171,618	3,367,851,994	26,682,462	19,303,432,005	3,339,824,486

[a] Data obtained from denominational source.

[f] Membership obtained from the denomination and used only in Chapter 5 analysis; not included in the Total sum on this page.

[k] Data available in the *YACC* used only in Chapter 5 analysis; not included in Total sum on this page.

[l] 2010 membership data is calculated from the average of Data Year 2009 obtained from the denomination and Data Year 2011; used only in Chapter 5 analysis; not included in Total sum on this page.

Appendix B-1: Church Member Giving, in Current Dollars, 1968–2021 (continued)

	Data Year 2013			Data Year 2014			Data Year 2015		
	Full/Confirmed Members	Congregational Finances	Benevolences	Full/Confirmed Members	Congregational Finances	Benevolences	Full/Confirmed Members	Congregational Finances	Benevolences
abc	186,521 [a]	249,467,329 [a]	41,692,466 [a]	166,551 [a]	214,939,212 [a]	38,078,517 [a]	174,453 [a]	222,125,335 [a]	43,021,344 [a]
alc	See ELCA	See ELCA	See ELCA	See ELCA	See ELCA	See ELCA	See ELCA	See ELCA	See ELCA
arp	32,340 [a]	52,793,241 [a]	4,574,180 [a]	29,987 [a]	52,308,523 [a]	4,520,547 [a]	29,317 [a]	59,919,840 [a]	4,843,213 [a]
bcc	22,646 [a]	37,159,631 [a]	5,124,016 [a]	22,862 [a]	44,519,455 [a]	4,805,105 [a]	18,585 [a]	41,239,581 [a]	1,673,442 [a]
ccd	306,256 [a]	373,477,803 [a]	39,242,516 [a]	293,567 [a]	364,275,745 [a]	37,720,153 [a]	273,258 [a]	349,213,983 [a]	37,425,704 [a]
cga	230,497 [f]	NA	NA	233,850 [f]	NA	NA	233,049 [f]	NA	NA
cgg	2,851 [a]	3,287,800 [a]	499,818 [a]	2,797 [a]	3,148,400 [a]	528,521 [a]	2,660 [a]	3,275,800 [a]	755,762 [a]
chb	115,183 [a]	66,190,332 [a]	15,869,158 [a]	NA [a]	NA [a]	NA [a]	112,656 [a]	59,900,015 [a]	18,237,315 [a]
chn	637,244 [a]	638,579,607 [a]	119,537,154 [a]	631,454 [a]	629,618,154 [a]	120,715,413 [a]	627,569 [a]	611,892,921 [a]	121,740,432 [a]
cccc	44,110 [a]	46,109,526 [a]	10,079,798 [a]	44,825 [a]	46,857,036 [a]	10,243,087 [a]	44,909 [a]	46,998,811 [a]	10,316,812 [a]
cpc	64,056 [a]	41,203,917 [a]	9,235,790 [a]	62,500 [a]	39,401,398 [a]	8,716,039 [a]	60,707 [a]	39,025,902 [a]	8,914,948 [a]
ecc	13,876 [a]	14,062,042 [a]	1,629,372 [a]	14,121 [a]	14,872,218 [a]	1,637,622 [a]	13,533 [a]	16,669,890 [a]	1,734,901 [a]
ecv	NA	NA	NA	NA	NA	NA	NA	NA	NA
elc	2,967,754 [a]	1,952,882,501 [a]	208,744,726 [a]	2,868,102 [a]	1,969,773,060 [a]	206,586,757 [a]	2,803,450 [a]	2,010,949,640 [a]	205,044,253 [a]
els	14,318 [a]	13,957,826 [a]	1,186,945 [a]	14,122 [a]	14,208,638 [a]	1,476,661 [a]	13,350 [a]	14,338,938 [a]	1,511,496 [a]
emc	See FEC	See FEC	See FEC	See FEC	See FEC	See FEC	See FEC	See FEC	See FEC
feb	2,152 [l]	NA	NA	2,409 [m]	NA	NA	NA	NA	NA
fec	7,659 [a]	19,581,497 [a]	1,095,001 [a]	8,041 [a]	21,632,741 [a]	1,463,381 [a]	8,475 [a]	24,300,736 [a]	1,525,753 [a]
fmc	62,966 [a]	131,979,029 [a]	16,820,895 [a]	62,062 [a]	131,579,040 [a]	17,739,068 [a]	61,708 [a]	136,843,420 [a]	15,471,071 [a]
fum	34,310 [a]	NA	NA	33,730 [m]	NA	NA	NA	NA	NA
ggb	46,909 [a]	36,334,280 [a]	3,854,726 [a]	44,440 [a]	39,957,705 [a]	3,500,181 [a]	49,128 [a]	42,822,936 [a]	3,444,391 [a]
lca	See ECLA	See ECLA	See ECLA	See ELCA	See ELCA	See ELCA	See ELCA	See ELCA	See ELCA
lms	1,685,597 [a]	1,290,994,013 [a]	128,693,151 [a]	1,641,679 [a]	1,229,158,978 [a]	118,292,783 [a]	1,609,100 [a]	1,289,412,334 [a]	123,986,821 [a]
mch	See MUS	See MUS	See MUS	See MUS	See MUS	See MUS	See MUS	See MUS	See MUS
mgc	See MUS	See MUS	See MUS	See MUS	See MUS	See MUS	See MUS	See MUS	See MUS
mus	97,541 [f]	NA	NA	94,500 [f]	NA	NA	79,150 [f]	NA	NA
mca	15,309 [a]	15,339,518 [a]	676,370 [a]	15,307 [a]	14,342,384 [a]	618,002 [a]	15,101 [a]	14,357,605 [a]	699,543 [a]
nab	NA	NA	NA	NA	NA	NA	NA	NA	NA
opc	23,027 [a]	46,909,402 [a]	7,158,600 [a]	22,806 [a]	46,800,500 [a]	7,388,100 [a]	22,917 [a]	49,470,400 [a]	7,383,500 [a]
pch	1,760,200 [a]	2,037,244,765 [a]	319,539,345 [a]	1,667,767 [a]	1,959,277,857 [a]	278,030,019 [a]	1,572,660 [a]	1,863,993,685 [a]	245,459,688 [a]
rca	145,410 [a]	277,362,930 [a]	45,334,098 [a]	144,006 [a]	285,323,545 [a]	46,946,039 [a]	139,767 [a]	293,937,657 [a]	46,387,495 [a]
sda	1,108,893 [a]	409,707,120 [a]	913,538,455 [a]	1,124,313 [a]	424,454,026 [a]	930,939,434 [a]	1,140,080 [a]	427,231,606 [a]	954,976,003 [a]
sbc	15,735,640 [a]	9,914,954,471 [a]	1,294,701,479 [a]	15,499,173 [a]	9,924,407,787 [a]	1,230,258,151 [a]	15,294,764 [a]	10,340,566,552 [a]	1,205,295,079 [a]
ucc	979,239 [a]	860,429,761 [a]	63,327,328 [a]	943,521 [a]	887,072,019 [a]	63,466,950 [a]	914,871 [a]	866,112,106 [a]	62,556,317 [a]
wel	297,111 [a]	272,882,578 [a]	56,940,343 [a]	294,215 [a]	278,515,025 [a]	58,323,202 [a]	291,378 [a]	284,320,518 [a]	60,052,858 [a]
Total	26,275,115	18,802,890,919	3,309,095,730	25,618,218	18,636,443,446	3,191,993,732	25,294,396	19,108,920,210	3,182,458,141

[a] Data obtained from denominational source.

[f] Membership obtained from the denomination and used only in Chapter 5 analysis; not included in the Total sum on this page.

[l] 2010 membership data is calculated from the average of Data Year 2009 obtained from the denomination and Data Year 2011; used only in Chapter 5 analysis; not included in Total sum on this page.

[m] 2014 membership is calculated for Data Years 2012 and 2013; used only in Chapter 5 analysis; not included in Total sum on this page..

Appendix B-1: Church Member Giving, in Current Dollars, 1968–2021 (continued)

	Data Year 2016			Data Year 2017			Data Year 2018		
	Full/Confirmed Members	Congregational Finances	Benevolences	Full/Confirmed Members	Congregational Finances	Benevolences	Full/Confirmed Members	Congregational Finances	Benevolences
abc	180,746 a	237,277,268 a	37,598,713 a	209,707 a	236,226,608 a	35,751,551 a	134,902 a	186,523,084 a	35,112,745 a
alc	See ELCA	See ELCA	See ELCA	See ELCA	See ELCA	See ELCA	See ELCA	See ELCA	See ELCA
arp	28,826 a	55,223,077 a	4,835,606 a	28,647 a	58,975,955 a	4,850,229 a	27,704 a	60,034,220 a	4,860,047 a
bcc	18,138 a	33,098,137 a	2,601,053 a	17,982 a	38,419,578 a	4,374,485 a	19,242 a	45,707,219 a	3,383,922 a
ccd	268,889 a	346,460,428 a	35,067,784 a	245,741 a	350,624,160 a	38,624,697 a	233,808 a	240,628,538 a	36,471,118 a
cga	226,808 f	NA	NA	237,044 n	NA	NA	247,280 f	NA	NA
cgg	2,619 n	NA	NA	2,578 a	3,298,000	674,103	2,502 a	3,310,000	784,781
chb	111,431 a	59,605,993 a	17,585,143 a	109,259 a	60,266,637 a	18,123,289 a	104,446 a	57,489,237 a	15,250,104 a
chn	624,202 a	625,440,639 a	123,920,181 a	618,643 a	629,952,118 a	121,783,695 a	612,029 a	629,964,351 a	124,972,309 a
cccc	45,006 a	47,000,325 a	10,439,095 a	45,565 a	47,928,982 a	10,645,343 a	46,790 a	49,066,172 a	10,770,623 a
cpc	58,843 a	45,501,036 a	9,305,056 a	57,721 a	37,494,507 a	9,495,443 a	56,142 a	40,946,861 a	9,174,753 a
ecc	12,441 a	14,196,017 a	1,828,937 a	11,756 a	15,922,402 a	1,640,804 a	12,751 a	16,750,277 a	1,644,305 a
ecv	NA	NA	NA	131,960 f	NA	NA	129,015 f	NA	NA
elc	2,733,430 a	1,990,925,510 a	204,374,951 a	2,685,833 a	2,006,241,276 a	210,863,529 a	2,644,146 a	2,062,715,258 a	205,284,506 a
els	13,306 a	13,699,692 a	1,344,073 a	13,113 a	14,003,326 a	1,013,509 a	13,207 a	14,577,543 a	1,240,975 a
emc	See FEC	See FEC	See FEC	See FEC	See FEC	See FEC	See FEC	See FEC	See FEC
feb	NA	NA	NA	NA	NA	NA	NA	NA	NA
fec	8,022 a	27,092,984 a	1,968,017 a	8,407 a	27,273,702 a	1,737,631 a	8,446 a	29,168,696 a	2,005,390 a
fmc	62,028 a	145,445,855 a	11,173,732 a	61,616 a	146,513,859 a	12,599,215 a	65,992 a	149,786,251 a	11,873,788 a
fum	NA	NA	NA	NA	NA	NA	NA	NA	NA
ggb	50,365 a	45,560,757 a	3,409,105 a	42,982 a	33,918,464 a	3,397,075 a	43,595 a	37,492,955 a	3,158,538 a
lca	See ECLA	See ECLA	See ECLA	See ECLA	See ECLA	See ECLA	See ECLA	See ECLA	See ECLA
lms	1,580,180 a	1,301,629,488 a	126,311,640 a	1,541,199 a	1,318,719,277 a	142,804,783 a	1,500,794 a	1,286,902,159 a	120,165,928 a
mch	See MUS	See MUS	See MUS	See MUS	See MUS	See MUS	See MUS	See MUS	See MUS
mgc	See MUS	See MUS	See MUS	See MUS	See MUS	See MUS	See MUS	See MUS	See MUS
mus	75,107 f	NA	NA	67,346 f	NA	NA	65,693 f	NA	NA
mca	14,778 a	15,048,553 a	570,560 a	14,848 a	15,634,709 a	570,562 a	14,054 a	16,546,436 a	556,116 a
nab	NA	NA	NA	NA	NA	NA	NA	NA	NA
opc	22,745 a	49,718,000 a	7,893,500 a	23,032 a	52,499,700 a	8,325,800 a	22,847 a	54,781,600 a	8,721,000 a
pch	1,482,767 a	1,831,353,192 a	251,037,863 a	1,415,053 a	1,790,982,886 a	244,141,485 a	1,352,678 o	1,978,204,314 o	211,496,303 o
rca	134,861 a	286,239,864 a	46,412,399 a	130,816 a	315,102,576 a	45,918,149 a	126,386 a	284,885,301 a	42,774,174 a
sda	1,157,131 a	419,262,330 a	975,273,380 a	1,168,683 a	503,050,620 a	955,505,472 a	*1,176,013* a	510,045,731 a	1,003,527,847 a
sbc	15,216,978 a	10,271,915,665 a	1,189,656,873 a	15,005,638 a	10,542,911,055 a	1,185,509,033 a	*14,813,234* g	10,639,488,930 a	1,171,604,679 a
ucc	880,383 a	859,020,596 a	60,992,331 a	853,778 a	905,788,695 a	58,151,694 a	824,866 a	912,643,121 a	54,910,992 a
wel	288,001 a	285,478,030 a	56,257,356 a	284,328 a	298,127,712 a	55,987,987 a	280,006 a	303,329,127 a	53,916,766 a
Total	24,993,497	19,006,193,436	3,179,857,348	24,596,925	19,449,876,804	3,172,489,563	24,136,580	19,610,987,381	3,133,661,709

a Data obtained from denominational source.

f Membership obtained from the denomination and used only in Chapter 5 analysis; not included in the Total sum on this page.

n Membership calculated from prior and following years. 2016 Church of God, general Conference (McDonough, GA): Data Years 2015 and 2017. 2017 Church of God (Anderson, IN): Data Years 2016 and 2018. Used only in Chapter 5 analysis; not included in Total sum on this page.

o Data obtained from denominational source. In 2018, the Presbyterian Church (USA) changed the reporting categories for information from congregations. In 2018 and going forward, the data in this series reflects the published PC(USA) data presented in order to be as consistent as possible, although not strictly comparable with the earlier multi-decade *Yearbook of American and Canadian Churches* series information for the PC(USA) and its antecedents.

Appendix B-1: Church Member Giving, in Current Dollars, 1968–2021 (continued)

	Data Year 2019			Data Year 2020			Data Year 2021		
	Full/Confirmed Members	Congregational Finances	Benevolences	Full/Confirmed Members	Congregational Finances	Benevolences	Full/Confirmed Members	Congregational Finances	Benevolences
abc	144,318 [a]	128,048,383 [a]	29,129,952 [a]	132,808 [a]	146,862,813 [a]	27,166,506 [a]	72,478 [a]	139,021,959 [a]	26,890,962 [a]
alc	See ELCA	See ELCA	See ELCA	See ELCA	See ELCA	See ELCA	See ELCA	See ELCA	See ELCA
arp	27,176 [a]	61,683,078 [a]	5,183,184 [a]	26,871 [a]	59,660,209 [a]	5,408,175 [a]	26,252 [a]	60,121,988 [a]	5,362,777 [a]
bcc	19,358 [a]	46,593,942 [a]	3,683,399 [a]	17,788 [a]	49,332,175 [a]	3,654,627 [a]	15,021 [a]	40,177,038 [a]	3,267,202 [a]
ccd	220,447 [a]	247,308,037 [a]	30,433,504 [a]	223,133 [a]	254,350,117 [a]	23,772,699 [a]	214,863 [a]	268,065,782 [a]	26,478,615 [a]
cga	257,958 [n]	NA	NA	209,574 [f]	NA	NA	203,068 [f]	NA	NA
cgg	2,493 [a]	3,311,000 [a]	818,842 [a]	2,482 [a]	3,272,000 [a]	868,360 [a]	2,672 [a]	3,866,500 [a]	856,674 [a]
chb	96,680 [a]	50,702,813 [a]	13,714,991 [a]	91,608 [a]	47,682,800 [a]	14,264,919 [a]	87,181 [a]	50,488,331 [a]	16,481,491 [a]
chn	603,557 [a]	632,306,856 [a]	119,505,614 [a]	593,494 [a]	624,978,693 [a]	116,250,111 [a]	575,889 [a]	596,172,848 [a]	116,773,473
cccc	47,052 [a]	49,160,349 [a]	10,792,514 [a]	46,199 [a]	48,870,481 [a]	10,606,835 [a]	45,785 [a]	48,854,181 [a]	10,274,697 [a]
cpc	55,179 [a]	39,669,235 [a]	8,798,510 [a]	53,741 [a]	37,646,856 [a]	8,252,043 [a]	53,056 [a]	28,607,479 [a]	11,570,589 [a]
ecc	12,522 [a]	17,605,560 [a]	1,451,484 [a]	11,802 [a]	19,771,360 [a]	1,594,363 [a]	11,162 [a]	17,728,986 [a]	1,648,473 [a]
ecv	137,291 [f]	NA	NA	63,026 [p]	NA	NA	59,752 [f]	NA	NA
elc	2,544,840 [a]	2,060,185,385 [a]	200,554,007 [a]	2,458,496 [a]	1,932,843,892 [a]	194,339,887 [a]	2,377,298 [a]	1,930,049,629 [a]	195,611,238 [a]
els	12,677 [a]	15,299,090 [a]	1,119,921 [a]	12,614 [a]	14,846,953 [a]	1,161,127 [a]	12,748 [a]	12,409,092 [a]	1,031,598 [a]
emc	See FEC	See FEC	See FEC	See FEC	See FEC	See FEC	See FEC	See FEC	See FEC
feb	NA	NA	NA	NA	NA	NA	NA	NA	NA
fec	8,582 [a]	32,290,783 [a]	1,999,865 [a]	8,105 [a]	32,989,243 [a]	1,992,790 [a]	7,823 [a]	33,670,378 [a]	1,840,000 [a]
fmc	66,163 [a]	156,128,262 [a]	10,358,264 [a]	64,659 [a]	153,607,904 [a]	14,116,618 [a]	64,863 [a]	169,826,447 [a]	12,250,517 [a]
fum	NA	NA	NA	NA	NA	NA	NA	NA	NA
ggb	47,195 [a]	48,169,269 [a]	3,027,816 [a]	45,636 [a]	51,170,764 [a]	3,024,618 [a]	56,737 [a]	48,936,339 [a]	2,963,391
lca	See ELCA	See ELCA	See ELCA	See ELCA	See ELCA	See ELCA	See ELCA	See ELCA	See ELCA
lms	1,466,431 [a]	1,264,000,965 [a]	114,736,785 [a]	1,429,663 [a]	1,245,235,540 [a]	103,758,300 [a]	1,395,639 [a]	1,334,214,152 [a]	139,782,134 [a]
mch	See MUS	See MUS	See MUS	See MUS	See MUS	See MUS	See MUS	See MUS	See MUS
mgc	See MUS	See MUS	See MUS	See MUS	See MUS	See MUS	See MUS	See MUS	See MUS
mus	62,361 [f]	NA	NA	61,760 [f]	NA	NA	59,026 [f]	NA	NA
mca	14,903 [a]	10,554,006 [a]	568,568 [a]	14,747 [a]	10,222,105 [a]	555,042 [a]	14,530 [a]	10,146,771 [a]	542,830 [a]
nab	NA	NA	NA	NA	NA	NA	NA	NA	NA
opc	23,175 [a]	56,418,100 [a]	9,013,000 [a]	23,304 [a]	58,673,500 [a]	8,921,700 [a]	23,664 [a]	65,791,300 [a]	9,352,600 [a]
pch	1,302,043 [o]	1,972,708,976 [o]	216,202,247 [o]	1,245,354 [o]	1,796,563,616 [o]	197,890,888 [o]	1,193,770 [a]	1,831,993,311 [a]	206,061,063 [a]
rca	122,961 [a]	359,965,003 [a]	45,067,530 [a]	117,387 [a]	332,442,886 [a]	51,773,071 [a]	92,828 [a]	276,011,961 [a]	36,530,509 [a]
sda	1,262,927 [a]	555,897,045 [a]	1,037,957,155 [a]	1,182,520 [a]	457,966,261 [a]	1,051,474,916 [a]	1,187,821 [a]	494,353,422 [a]	1,158,208,941 [a]
sbc	14,525,579 [a]	10,517,372,272 [a]	1,123,298,287 [a]	14,089,947 [g]	10,479,942,428 [a]	1,046,655,912 [a]	13,680,493 [a]	10,711,228,153 [a]	1,119,075,812 [a]
ucc	802,356 [a]	915,463,799 [a]	51,535,392 [a]	773,539 [a]	837,482,178 [a]	46,095,281 [a]	745,230 [a]	835,858,118 [a]	44,631,304 [a]
wel	276,982 [a]	309,312,944 [a]	60,639,701 [a]	273,334 [a]	304,561,498 [a]	71,319,467 [a]	270,529 [a]	329,059,911 [a]	81,104,599 [a]
Total	23,705,596	19,550,155,152	3,099,590,532	22,939,231	19,000,976,272	3,004,918,255	22,228,332	19,336,654,076	3,228,591,489

a Data obtained from denominational source.
f Membership obtained from the denomination and used only in Chapter 5 analysis; not included in the Total sum on this page.
n 2019 membership data is calculated from Data Years 2017 and 2018; used only in Chapter 5 analysis; not included in Total sum on this page.
o Data obtained from denominational source. In 2018, the Presbyterian Church (USA) changed the reporting categories for information from congregations. In 2018 and going forward, the data in this series reflects the published PC(USA) data presented in order to be as consistent as possible, although not strictly comparable with the earlier multi-decade *Yearbook of American and Canadian Churches* series information for the PC(USA) and its antecedents.
p "Less than half of our 860 churches completed the survey likely because of pandemic." Data used only in Chapter 5 analysis; not included in Total sum on this page.

Appendix B-2: Church Member Giving for 36 Denominations, in Current Dollars, 2020–2021

	Data Year 2020 [a]			**Data Year 2021** [a]		
	Full/Confirmed Members	Congregational Finances	Benevolences	Full/Confirmed Members	Congregational Finances	Benevolences
Allegheny Wesleyan Methodist Connection (Original Allegheny Conference)	1,012 [a]	3,500,188 [a]	1,032,060 [a]	973 [a]	3,314,363 [a]	1,159,751 [a]
Brethren Church (Ashland, Ohio)	6,716 [a]	10,299,583 [a]	1,493,764 [a]	5,911 [a]	6,691,237 [a]	1,630,768 [a]
Alliance (Christian and Missionary Alliance)	204,682 [a]	454,192,262 [a]	44,194,093 [a]	194,050 [a]	463,791,125 [a]	49,670,895 [a]
Church of Christ (Holiness) U.S.A.	12,741 [a]	9,168,095 [a]	453,916 [a]	12,080 [a]	11,008,356 [a]	268,183 [a]
Church of the Lutheran Brethren of America	6,331 [a]	18,993,280 [a]	1,745,000 [a]	7,623 [a]	22,758,820 [a]	2,245,000 [a]
Church of the Lutheran Confession	5,466 [a]	7,105,013 [a]	1,200,183 [a]	5,367 [a]	7,841,163 [a]	1,278,307 [a]
Churches of God General Conference	26,074 [a]	34,189,262 [a]	5,662,312 [a]	24,091 [a]	41,403,869 [a]	5,627,137 [a]
The Episcopal Church	1,217,433 [a]	1,827,993,488 [a]	311,075,028 [a]	1,083,483 [a]	1,949,531,972 [a]	312,839,447 [a]
Missionary Church USA	32,983 [a]	89,405,061 [a]	13,253,176 [a]	31,427 [a]	93,825,380 [a]	15,524,854 [a]
Presbyterian Church in America	298,694 [a]	780,864,814 [a]	150,333,606 [a]	295,953 [a]	804,546,398 [a]	151,622,186 [a]
The United Methodist Church	6,307,795 [a]	4,988,303,620 [a]	763,101,881 [a]	6,080,352 [a]	5,110,280,914 [a]	806,394,852 [a]
The Wesleyan Church	116,491 [a]	330,664,376 [a]	53,604,559 [a]	109,169 [a]	298,655,379 [a]	49,935,348 [a]

[a] Data obtained from denominational sources.

Appendix B-3.1: Church Member Giving for 11 Denominations, in Current Dollars, 1921–1952

Year	Total Contributions	Members	Per Capita Giving
1921	$281,173,263	17,459,611	$16.10
1922	345,995,802	18,257,426	18.95
1923	415,556,876	18,866,775	22.03
1924	443,187,826	19,245,220	23.03
1925	412,658,363	19,474,863	21.19
1926	368,529,223	17,054,404	21.61
1927	459,527,624	20,266,709	22.67
1928	429,947,883	20,910,584	20.56
1929	445,327,233	20,612,910	21.60
1930	419,697,819	20,796,745	20.18
1931	367,158,877	21,508,745	17.07
1932	309,409,873	21,757,411	14.22
1933	260,366,681	21,792,663	11.95
1934	260,681,472	22,105,624	11.79
1935	267,596,925	22,204,355	12.05
1936	279,835,526	21,746,023	12.87
1937	297,134,313	21,906,456	13.56
1938	307,217,666	22,330,090	13.76
1939	302,300,476	23,084,048	13.10
1940	311,362,429	23,671,660	13.15
1941	336,732,622	23,120,929	14.56
1942	358,419,893	23,556,204	15.22
1943	400,742,492	24,679,784	16.24
1944	461,500,396	25,217,319	18.30
1945	551,404,448	25,898,642	21.29
1946	608,165,179	26,158,559	23.25
1947	684,393,895	27,082,905	25.27
1948	775,360,993	27,036,992	28.68
1949	875,069,944	27,611,824	31.69
1950	934,723,015	28,176,095	33.17
1951	1,033,391,527	28,974,314	35.67
1952	1,121,802,639	29,304,909	38.28

Source: *Yearbook of American Churches*, 1949 and 1955 editions.
See Introduction to Appendix B-3, p. 180.

Appendix B-3.2: Church Member Giving for 11 Denominations, in Current Dollars, 1953–1967

	Data Year 1953		Data Year 1954		Data Year 1955	
	Total Contributions	Per Capita Total Contributions	Total Contributions	Per Capita Total Contributions	Total Contributions	Per Capita Total Contributions
American Baptist (Northern)	$66,557,447 [a]	$44.50 [b]	$65,354,184	$43.17	$67,538,753 [d]	$44.19 [d]
Christian Church (Disciples of Christ)	60,065,545 [c]	32.50 [b]	65,925,164	34.77	68,661,162 [d]	35.96 [d]
Church of the Brethren	7,458,584	43.78	7,812,806	45.88	9,130,616	53.00
The Episcopal Church	84,209,027	49.02	92,079,668	51.84	97,541,567 [d]	50.94 [b]
Evangelical Lutheran Church in America						
The American Lutheran Church						
American Lutheran Church	30,881,256	55.24	34,202,987	58.83	40,411,856	67.03
The Evangelical Lutheran Church	30,313,907	48.70	33,312,926	51.64	37,070,341	55.29
United Evangelical Lutheran Church	1,953,163	55.85	2,268,200	50.25	2,635,469	69.84
Lutheran Free Church	Not Reported: YAC 1955, p. 264		2,101,026	44.51	2,708,747	55.76
Evan. Lutheran Churches, Assn. of	Not Reported: YAC 1955, p. 264		Not Reported: YAC 1956, p. 276		Not Reported: YAC 1957, p. 284	
Lutheran Church in America						
United Lutheran Church	67,721,548	45.68	76,304,344	50.25	83,170,787	53.46
General Council Evang. Luth. Ch.						
General Synod of Evang. Luth. Ch.						
United Syn. Evang. Luth. South						
American Evangelical Luth. Ch.	Not Reported: YAC 1955, p. 264		Not Reported: YAC 1956, p. 276		Not Reported: YAC 1957, p. 284	
Augustana Lutheran Church	18,733,019	53.98	22,203,098	62.14	22,090,350	60.12
Finnish Lutheran Ch. (Suomi Synod)	744,971	32.12	674,554	29.47	1,059,682	43.75
Moravian Church in Am. No. Prov.	1,235,534	53.26	1,461,658	59.51	1,241,008	49.15
Presbyterian Church (U.S.A.)						
United Presbyterian Ch. In U.S.A.						
Presbyterian Church in the U.S.A.	141,057,179	56.49	158,110,613	61.47	180,472,698	68.09
United Presbyterian Ch. In N.A.	13,204,897	57.73	14,797,353	62.37	16,019,616	65.39
Presbyterian Church in the U.S.	56,001,996	73.99	59,222,983	75.54	66,033,260	81.43
Reformed Church in America	13,671,897	68.57	14,740,275	71.87	17,459,572	84.05
Southern Baptist Convention	278,851,129	39.84	305,573,654	42.17	334,836,283	44.54
United Church of Christ						
Congregational Christian	64,061,866	49.91	71,786,834	54.76	80,519,810	60.00
Congregational						
Evangelical and Reformed	31,025,133	41.24	36,261,267	46.83	41,363,406	52.74
Evangelical Synod of N.A./German						
Reformed Church in the U.S.						
The United Methodist Church						
The Evangelical United Brethren	36,331,994	50.21	36,609,598	50.43	41,199,631	56.01
The Methodist Church	314,521,214	34.37	345,416,448	37.53	389,490,613	41.82
Methodist Episcopal Church						
Methodist Episcopal Church South						
Methodist Protestant Church						
Total	$1,318,601,306		$1,446,219,640		$1,600,655,227	

[a] In data year 1953, $805,135 has been subtracted from the 1955 Yearbook of American Churches (YAC) (Edition for 1956) entry. See 1956 YAC (Edition for 1957), p. 276, n.1.

[b] This Per Capita Total Contributions figure was calculated by dividing (1) revised Total Contributions as listed in this Appendix, by (2) Membership that, for purposes of this report, had been calculated by dividing the revised Total Contributions by the Per Capita Total Contributions figures that were published in the *YAC* series.

[c] In data year 1953, $5,508,883 has been added to the 1955 *YAC* (Edition for 1956) entry. See 1956 *YAC* (Edition for 1957), p. 276, n. 4.

[d] Total Contributions and Per Capita Total Contributions, respectively, prorated based on available data as follows: American Baptist Churches, 1954 and 1957 data; Christian Church (Disciples of Christ), 1954 and 1956 data; and The Episcopal Church, 1954 and 1956 data.

Appendix B-3.2: Church Member Giving for 11 Denominations, in Current Dollars, 1953-1967 (continued)

	Data Year 1956		Data Year 1957		Data Year 1958	
	Total Contributions	Per Capita Total Contributions	Total Contributions	Per Capita Total Contributions	Total Contributions	Per Capita Total Contributions
American Baptist (Northern)	$69,723,321 [e]	$45.21 [e]	$71,907,890	$46.23	$70,405,404	$45.03
Christian Church (Disciples of Christ)	71,397,159	37.14	73,737,955	37.94	79,127,458	41.17
Church of the Brethren	10,936,285	63.15	11,293,388	64.43	12,288,049	70.03
The Episcopal Church	103,003,465	52.79	111,660,728	53.48	120,687,177	58.33
Evangelical Lutheran Church in America						
The American Lutheran Church						
American Lutheran Church	45,316,809	72.35	44,518,194	68.80	47,216,896	70.89
The Evangelical Lutheran Church	39,096,038	56.47	44,212,046	61.95	45,366,512	61.74
United Evangelical Lutheran Church	2,843,527	73.57	2,641,201	65.46	3,256,050	77.38
Lutheran Free Church	2,652,307	53.14	3,379,882	64.70	3,519,017	66.31
Evan. Lutheran Churches, Assn. of	Not Reported: YAC 1958, p. 292		Not Reported: YAC 1959, p. 277		Not Reported: YAC 1960, p. 276	
Lutheran Church in America						
United Lutheran Church	93,321,223	58.46	100,943,860	61.89	110,179,054	66.45
General Council Evang. Luth. Ch.						
General Synod of Evang. Luth. Ch.						
United Syn. Evang. Luth. South						
American Evangelical Luth. Ch.	Not Comparable YAC 1958, p. 292		935,319	59.45	1,167,503	72.98
Augustana Lutheran Church	24,893,792	66.15	28,180,152	72.09	29,163,771	73.17
Finnish Lutheran Ch. (Suomi Synod)	1,308,026	51.56	1,524,299	58.11	1,533,058	61.94
Moravian Church in Am. No. Prov.	1,740,961	67.53	1,776,703	67.77	1,816,281	68.14
Presbyterian Church (U.S.A.)						
United Presbyterian Ch. In U.S.A.					243,000,572	78.29
Presbyterian Church in the U.S.A.	204,208,085	75.02	214,253,598	77.06		
United Presbyterian Ch. In N.A.	18,424,936	73.3	19,117,837	74.24		
Presbyterian Church in the U.S.	73,477,555	88.56	78,426,424	92.03	82,760,291	95.18
Reformed Church in America	18,718,008	88.56	19,658,604	91.10	21,550,017	98.24
Southern Baptist Convention	372,136,675	48.17	397,540,347	49.99	419,619,438	51.04
United Church of Christ						
Congregational Christian	89,914,505	65.18	90,333,453	64.87	97,480,446	69.55
Congregational						
Evangelical and Reformed	51,519,531	64.88	55,718,141	69.56	63,419,468	78.56
Evangelical Synod of N.A./German						
Reformed Church in the U.S.						
The United Methodist Church						
The Evangelical United Brethren	44,727,060	60.57	45,738,332 [e]	61.75 [e]	46,749,605 [e]	62.93 [e]
The Methodist Church	413,893,955	43.82	462,826,269 [e]	48.31 [e]	511,758,582	52.80
Methodist Episcopal Church						
Methodist Episcopal Church South						
Methodist Protestant Church						
Total	$1,753,253,223		$1,880,324,622		$2,012,064,649	

[e] Total Contributions and Per Capita Total Contributions, respectively, prorated based on available data as follows: American Baptist Churches, 1954 and 1957 data; The Evangelical United Brethren, 1956 and 1960 data; and The Methodist Church, 1956 and 1958 data.

Appendix B-3.2: Church Member Giving for 11 Denominations, in Current Dollars, 1953-1967 (continued)

	Data Year 1959		Data Year 1960		Data Year 1961	
	Total Contributions	Per Capita Total Contributions	Total Contributions	Per Capita Total Contributions	Total Contributions	Per Capita Total Contributions
American Baptist (Northern)	$74,877,669	$48.52	$73,106,232	$48.06	$104,887,025	$68.96
Christian Church (Disciples of Christ)	Not Comparable YAC 1961, p. 273		86,834,944	63.26	89,730,589	65.31
Church of the Brethren	12,143,983	65.27	12,644,194	68.33	13,653,155	73.33
The Episcopal Church	130,279,752	61.36	140,625,284	64.51	154,458,809	68.30
Evangelical Lutheran Church in America						
The American Lutheran Church					113,645,260	73.28
American Lutheran Church	50,163,078	73.52	51,898,875	74.49		
The Evangelical Lutheran Church	49,488,063	65.56	51,297,348	66.85		
United Evangelical Lutheran Church	Not Reported: YAC 1961, p. 273		Not Reported: YAC 1963, p. 273			
Lutheran Free Church	3,354,270	61.20	3,618,418	63.98	4,316,925	73.46
Evan. Lutheran Churches, Assn. of	Not Reported: YAC 1961, p. 273		Not Reported: YAC 1963, p. 273			
Lutheran Church in America						
United Lutheran Church	114,458,260	68.29	119,447,895	70.86	128,850,845	76.18
General Council Evang. Luth. Ch.						
General Synod of Evang. Luth. Ch.						
United Syn. Evang. Luth. South						
American Evangelical Luth. Ch.	1,033,907	63.83	1,371,600	83.63	1,209,752	74.89
Augustana Lutheran Church	31,279,335	76.97	33,478,865	80.88	37,863,105	89.37
Finnish Lutheran Ch. (Suomi Synod)	1,685,342	68.61	1,860,481	76.32	1,744,550	70.60
Moravian Church in Am. No. Prov.	2,398,565	89.28	2,252,536	82.95	2,489,930	90.84
Presbyterian Church (U.S.A.)						
United Presbyterian Ch. In U.S.A.	259,679,057	82.30	270,233,943	84.31	285,380,476	87.90
Presbyterian Church in the U.S.A.						
United Presbyterian Ch. In N.A.						
Presbyterian Church in the U.S.	88,404,631	99.42	91,582,428	101.44	96,637,354	105.33
Reformed Church in America	22,970,935	103.23	23,615,749	104.53	25,045,773	108.80
Southern Baptist Convention	453,338,720	53.88	480,608,972	55.68	501,301,714	50.24
United Church of Christ						
Congregational Christian	100,938,267	71.12	104,862,037	73.20	105,871,158	73.72
Congregational						
Evangelical and Reformed	65,541,874	80.92	62,346,084	76.58	65,704,662	80.33
Evangelical Synod of N.A./German						
Reformed Church in the U.S.						
The United Methodist Church						
The Evangelical United Brethren	47,760,877 d	64.10	48,772,149 d	65.28	50,818,912 d	68.12
The Methodist Church	532,854,842 d	53.97	553,951,102 d	55.14	581,504,618 d	57.27
Methodist Episcopal Church						
Methodist Episcopal Church South						
Methodist Protestant Church						
Total	$2,042,651,427		$2,214,409,136		$2,365,114,612	

d Total Contributions averaged from available data as follows: The Evangelical United Brethren, 1956 and 1960 data; The United Methodist Church, 1958 and 1960 data.

Appendix B-3.2: Church Member Giving for 11 Denominations, in Current Dollars, 1953-1967* (continued)

	Data Year 1962		Data Year 1963		Data Year 1964	
	Total Contributions	Per Capita Total Contributions	Total Contributions	Per Capita Total Contributions	Total Contributions	Per Capita Total Contributions
American Baptist (Northern)	$105,667,332	$68.42	$99,001,651	$68.34	$104,699,557	$69.99
Christian Church (Disciples of Christ)	91,889,457	67.20	96,607,038	75.81	102,102,840	86.44
Church of the Brethren	14,594,572	77.88	14,574,688	72.06	15,221,162	76.08
The Episcopal Church	155,971,264	69.80	171,125,464	76.20	175,374,777	76.66
Evangelical Lutheran Church in America						
The American Lutheran Church	114,912,112	72.47	136,202,292	81.11	143,687,165	83.83
American Lutheran Church						
The Evangelical Lutheran Church						
United Evangelical Lutheran Church						
Lutheran Free Church	4,765,138	78.68				
Evan. Lutheran Churches, Assn. of						
Lutheran Church in America	185,166,857	84.98	157,423,391	71.45	170,012,096	76.35
United Lutheran Church						
General Council Evang. Luth. Ch.						
General Synod of Evang. Luth. Ch.						
United Syn. Evang. Luth. South						
American Evangelical Luth. Ch.						
Augustana Lutheran Church						
Finnish Lutheran Ch. (Suomi Synod)						
Moravian Church in Am. No. Prov.	2,512,133	91.92	2,472,273	89.29	2,868,694	103.54
Presbyterian Church (U.S.A.)						
United Presbyterian Ch. In U.S.A.	288,496,652	88.08	297,582,313	90.46	304,833,435	92.29
Presbyterian Church in the U.S.A.						
United Presbyterian Ch. In N.A.						
Presbyterian Church in the U.S.	99,262,431	106.96	102,625,764	109.46	108,269,579	114.61
Reformed Church in America	25,579,443	110.16	26,918,484	117.58	29,174,103	126.44
Southern Baptist Convention	540,811,457	53.06	556,042,694	53.49	591,587,981	55.80
United Church of Christ	164,858,968	72.83	162,379,019	73.12	169,208,042	75.94
Congregational Christian						
Congregational						
Evangelical and Reformed						
Evangelical Synod of N.A./German						
Reformed Church in the U.S.						
The United Methodist Church						
The Evangelical United Brethren	54,567,962	72.91	49,921,568	67.37	56,552,783	76.34
The Methodist Church	599,081,561	58.53	613,547,721	59.60	608,841,881	59.09
Methodist Episcopal Church						
Methodist Episcopal Church South						
Methodist Protestant Church						
Total	$2,448,137,339		$2,486,424,360		$2,582,434,095	

* Note: Data for the years 1965 through 1967 was not available in a form that could be readily analyzed for the present purposes, and therefore, data for 1965-1967 was estimated as described in the introductory comments to Appendix B. See Appendix B-1 for 1968-1991 data except for The Episcopal Church and The United Methodist Church, available data for which is presented in the continuation of Appendix B-3 in the table immediately following.

Appendix B-3.3: Church Member Giving for 11 Denominations, in Current Dollars, The Episcopal Church and The United Methodist Church, 1968–2021

The Episcopal Church			The United Methodist Church					
Data Year	Total Contributions	Full/Confirmed Membership	Data Year	Total Contributions	Full/Confirmed Membership	Connectional Clergy Support	Unadjusted Congregational Finances e	Unadjusted Benevolences e
1968	$202,658,092 c	2,322,911 c	1968	$763,000,434 a	10,849,375 b	NA	NA	NA
1969	209,989,189 c	2,238,538	1969	800,425,000	10,671,774	$44,416,000	$659,855,000	$140,570,000
1970	248,702,969	2,208,773	1970	819,945,000	10,509,198	48,847,000	682,900,000	137,045,000
1971	257,523,469	2,143,557	1971	843,103,000	10,334,521	52,731,000	652,709,000	190,394,000
1972	270,245,645	2,099,896	1972	885,708,000	10,192,265	56,968,000	684,512,000	201,196,000
1973	296,735,919 c	2,079,873 c	1973	935,723,000	10,063,046	62,498,997	723,680,000	212,043,000
1974	305,628,925	2,069,793	1974	1,009,760,804	9,957,710	67,344,298	794,385,263	215,375,541
1975	352,243,222	2,051,914 c	1975	1,081,080,372	9,861,028	75,220,496	831,974,304	249,106,068
1976	375,942,065	2,021,057	1976	1,162,828,991	9,785,534	82,681,376	896,427,840	266,401,151
1977	401,814,395	2,114,638	1977	1,264,191,548	9,731,779	94,705,448	972,038,703	292,152,845
1978	430,116,564	1,975,234	1978	1,364,460,266	9,653,711	107,508,214	1,050,480,562	313,979,704
1979	484,211,412	1,962,062	1979	1,483,481,986	9,584,771	116,405,701	1,140,043,707	343,438,279
1980	507,315,457	1,933,080 c	1980	1,632,204,336	9,519,407	126,442,425	1,271,637,950	360,566,386
1981	697,816,298	1,930,690	1981	1,794,706,741	9,457,012	136,991,942	1,389,977,880	404,728,861
1982	778,184,068	1,922,923 c	1982	1,931,796,533	9,405,164	162,884,181	1,493,668,825	438,127,708
1983	876,844,252	1,906,618	1983	2,049,437,917	9,291,936	172,569,488	1,585,113,419	464,324,498
1984	939,796,743	1,896,056	1984	2,211,306,198	9,266,853	188,372,446	1,700,916,514	510,389,684
1985	1,043,117,983	1,881,250	1985	2,333,928,274	9,192,172	203,047,650	1,789,454,589	544,473,685
1986	1,134,455,479	1,772,271 c	1986	2,460,079,431	9,124,575	211,121,271	1,898,162,151	561,917,280
1987	1,181,378,441	1,741,036	1987	2,573,518,234 c	9,055,145	217,708,718	1,995,818,424 c	577,699,810 c
1988	1,209,378,098	1,725,581	1988	2,697,918,285	8,979,139	230,013,885	2,096,540,363	601,377,922
1989	1,309,243,747	1,714,122	1989	2,845,998,177	8,904,824	245,281,392	2,207,326,260	638,671,917
1990	1,377,794,610	1,698,240	1990	2,967,535,538 c	8,853,455 c	261,434,709	2,306,767,011 c	660,768,527 c
1991	1,541,141,356 c	1,613,825 c	1991	3,099,522,282	8,789,101	269,248,639	2,421,078,608	678,443,674
1992	1,582,055,527 c	1,615,930 c	1992	3,202,700,721 c	8,726,951 c	278,990,363	2,495,335,729 c	707,364,992 c
1993	1,617,623,255 c	1,580,339 c	1993	3,303,255,279	8,646,595	284,654,147	2,583,890,618	719,364,661
1994	1,679,250,095 c	1,578,282 c	1994	3,430,351,778	8,584,125	293,637,514	2,698,513,430	731,838,348
1995	1,840,431,636 c	1,584,225 c	1995	3,568,359,334 c	8,538,808 c	295,102,097	2,825,152,360 c	743,206,974 c
1996	1,731,727,725 c	1,637,584 c	1996	3,744,692,223	8,496,047 c	296,944,022	2,984,250,917	760,441,306
1997	1,832,000,448 c	1,757,972 c	1997	3,990,329,491 c	8,452,042 c	310,347,506	3,192,213,867 c	798,115,624 c
1998	1,977,012,320 c	1,807,651 c	1998	4,219,596,499 c	8,411,503 c	319,721,285	3,388,300,027 c	831,296,472 c
1999	2,146,835,718 c	1,843,108 c	1999	4,523,284,851	8,377,662	328,089,751	3,639,161,294	884,123,557
2000	2,143,238,797 c	1,877,271 c	2000	4,761,148,280	8,341,375	338,798,893	3,854,328,165	906,820,115
2001	2,070,493,919 c	1,897,004 c	2001	5,043,693,838 c	8,298,460 c	359,734,860	4,067,476,116 c	976,217,722 c
2002	2,090,536,512 c	1,902,525 c	2002	5,242,691,229 c	8,251,042	401,465,727	4,236,235,774 c	1,006,455,455 c
2003	2,133,772,253	1,866,157	2003	5,376,057,236 c	8,186,274 c	444,210,401	4,329,518,407 c	1,046,538,829 c
2004	2,132,774,534	1,834,530	2004	5,541,540,536	8,120,186 d	462,206,590	4,448,116,006	1,093,424,530
2005	2,180,974,503 c	1,796,017 c	2005	5,861,722,397 c	8,040,577 c	466,588,268	4,621,323,160 c	1,240,399,237 c
2006	2,187,308,798 c	1,749,073 c	2006	6,012,378,898	7,976,985 c	481,453,754	4,825,846,715	1,186,532,183
2007	2,221,167,438	1,720,477	2007	6,295,942,455 c	7,899,147 c	478,982,491	5,080,054,998 c	1,215,887,457 c
2008	2,294,941,221	1,666,202	2008	6,300,722,381 c	7,819,668 c	477,863,600	5,079,086,476 c	1,221,635,905 c
2009	2,182,330,459	1,624,025	2009	6,218,009,630 c	7,724,821 c	Not Available	5,313,185,468 c	904,824,162 c
2010	2,088,449,676	1,576,721	2010	6,158,084,527 c	7,615,750 c	Not Available	5,242,248,358 c	915,836,169 c
2011	2,080,612,044 c	1,542,072 c	2011	6,189,661,943 c	7,526,497 c	Not Available	5,278,681,549 c	910,980,394 c
2012	2,084,487,182 c	1,516,117 c	2012	6,216,393,709 c	7,439,145 c	Not Available	5,290,790,835 c	925,602,874 c
2013	2,136,588,352 c	1,491,423 c	2013	6,231,445,829 c	7,344,124 c	Not Available	5,296,791,114 c	934,654,715 c
2014	2,154,850,845 c	1,450,472 c	2014	6,315,279,161 c	7,228,844 c	Not Available	5,377,857,003 c	937,422,158 c
2015	2,218,134,990 c	1,434,461 c	2015	6,338,036,534 c	7,114,433 c	Not Available	5,402,098,517 c	935,938,017 c
2016	2,196,475,669 c	1,399,523 c	2016	6,332,354,673 c	6,995,358 c	Not Available	5,394,678,897 c	937,675,776 c
2017	2,226,690,846 c	1,368,631 c	2017	6,392,738,477 c	6,849,034 c	Not Available	5,429,444,860 c	963,293,617 c
2018	2,267,187,403 c	1,324,977 c	2018	6,409,819,537 c	6,710,133 c	Not Available	5,476,994,058 c	932,825,479 c
2019	2,291,275,165 c	1,285,650 c	2019	6,378,669,727 c	6,527,408 c	Not Available	5,482,650,341 c	896,019,386 c
2020	2,139,068,516 c	1,217,433 c	2020	5,751,405,501 c	6,307,795 c	Not Available	*4,988,303,620* c	763,101,881 c
2021	2,262,371,419 c	1,083,483 c	2021	5,916,675,766 c	6,080,352 c	Not Available	5,110,280,914 c	806,394,852 c

a The Evangelical United Brethren Data Not Reported: YAC 1970, p. 198-200. This figure is the sum of The Methodist Church in 1968, and the Evangelical United Brethren data for 1967.

b This membership figure is an average of the sum of 1967 membership for The Methodist Church and the Evangelical United Brethren and 1969 data for The United Methodist Church.

c Data obtained directly from denominational source.

d Data obtained from the denomination included this note: "Combines 2004 local church data with 2004 clergy data. In the past 2004 lay would be combined with 2005 clergy. We've been delayed in finalizing clergy figures for 2005… [Based on a check of] the past few years, that will mean a difference of less than 300 for the total number."

e The numbers in this column are used in Chapter 5 as the basis for Figure 15. The numbers for 2019 and 2020 also appear in Appendix B-2.

Appendix B-4: Membership for Seven Denominations, 1968-2021

Year	American Baptist Churches (Total Mem.)	Assemblies of God	Baptist General Conference/ Converge Worldwide	Christian and Missionary Alliance	Church of God (Cleveland, TN)	Roman Catholic Church	Salvation Army (Inclusive Mem.)
1968	1,583,560	610,946	100,000	71,656	243,532	47,468,333	329,515
1969	1,528,019	626,660	101,226	70,573	257,995	47,872,089	331,711
1970	1,472,478	625,027	103,955	71,708	272,276	48,214,729	326,934
1971	1,562,636	645,891	108,474	73,547	287,099	48,390,990	335,684
1972	1,484,393	679,813	111,364	77,991	297,103	48,460,427	358,626
1973	1,502,759	700,071	109,033	77,606	313,332	48,465,438	361,571
1974	1,579,029	751,818	111,093	80,412	328,892	48,701,835	366,471
1975	1,603,033	785,348	115,340	83,628	343,249	48,881,872	384,817
1976	1,593,574	898,711	117,973	83,978	365,124	49,325,752	380,618
1977	1,584,517	939,312	120,222	88,763	377,765	49,836,176	396,238
1978	1,589,610	932,365	131,000	88,903	392,551	49,602,035	414,035
1979	1,600,521	958,418	126,800	96,324	441,385	49,812,178	414,659
1980	1,607,541	1,064,490	133,385	106,050	435,012	50,449,842	417,359
1981	1,621,795	1,103,134	127,662	109,558	456,797	51,207,579	414,999
1982	1,637,099	1,119,686	129,928	112,745	463,992	52,088,774 [a]	419,475
1983	1,620,153	1,153,935	131,594 [a]	117,501	493,904	52,392,934	428,046
1984	1,559,683	1,189,143	131,162 [a]	120,250	505,775	52,286,043	420,971
1985	1,576,483	1,235,403	130,193 [a]	123,602	521,061 [b]	52,654,908	427,825
1986	1,568,778 [a]	1,258,724	132,546 [a]	130,116	536,346 [b]	52,893,217	432,893
1987	1,561,656 [a]	1,275,146	136,688 [a]	131,354	551,632 [b]	53,496,862	434,002
1988	1,548,573 [a]	1,275,148	134,396 [a]	133,575	556,917 [b]	54,918,949 [a]	433,448
1989	1,535,971 [a]	1,266,982	135,125 [a]	134,336	582,203	57,019,948	445,566
1990	1,527,840 [a]	1,298,121	133,742 [a]	138,071	620,393	58,568,015	445,991
1991	1,534,078 [a]	1,324,800	134,717 [a]	141,077	646,201 [b]	58,267,424	446,403
1992	1,538,710 [a]	1,337,321	134,658 [a]	142,346	672,008	59,220,723	450,028 [a]
1993	1,516,505	1,340,400	134,814 [a]	147,367	700,517	59,858,042	450,312 [a]
1994	1,507,934 [a]	1,354,337	135,128	147,560 [a]	722,541	60,190,605	443,246
1995	1,517,400	1,377,320	135,008	147,955	753,230	60,280,454	453,150
1996	1,503,267 [a]	1,407,941	136,120	143,157	773,483 [a]	61,207,914	462,744 [a]
1997	1,478,534 [a]	1,419,717	134,795	146,153	815,042 [a]	61,563,769 [a]	468,262 [a]
1998	1,507,824 [a]	1,453,907	141,445	163,994	839,857 [a]	62,018,436	471,416
1999	1,454,388	1,492,196	142,871 [a]	164,196	870,039	62,391,484	472,871
2000	1,436,909	1,506,834	141,781 [a]	185,133	895,536	63,683,030 [a]	476,887 [a]
2001	1,442,824	1,532,876	144,365 [a]	191,318	920,664 [a]	65,270,444	454,982
2002	1,484,291	1,585,428	145,148	190,573	944,857	66,407,105	457,807 [a]
2003	1,433,075	1,584,076	145,436 [a]	194,074	961,390	67,259,768 [a]	449,634 [a]
2004	1,418,403 [a]	1,594,062	145,000 [a]	197,764	989,965	67,820,833	427,027
2005	1,396,700	1,612,336	140,494 [a]	201,009	1,013,488	69,135,254	422,543 [a]
2006	1,371,278	1,627,932	140,000 [a]	189,969	1,032,550	67,515,016	414,054 [a]
2007	1,358,351 [a]	1,641,341	147,500	195,481	1,053,642	67,117,016	413,028
2008	1,331,127	1,662,632	167,500 [a]	194,473	1,072,169	68,115,001	405,967 [a]
2009	1,310,505	1,710,560	190,100 [a]	197,653	1,076,254	68,503,456	400,055
2010	1,308,054	1,753,881	210,500 [a]	198,118	1,074,047	68,293,869 [a]	413,961
2011	1,300,744	1,755,872 [a]	217,200 [a]	202,285 [a]	1,088,756	68,229,841 [a]	416,526
2012	1,235,507 [a]	1,780,468 [a]	271,738 [a]	214,264 [a]	1,119,250 [a]	69,436,660 [a]	417,901 [a]
2013	1,236,550 [a]	1,805,381 [a]	295,403 [a]	212,185 [a]	1,138,052 [a]	69,470,686 [a]	417,834 [a]
2014	1,196,828 [a]	1,812,126 [a]	318,123 [a]	212,945 [a]	1,150,324 [a]	71,128,395 [a]	414,267 [a]
2015	1,185,925 [a]	1,817,450 [a]	322,063 [a]	211,727 [a]	1,166,684 [a]	70,412,021 [a]	412,677 [a]
2016	1,160,502 [a]	1,818,941 [a]	319,485 [a]	216,280 [a]	1,176,149 [a]	71,163,054 [a]	400,031 [a]
2017	1,248,984 [a]	1,853,273 [a]	339,675 [a]	215,004 [a]	1,189,701 [a]	71,417,568 [a]	399,919 [a]
2018	1,241,311 [a]	1,856,653 [a]	339,707 [a]	210,261 [a]	1,199,107 [a]	70,514,657 [a]	381,372 [a]
2019	1,221,369 [a]	1,810,093 [a]	324,163 [a]	208,954 [a]	1,210,011 [a]	70,039,079 [a]	359,582 [a]
2020	1,201,289 [a]	1,766,477 [a]	324,163 [a]	204,682 [a]	1,224,078 [a]	69,155,765 [a]	326,649 [a]
2021	1,107,712 [a]	1,683,579 [a]	324,163 [a]	194,050 [a]	1,288,628 [a]	69,214,513 [a]	319,125 [a]

[a] Data obtained from a denominational source.
[b] Extrapolated from *YACC* series.

Note regarding American Baptist Churches (ABC) in the U.S.A. Total Membership data: Total Membership is used for the ABC for analyses that consider membership as a percentage of U.S. population. The ABC denominational office is the source for this data in the years 1968 and 1970. The year 1978 Total Membership data figure is an adjustment of *YACC* data based on 1981 *YACC* information.

Appendix B-5: Overseas Missions Income in Current Dollars, 34 Denominations, 2003 and 2004

	2003 Overseas Missions Income				2004 Overseas Missions Income			
Denomination	Line 1.	Line 2.	Line 3.	Line 4.	Line 1.	Line 2.	Line 3.	Line 4.
Allegheny Wesleyan Methodist Connection	$262,260	$0	$0	$262,260	$266,299	$0	$0	$266,299
American Baptist Churches in the U.S.A. [1]	$20,562,505	$12,048,667	$0	$8,513,838	$17,250,939	$7,759,091	$0	$9,491,848
Associate Reformed Presbyterian Church (General Synod)	$3,508,682	$0	$175,690	$3,332,992	$4,453,573	$15,183	$483,815	$3,954,575
Brethren in Christ Church	$1,651,911	$45,000	$0	$1,606,911	$1,850,963	$50,000	$0	$1,800,963
Christian Church (Disciples of Christ)	$5,960,892	$1,881,873	$0	$4,079,019	$5,347,401	$1,515,309	$0	$3,832,092
Christian and Missionary Alliance [2]	$43,160,960	$0	$0	$43,160,960	$43,534,066	$0	$0	$43,534,066
Church of the Brethren [3]	$1,767,447	$203,824	$0	$1,563,623	$1,702,267	$143,947	$0	$1,558,320
Church of God General Conference (Oregon, Ill., and Morrow, Ga.)	$67,193	$0	$0	$67,193	$113,497	$0	$0	$113,497
Church of the Lutheran Confession	$182,156	$27,000	$0	$155,156	$246,896	$40,000	$0	$206,896
Church of the Nazarene	$46,334,499	$694,019	$0	$45,640,480	$49,715,273	$1,542,188	$0	$48,173,085
Churches of God General Conference [4]	$899,679	$0	$0	$899,679	$1,068,665	$21,517	$0	$1,047,148
Conservative Congregational Christian Conference [5]	$147,805	$0	$0	$147,805	$149,299	$0	$0	$149,299
Cumberland Presbyterian Church	$303,000	$12,236	$0	$290,764	$338,314	$14,974	$0	$323,340
The Episcopal Church [6]	$21,120,265	$3,507,225	$4,419,185	$13,193,855	$23,281,000	$3,000,000	$5,500,000	$14,781,000
Evangelical Congregational Church	$1,264,969	$219,732	$0	$1,045,237	$1,135,224	$193,815	$0	$941,409
Evangelical Covenant Church	$7,913,682	$0	$0	$7,913,682	$8,591,574	$0	$0	$8,591,574
Evangelical Lutheran Church in America [7]	$22,590,206	$2,952,825	$0	$19,637,381	$27,173,066	$3,741,985	$0	$23,431,081
Evangelical Lutheran Synod	$912,460	$665,873	$0	$246,587	$945,470	$679,229	$0	$266,241
Fellowship of Evangelical Churches	$912,689	$0	$0	$912,689	$847,526	$0	$0	$847,526
Free Methodist Church of North America	$9,848,924	$727,325	$0	$9,121,599	$10,817,138	$630,519	$0	$10,186,619
General Association of General Baptists	$1,893,585	$34,719	$0	$1,858,866	$1,817,715	$49,178	$0	$1,768,537
Lutheran Church-Missouri Synod [8]	$14,960,928	$1,881,887	$0	$13,079,041	$15,548,240	$2,370,861	$0	$13,177,379
Moravian Church in America, Northern Province [9]				$467,570				$528,733
The Orthodox Presbyterian Church [10]	$1,254,678	$40,229		$1,214,449	$1,417,758	$43,504	$0	$1,374,254
Presbyterian Church in America	$24,070,885	$0	$0	$24,070,885	$24,319,185	$0	$0	$24,319,185
Presbyterian Church (U.S.A.) [11]	$34,348,000	$11,046,000	$47,000	$23,255,000	$36,900,000	$12,190,000	$122,000	$24,588,000
Primitive Methodist Church in the U.S.A. [12]	$542,252	$5,349	$0	$536,903	$532,337	$5,697	$0	$526,640
Reformed Church in America	$8,159,552	$307,088	$0	$7,852,464	$7,610,120	$325,560	$0	$7,284,560
Seventh-day Adventist, North Am. Division [13]	$50,790,392	$2,565,158	$0	$48,225,234	$48,209,196	$1,456,611	$0	$46,752,585
Southern Baptist Convention [14]	$239,663,000	$0	$0	$239,663,000	$242,140,000	$0	$0	$242,140,000
United Church of Christ	$12,990,011	$4,616,927	$0	$8,373,084	$12,125,594	$4,189,916	$0	$7,935,678
The United Methodist Church [15]	$124,800,000	$20,000,000	$22,800,000	$82,000,000	$138,700,000	$19,800,000	$27,700,000	$91,200,000
The Wesleyan Church	$8,507,914	$0	$0	$8,507,914	$8,881,386	$0	$0	$8,881,386
Wisconsin Evangelical Lutheran Synod	$11,534,079	$754,916	$0	$10,779,164	$10,707,496	$402,633	$0	$10,304,863

See endnotes on the page after the tables.

Appendix B-5 Overseas Missions Income, 34 Denominations, in Current Dollars, 2005 and 2006

	2005 Overseas Missions Income				2006 Overseas Missions Income			
Denomination	Line 1	Line 2	Line 3	Line 4	Line 1	Line 2	Line 3	Line 4
Allegheny Wesleyan Methodist Connection	$399,514	$0	$0	$399,514	$286,781	$0	$0	$286,781
American Baptist Churches in the U.S.A. [1]	$18,837,736	$7,741,255	$0	$11,096,481	$14,701,486	$5,922,316	$0	$8,779,170
Associate Reformed Presbyterian Church (General Synod)	$4,920,208	$139,231	$264,675	$4,516,302	$4,682,925	$689,152	$172,476	$3,821,297
Brethren in Christ Church	$1,980,000	$60,000	$0	$1,920,000	$2,200,000	$82,406	$0	$2,117,594
Christian Church (Disciples of Christ)	$5,810,205	$1,587,428	$0	$4,222,777	$6,134,200	$1,712,531	$0	$4,421,669
Christian and Missionary Alliance [2]	$54,267,422	$0	$0	$54,267,422	$52,505,044	$0	$0	$52,505,044
Church of the Brethren [3]	$2,417,349	$147,215	$0	$2,270,134	$2,087,021	$199,819	$0	$1,887,202
Church of God General Conference (Oregon, Ill., and Morrow, Ga.)	$80,000	$0	$0	$80,000	$63,355	$0	$0	$63,355
Church of the Lutheran Confession	$329,823	$20,000	$0	$309,823	$314,804	$125,987	$0	$188,817
Church of the Nazarene	$54,653,601	$1,899,919	$0	$52,753,682	$52,721,095	$1,751,130	$0	$50,969,965
Churches of God General Conference [4]	$1,146,044	$15,944	$0	$1,130,100	$1,282,333	$48,490	$0	$1,233,843
Conservative Congregational Christian Conference [5]	$166,875	$0	$0	$166,875	$123,509	$0	$0	$123,509
Cumberland Presbyterian Church	$306,428	$13,082	$0	$293,346	$306,035	$15,728	$0	$290,307
The Episcopal Church [6]	$23,871,967	$3,000,000	$5,500,000	$15,371,967	$24,334,083	$3,000,000	$6,527,290	$14,806,793
Evangelical Congregational Church	$767,359	$42,270	$0	$725,089	$1,326,393	$0	$0	$1,326,393
Evangelical Covenant Church	$9,008,719	$0	$0	$9,008,719	$8,530,245	$0	$0	$8,530,245
Evangelical Lutheran Church in America [7]	$29,109,564	$3,025,562	$0	$26,084,001	$25,484,714	$3,942,905	$0	$21,541,809
Evangelical Lutheran Synod	$1,211,101	$988,897	$0	$222,204	$1,214,815	$884,164	$0	$330,651
Fellowship of Evangelical Churches	$785,676	$0	$0	$785,676	$700,159	$0	$0	$700,159
Free Methodist Church of North America	$10,831,707	$111,467	$0	$10,720,240	$12,578,589	$699,714	$0	$11,878,875
General Association of General Baptists	$1,945,215	$20,707	$0	$1,924,508	$2,082,916	$34,346	$0	$2,048,570
Lutheran Church-Missouri Synod [8]	$18,897,894	$1,722,316	$0	$17,175,578	$16,170,108	$2,737,162	$0	$13,432,946
Moravian Church in America, Northern Province [9]	$568,497	$86,340	$0	$482,157	$561,849	$49,021	$0	$512,828
The Orthodox Presbyterian Church [10]	$2,212,525	$355,996	$0	$1,856,529	$2,064,820	$358,528	$0	$1,706,292
Presbyterian Church in America	$25,890,591	$0	$0	$25,890,591	$27,627,770	$0	$0	$27,627,770
Presbyterian Church (U.S.A.) [11]	$47,223,000	$15,540,000	$65,000	$31,618,000	$35,539,000	$14,575,000	$0	$20,964,000
Primitive Methodist Church in the U.S.A. [12]	$503,286	$5,441	$0	$497,845	$568,032	$1,916	$0	$566,116
Reformed Church in America	$10,727,347	$0	$0	$10,727,347	$7,891,745	$405,218	$0	$7,486,527
Seventh-day Adventist, North Am. Division [13]	$53,745,101	$1,614,134	$0	$52,130,967	$51,459,266	$2,553,650	$0	$48,905,616
Southern Baptist Convention [14]	$259,394,000	$0	$0	$259,394,000	$275,747,000	$0	$0	$275,747,000
United Church of Christ	$11,299,684	$3,647,313	$0	$7,652,371	$10,834,552	$3,295,428	$0	$7,539,124
The United Methodist Church [15]	$177,000,000	$23,400,000	$26,000,000	$127,600,000	$120,400,000	$21,600,000	$15,700,000	$83,100,000
The Wesleyan Church	$9,769,938	$0	$0	$9,769,938	$13,105,882	$0	$0	$13,105,882
Wisconsin Evangelical Lutheran Synod	$8,957,945	$163,652	$0	$8,794,293	$10,886,785	$418,225	$0	$10,468,560

See endnotes on the page after the tables.

Appendix B-5: Overseas Missions Income in Current Dollars, 34 Denomination, 2007 and 2008

	2007 Overseas Missions Income				2008 Overseas Missions Income			
Denomination	Line 1.	Line 2.	Line 3.	Line 4.	Line 1.	Line 2.	Line 3.	Line 4.
Allegheny Wesleyan Methodist Connection	$332,511	$0	$0	$332,511	$306,946	$0	$0	$306,946
American Baptist Churches in the U.S.A. [1]	$15,703,238	$5,837,228	$0	$9,866,010	$16,099,000	$6,253,000	$0	$9,846,000
Associate Reformed Presbyterian Church (General Synod)	$5,088,825	$254,533	$14,670	$4,819,622	$5,838,994	$0	$0	$5,838,994
Brethren in Christ Church	$2,264,672	$92,850	$0	$2,171,822	$2,569,054	$116,556	$0	$2,452,498
Christian Church (Disciples of Christ)	$6,645,790	$1,871,786	$0	$4,774,004	$6,436,974	$1,909,503	$0	$4,527,471
Christian and Missionary Alliance [2]	$55,964,407	$0	$0	$55,964,407	$52,012,830	$0	$0	$52,012,830
Church of the Brethren [3]	$1,943,631	$206,977	$0	$1,736,654	$1,807,162	$58,642	$0	$1,748,520
Church of God General Conference (Oregon, Ill., and Morrow, Ga.)	$103,495	$0	$0	$103,495	$101,028	$0	$0	$101,028
Church of the Lutheran Confession	$313,700	$36,100	$0	$277,600	$361,641	$1,318	$0	$360,323
Church of the Nazarene	$52,195,781	$1,604,626	$0	$50,591,155	$54,573,954	$812,861	$0	$53,761,093
Churches of God General Conference [4]	$1,148,045	$29,124	$0	$1,118,921	$1,153,166	($34,087)	$0	$1,187,253
Conservative Congregational Christian Conference [5]	$169,508	$0	$0	$169,508	$84,460	$0	$0	$84,460
Cumberland Presbyterian Church	$368,334	$15,690	$0	$352,644	$322,815	$21,570	$0	$301,245
The Episcopal Church [6]	$26,940,269	$3,400,000	$8,511,710	$15,028,559	$27,589,783	$3,517,957	$9,472,472	$14,599,354
Evangelical Congregational Church	$1,464,523	$0	$0	$1,464,523	$1,583,478	$0	$0	$1,583,478
Evangelical Covenant Church	$7,954,834	$0	$0	$7,954,834	NA	NA	NA	NA
Evangelical Lutheran Church in America [7]	$26,161,433	$4,414,055	$0	$21,747,378	$27,518,419	$3,358,245	$0	$24,160,174
Evangelical Lutheran Synod	$1,389,221	$885,203	$0	$504,018	$1,070,241	$450,487	$0	$619,754
Fellowship of Evangelical Churches	$700,590	$0	$0	$700,590	$724,626	$0	$0	$724,626
Free Methodist Church of North America	$13,705,466	$1,226,998	$0	$12,478,468	$13,581,459	$336,594	$0	$13,244,864
General Association of General Baptists	$2,246,653	$67,605	$0	$2,179,048	$2,158,514	$52,673	$0	$2,105,841
Lutheran Church-Missouri Synod [8]	$16,086,361	$2,899,441	$0	$13,186,920	$17,473,964	$2,968,153	$0	$14,505,811
Moravian Church in America, Northern Province [9]	$542,968	$18,819	$0	$524,149	$504,041	$30,521	$0	$473,520
The Orthodox Presbyterian Church [10]	$1,899,674	$75,285	$0	$1,824,389	$1,820,552	$20,247	$0	$1,800,305
Presbyterian Church in America	$28,456,453	$0	$0	$28,456,453	$29,173,722	$0	$0	$29,173,722
Presbyterian Church (U.S.A.) [11]	$45,301,000	$4,935,000	$0	$40,366,000	$24,839,000	$4,920,000	$0	$19,919,000
Primitive Methodist Church in the U.S.A. [12]	$568,612	$1,802	$0	$566,810	$543,570	$1,132	$0	$542,438
Reformed Church in America	$7,931,523	$319,910	$0	$7,611,613	$8,160,053	$517,484	$0	$7,642,569
Seventh-day Adventist, North Am. Division [13]	$53,772,765	$1,734,653	$0	$52,038,112	$53,959,359	$2,457,879	$0	$51,501,480
Southern Baptist Convention [14]	$278,313,000	$0	$0	$278,313,000	$254,860,000	$0	$0	$254,860,000
United Church of Christ	$9,800,591	$2,493,501	$0	$7,307,090	$9,943,495	$2,698,518	$0	$7,244,977
The United Methodist Church [15]	$126,600,000	$21,400,000	$25,700,000	$79,500,000	$148,300,000	$23,800,000	$10,000,000	$114,500,000
The Wesleyan Church	$13,554,996	$0	$0	$13,554,996	$13,669,461	$0	$0	$13,669,461
Wisconsin Evangelical Lutheran Synod	$11,173,147	$500,952	$0	$10,672,195	$12,107,158	$471,779	$0	$11,635,379

See endnotes on the page after the tables.

Appendix B-5: Overseas Missions Income in Current Dollars, 33 Denominations, 2009 and 2010

	2009 Overseas Missions Income				2010 Overseas Missions Income			
Denomination	Line 1.	Line 2.	Line 3.	Line 4.	Line 1.	Line 2.	Line 3.	Line 4.
Allegheny Wesleyan Methodist Connection	$275,139	$0	$0	$275,139	$313,920	$0	$0	$313,920
American Baptist Churches in the U.S.A. [1]	$14,526,000	$4,941,000	$0	$9,585,000	$16,628,000	$4,507,000	$0	$12,121,000
Associate Reformed Presbyterian Church (General Synod)	$4,359,553	$124,682	$0	$4,234,871	$4,367,714	$122,084	$0	$4,245,630
Brethren in Christ Church	$2,612,767	$139,173	$0	$2,473,594	$2,614,574	$107,127	$0	$2,507,447
Christian Church (Disciples of Christ)	$5,826,676	$1,848,084	$0	$3,978,592	$5,964,111	$1,668,436	$0	$4,295,675
Christian and Missionary Alliance [2]	$52,888,984	$0	$0	$52,888,984	$53,693,745	$0	$0	$53,693,745
Church of the Brethren [3]	$2,022,629	$118,492	$0	$1,904,137	$2,120,575	$98,945	$0	$2,021,630
Church of God General Conference (Oregon, Ill., and Morrow, Ga./ McDonough, Ga.)	$166,433	$0	$0	$166,433	$108,017	$2,002	$0	$106,015
Church of the Lutheran Confession	$402,162	$0	$0	$402,162	$405,811	$0	$0	$405,811
Church of the Nazarene	$45,059,581	$1,688,702	$0	$43,370,879	$50,869,056	$3,600,786	$0	$47,268,270
Churches of God General Conference [4]	$1,355,136	$19,538	$0	$1,335,598	$1,718,312	$21,024	$0	$1,697,288
Conservative Congregational Christian Conference [5]	$18,397	$0	$0	$18,397	$10,124	$0	$0	$10,124
Cumberland Presbyterian Church	$300,535	$23,123	$0	$277,412	$326,906	$17,906	$0	$309,000
The Episcopal Church [6]	$30,493,164	$4,373,291	$10,508,830	$15,611,043	$38,106,292	$4,429,106	$13,625,923	$20,051,263
Evangelical Congregational Church	$1,462,048	$0	$0	$1,462,048	$1,416,294	$0	$0	$1,416,294
Evangelical Covenant Church	NA	NA	NA	NA	NA	NA	NA	NA
Evangelical Lutheran Church in America [7]	$27,574,196	$2,908,702	$0	$24,665,494	$25,482,057	$2,573,432	$0	$22,908,625
Evangelical Lutheran Synod	$1,964,975	$820,864	$0	$1,144,111	$1,327,743	$675,405	$0	$652,338
Fellowship of Evangelical Churches	$804,057	$0	$0	$804,057	$839,881	$0	$0	$839,881
Free Methodist Church of North America-USA	$12,032,082	$311,563	$0	$11,720,519	$12,354,513	$128,003	$0	$12,226,510
General Association of General Baptists	$1,978,712	$32,563	$0	$1,946,149	$1,724,984	$27,225	$0	$1,697,759
Lutheran Church-Missouri Synod [8]	$17,687,922	$2,196,136	$0	$15,491,786	$16,992,475	$984,639	$0	$16,007,836
Moravian Church in America, Northern Province [9]	$531,872	$28,055	$0	$503,817	$516,738	$23,570	$0	$493,168
The Orthodox Presbyterian Church [10]	$2,293,701	$314,657	$0	$1,979,044	$2,329,475	$523,507	$0	$1,805,968
Presbyterian Church in America	$27,219,278	$0	$0	$27,219,278	$25,327,324	$0	$0	$25,327,324
Presbyterian Church (U.S.A.) [11]	$27,182,967	$5,196,136	$0	$21,986,831	$35,638,050	$4,175,670	$0	$31,462,380
Primitive Methodist Church in the U.S.A. [12]	$430,150	$620	$0	$429,530	$405,337	$567	$0	$404,770
Reformed Church in America	$8,367,356	$179,496	$0	$8,187,860	$9,105,639	$235,004	$0	$8,870,635
Seventh-day Adventist, North Am. Division [13]	$52,019,434	$2,480,790	$0	$49,538,644	$51,744,014	$1,351,563	$0	$50,392,451
Southern Baptist Convention [14]	$255,427,000	$0	$0	$255,427,000	$264,924,000	$0	$0	$264,924,000
United Church of Christ	$9,531,462	$3,317,710	$0	$6,213,752	$9,380,301	$3,567,773	$0	$5,812,528
The United Methodist Church [15]	$124,120,000	$17,800,000	$9,400,000	$96,920,000	$166,640,000	$21,200,000	$10,200,000	$135,240,000
The Wesleyan Church	$14,139,092	$0	$0	$14,139,092	$14,780,950	$0	$0	$14,780,950
Wisconsin Evangelical Lutheran Synod	$10,706,565	($324,254)	$0.00	$11,030,819	$9,367,119	$99,538	$0	$9,267,581

See endnotes on the page after the tables.

Overseas Missions Income Data for Three Additional Denominations, in Current Dollars, 2003–2021

Denomination	2003 Overseas Missions Income, Line 4	2004 Overseas Missions Income, Line 4	2005 Overseas Missions Income, Line 4	2006 Overseas Missions Income, Line 4	2007 Overseas Missions Income, Line 4	2008 Overseas Missions Income, Line 4	2009 Overseas Missions Income, Line 4	2010 Overseas Missions Income, Line 4	2011 Overseas Missions Income, Line 4	2012 Overseas Missions Income, Line 4	2013 Overseas Missions Income, Line 4
Friends United Meeting	$1,314,527	$276,887 (partial year)	$863,445	$859,750	$937,142	$1,076,400	$888,142	$1,144,101	$965,104	$989,168	NA
Evangelical Covenant Church	See above	See above	See above	See above	See above	NA	NA	NA	NA	$9,876,142	$9,525,352
Mennonite Church-USA	$4,155,596	$3,854,139	$3,937,548	$3,876,657	$3,982,834	$4,176,371	$3,604,953	$3,261,148	$3,078,309	$3,617,736	$2,900,278

Appendix B-5: Overseas Missions Income in Current Dollars, 33 Denom., 2011 and 32 Denom., 2012

	2011 Overseas Missions Income				2012 Overseas Missions Income			
Denomination	Line 1.	Line 2.	Line 3.	Line 4.	Line 1.	Line 2.	Line 3.	Line 4.
Allegheny Wesleyan Methodist Connection 1	$244,376	$0	$0	$244,376	$284,379	$0	$0	$284,379
American Baptist Churches in the U.S.A.	$14,229,000	$4,226,000	$0	$10,003,000	$15,341,000	$4,849,000	$0	$10,492,000
Associate Reformed Presbyterian Church (General Synod)	$4,161,822	$40,172	$0	$4,121,650	$4,463,159	$140,136	$189,136	$4,133,887
Brethren in Christ Church	$2,445,941	$88,182	$0	$2,357,759	$2,679,772	$204,652	$0	$2,475,120
Christian Church (Disciples of Christ) 2	$5,384,548	$2,361,965	$0	$3,022,583	$4,913,966	$2,167,587	$0	$2,746,379
Christian and Missionary Alliance 3	$51,740,315	$0	$0	$51,740,315	$48,974,794	$0	$0	$48,974,794
Church of the Brethren	$1,855,666	$42,627	$0	$1,813,039	NA	NA	NA	NA
Church of God General Conference (Oregon, Ill., and Morrow, Ga./ McDonough, Ga.)	$82,803	$1,522	$0	$81,281	$81,267	$4,099	$0	$77,168
Church of the Lutheran Confession	$389,457	$0	$0	$389,457	$176,342	$0	$0	$176,342
Church of the Nazarene 4	$46,983,907	$2,214,694	$0	$44,769,213	$43,697,325	$731,913	$0	$42,965,412
Churches of God General Conference 5	$1,344,352	$14,421	$0	$1,329,931	$1,498,459	$15,811	$0	$1,482,648
Conservative Congregational Christian Conference	$21,855	$0	$0	$21,855	$1,750	$0	$0	$1,750
Cumberland Presbyterian Church 5	$441,629	$12,241	$0	$429,388	$1,406,000	$11,740	$0	$1,394,260
The Episcopal Church 6	$35,085,747	$3,915,786	$11,800,789	$19,369,172	$36,202,067	$4,916,844	$15,922,524	$15,362,699
Evangelical Congregational Church	$1,502,493	$0	$0	$1,502,493	$1,236,345	$0	$0	$1,236,345
Evangelical Covenant Church	NA	NA	NA	NA	See Three Additional Denominations Table (Total Contributions not available)			
Evangelical Lutheran Church in America 7	$26,199,965	$1,812,519	$0	$24,387,446	$25,883,084	$2,006,051	$0	$23,877,033
Evangelical Lutheran Synod	$699,851	$445,562	$0	$254,289	$916,940	$652,029	$0	$264,911
Fellowship of Evangelical Churches	$719,573	$0	$0	$719,573	$602,397	$0	$0	$602,397
Free Methodist Church of North America-USA	$13,790,352	$156,929	$0	$13,633,423	$13,143,094	$121,681	$0	$13,021,413
General Association of General Baptists	$1,699,280	$28,352	$0	$1,670,928	$2,181,279	$30,044	$0	$2,151,235
Lutheran Church-Missouri Synod 8	$19,170,000	$506,663	$0	$18,663,337	$20,298,197	$82,380	$0	$20,215,817
Moravian Church in America, Northern Province 9	$510,848	$19,684	$0	$491,164	$460,698	$20,710	$0	$439,988
The Orthodox Presbyterian Church 10	$1,870,011	$28,521	$0	$1,841,490	$1,931,535	$133,268	$0	$1,798,267
Presbyterian Church in America	$24,971,256	$0	$0	$24,971,256	$24,436,050	$0	$0	$24,436,050
Presbyterian Church (U.S.A.) 11	$26,311,242	$3,359,214	$0	$22,952,028	$26,083,759	$3,069,365	$0	$23,014,394
Primitive Methodist Church in the U.S.A. 12	$341,040	$573	$0	$340,467	$419,227	$416	$0	$418,811
Reformed Church in America	$6,858,714	$231,324	$0	$6,627,390	$7,235,908	$235,036	$0	$7,000,872
Seventh-day Adventist, North Am. Division 13	$57,206,455	$1,914,301	$0	$55,292,154	$53,011,220	$2,365,375	$0	$50,645,845
Southern Baptist Convention 14	$256,882,000	$0	$0	$256,882,000	$262,104,000	$0	$0	$262,104,000
United Church of Christ	$9,036,727	$3,357,817	$0	$5,678,910	$8,654,039	$3,410,790	$0	$5,243,249
The United Methodist Church 15	$132,000,000	$21,200,000	$8,200,000	$102,600,000	$107,900,000	$19,450,000	$7,100,000	$81,350,000
The Wesleyan Church	$14,788,726	$0	$0	$14,788,726	$16,556,897	$0	$0	$16,556,897
Wisconsin Evangelical Lutheran Synod	$9,899,138	$411,524	$0	$9,487,614	$8,597,168	($36,360)	$0	$8,633,528

See endnotes on the page after the tables.

Overseas Missions Income Data for Three Additional Denominations (continued)

Denomination	2014 Overseas Missions Income, Line 4	2015 Overseas Missions Income, Line 4	2016 Overseas Missions Income, Line 4	2017 Overseas Missions Income, Line 4	2018 Overseas Missions Income, Line 4	2019 Overseas Missions Income, Line 4	2020 Overseas Missions Income, Line 4	2021 Overseas Missions Income, Line 4
Friends United Meeting	NA	NA	NA	NA	NA	NA	NA	NA
Evangelical Covenant Church	$10,534,289	$11,645,103	$11,444,726	$10,717,240	$10,997,034	$ 11,981,066	$ 10,338,035	$ 9,141,379
Mennonite Church-USA	$3,220,289	$3,529,226	$3,139,149	$3,407,686	$2,697,983	$ 2,811,824	$2,062,733	NA

Appendix B-5: Overseas Missions Income in Current Dollars, 32 Denominations, 2013 and 2014

	2013 Overseas Missions Income				2014 Overseas Missions Income			
Denomination	Line 1.	Line 2.	Line 3.	Line 4.	Line 1.	Line 2.	Line 3.	Line 4.
Allegheny Wesleyan Methodist Connection	$266,255	$0	$0	$266,255	$270,953	$0	$0	$270,953
American Baptist Churches in the U.S.A. [1]	$15,592,000	$5,610,000	$0	$9,982,000	$15,976,000	$2,999,000	$0	$12,977,000
Associate Reformed Presbyterian Church (General Synod)	$4,561,525	$148,604	$22,395	$4,390,526	$4,262,053	$35,520	$0	$4,226,533
Brethren in Christ Church	$2,755,069	$99,052	$0	$2,656,017	$3,480,009	$179,130	$0	$3,300,879
Christian Church (Disciples of Christ)	$5,340,429	$2,615,209	$0	$2,725,220	$5,133,907	$2,549,424	$0	$2,584,483
Christian and Missionary Alliance [2]	$50,426,684	$0	$0	$50,426,684	$54,324,052	$0	$0	$54,324,052
Church of the Brethren [3]	NA	NA	NA	NA	NA	NA	NA	NA
Church of God General Conference (Oregon, Ill., and Morrow, Ga./ McDonough, Ga.)	$103,719	$1,512	$0	$102,207	$87,598	$1,512	$0	$86,086
Church of the Lutheran Confession	$208,419	$0	$0	$208,419	$204,023	$0	$0	$204,023
Church of the Nazarene	$44,098,660	$2,296,109	$0	$41,802,551	$46,043,804	$3,164,671	$0	$42,879,133
Churches of God General Conference [4]	$1,492,307	$25,688	$0	$1,466,619	$1,449,958	$17,002	$0	$1,432,956
Conservative Congregational Christian Conference [5]	$2,996	$0	$0	$2,996	$9,600	$0	$0	$9,600
Cumberland Presbyterian Church	$363,138	$12,491	$0	$350,647	$795,199	$27,116	$0	$768,083
The Episcopal Church [6]	$34,317,830	$3,918,434	$11,303,627	$19,095,769	$42,519,216	$5,175,771	$16,860,773	$20,482,672
Evangelical Congregational Church	$1,188,936	$0	$0	$1,188,936	$1,271,216	$0	$0	$1,271,216
Evangelical Covenant Church	See Three Additional Denominations Table (Total Contributions not available)				See Three Additional Denominations Table (Total Contributions not available)			
Evangelical Lutheran Church in America [7]	$27,285,548	$1,919,062	$0	$25,366,486	$29,391,319	$3,071,768	$0	$26,319,551
Evangelical Lutheran Synod	$992,024	$745,321	$0	$246,703	$824,449	$559,004	$0	$265,445
Fellowship of Evangelical Churches	$465,828	$0	$0	$465,828	$257,376	$0	$0	$257,376
Free Methodist Church of North America-USA	$12,374,111	$166,159	$0	$12,207,952	$13,434,196	$370,611	$0	$13,063,585
General Association of General Baptists	$2,153,058	$35,913	$0	$2,117,145	$1,046,835	$34,092	$0	$1,012,743
Lutheran Church-Missouri Synod [8]	$21,314,084	$41,667	$0	$21,272,417	$23,289,391	$7,750	$0	$23,281,641
Moravian Church in America, Northern Province [9]	$466,365	$18,539	$0	$447,826	$501,040	$22,390	$0	$478,650
The Orthodox Presbyterian Church [10]	$2,121,563	$15,724	$0	$2,105,839	$2,191,730	$80,552	$0	$2,111,178
Presbyterian Church in America	$25,049,022	$0	$0	$25,049,022	$25,131,181	$0	$0	$25,131,181
Presbyterian Church (U.S.A.) [11]	$24,258,507	$3,939,756	$0	$20,318,751	$21,961,358	$4,072,441	$0	$17,888,917
Primitive Methodist Church in the U.S.A. [12]	$441,154	$388	$0	$440,766	$340,000	$206	$0	$339,794
Reformed Church in America	$8,070,590	$254,222	$0	$7,816,368	$7,065,632	$220,816	$0	$6,844,816
Seventh-day Adventist, North Am. Division [13]	$53,641,885	$446,987	$0	$53,194,898	$53,674,153	$5,652,242	$0	$48,021,911
Southern Baptist Convention [14]	$265,429,000	$0	$0	$265,429,000	$265,633,000	$0	$0	$265,633,000
United Church of Christ	$8,065,706	$3,301,836	$0	$4,763,870	$7,845,446	$3,605,681	$0	$4,239,765
The United Methodist Church [15]	$110,600,000	$18,400,000	$5,500,000	$86,700,000	$98,000,000	$15,800,000	$5,800,000	$76,400,000
The Wesleyan Church	$16,309,860	$0	$0	$16,309,860	$16,186,471	$0	$0	$16,186,471
Wisconsin Evangelical Lutheran Synod	$8,515,044	$1,113,148	$0	$7,401,896	$9,767,440	$1,615,742	$0	$8,151,698

See endnotes on the page after the tables.

Appendix B-5: Overseas Missions Income in Current Dollars, 31 Denom., 2015 and 30 Denom., 2016

	2015 Overseas Missions Income				2016 Overseas Missions Income			
Denomination	Line 1.	Line 2.	Line 3.	Line 4.	Line 1	Line 2	Line 3	Line 4
Allegheny Wesleyan Methodist Connection	$279,143	$0	$0	$279,143	$266,163	$0	$0	$266,163
American Baptist Churches in the U.S.A. [1]	*$15,973,207*	*$3,567,552*	*$0*	*$12,405,655*	$16,801,364	$4,343,603	$0	$12,457,761
Associate Reformed Presbyterian Church (General Synod)	$4,637,798	$143,555	$0	$4,494,243	$4,770,826	$185,102	$0	$4,585,724
Brethren in Christ Church	$2,026,048	$28,574	$0	$1,997,474	$2,468,450	$189,619	$0	$2,278,831
Christian Church (Disciples of Christ)	$5,380,712	$2,736,363	$0	$2,644,349	$5,466,735	$2,961,475	$0	$2,505,260
Christian and Missionary Alliance [2]	$56,270,007	$0	$0	$56,270,007	$57,675,292	$0	$0	$57,675,292
Church of the Brethren [3]	NA	NA	NA	NA	NA	NA	NA	NA
Church of God General Conference (McDonough, Ga.)	$219,873	$1,512	$0	$218,361	NA	NA	NA	NA
Church of the Lutheran Confession	$164,708	$0	$0	$164,708	$176,019	$0	$0	$176,019
Church of the Nazarene	$45,556,416	$1,781,779	$0	$43,774,637	$43,421,673	$1,312,677	$0	$42,108,996
Churches of God General Conference [4]	$1,349,603	$16,835	$0	$1,332,768	$1,426,050	$10,607	$0	$1,415,443
Conservative Congregational Christian Conference [5]	$7,700	$0	$0	$7,700	$3,396	$0	$0	$3,396
Cumberland Presbyterian Church	$434,896	$27,116	$0	$407,780	$538,979	$0	$0	$538,979
The Episcopal Church [6]	$36,564,163	$3,830,237	$16,264,274	$16,469,652	$39,861,331	$4,513,849	$19,167,085	$16,180,397
Evangelical Congregational Church	$1,294,221	$0	$0	$1,294,221	$1,255,320	$0	$0	$1,255,320
Evangelical Covenant Church	See Three Additional Denominations Table (Total Contributions not available)				See Three Additional Denominations Table (Total Contributions not available)			
Evangelical Lutheran Church in America [7]	$28,807,175	$4,290,069	$0	$24,517,106	$29,713,464	$4,155,238	$0	$25,558,226
Evangelical Lutheran Synod	$806,121	$460,532	$0	$345,589	$1,334,120	$722,870	$0	$611,250
Fellowship of Evangelical Churches	$371,631	$0	$0	$371,631	$631,525	$0	$0	$631,525
Free Methodist Church of North America-USA	$14,233,540	$740,595	$0	$13,492,945	$13,875,655	$226,160	$0	$13,649,495
General Association of General Baptists	$1,833,807	$34,112	$0	$1,799,695	$1,676,651	$34,887	$0	$1,641,764
Lutheran Church-Missouri Synod [8]	$24,534,348	$339,798	$0	$24,194,550	$27,823,293	$646,609	$0	$27,176,684
Moravian Church in America, Northern Province [9]	$587,255	$24,213	$0	$563,042	$595,799	$25,028	$0	$570,771
The Orthodox Presbyterian Church [10]	$2,350,703	$20,008	$0	$2,330,695	$2,552,336	$310,749	$0	$2,241,587
Presbyterian Church in America	$25,870,900	$0	$0	$25,870,900	$25,838,573	$0	$0	$25,838,573
Presbyterian Church (U.S.A.) [11]	$25,607,238	$4,748,278	$0	$20,858,960	$24,122,349	$4,883,000	$0	$19,239,349
Primitive Methodist Church in the U.S.A. [12]	NA	NA	NA	NA	NA	NA	NA	NA
Reformed Church in America	$7,409,517	$232,352	$0	$7,177,165	$7,302,566	$292,317	$0	$7,010,249
Seventh-day Adventist, North Am. Division [13]	$42,448,228	($104,922)	$0	$42,553,150	$47,146,045	$4,726,537	$0	$42,419,508
Southern Baptist Convention [14]	$285,896,000	$0	$0	$285,896,000	$272,292,000	$0	$0	$272,292,000
United Church of Christ	$7,551,108	$3,142,272	$0	$4,408,836	$8,155,048	$3,360,576	$0	$4,794,472
The United Methodist Church [15]	$93,305,845	$20,612,310	$2,700,000	$69,993,535	$91,869,138	$13,580,758	$2,221,845	$76,066,535
The Wesleyan Church	$16,269,347	$0	$0	$16,269,347	$16,240,598	$0	$0	$16,240,598
Wisconsin Evangelical Lutheran Synod	$9,144,388	$762,300	$0	$8,382,088	$9,418,827	$1,499,819	$0	$7,919,008

See endnotes on the page after the tables.

Appendix B-5: Overseas Missions Income, in Current Dollars, 29 Denominations, 2017 and 2018

	2017 Overseas Missions Income				2018 Overseas Missions Income			
Denomination	Line 1.	Line 2.	Line 3.	Line 4.	Line 1.	Line 2.	Line 3.	Line 4.
Allegheny Wesleyan Methodist Connection	$280,063	$0	$0	$280,063	$218,722	$0	$0	$218,722
American Baptist Churches in the U.S.A. [1]	$15,584,519	$3,301,661	$0	$12,282,858	$15,987,302	$2,644,464	$0	$13,342,838
Associate Reformed Presbyterian Church (General Synod)	$4,558,852	$117,470	$0	$4,441,382	$4,860,047	$28,983	$0	$4,831,064
Brethren in Christ Church	$4,197,380	$524,078	$0	$3,673,302	$1,950,969	$0	$0	$1,950,969
Christian Church (Disciples of Christ)	$5,125,436	$2,735,573	$0	$2,389,863	$4,943,884	$2,849,301	$0	$2,094,583
Christian and Missionary Alliance [2]	$54,784,666	$0	$0	$54,784,666	$53,675,476	$0	$0	$53,675,476
Church of the Brethren [3]	NA	NA	NA	NA	NA	NA	NA	NA
Church of God General Conference (McDonough, Ga.)	$131,539	$1,512	$0	$130,027	$189,161	$1,512	$0	$187,649
Church of the Lutheran Confession	$272,236	$0	$0	$272,236	$281,732	$0	$0	$281,732
Church of the Nazarene	$48,040,431	$2,065,846	$0	$45,974,585	NA	NA	NA	NA
Churches of God General Conference [4]	$1,563,015	$15,541	$0	$1,547,474	$1,481,436	$20,461	$0	$1,460,975
Conservative Congregational Christian Conference [5]	$4,887	$0	$0	$4,887	$4,613	$0	$0	$4,613
Cumberland Presbyterian Church	$661,238	$45,766	$0	$615,472	$575,683	$51,020	$0	$524,663
The Episcopal Church [6]	$27,021,338	$6,214,908	$7,833,168	$12,973,262	$26,542,708	$6,635,677	$6,954,425	$12,952,606
Evangelical Congregational Church	$1,228,990	$0	$0	$1,228,990	$1,148,753	$0	$0	$1,148,753
Evangelical Covenant Church	See Three Additional Denominations Table (Total Contributions not available)				See Three Additional Denominations Table (Total Contributions not available)			
Evangelical Lutheran Church in America [7]	$30,917,663	$1,275,030	$0	$29,642,633	$31,803,057	$1,325,649	$0	$30,477,408
Evangelical Lutheran Synod	$1,345,472	$613,472	$0	$732,000	$1,032,944	$337,690	$0	$695,254
Fellowship of Evangelical Churches	$497,396	$0	$0	$497,396	$881,367	$0	$0	$881,367
Free Methodist Church of North America-USA	$13,416,036	$347,737	$0	$13,068,299	$13,423,440	$206,126	$0	$13,217,314
General Association of General Baptists	$2,084,599	$38,499	$0	$2,046,100	$1,661,301	$43,225	$0	$1,618,076
Lutheran Church-Missouri Synod [8]	$26,965,192	$986,628	$0	$25,978,564	$26,049,758	$735,179	$0	$25,314,579
Moravian Church in America, Northern Province [9]	$594,099	$25,324	$0	$568,775	$594,880	$12,833	$0	$582,047
The Orthodox Presbyterian Church [10]	$2,194,822	$16,967	$0	$2,177,855	$2,813,313	$269,272	$0	$2,544,041
Presbyterian Church in America	$25,152,705	$0	$0	$25,152,705	$24,703,928	$0	$0	$24,703,928
Presbyterian Church (U.S.A.) [11]	$27,753,626	$7,357,549	$0	$20,396,077	$22,061,055	$4,533,760	$0	$17,527,295
Primitive Methodist Church in the U.S.A. [12]	NA	NA	NA	NA	NA	NA	NA	NA
Reformed Church in America	$8,051,458	$292,055	$0	$7,759,403	$4,550,024	$226,253	$0	$4,323,771
Seventh-day Adventist, North Am. Division [13]	NA	NA	NA	NA	NA	NA	NA	NA
Southern Baptist Convention [14]	$274,512,000	$0	$0	$274,512,000	$279,410,000	$0	$0	$279,410,000
United Church of Christ	$7,724,904	$3,309,441	$0	$4,415,463	$7,275,281	$3,382,392	$0	$3,892,889
The United Methodist Church [15]	$77,253,400	$14,870,060	$950,170	$61,433,170	$90,284,345	$17,082,738	$5,410,323	$67,791,284
The Wesleyan Church	$15,129,898	$0	$0	$15,129,898	$16,170,162	$0	$0	$16,170,162
Wisconsin Evangelical Lutheran Synod	$11,439,447	$3,879,322	$0	$7,560,125	$10,077,537	$254,461	$0	$9,823,076

See endnotes on the page after the tables.

Line Descriptions on empty tomb, inc. Overseas Missions Income Data Request Form:

Line 1.: What was the amount of income raised in the U.S. during the calendar or fiscal year indicated for overseas ministries?

Line 2.: How many dollars of the total amount on Line 1. came from endowment, foundation, and other investment income?

Line 3.: Of the total amount on Line 1., what is the dollar value of government grants, either in dollars or in-kind goods for distribution?

Line 4.: Balance of overseas ministries income: Line 1. minus Lines 2. and 3.

Appendix B-5: Overseas Missions Income, in Current Dollars, 29 Denominations, 2019 and 2020

	2019 Overseas Missions Income				2020 Overseas Missions Income			
Denomination	Line 1.	Line 2.	Line 3.	Line 4.	Line 1.	Line 2.	Line 3.	Line 4.
Allegheny Wesleyan Methodist Connection	$197,899	$0	$0	$197,899	$176,878	$0	$0	$176,878
American Baptist Churches in the U.S.A. [1]	$16,072,895	$2,405,584	$0	$13,667,311	$15,768,384	$2,732,274	$0	$13,036,110
Associate Reformed Presbyterian Church (General Synod)	$5,183,184	$238,841	$0	$4,944,343	$5,408,175	$151,878	$447,000	$4,809,297
Brethren in Christ Church	$3,628,839	$757,503	$0	$2,871,335	$3,368,264	$611,422	$0	$2,756,842
Christian Church (Disciples of Christ)	$4,805,669	$2,633,423	$0	$2,172,246	$4,443,628	$2,400,214	$0	$2,043,414
Christian and Missionary Alliance [2]	$58,801,870	$0	$0	$58,801,870	$54,542,430	$0	$0	$54,542,430
Church of the Brethren [3]	NA	NA	NA	NA	NA	NA	NA	NA
Church of God General Conference (McDonough, Ga.)	$139,393	$1,512	$0	$137,881	$187,649	$1,512	$0	$186,137
Church of the Lutheran Confession	$257,230	$0	$0	$257,230	$282,667	$0	$0	$282,667
Church of the Nazarene	NA	NA	NA	NA	NA	NA	NA	NA
Churches of God General Conference [4]	$1,199,625	$8,071	$0	$1,191,554	$1,231,384	$6,738	$0	$1,224,646
Conservative Congregational Christian Conference [5]	$4,088	$0	$0	$4,088	$14,540	$0	$0	$14,540
Cumberland Presbyterian Church	$739,962	$33,539	$0	$706,423	$766,892	$47,024	$0	$719,868
The Episcopal Church [6]	$31,182,884	$10,795,721	$6,678,000	$13,709,163	$31,138,446	$7,784,612	$6,678,288	$16,675,546
Evangelical Congregational Church	$1,100,402	$0	$0	$1,100,402	$1,143,819	$0	$0	$1,143,819
Evangelical Covenant Church	See Three Additional Denominations Table (Total Contributions not available)				See Three Additional Denominations Table (Total Contributions not available)			
Evangelical Lutheran Church in America [7]	$27,524,026	$2,172,045	$0	$25,351,981	$27,953,648	$2,141,399	$0	$25,812,249
Evangelical Lutheran Synod	$1,118,104	$718,877	$0	$399,227	$1,068,328	$684,283	$0	$384,045
Fellowship of Evangelical Churches	$590,548	$0	$0	$590,548	$583,473	$0	$0	$583,473
Free Methodist Church of North America-USA	$12,979,053	$71,831	$0	$12,907,222	$12,224,724	$241,205	$0	$11,983,519
General Association of General Baptists	$1,673,422	$41,760	$0	$1,631,662	$2,045,969	$186,684	$0	$1,859,285
Lutheran Church-Missouri Synod [8]	$21,454,780	$673,018	$0	$20,781,762	$21,608,510	$783,835	$0	$20,824,675
Moravian Church in America, Northern Province [9]	$597,601	$17,688	$0	$579,913	$544,027	$14,673	$0	$529,354
The Orthodox Presbyterian Church [10]	$2,921,756	$87,975	$0	$2,833,781	$2,589,666	$17,849	$0	$2,571,817
Presbyterian Church in America	$26,549,871	$0	$0	$26,549,871	$25,248,587	$0	$0	$25,248,587
Presbyterian Church (U.S.A.) [11]	$21,105,144	$4,559,463	$0	$16,545,681	$17,947,692	$4,805,640	$0	$13,142,052
Primitive Methodist Church in the U.S.A. [12]	NA	NA	NA	NA	NA	NA	NA	NA
Reformed Church in America	$7,028,491	$396,990	$0	$6,631,501	$6,237,822	$349,876	$0	$5,887,946
Seventh-day Adventist, North Am. Division [13]	NA	NA	NA	NA	NA	NA	NA	NA
Southern Baptist Convention [14]	$277,463,000	$0	$0	$277,463,000	$284,550,000	$0	$0	$284,550,000
United Church of Christ	$7,444,999	$3,487,644	$0	$3,957,355	$6,864,348	$3,376,204	$0	$3,488,144
The United Methodist Church [15]	$76,920,894	$14,865,439	$7,507,274	$54,548,181	$80,746,345	$18,299,687	$2,493,344	$59,953,314
The Wesleyan Church	$15,860,834	$0	$0	$15,860,834	$16,268,002	$0	$0	$16,268,002
Wisconsin Evangelical Lutheran Synod	$11,163,440	$372,991	$0	$10,790,449	$11,639,536	$473,505	$0	$11,166,031

See endnotes on the page after the tables.

Appendix B-5: Overseas Missions Income, in Current Dollars, 28 Denominations, 2021

	2021 Overseas Missions Income			
Denomination	Line 1.	Line 2.	Line 3.	Line 4.
Allegheny Wesleyan Methodist Connection	$220,202	$0	$0	$220,202
American Baptist Churches in the U.S.A. [1]	NA	NA	NA	NA
Associate Reformed Presbyterian Church (General Synod)	$5,362,777	$203,602	$0	$5,159,175
Brethren in Christ Church	$4,152,450	$669,633	$0	$3,482,817
Christian Church (Disciples of Christ)	$4,764,139	$2,533,283	$0	$2,230,856
Christian and Missionary Alliance [2]	$55,293,355	$0	$0	$55,293,355
Church of the Brethren [3]	NA	NA	NA	NA
Church of God General Conference (McDonough, Ga.)	$200,476	$1,512	$0	$198,964
Church of the Lutheran Confession	$225,968	$0	$0	$225,968
Church of the Nazarene	NA	NA	NA	NA
Churches of God General Conference [4]	$1,104,374	$7,174	$0	$1,097,200
Conservative Congregational Christian Conference [5]	$9,600	$0	$0	$9,600
Cumberland Presbyterian Church	$783,872	$50,225	$0	$733,647
The Episcopal Church [6]	$36,882,945	$9,220,736	$10,171,000	$17,491,209
Evangelical Congregational Church	$1,193,416	$0	$0	$1,193,416
Evangelical Covenant Church	See Three Additional Denominations Table (Total Contributions not available)			
Evangelical Lutheran Church in America [7]	$26,812,284	$2,931,333	$0	$23,880,951
Evangelical Lutheran Synod	$1,212,065	$492,005	$0	$720,060
Fellowship of Evangelical Churches	$507,130	$0	$0	$507,130
Free Methodist Church of North America-USA	$13,783,377	$51,792	$0	$13,731,585
General Association of General Baptists	$1,722,045	$46,518	$0	$1,675,527
Lutheran Church-Missouri Synod [8]	$20,687,900	$1,391,161	$0	$19,296,739
Moravian Church in America, Northern Province [9]	$569,700	$34,245	$0	$535,455
The Orthodox Presbyterian Church [10]	$3,531,211	$491,031	$0	$3,040,180
Presbyterian Church in America	$25,367,761	$0	$0	$25,367,761
Presbyterian Church (U.S.A.) [11]	$17,240,149	$5,467,230	$0	$11,772,919
Primitive Methodist Church in the U.S.A. [12]	NA	NA	NA	NA
Reformed Church in America	$7,494,470	$311,760	$0	$7,182,710
Seventh-day Adventist, North Am. Division [13]	NA	NA	NA	NA
Southern Baptist Convention [14]	$283,094,000	$0	$0	$283,094,000
United Church of Christ	$7,362,651	$3,660,711	$0	$3,701,940
The United Methodist Church [15]	$57,500,106	$4,380,702	$0	$53,119,404
The Wesleyan Church	$11,833,336	$0	$0	$11,833,336
Wisconsin Evangelical Lutheran Synod	$14,126,407	$2,281,223	$0	$11,845,184

See endnotes on the page after the tables.

Notes to Appendix B-5: Overseas Missions Income, 2003 through 2021

[1] American Baptist Churches in the U.S.A.: An October 21, 2016, review of Overseas Missions Income data for the American Baptist Churches in the U.S.A. (ABCUSA) resulted in the following note. The Overseas Missions Income tables compare Overseas Missions Income as a percent of Total Contributions. As noted in the Introduction to Appendix B, for the ABCUSA, the membership data used in the calculation for giving as a percent of income was the number of members in congregations reporting Congregational Finances financial data. This partial Congregational Finances figure was added to Total Benevolences to produce a working Total Contributions figure for the communion. This working Total Contributions figure was divided by the number of members in reporting congregations, resulting in the per member giving figure for the ABCUSA. However, this working Total Contributions figure did not reflect the income of non-reporting congregations. As a result, the percent of Overseas Missions Income, the total the national office received from all congregations and individuals, as a percent of Total Contributions presented in the tables was likely higher than it would have been if a Total Contributions figure had included the income of non-reporting churches as well. For example, in 2014, the members in congregations reporting Congregational Finances numbered 166,551, or 13.92%, of the Total Membership figure of 1,196,828. Assuming non-reporting congregations received a similar level of Congregational Finances as did the reporting congregations, the reported Congregational Finances figure of $214,939,212 was divided by 13.92% to yield an adjusted Congregational Finances figure of $1,544,543,517, an estimate of the Congregational Finances donated by the 1.2 million ABCUSA Total Full/Confirmed Members. By adding this adjusted Congregational Finances figure to the reported Total Benevolences figure of $38,078,517, which latter figure included donations from the total membership for some Benevolences categories, an adjusted Total Contributions figure was estimated as $1,582,622,034. When 2014 Overseas Missions Income of $12,977,000 was divided by the adjusted Total Contributions figure of $1,582,622,034, the resulting percent of Overseas Missions as a percent of Total Contributions was now 0.82%, rather than the 2014 percent figure of 5.1% presented in the table. A similar adjustment could be made to the ABCUSA figures for data years 2003 through 2013, and for subsequent years after 2014.

[2] Christian and Missionary Alliance: "Since both domestic and overseas works are budgeted through the same source (our 'Great Commission Fund'), the amount on lines 1 and 4 are actual amounts spent on overseas missions. Total Congregational Contributions no longer includes building fund income, as of Data Year 2012."

[3] Church of the Brethren (through Data Year 2011): "This amount is national denominational mission and service, i.e., direct staffing and mission support, and does not include other projects funded directly by congregations or districts, or independent missionaries sponsored by congregations and individuals that would not be part of the denominational effort."

[4] Churches of God General Conference: "[Data Year] 2008 line 2 represents a net loss in investment income included in line 1. By adding this net loss amount back, line 4 represents the amount received in contributions from donors."

[5] Conservative Congregational Christian Conference: "The structure of this communion limits the national office coordination of overseas ministries activity. By design, congregations are to conduct missions directly, through agencies of their choice. The national office does not survey congregations about these activities. The one common emphasis of affiliated congregations is a focus on Micronesia, represented by the reported numbers. Data Year 2010: The amount raised is down because we didn't have any missionary that we sent overseas."

[6] The Episcopal Church: "The Episcopal Church (aka, The Domestic and Foreign Missionary Society) does not specifically raise money to support our non-domestic ministries. Many of the activities included in our budget are, however, involved, directly or indirectly with providing worldwide mission...Many other expenditures (e.g., for ecumenical and interfaith relations; for federal chaplaincies; for management's participation in activities of the worldwide Anglican Communion) contain an overseas component; but we do not separately track or report domestic vs. overseas expenses in those categories."

[7] Evangelical Lutheran Church in America: "Some assumptions were made in arriving with the total income, and those remain consistent from year to year."

[8] Lutheran Church—Missouri Synod: "The Lutheran Church-Missouri Synod (LCMS) is a confessing, orthodox Lutheran church comprising nearly 6,000 congregations and approximately 600,000 households (1.98 million baptized individuals) across North America. LCMS witness and mercy work is carried out by two distinct offices: The Office of International Mission and the Office of National Mission. The majority of funding was supplied by voluntary charitable gifts from individuals, congregations, and organizations connected to the Synod.

In more recent years, the 35 districts (regional jurisdictions) of the LCMS, along with a growing number of congregations and Lutheran mission societies, began sponsoring various mission fields and projects directly. That support did not flow through the LCMS. More information regarding the international work of the 35 LCMS districts can be found at <www.lcmsdistricts.org> and the 75-plus members of Association of Lutheran Mission Agencies at <www.alma-online.org>. Therefore, millions of dollars of additional support from LCMS members is raised and spent for international ministry each year which are not part of this report. Since these funds are not sent through the LCMS national office—and thus are not part of Synod's annual auditing process—the total amount cannot be verified and incorporated into this report."

[9] Moravian Church in America, Northern Province: "Data provided by the Board of World Mission, an interprovincial agency of the North American Moravian Church. The Overseas Missions Income figure was estimated for the Northern Province by the Board of World Mission of the Moravian Church. The Northern Province is the only one of the three Moravian Provinces that reports Total Contributions to the *Yearbook of American and Canadian Churches* series."

[10] Orthodox Presbyterian Church: "These figures, as in past years, reflect only what was given through our denominational Committee on Foreign Missions. In addition, $66,751 [in 2015] was given through our Committee on Diaconal Ministries for diaconal and disaster relief ministries administered by our missionaries on various overseas fields. Local churches and individuals also give directly to a variety of overseas missions causes."

[11] Presbyterian Church (U.S.A.): For Data Year 2005: "Nos. 1 & 4 Year 2005: Higher for Asian Tsunami Relief."

[12] Primitive Methodist Church in the U.S.A. (through Data Year 2014): "This only includes monies passing through our Denominational Mission Board (International). Many churches send money directly to a mission field."

[13] Seventh-day Adventist, North American Division (NAD): "This estimate, prepared by the General Conference Treasury Department and NAD Stewardship Department, is for the U.S. portion of the total donated by congregations in Canada, the U.S., Bermuda, and Guam."

[14] Southern Baptist Convention (SBC): Data Year 2017: The SBC International Mission Board changed from a calendar year to an October 1-September 30 fiscal year in 2017; the FY 2017 IMB numbers include the note for the 2017 Fiscal Year of October 1, 2016 through September 30, 2017: "Oct. 1-Dec. 31, 2016 Quarter numbers are repeated from the 2016 Calendar Year."

[15] The United Methodist Church: "The above represents total income received by the General Board of Global Ministries of The United Methodist Church, Inc."

Appendix B-6: Estimates of Giving

Year	A. Form 990 Direct Public Support '000s $	B. Form 990 Indirect Public Support '000s $	C. Form 990 Donor-Advised Funds '000s $	D. Form 990-EZ Contributions, Gifts and Grants '000s $	E. *Giving USA* Gifts to Foundations Billion $s	F. *Giving USA* Giving by Corporations Billion $s	G. *Giving USA* Giving by Foundations Billion $s	H. *Giving USA* Giving by Bequests Billion $s	I. *Giving USA* Individual Giving, Million $s	J. IRS Other than Cash Contributions '000s $	K. CE Giving to "Church, Religious Organizations" '000s $
1989	35,828,100	7,008,648		463,432	4.41	5.46	6.55	6.84	79,450	7,550,914	31,739,713
1990	39,395,074	8,055,551		644,613	3.83	5.46	7.23	6.79	79,000	7,494,016	30,673,887
1991	40,282,952	7,717,705		685,538	4.46	5.25	7.72	7.68	81,930	9,681,786	36,444,100
1992	43,986,785	9,110,478		813,604	5.01	5.91	8.64	9.54	87,200	9,632,779	35,159,679
1993	47,507,722	8,335,206		769,751	6.26	6.47	9.53	8.86	91,720	12,278,893	35,495,384
1994	49,238,498	8,722,141		780,896	6.33	6.98	9.66	11.13	92,280	14,739,299	37,189,109
1995	64,148,723	9,746,924		820,036	8.46	7.35	10.56	10.41	94,780	13,521,937	39,741,542
1996	69,419,764	10,230,304		988,638	12.63	7.51	12.00	12.03	107,350	21,298,819	39,053,447
1997	74,681,875	10,945,060		977,961	13.96	8.62	13.92	16.25	123,670	27,961,174	41,201,034
1998	83,359,695	12,711,938		1,053,669	19.92	8.46	17.01	13.41	137,680	29,255,985	44,831,015
1999	91,696,783	13,519,909		1,011,289	28.76	10.23	20.51	17.82	154,630	38,286,580	49,102,106
2000	103,453,445	15,176,512		1,086,099	24.71	10.74	24.58	20.25	174,090	47,256,104	48,737,216
2001	108,065,595	14,561,940		1,087,365	25.67	11.66	27.22	20.15	173,060	37,997,546	57,321,111
2002	102,802,550	15,223,713		1,095,317	19.16	10.79	26.98	21.16	173,790	34,293,125	62,476,667
2003	112,808,019	16,330,097		1,188,783	21.62	11.06	26.84	18.08	181,470	38,041,067	65,108,080
2004	124,575,951	16,947,398		1,397,630	20.32	11.36	28.41	18.53	201,960	43,373,209	65,712,121
2005	140,348,374	21,624,408		1,469,440	24.46	15.20	32.41	24.00	220,820	48,056,520	82,948,394
2006	150,214,837	26,049,161	10,368,453	1,551,098	27.10	14.52	34.91	21.90	224,760	52,631,443	89,469,764
2007	157,337,807	31,074,073	10,902,610	1,465,577	37.67	14.22	40.00	23.79	233,050	58,747,438	82,288,294
2008	145,209,711 *	26,844,533 *		13,851,212	30.14	12.40	42.21	31.24	213,760	40,421,411	89,915,680
2009	141,663,143 *	30,839,484 *		9,420,321	32.39	13.79	41.09	19.12	200,780	31,816,050	87,565,736
2010	154,613,448 *	26,987,759 *		3,871,551	26.07	15.82	40.95	23.40	207,990	44,321,908	80,055,360
2011	164,945,919 *	30,339,263 *		3,991,230	*30.20*	15.58	43.83	25.18	*213,910*	43,639,867	79,385,052
2012	179,838,212 *	29,221,473 *		4,281,733	40.13	17.22	46.37	24.63	244,380	49,047,100	91,358,669
2013	195,176,086 *	31,231,701 *		4,406,935	*39.49*	*15.87*	*48.54*	*23.81*	242,430	51,591,496	87,867,207
2014	210,351,749 *	35,307,105 *		4,911,898	*42.83*	18.26	*53.11*	*31.72*	252,250	65,330,485	89,460,486
2015	217,999,055 *	35,502,853 *		4,789,853	*36.26*	19.08	*54.26*	*35.14*	264,690	70,869,799	100,672,774
2016	240,766,353 *	36,843,729 *		4,767,424	*36.73*	*19.41*	*59.08*	*34.46*	279,380	79,569,011	96,814,559
2017	256,439,252 *	50,711,354 *		4,936,911	*47.52*	17.83	*65.86*	*38.03*	*302,790*	88,062,488	99,392,265
2018	252,548,001 *	39,435,611 *		5,123,282	*49.78*	*18.72*	*69.44*	*40.33*	*302,800*	83,501,257	103,732,973
2019	283,021,299 *	41,257,282 *		4,860,632	43.26	24.03	74.00	38.03	300,940	74,799,416	106,415,137

* Form 990 categories changed for the 2008 Form 990. For purposes of this analysis, the 2008-2019 category, "All other contributions, gifts, etc." is regarded as "Direct Public Support." "Indirect Public Support" is the sum of:
2008 data for: "Federated campaigns," $3,392,058; "Fundraising events," $5,919,225; "Related organizations," $17,533,250
2009 data for: "Federated campaigns," $3,070,589; "Fundraising events," $6,149,135; "Related organizations," $21,619,760
2010 data for: "Federated campaigns," $2,883,698; "Fundraising events," $7,123,029; "Related organizations," $16,981,032
2011 data for: "Federated campaigns," $2,863,639; "Fundraising events," $6,944,343; "Related organizations," $20,531,281
2012 data for: "Federated campaigns," $2,740,782; "Fundraising events," $7,680,228; "Related organizations," $18,800,463
2013 data for: "Federated campaigns," $2,695,700; "Fundraising events," $8,541,301; "Related organizations," $19,994,700
2014 data for: "Federated campaigns," $2,641,761; "Fundraising events," $9,332,117; "Related organizations," $23,333,227
2015 data for: "Federated campaigns," $2,360,782; "Fundraising events," $9,747,800; "Related organizations," $23,394,271
2016 data for: "Federated campaigns," $2,099,763; "Fundraising events," $9,823,092; "Related organizations," $24,920,874
2017 data for: "Federated campaigns," $2,278,088; "Fundraising events," $10,492,935; "Related organizations," $37,940,331
2018 data for: "Federated campaigns," $1,878,539; "Fundraising events," $10,522,222; "Related organizations," $27,034,850
2019 data for: "Federated campaigns," $1,913,023; "Fundraising events," $9,220,752; "Related organizations," $30,123,507

Source: Columns A., B., and C.

1989	"Form 990 Returns of Nonprofit Charitable Section 501(c)(3) Organizations: Selected Income Statement and Balance Sheet Items, by Size of Total Assets, 1989"; downloaded 6/12/2007; <http://www.irs.gov/pub/irs-soi/89eo01as.xls>; p. 2 of 6/13/2007 12:26 PM printout.
1990	"Table 1.--1990, Form 990 Returns of Organizations Tax-Exempt Under Internal Revenue Code Sections 501(c)(3)-(9): Selected Income Statement and Balance Sheet Items, by Code Section"; downloaded 6/12/2007; <http://www.irs.gov/pub/irs-soi/90np01fr.xls>; p. 3 of 6/13/2007 1:48 PM printout.
1991	"Form 990 Returns of Nonprofit Charitable Internal Revenue Code Section 501(c)(3) Organizations: Selected Income Statement and Balance Sheet Items, by Asset Size, 1991"; Internal Revenue Service, SOI Bulletin, Pub. 1136 (Rev. 8-96); downloaded 6/12/2007; <http://www.irs.gov/pub/irs-soi/91eo01as.xls>; p. 2 of 6/13/2007 2:48 PM printout.
1992-1999	"Table 1.--[Year], Form 990 Returns of Nonprofit Charitable Internal Revenue Code Section 501(c)(3) Organizations: Selected Income Statement and Balance Sheet Items, by Asset Size"; Internal Revenue Service, Statistics of Income Bulletin, Pub. 1136; downloaded 6/12/2007;
1992	(Rev. 8-96); <http://www.irs.gov/pub/irs-soi/92eo01as.xls>; p. 2 of 6/13/2007 3:21 PM printout.
1993	(Rev. 4-97); <http://www.irs.gov/pub/irs-soi/93eo01as.xls>; p. 2 of 6/13/2007 3:39 PM printout.
1994	Spring 1998 (Rev. 5-98); <http://www.irs.gov/pub/irs-soi/94eo01as.xls>; p. 2 of 6/13/2007 4:12 PM printout.
1995	Winter 1998/1999 (Rev. 2/99); <http://www.irs.gov/pub/irs-soi/95eotab1.xls>; p. 2 of 6/14/2007 9:25 AM printout.
1996	Winter 1999/2000 (Rev. 2/00); <http://www.irs.gov/pub/irs-soi/96eo01c3.xls>; p. 1 of 6/14/2007 9:55 AM printout.
1997	Fall 2000 (Rev. 11-2000); <http://www.irs.gov/pub/irs-soi/97eotb1.xls>; p. 1 of 6/14/2007 10:09 AM printout.
1998	Fall 2001 (Rev. 11-01); <http://www.irs.gov/pub/irs-soi/98eo01as.xls>; p. 1 of 6/14/2007 10:17 AM printout.
1999	Fall 2002 (Rev. 12-02); <http://www.irs.gov/pub/irs-soi/99eo01as.xls>; p. 1 of 6/14/2007 10:29 AM printout.

Appendix B-6: Estimates of Giving (continued)

2000	"Table 1.--2000, Form 990 Returns of Nonprofit Charitable Section 501(c)(3) Organizations: Selected Balance Sheet and Income Statement Items, by Size of Total Assets"; IRS, Statistics of Income Bulletin, Fall 2003, Pub. 1136, (Rev. 12-03); downloaded 6/12/2007; <http://www.irs.gov/pub/irs-soi/00eo01ta.xls>; p. 2 of 6/14/2007 10:43 AM printout.
2001	Form 990 Returns of Nonprofit Charitable Section 501(c)(3) Organizations: Selected Balance Sheet and Income Statement Items, by Asset Size, Tax Year 2001"; downloaded 6/12/2007; <http://www.irs.gov/pub/irs-soi/01eo01as.xls>; p. 1 of 6/14/2007 10:55 AM printout.
2002	"Table 1.--Form 990 Returns of Nonprofit Charitable Section 501(c)(3) Organizations: Selected Balance Sheet and Income Statement Items, by Asset Size, Tax Year 2002"; IRS, Statistics of Income Bulletin, Fall 2005, Pub. 1136, (Rev.12-05); downloaded 6/12/2007; <http://www.irs.gov/pub/irs-soi/02eo01as.xls>; p. 2 of 6/14/2007 4:31 PM printout.
2003	"Table 1: Form 990 Returns of Nonprofit Charitable Section 501 (c)(3) Organizations: Selected Balance Sheet and Income Statement Items, by Asset Size, Tax Year 2003"; IRS SOI Division, August 2006; downloaded 6/12/2007; <http://www.irs.gov/pub/irs-soi/03eo01as.xls>; p. 1 of 6/14/2007 4:42 PM printout.
2004-2005	Table 1: Form 990 Returns of 501(c)(3) Organizations: Balance Sheet and Income Statement Items, By Asset Size,Tax Year [Year]; IRS, SOI Division,
2004	August 2007; downloaded 3/15/2008; <http://www.irs.gov/pub/irs-soi/04eo01as.xls>; p. 1 of 3/15/2008 9:59 AM printout.
2005	August 2008; downloaded 3/5/2009; <http://www.irs.gov/pub/irs-soi/05eo01as.xls>; p. 1 of 3/5/2009 3:59 PM printout.
2006-2008	"Table 1. Form 990 Returns of 501(c)(3) Organizations: Balance Sheet and Income Statement Items, by Asset Size, Tax Year [Year]"; IRS, SOI Division,
2006	August 2009; downloaded 4/29/2010; <http://www.irs.gov/pub/irs-soi/06eo01as.xls>; p. 1 of 4/29/2010 3:27 PM printout.
2007	July 2010; downloaded 4/28/2011; <http://www.irs.gov/pub/irs-soi/07eo01.xls>; p. 1 of 4/29/2011 9:10 AM printout.
2008	July 2011; downloaded 3/26/2012; <http://www.irs.gov/pub/irs-soi/08eo01.xls>; p. 1 of 3/26/2012 2:58 PM printout.
2009	"Table 1--Selected Form 990 Data for 501(c)(3) Organizations, 2009"; IRS; downloaded 2/12/13; <http://www.irs.gov/PUP/taxstats/charitablestats/09eo01.xls>; p. 1 of 2/12/13 10:13 AM printout.
2010	"Table 1. Form 990 Returns of 501(c)(3) Organizations: Balance Sheet and Income Statement Items, by Asset Size, Tax Year 2010"; IRS, Statistics of Income Division, July 2013; downloaded 11/11/13; <http://www.irs.gov/pub/irs-soi/10eo01.xls>; p. 1 of 11/17/13 2:04 PM printout.
2011	"Table 1. Form 990 Returns of 501(c)(3) Organizations: Balance Sheet and Income Statement Items, by Asset Size, Tax Year 2011"; IRS, Statistics of Income Division, July 2014; download 11eo01.xls; downloaded November 13, 2014; <http://www.irs.gov/pub/irs-soi/11eo01.xls>; p. 1 of 11/13/2014 2:14 PM printout
2012	"Table 1. Form 990 Returns of 501(c)(3) Organizations: Balance Sheet and Income Statement Items, by Asset Size, Tax Year 2012"; IRS, Statistics of Income Division, July 2016; download 12eo01.xls; downloaded April 26, 2016; <https://www.irs.gov/pub/irs-soi/12eo01.xls>; p. 1 of 4/26/2016 5:30 PM printout.
2013	"Table 1. Form 990 Returns of 501(c)(3) Organizations: Balance Sheet and Income Statement Items, by Asset Size, Tax Year 2013"; IRS, Statistics of Income Division, July 2016; download 13eo01.xls; downloaded February 2, 2017; <https://www.irs.gov/pub/irs-soi/13eo01.xls>; p. 1 of 2/3/2017 2:54 PM printout.
2014	"Table 1. Form 990 Returns of 501(c)(3) Organizations: Balance Sheet and Income Statement Items, by Asset Size, Tax Year 2014"; IRS, Statistics of Income Division, July 2017; download 14eo01.xls; downloaded August 21, 2018; <https://www.irs.gov/pub/irs-soi/14eo01.xls>; p. 1 of 8/21/2018 5:19 PM printout.
2016	"Table 1. Form 990 Returns of 501(c)(3) Organizations: Balance Sheet and Income Statement Items, by Asset Size, Tax Year 2015"; IRS, Statistics of Income Division, July 2018; download 15eo01.xlsx; downloaded March 5, 2019; <https://www.irs.gov/pub/irs-soi/15eo01.xlsx>; p. 1 of 3/5/2019 3:42 PM printout.
2016	"Table 1. Form 990 Returns of 501(c)(3) Organizations: Balance Sheet and Income Statement Items, by Asset Size, Tax Year 2016"; IRS, Statistics of Income Division, September 2019; download 16eo01.xlsx; downloaded April 27, 2020. <https://www.irs.gov/pub/irs-soi/16eo01.xlsx>; p. 1 of 4/27/2020 6:35 PM printout.
2017	"Table 1. Form 990 Returns of 501(c)(3) Organizations: Balance Sheet and Income Statement Items, by Asset Size, Tax Year 2017"; IRS, Statistics of Income Division, August 2020; download 17eo01.xlsx; downloaded December 13, 2021; <https://www.irs.gov/pub/irs-soi/17eo01.xlsx>; p. 1 of 12/13/2021 4:14 PM printout.
2018	"Table 1. Form 990 Returns of 501(c)(3) Organizations: Balance Sheet and Income Statement Items, by Asset Size, Tax Year 2018"; IRS, Statistics of Income Division, August 2020; download 18eo01.xlsx; downloaded October 21, 2022; <https://www.irs.gov/pub/irs-soi/18eo01.xlsx>; p. 1 of 10/21/2022 5:44 PM printout.
2019	"Table 1. Form 990 Returns of 501(c)(3) Organizations: Balance Sheet and Income Statement Items, by Asset Size, Tax Year 2019"; IRS, Statistics of Income Division, April 2023; download 19eo01.xlsx; downloaded February 13, 2024; <https://www.irs.gov/pub/irs-soi/19eo01.xlsx>; p. 1 of 2/13/2024 5:53 PM printout.

Source: Col. D.

1989	"Form 990EZ Returns of Organizations Tax-Exempt Under Internal Revenue Code Sections 501(c)(3)-(9): Selected Income Statement and Balance Sheet Items, by Code Section, 1989"; IRS, SOI Tax Stats; downloaded 6/15/2007; <http://www.irs.gov/pub/irs-soi/89eo04cs.xls>; p. 1 of 6/16/2007 8:56 AM printout.
1990	"Table 2.--1990, Form 990EZ Returns of Organizations Tax-Exempt Under Internal Revenue Code Sections 501(c)(3)-(9): Selected Income Statement and Balance Sheet Items, by Code Section"; IRS, SOI Tax Stats; downloaded 6/15/2007; <http://www.irs.gov/pub/irs-soi/90np02ro.xls>; p.1 of 6/16/2007 9:11 AM printout.
1991	"Form 990EZ Returns of Organizations Tax-Exempt Under Internal Revenue Code Sections 501(c)(3)-(9): Selected Income Statement and Balance Sheet Items, by Code Section, 1991"; IRS, SOI Bulletin, Pub. 1136 (Rev. 8-96); downloaded 6/15/2007; <http://www.irs.gov/pub/irs-soi/91eo04cs.xls>; p.1 of 6/16/2007 9:22 AM printout.
1992-1993	"Table 4.--[Year], Form 990EZ Returns of Organizations Tax-Exempt Under Internal Revenue Code Sections 501(c)(3)-(9): Selected Income Statement and Balance Sheet Items, by Code Section"; IRS, SOI Bulletin, Pub.1136; downloaded 6/15/2007;
1992	(Rev. 8-96); <http://www.irs.gov/pub/irs-soi/92eo04cs.xls>; p.1 of 6/16/2007 9:39 AM printout.
1993	(Rev. 4-97); <http://www.irs.gov/pub/irs-soi/93eo04cs.xls>; p.1 of 6/16/2007 9:48 AM printout.
1994-1995	"Table 4.--[Year], Form 990-EZ Returns of Organizations Tax-Exempt Under Internal Revenue Code Sections 501 (c)(3)-(9): Selected Balance Sheet and Income Statement Items, by Code Section"; IRS, SOI Bulletin, Pub. 1136; downloaded 6/15/2007;
1994	Spring 1998, (Rev. 5-98); <http://www.irs.gov/pub/irs-soi/94eo04cs.xls>; p. 1 of 6/16/2007 9:58 AM printout.
1995	Winter 1998/99, (Rev. 2/99); <http://www.irs.gov/pub/irs-soi/95eotab4.xls>; p. 1 of 6/16/2007 10:09 AM printout.
1996	"Table 3.--1996, Form 990-EZ Returns of Nonprofit Charitable Section 501(c)(3) Organizations: Selected Balance Sheet and Income Statement Items, by Asset Size"; IRS, SOI Bulletin, Winter 1999/2000; Pub. 1136, (Rev. 2/00); downloaded 6/15/2007; <http://www.irs.gov/pub/irs-soi/96eo03c3.xls>; p. 1 of 6/16/2007 10:28 AM printout.
1997-2000	"Table 4.--[Year], Form 990-EZ Returns of Organizations Tax-Exempt Under Internal Revenue Code Sections 501(c)(3)-(9): Selected Balance Sheet and Income Statement Items, by Code Section"; IRS, SOI Bulletin, Pub. 1136; downloaded 6/15/2007;
1997	Fall 2000, (Rev. 11-2000); <http://www.irs.gov/pub/irs-soi/97eotb4.xls>; p. 1 of 6/16/2007 10:36 AM printout.
1998	Fall 2001, (Rev. 11-2001); <http://www.irs.gov/pub/irs-soi/98eo04cs.xls>; p. 1 of 6/16/2007 10:43 AM printout.
1999	Fall 2002, (Rev. 12-02); <http://www.irs.gov/pub/irs-soi/99eo04cs.xls>; p. 1 of 6/16/2007 11:22 AM printout.
2000	Fall 2003, (Rev. 12-03); <http://www.irs.gov/pub/irs-soi/00eo04cs.xls>; p. 1 of 6/16/2007 11:29 AM printout.
2001	"Form 990-EZ Returns of Organizations Tax-Exempt Under Internal Revenue Code Sections 501(c)(3)-(9): Selected Balance Sheet and Income Statement Items, by Code Section, Tax Year 2001"; IRS, SOI Tax Stats, downloaded 6/15/2007; <http://www.irs.gov/pub/irs-soi/01eo04cs.xls>; p. 1 of 6/16/2007 11:34 AM printout.
2002	"Table 4.--Form 990-EZ Returns of Organizations Tax-Exempt Under Internal Revenue Code Sections 501(c)(3)-(9): Selected Balance Sheet and Income Statement Items, by Code Section, Tax Year 2002"; IRS, SOI Bulletin, Fall 2005, Pub. 1136 (Rev. 12-05); downloaded 6/15/2007; <http://www.irs.gov/pub/irs-soi/02eo04ty.xls>; p. 1 of 6/17/2007 7:50 AM printout.
2003	"Table 4: Form 990-EZ Returns of Organizations Tax-Exempt Under Internal Revenue Code Sections 501(c)(3)-(9): Selected Balance Sheet and Income Statement Items, by Code Section, Tax Year 2003"; IRS, SOI Division, August 2006; downloaded 6/15/2007; <http://www.irs.gov/pub/irs-soi/03eo04ty.xls>; p. 1 of 6/17/2007 8:07 AM printout.
2004	"Table 4: Form 990-EZ Returns of 501(c)(3)-(9) Organizations: Balance Sheet and Income Statement Items, by Code Section, Tax Year 2004"; IRS, SOI Division, August 2007; downloaded 3/14/2008; <http://www.irs.gov/pub/irs-soi/04eo04ty.xls>; p. 1 of 3/14/2008 3:50 PM printout.
2005	"Table 4: Form 990-EZ Returns of 501(c)(3)-(9) Organizations: Selected [I]tems, by Code Section, Tax Year 2005"; IRS, SOI Division, August 2008; downloaded 3/5/2009; <http://www.irs.gov/pub/irs-soi/05eo04ty.xls>; p. 1 of 3/5/2009 4:11 PM printout.

Appendix B-6: Estimates of Giving (continued)

2006-2008	"Table 4: Form 990-EZ Returns of 501(c)(3)-(9) Organizations: Selected Items, by Code Section, Tax Year [Year]"; IRS, SOI Division.
2006	August 2009; <http://www.irs.gov/pub/irs-soi/06eo04ty.xls>; p. 1 of 4/29/2010 5:34 PM printout.
2007	July 2010; <http://www.irs.gov/pub/irs-soi/07eo04.xls>; p. 1 of 4/29/2010 3:41 PM printout.
2008	July 2011; <http://www.irs.gov/pub/irs-soi/08eo04.xls>; p. 1 of 3/23/2012 9:00 PM printout.
2009	"Table 4–Selected Form 990-EZ Data 501(c)(4[sic])-Orgs, 2009"; IRS; downloaded 2/9/13; <http://www.irs.gov/PUP/taxstats/charitablestats/09eo04.xls>; p. 1 of 2/9/2013 1:47 PM printout.
2010	"Table 4. Form 990-EZ Returns of 501(c)(3)-(9) Organizations: Selected Items, by Code Section, Tax Year 2010"; IRS, Statistis of Income Division, July 2013 downloaded 11/11/13; <http://www.irs.gov/pub/irs-soi/10eo04.xls>; p. 1 of 11/11/2013 12:11 PM printout.
2011	"Table 4. Form 990-EZ Returns of 501(c)(3)-(9) Organizations: Selected Items, by Code Section, Tax Year 2011"; IRS, Statistics of Income Division, July 2014; download 11eo04.xls; downloaded November 12, 2014; <http://www.irs.gov/pub/irs-soi/11eo04.xls>; p. 1 of 11/12/2014 5:01 PM printout.
2012	"Table 4. Form 990-EZ Returns of 501(c)(3)-(9) Organizations: Selected Items, by Code Section, Tax Year 2012"; IRS, Statistics of Income Division, July 2015; download 12eo04.xls; downloaded April 26, 2016; <https://www.irs.gov/pub/irs-soi/12eo04.xls>; p. 1 of 4/27/2016 11:31 AM printout.
2013	"Table 4. Form 990-EZ Returns of 501(c)(3)-(9) Organizations: Selected Items, by Code Section, Tax Year 2013"; IRS, Statistics of Income Division, July 2016; download 13eo04.xls; downloaded February 2, 2017; <https://www.irs.gov/pub/irs-soi/13eo04.xls>; p. 1 of 2/2/2017 5:15 PM printout.
2014	"Table 4. Form 990-EZ Returns of 501(c)(3)-(9) Organizations: Selected Items, by Code Section, Tax Year 2014"; IRS, Statistics of Income Division, July 2017; download 14eo04.xls; downloaded August 21, 2018; <https://www.irs.gov/pub/irs-soi/14eo04.xls>; p. 1 of 8/22/2018 4:42 PM printout.
2015	"Table 4. Form 990-EZ Returns of 501(c)(3)-(9) Organizations: Selected Items, by Code Section, Tax Year 2015"; IRS, Statistics of Income Division, July 2018; download 15eo04.xlsx; downloaded March 5, 2019; <https://www.irs.gov/pub/irs-soi/15eo04.xls>; p. 1 of 3/5/2019 1:13 PM printout.
2016	"Table 4. Form 990-EZ Returns of 501(c)(3)-(9) Organizations: Selected Items, by Code Section, Tax Year 2016"; IRS, Statistics of Income Division, September 2019; download 16eo04.xlsx; downloaded April 27, 2020; <https://www.irs.gov/pub/irs-soi/16eo04.xlsx>; p. 1 of 4/27/2020 5:05 PM printout.
2017	"Table 4. Form 990-EZ Returns of 501(c)(3)-(9) Organizations: Selected Items, by Code Section, Tax Year 2017"; IRS, Statistics of Income Division, August 2020; download 17eo04.xlsx; downloaded December 13, 2021; <https://www.irs.gov/pub/irs-soi/17eo04.xlsx>; p. 1 of 12/13/2021 2:53 PM printout.
2018	"Table 4. Form 990-EZ Returns of 501(c)(3)-(9) Organizations: Selected Items, by Code Section, Tax Year 2018"; IRS, Statistics of Income Division, August 2020; download 18eo01.xlsx; downloaded October 21, 2022; <https://www.irs.gov/pub/irs-soi/18eo04.xlsx>; p. 1 of 10/21/2022 4:59 PM printout.
2019	"Table 4. Form 990-EZ Returns of 501(c)(3)-(9) Organizations: Selected Items, by Code Section, Tax Year 2019"; IRS, Statistics of Income Division, April 2023; download 19eo04.xlsx; <https://www.irs.gov/pub/irs-soi/19eo04.xlsx>; p. 1 of 2/13/2024 5:11 PM printout.

Source: Col. E.

1989-2019	*Giving USA 2023: The Annual Report on Philanthropy for the Year 2022* (2023). Chicago: Giving USA Foundation, p. 301.

Source: Columns F., G., H., and I.

1989-2019	*Giving USA 2023*, p.298.

Source: Col. J.

1989	Internal Revenue Service, Statistics of Income—1989, Individual Income Tax Returns, "Table 2.1—Returns with Itemized Deductions: Sources of Income, Adjustments, Itemized Deductions by Type, Exemptions, and Tax Items by Size of Adjusted Gross Income" (Internal Revenue Service: Washington, DC, 1992), p. 41.
1990-2001	"Table 1.--Individual Income Tax Returns, Selected Deductions, 1990-2001"; IRS Statistics of Income Winter 2003-2004 Bulletin, Pub 1136; <http://www.irs.gov/pub/irs-soi/01in01sd.xls>; pp. 1-2 of 9/6/2005 8:59 AM printout.
2002	"Table 3.--2002, Individual Income Tax Returns with Itemized Deductions, by Size of Adjusted Gross Income"; IRS, Statistics of Income Bulletin, Fall 2004, Pub. 1136, (Rev. 12-04); <http://www.irs.gov/pub/irs-soi/02in03ga.xls>; p. 5 of 9/6/2005 10:58 AM printout.
2003	"Table 3.---2003, Individual Income Tax Returns with Itemized Deductions, by Size of Adjusted Gross Income"; IRS, Statistics of Income Bulletin, Fall 2005, Pub. 1136, (Rev. 12-05); <http://www.irs.gov/pub/irs-soi/03in03ag.xls>; p. 5 of 6/6/2006 3:38 PM printout.
2004	"Table 3--Returns with Itemized Deductions: Sources of Income, Adjustments, Itemized Deductions by Type, Exemptions, and Tax Items, by Size of Adjusted Gross Income, Tax year 2004"; IRS, Statistics of Income Division, July 2006; <http://www.irs.gov/pub/irs-soi/04in03id.xls>; p. 3 of 8/12/2007 1:33 PM printout.
2005-2011	"Table 3. Returns with Itemized Deductions: Itemized Deductions by Type and by Size of Adjusted Gross Income, Tax Year [Year]"; IRS;
2005	<http://www.irs.gov/pub/irs-soi/05in03id.xls>; p. 3 of 4/10/2008 7:07 PM printout.
2006	<http://www.irs.gov/pub/irs-soi/06in03id.xls>; p. 3 of 3/10/2009 11:34AM printout.
2007	<http://www.irs.gov/pub/irs-soi/07in03id.xls>; p. 3 of 4/28/2010 4:48 PM printout.
2008	<http://www.irs.gov/pub/irs-soi/08in03id.xls>; p. 3 of 4/28/2011 12:09 PM printout.
2009	<http://www.irs.gov/pub/irs-soi/09in03id.xls>; p. 3 of 4/9/2012 5:05 PM printout.
2010	<http://www.irs.gov/pub/irs-soi/10in03id.xls>; p. 3 of 2/28/2013 4:58 PM printout.
2011	<http://www.irs.gov/pub/irs-soi/11in03id.xls>; p. 3 of 11/16/2014 3:14 PM printout.
2012	"Table 2.1. Returns with Itemized Deductions: Sources of Income, Adjustments, Itemized Deductions by Type, Exemptions, and Tax Items, by Size of Adjusted Gross Income, Tax Year 2012"; IRS, Statistics of Income Division, Publication 1304, July 2014; download 12in21id.xls; <https://www.irs.gov/pub/irs-soi/12in21id.xls>; p. 7 of 5/6/2016 4:59 PM printout.
2013	"Table 2.1. Returns with Itemized Deductions: Sources of Income, Adjustments, Itemized Deductions by Type, Exemptions, and Tax Items, by Size of Adjusted Gross Income, Tax Year 2013"; IRS, Statistics of Income Division, Publication 1304, July 2016; download 13in21id.xls; <https://www.irs.gov/pub/irs-soi/13in21id.xls>; p. 7 of 5/8/2016 3:20 PM printout.
2014	"Table 2.1. Returns with Itemized Deductions: Sources of Income, Adjustments, Itemized Deductions by Type, Exemptions, and Tax Items, by Size of Adjusted Gross Income, Tax Year 2014"; IRS, Statistics of Income Division, Publicaton 1304, August 2016; download 14in21id.xls; <https://www.irs.gov/pub/irs-soi/14in21id.xls>; p. 8 of 2/14/2017 4:07 PM printout.
2015	"Table 2.1. Returns with Itemized Deductions: Sources of Income, Adjustments, Itemized Deductions by Type, Exemptions, and Tax Items, by Size of Adjusted Gross Income, Tax Year 2015"; IRS, Statistics of Income Division, Publicaton 1304, September 2017; download 15in21id.xls; <https://www.irs.gov/pub/irs-soi/15in21id.xls>; p. 8 of 3/7/2019 9:33 AM printout.
2016	"Table 2.1. Returns with Itemized Deductions: Sources of Income, Adjustments, Itemized Deductions by Type, Exemptions, and Tax Items, by Size of Adjusted Gross Income, Tax Year 2016"; IRS, Statistics of Income Division, Publicaton 1304, August 2018; download 16in21id.xls; <https://www.irs.gov/pub/irs-soi/16in21id.xls>; p. 8 of 3/7/2019 3:50 PM printout.
2017	"Table 2.1. Returns with Itemized Deductions: Sources of Income, Adjustments, Itemized Deductions by Type, Exemptions, and Tax Items, by Size of Adjusted Gross Income, Tax Year 2017"; IRS, Statistics of Income Division, Publicaton 1304, September 2019; download 17in21id.xls; <https://www.irs.gov/pub/irs-soi/17in21id.xls>; p. 8 of 5/3/2020 5:08 PM printout.
2018	"Table 2.1. Returns with Itemized Deductions: Sources of Income, Adjustments, Itemized Deductions by Type, Exemptions, and Tax Items, by Size of Adjusted Gross Income, Tax Year 2018"; IRS, Statistics of Income Division, Publicaton 1304, September 2020; download 18in21id.xls; <https://www.irs.gov/pub/irs-soi/18in21id.xls>; p. 8 of 1/5/2022 5:02 PM printout.
2019	"Table 2.1. Returns with Itemized Deductions: Sources of Income, Adjustments, Itemized Deductions by Type, Exemptions, and Tax Items, by Size of Adjusted Gross Income, Tax Year 2019"; IRS, Statistics of Income Division, Publicaton 1304, November 2021; download 19in21id.xls; <https://www.irs.gov/pub/irs-soi/19in21id.xls>; p. 8 of 1/10/2022 4:45 PM printout.

Source: Col. K.

1989-2019	U.S. Department of Labor, Bureau of Labor Statistics, "Table 1800.Region of residence: Average annual expenditures and characteristics, Consumer Expenditure Survey, [Year]." See chapter 7, endnote 12, for detail.

APPENDIX C: *Income, Deflators, and U.S. Population*

Appendix C.1 presents U.S. Per Capita Disposable Personal Income for 1921 through 2022.

The Implicit Price Index for Gross National Product is provided for 1921 through 2022. The deflator series keyed to 2012 dollars provided deflators from 1929, only, through 2022. Therefore, the 1921 through 1928 data was converted to inflation-adjusted 1958 dollars using the series keyed to 1958=100, and the inflation-adjusted 1958 dollar values were then converted to inflation-adjusted 2012 dollars using the series keyed to 2012 dollars.

Appendix C.2 presents U.S. Population for 1921 through 2022.

SOURCES

Income, 1897-1918

Raymond W. Goldsmith, Dorothy S. Brady and Horst Mendershausen, *A Study of Saving in the United States,* Vol. 3 (Princeton, NJ: Princeton University Press, 1956; reprint, New York: Greenwood Press, 1969), Table N-1, p. 427 (page citations are to the reprint editions).

Income, 1919-1928, Deflator 1921-1928, and U.S. Population, 1897-1928

Historical Statistics of the United States: Colonial Times to 1970, Bicentennial Edition, Part 1 (Washington, DC: Bureau of the Census, 1975):

1919-28 Disposable Personal Income: Series F 9, p. 224 (F 6-9).

1921-28 Implicit Price Index GNP (1958=100): Series F 5, p. 224 (F 1-5).

1897-28 U.S. Population: Series A-7, p. 8 (A 6-8).

Income, 1929-2022

Per Capita Disposable Personal Income in Current Dollars: U.S. Department of Commerce, Bureau of Economic Analysis; "Table 7.1. Selected Per Capita Product and Income Series in Current and Chained Dollars"; Line 4: "Disposable personal income"; National Income and Product Accounts Tables; <https://apps.bea.gov/national/Release/XLS/Survey/Section7All_xls.xlsx>; data published on April 27, 2023.

Deflator, 2012 Dollars, 1929-2022

Gross National Product: Implicit Price Deflators for Gross National Product [2012=100]: U.S. Bureau of Economic Analysis; "Table 1.1.9. Implicit Price Deflators for Gross Domestic Product"; Line 27: "Gross national product"; National Income and Product Accounts Tables; <https://apps.bea.gov/national/Release/XLS/Survey/Section1All_xls.xlsx>; data published on April 27, 2023.

Population, 1929-2022

U.S. Bureau of Economic Analysis; "Table 7.1. Selected Per Capita Product and Income Series in Current and Chained Dollars"; Line 18: "Population (midperiod, thousands)"; National Income and Product Accounts Tables; <https://apps.bea.gov/national/Release/XLS/Survey/Section7All_xls.xlsx>; data published on April 27, 2023.

Aggregate Income, 1929-2022

U.S. Bureau of Economic Analysis; "Table 2.1. Personal Income and Its Disposition"; Line 27: "Disposable personal income"; National Income and Product Accounts Tables; <https://apps.bea.gov/national/Release/XLS/Survey/Section2All_xls.xlsx>; data published on April 27, 2023.

Appendix C-1: Per Capita Disposable Personal Income and Deflators, 1921-2022

Year	Current $ Per Capita Disposable Personal Income	Implicit Price Deflator GNP [1958=100]	Implicit Price Deflator GNP [2012=100]
1921	$555	54.5	16.157
1922	$548	50.1	16.157
1923	$623	51.3	16.157
1924	$626	51.2	16.157
1925	$630	51.9	16.157
1926	$659	51.1	16.157
1927	$650	50.0	16.157
1928	$643	50.8	16.157
1929	$686		9.398
1930	$609		9.054
1931	$521		8.124
1932	$397		7.174
1933	$369		6.976
1934	$421		7.359
1935	$469		7.510
1936	$530		7.600
1937	$564		7.925
1938	$517		7.698
1939	$551		7.621
1940	$588		7.712
1941	$716		8.233
1942	$903		8.887
1943	$1,020		9.292
1944	$1,099		9.512
1945	$1,117		9.760
1946	$1,169		11.023
1947	$1,212		12.234
1948	$1,325		12.921
1949	$1,303		12.898
1950	$1,416		13.059
1951	$1,537		13.983
1952	$1,596		14.224
1953	$1,667		14.397
1954	$1,675		14.531
1955	$1,763		14.778
1956	$1,851		15.282
1957	$1,921		15.788
1958	$1,955		16.148
1959	$2,036		16.371
1960	$2,080		16.595
1961	$2,141		16.772
1962	$2,236		16.977
1963	$2,315		17.173
1964	$2,481		17.435
1965	$2,640		17.756
1966	$2,818		18.254
1967	$2,982		18.783
1968	$3,208		19.584
1969	$3,432		20.543
1970	$3,715		21.628
1971	$4,002		22.726

Year	Current $ Per Capita Disposable Personal Income	Implicit Price Deflator GNP [2012=100]
1972	$4,291	23.709
1973	$4,758	25.011
1974	$5,146	27.257
1975	$5,657	29.784
1976	$6,098	31.429
1977	$6,634	33.384
1978	$7,340	35.733
1979	$8,057	38.699
1980	$8,888	42.190
1981	$9,823	46.187
1982	$10,494	49.039
1983	$11,216	50.965
1984	$12,330	52.804
1985	$13,027	54.474
1986	$13,691	55.576
1987	$14,297	56.966
1988	$15,414	58.978
1989	$16,403	61.297
1990	$17,264	63.604
1991	$17,734	65.767
1992	$18,714	67.264
1993	$19,245	68.856
1994	$19,943	70.324
1995	$20,792	71.806
1996	$21,658	73.124
1997	$22,570	74.384
1998	$23,806	75.225
1999	$24,684	76.290
2000	$26,274	78.020
2001	$27,255	79.777
2002	$28,160	81.019
2003	$29,230	82.619
2004	$30,674	84.836
2005	$31,732	87.499
2006	$33,558	90.199
2007	$34,899	92.640
2008	$36,021	94.421
2009	$35,568	95.018
2010	$36,654	96.162
2011	$38,059	98.165
2012	$39,732	100.000
2013	$39,474	101.747
2014	$41,276	103.652
2015	$42,672	104.681
2016	$43,556	105.727
2017	*$45,252*	*107.736*
2018	*$47,473*	*110.324*
2019	*$49,585*	*112.300*
2020	*$53,034*	*113.765*
2021	*$56,065*	*118.871*
2022	$55,781	127.194

Appendix C-2: U.S. Population, 1921-2022

Year	U.S. Population
1921	108,538,000
1922	110,049,000
1923	111,947,000
1924	114,109,000
1925	115,829,000
1926	117,397,000
1927	119,035,000
1928	120,509,000
1929	121,878,000
1930	123,188,000
1931	124,149,000
1932	124,949,000
1933	125,690,000
1934	126,485,000
1935	127,362,000
1936	128,181,000
1937	128,961,000
1938	129,969,000
1939	131,028,000
1940	132,122,000
1941	133,402,000
1942	134,860,000
1943	136,739,000
1944	138,397,000
1945	139,928,000
1946	141,389,000
1947	144,126,000
1948	146,631,000
1949	149,188,000
1950	151,684,000
1951	154,287,000
1952	156,954,000
1953	159,565,000
1954	162,391,000
1955	165,275,000
1956	168,221,000
1957	171,274,000
1958	174,141,000
1959	177,130,000
1960	180,760,000
1961	183,742,000
1962	186,590,000
1963	189,300,000
1964	191,927,000
1965	194,347,000
1966	196,599,000
1967	198,752,000
1968	200,745,000
1969	202,736,000
1970	205,089,000
1971	207,692,000
1972	209,924,000
1973	211,939,000
1974	213,898,000
1975	215,981,000
1976	218,086,000
1977	220,289,000
1978	222,629,000
1979	225,106,000
1980	227,726,000
1981	230,008,000
1982	232,218,000
1983	234,333,000
1984	236,394,000
1985	238,506,000
1986	240,683,000
1987	242,843,000
1988	245,061,000
1989	247,387,000
1990	250,181,000
1991	253,530,000
1992	256,922,000
1993	260,282,000
1994	263,455,000
1995	266,588,000
1996	269,714,000
1997	272,958,000
1998	276,154,000
1999	279,328,000
2000	282,398,000
2001	285,225,000
2002	287,955,000
2003	290,626,000
2004	293,262,000
2005	295,993,000
2006	298,818,000
2007	301,696,000
2008	304,543,000
2009	307,240,000
2010	309,839,000
2011	312,295,000
2012	314,725,000
2013	317,099,000
2014	319,601,000
2015	322,113,000
2016	324,609,000
2017	326,860,000
2018	328,794,000
2019	330,513,000
2020	*331,788,000*
2021	*332,351,000*
2022	333,595,000

Printed in the USA
CPSIA information can be obtained
at www.ICGtesting.com
LVHW080029250824
789166LV00010B/177